PRACTICE EXTENDED

Practice Extended

BEYOND LAW AND LITERATURE

Robert A. Ferguson

 COLUMBIA UNIVERSITY PRESS NEW YORK

COLUMBIA UNIVERSITY PRESS
Publishers Since 1893
New York   Chichester, West Sussex

cup.columbia.edu

Permissions material for excerpted sources can be found on pages ix–x.

Library of Congress Cataloging-in-Publication Data
Names: Ferguson, Robert A., 1942–
Title: Practice extended : beyond law and literature / Robert A. Ferguson.
Description: New York : Columbia University Press, 2016. | Includes
   bibliographical references and index.
Identifiers: LCCN 2015025715 | ISBN 9780231175364 (cloth : alk. paper) |
   ISBN 9780231540599 (e-book)
Subjects: LCSH: Law and literature. | Law in literature. | Judicial opinion.
   | Lawyers as authors. | Law and culture. | Law and ethics. | Legal stories—History and criticism.
Classification: LCC PN56.L33 F47 2016 | DDC 809/.933554—dc23
LC record available at http://lccn.loc.gov/2015025715

c 10 9 8 7 6 5 4 3 2 1

Cover design: Archie Ferguson

References to websites (URLs) were accurate at the time of writing.
Neither the author nor Columbia University Press is responsible for URLs
that may have expired or changed since the manuscript was prepared.

FOR MY COLLEAGUES AT COLUMBIA LAW SCHOOL

WE ALL MARCH TO A DIFFERENT DRUM BUT SOMEHOW MAKE GOOD MUSIC

TOGETHER.

CONTENTS

ACKNOWLEDGMENTS   *IX*

INTRODUCTION
▸   The Letters in Law   *1*

PART ONE
Literary Components in the Legal Imagination   *11*

ONE
▸   The U.S. Constitution as Literature   *17*

TWO
▸   The Place of Mercy in Legal Discourse   *35*

THREE
▸   Immigration Law: An Answer to Intractability   *65*

PART TWO
The Nature of Judgment   *85*

FOUR
▸   Holmes and the Judicial Figure   *93*

FIVE
▸   The Opinion as Literary Genre   *115*

SIX
▸   *Ulysses* in Government Hands   *130*

PART THREE

The Public Uses of Eloquence   *151*

SEVEN

▸ Lawyer Lincoln: The Making of Eloquence   *159*

EIGHT

▸ Memorialization and the Spirit of Law   *188*

NINE

▸ Precision in Persuasion   *196*

PART FOUR

When Law Fails   *211*

TEN

▸ The *Somers* Mutiny and the American Ship of State   *217*

ELEVEN

▸ Invading Panama: Circumstance and the Rule of Law   *241*

CODA

▸ How to Read a Courtroom Novel   *265*

NOTES   *279*

CASES CITED   *331*

INDEX   *333*

ACKNOWLEDGMENTS

TWO ANONYMOUS EVALUATORS, IN FAVOR of publication, left quiet comments that nonetheless led me to redo this book completely and make it much better than it was. Philip Leventhal, Whitney Johnson, and Kathryn Jorge made invaluable suggestions and additions at each stage of the process and shepherded the book through Columbia University Press with professional élan.

A generation of scholars, beyond the dedication to this book, have helped with these essays, but the commitment, wisdom, tact, perspicacity, and energy of my research assistants deserve special mention and all of my gratitude. They are Amy Connors, Ethan Frechette, Megan Heller, Dina Hoffer, Alexander Lemann, Ian MacDougall, David Pucino, Caitlin Smith, and Brian Snyder. Gabriel Soto, my assistant, faithfully arranged aspects of these materials.

Many have read, but two stand out as Emerson's "good reader that makes the good book": John Paul Russo and Kenji Yoshino. A third encompasses all. Priscilla Parkhurst Ferguson reads everything including myself.

.   .   .

Grateful acknowledgment is made to the following publishers and journals for permission to use previously published material in revised versions of the current chapters of this book:

Chapter 1, "The U.S. Constitution as Literature," is a revised version of Robert A. Ferguson, "'We Do Ordain and Establish': The Constitution as Literary Text," *William & Mary Law Review* 29, no. 1 (Fall 1987): 3–25. Used with permission by the *William & Mary Law Review*.

Chapter 2, "The Place of Mercy in Legal Discourse" is revised version of
Robert A. Ferguson, "The Place of Mercy in Legal Discourse," in *Merciful
Judgments and Contemporary Society: Legal Problems, Legal Possibilities*, ed.
Austin Sarat (Cambridge: Cambridge University Press, 2012), 19–82. Used
with permission by Cambridge University Press.

Chapter 3, "Immigration Law: An Answer to Intractability," is a revised
version of Robert A. Ferguson, "Immigrant Plight/Immigration Law: A
Study in Intractability," *Columbia Journal of Race and Law* 2, no. 2 (2012):
241–66. Used with permission by *Columbia Journal of Race and Law*.

Chapter 4, "Holmes and the Judicial Figure," is a revised version of
"Holmes and the Judicial Figure," *University of Chicago Law Review* 55,
no. 2 (Spring 1988): 506–47. Used with permission by *University of Chicago
Law Review*.

Chapter 5, "The Opinion as Literary Genre," is a revised version of
"The Judicial Opinion as Literary Genre," *Yale Journal of Law & Human-
ities* 2, no. 1 (1990), 201–19. Used with permission by *Yale Journal of Law
& The Humanities*.

Chapter 6, "*Ulysses* in Government Hands," is a revised version of
"Judicial Rhetoric and *Ulysses* in Government Hands," *Rhetoric and Pub-
lic Affairs* 15, no. 3 (Fall 2012): 435–66. Used with permission by Michigan
State University Press.

Chapter 7, "Lawyer Lincoln: The Making of Eloquence," is a revised
version of "Hearing Lincoln and the Making of Eloquence," *American
Literary History* 21, no. 4 (2009): 687–724. Used with permission by
Oxford University Press.

Chapter 11, "Invading Panama: Circumstance and the Rule of Law,"
is a revised version of "Invading Panama: The Power of Circumstance in
the Rule of Law," in *Transformations in American Legal History: Essays
in Honor of Morton J. Horwitz*, vol. 2, *Law, Ideology, and Methods*, ed.
Daniel W. Hamilton and Alfred L. Brophy (Cambridge, Mass.: Harvard
Law School, 2010), 344–71. Used with permission by the editors.

The coda, "How to Read a Courtroom Novel," is a revised version of
"The Curves of Justice: Spatial Metaphors in the Courtroom Novel,"
English Language Notes 48, no. 2 (Fall/Winter 2010): 129–41. Used
with permission by *English Language Notes* (http://english.colorado.
edu/eln/).

PRACTICE EXTENDED

Introduction

THE LETTERS IN LAW

LAW CLOSES THINGS THAT ONCE were open. Literature opens things that were once closed. Many interpreters in the relatively new field of law and literature make this claim without drawing an obvious conclusion from it.[1] The openness of literature makes the term "law and literature" a misnomer. Imaginative literature contributes to a legal problem only when other disciplines make its claims credible. Take, for example, Herman Melville's nineteenth-century classic novella *Billy Budd*, with its summary execution of "the Handsome Sailor." The work still reaches law today through its philosophical challenge of the danger in legal positivism, a too-slavish regard for the letter of the law.[2]

At stake in this connection is a similarity within many differences. Law, like literature, manipulates its letters for a particular effect but with very different purposes in mind. It must deal with the world it finds and it must hold to tight rules of procedure and decision making to justify the authority it wields. The novel—or any well-told story—creates its own world. "Principles and systems" do not control it.[3] Fiction defines behavior in any manner it wants to as long as it convinces its readership. To convince its audience, which is no simple task, it must enlist other disciplines for the verisimilitude that makes an imaginary world believable.

Disciplinary verifications vary with the story told. They can include history, geography, philosophy, sociology, anthropology, theology, visual studies, biology, psychology, and yes, law. The combinations supply "this-ness," a "resultant impression of life-likeness."[4] Of course, legal discourse also depends "on a mass of non-legal considerations."[5] It draws on the commonalities in regular life for effect, one reason we refer to "a common law." Only recently, however, have we come to recognize how extensively "the realities" in fiction open into the commonalities of law.

Practice Extended: Beyond Law and Literature seeks an expanded view of those interdisciplinary possibilities with three main goals. It tests literary challenges through the other disciplines that fiction uses so casually to talk about law. It supplies alternative points of view when law hides behind or mystifies its authority. It seeks "the crafty reader," one willing to "set a standard for serious reading of an important document."[6] All three objectives share a larger premise that encourages every citizen to be that crafty reader. A rule of law depends on an informed public capable of evaluating the legal decisions that govern it.

The eleven chapters that follow are arranged in four thematic sections to further these goals. Part 1, "Literary Components in the Legal Imagination," clarifies literary techniques and dependence in legal expression. It also reveals why law frequently misuses fictional representations even when they are relevant to a case. Connections between law and literature can just as easily turn into misconnections. Part 2, "The Nature of Judgment," illuminates the ambivalent role of the judicial figure in American life. Knowing the generic forms in judicial decision making also exposes misuse of them. Part 3, "The Public Uses of Legal Eloquence," reveals and analyzes the mysterious links between legal communication and public understanding, the means by which a rule of law is recognized. Part 4, "When Law Fails," asks a larger question: What do we do when law does not do its job?

Law rarely does its job well in fiction. Perhaps that is why public distrust of law has turned an elitist form of fiction into a best-selling genre. The courtroom novel thrives today even though the basic components have always remained the same. A final coda, "How to Read a Courtroom Novel," details the intricacies involved. Law rarely talks about injustice; fiction always will. Where should a reader draw the line between what law does and what novelists say about it?

A few preliminaries are in order. The trajectory of the four thematic sections becomes more obvious if we see what law and literature analysis can and cannot do. There is a world of difference between "justice itself" and "justice represented in fiction." *Homo sapiens* is a very different beast than *Homo fictus*, if just because we can only know the latter perfectly.[7]

Law cannot know perfectly. It stumbles to its realizations through the imperfect lens of implied intent. The qualified certainty it achieves in judgment is rigorously circumscribed by procedures, presumptions, evidentiary limitations, and rules of standing.

A novel bypasses all the problems in circumstantiality. It lets us figure out everything on our own and at our leisure. It supplies all of the information we need and, just as significantly, with no more information available elsewhere! We learn what each character believes and does through the set world created by the novelist. All of the evidence is gathered on the page. Nothing important is left out that a reader cannot furnish. Nor does an ending in courtroom fiction leave matters dangling. Closure is always strategic in fiction; it frequently has to be more circumspect and tactical in legal decision making.[8]

Law cannot work with the certainty that fiction gives to its own sealed world. It must rule out myriad details, mere accident, and limited knowledge in the jumble of life to decide what has happened and what should be done about it. Often enough, it can do nothing about what has happened, and when it can, the answers may be unfulfilling.

Why is the field of law and literature therefore a vexed interdisciplinary endeavor? The imputed connection makes sense only when real expertise cobbles three or more disciplines together with intellectual restraint and respect for methodologies in what becomes "law and the humanities."[9] The alliterative rhythms of "law & literature"—the ampersand helps the phrase trip off the tongue—will forever be the moniker of a movement but not the reality of inquiries relevant to the field.[10]

Nor are these confusions without others. Strict interdisciplinary investigation always depends on the integrity of multidisciplinary effect. Literary answers come through the vraisemblance or reality check that the selective artifacts of history, psychology, philosophy, political science, and other disciplines give it on an arranged basis—a basis fused into a common understanding of humanity. Law needs to corral, order, and separate these disciplines in the workings of what it calls legal reason.[11]

If law has lost some autonomy to other disciplines in new areas of investigation (such as civil rights, family law, environmental law, and intellectual property), it accepts interdisciplinarity only for its own needs and on its own terms. It remains the dominant discipline whenever and wherever it is engaged in a social problem.[12] Authority, power, clarity, and lack of ambiguity reside here. Legal language takes priority. It trumps other expressions of expertise by claiming its own overriding importance in deciding people's lives and fortunes. Even so, and even if they do not change the imbalances in interdisciplinarity, some qualifications need to be drawn over legal insistences in explanation.

What are some of those qualifications? Law, a jealous mistress, insists unreasonably on its hermeneutic reliability when its purposes are under discussion, and it willingly admits to difficulty only over future directions and only then when the difficulties in question are not before it for consideration. The closed nature of legal thought needs to be pried open when it refuses to face uncertainty or oversimplifies matters to reach a decision.

The exuberance of the law & literature movement has not always been that opener. The anthropologist Clifford Geertz gives part of the explanation in *The Interpretation of Cultures*. He warns that "certain ideas burst upon the intellectual landscape with a tremendous force" and "seem also to promise that they will resolve all fundamental problems, clarify all obscure issues... crowding out almost everything else for a while." Gradually things settle down. "A few zealots [will] persist in the old key-to-the-universe view of it," but for most the new approach turns into a tool for situational use. The new idea becomes instead "a permanent and enduring part of our intellectual armory," losing "the grandiose, all-promising scope, the infinite versatility of apparent application, it once had."[13]

The adjustments in connections between law and literature from strategic to situational use have been slow at times because of the critical expertise that allows scholars to conflate the disciplines in a linear way without recognizing the boundaries of either. Notice, in this regard, that all emerging interdisciplinary investigations that have to do with legal inquiry put law first in declarative mode: law and economics, law and society, law and history, law and philosophy, critical legal race studies, law and gender studies, law and empirical studies, and naturally enough, law and literature.

Where does one challenge these hegemonic claims of law? There are some weaknesses to worry about. Too much of legal scholarship works through pack mentalities. It loves "movements," celebrates schools, argues in armed camps over minute intricacies in constitutionalism, and strains for a new vocabulary to replace established uses, whether the new terms are needed or not.[14] Language is an independent control in law, its own reality, and professional impulses turn it into an exclusive and excluding compulsion.

Most disciplines look to phenomenon to determine interpretation. Law thinks that its language can dictate the awareness of phenomenon, an orientation with costs. Court opinions, legal injunctions, and constabulary authority—coupled to the communal need to obey without question—confirm linguistic formalism in legal thought and guarantee its centrality. Law loves its internal quarrels over these formalistic tendencies, over the assumed structure in decision making through deductive mechanisms and hierarchical classifications in language. Adversarial woofing over terminology fills legal journals. Whole careers and reputations are made and lost on the scholasticism of linguistic variation and import.

A unique publishing mechanism feeds these intellectual attributes. Law professors publish in student-run journals, and most major law schools have a goodly number of journals to choose from. My own institution, Columbia Law School, now has more editorial openings for its journals than it has students! With such a plethora of possibilities available, the demand for good articles is greater than the supply and the rules used for transmission make it an imperious market.

Think of the rules that prevail. Law professors can submit their essays to a number of journals at once while setting severe time constraints on decision making in the editorial process. The hurried competition for acceptance by journals has pernicious consequences. Well-placed faculty writers can bully second and third-year law student editors into accepting their work quickly without the least modicum of peer review.

Everything about this process of publication encourages intellectual sloppiness and excess. Career advancement can depend on quick acceptance for a submitter and, further down the line, for student recipients. Cooperative prominence on a student journal may pave the path to judicial clerkships and academic careers. Rapid turnover in student editors also limits journalistic expertise and judgment in the market for articles. Students typically work on journals for a year and a half at most before moving on. The editorial boards that decide publication of an article serve even less time, usually a scant twelve months.

A required writing style in law journals makes things worse. The prescribed jog-trot steps in law review composition contribute to authorial indulgence with mind-numbing repetition instead of creative organization. Constant duplication and sign-posting in articles, part by tedious part, is the established mode in law review writing, and the plodding sequence of this intellectual straitjacket welcomes assertion over substance. The number of times an expression is repeated becomes the mark of its interest. Sought-after controversy adds to the mix. The more contentious the assertion endlessly offered, the greater will be the rejoinders in many subsequent journal articles.

And rejoinder is a goal. Reputations in the legal academy flourish on the number of journal citations received. Easy publication without peer review boosts those numbers. Two to four times a year, new articles in the many law journals of law schools—each article with literally hundreds of footnotes—comment pell-mell on previous articles. A touch of a finger then spits out footnote count information to hiring and promotional committee computers. These footnote counts support school evaluations without recourse to what was actually written in the articles or the validity of the citation.

None of these weaknesses can be strictly called an institutional disaster, but the tendencies are bad for creative thinking, and the more rigorous vetting process of the literary academy could bring needed freshness to legal writing. Law likes to do things as it has done them before. That reactive process comes with the corollary of rigidity in formal writing. As one literary critic summarizes the dangers in habitual performance, "the point to make about convention is not that it is untruthful per se, but that it has a way of becoming, by repetition, steadily more and more conventional."[15]

Literature and literary criticism admittedly have their own problems, but they do a better job of avoiding mindless routine. The writing in imaginative texts can be a useful model for law in rethinking its style if not its substance. Literary enterprise never forgets "the great virtuoso of exceptionalism." Creativity of this sort is the particular hallmark of fiction; "it always wriggles out of the rules thrown around it."[16] Law can learn from this inventive spirit without losing sight of the important rules that govern it.

That said, the novel is no panacea for legal reform. No one should forget that fiction leans toward protest narrative when the subject is law. A different reality, and by no means a better reality, is at work. The legal process differs not just in scope but in kind from that pictured in the realm of story.

Its great virtue lies not in moments of crisis, as newspaper reporters and novelists would have it, but in the quotidian.

Who notices when law gets it right beyond those involved? Mundane procedural integrity and consistency rule the roost in the average working courtroom through the justice that is plausible. That is what everyone wants in life; never, though, as the reader of a novel. No work of fiction can survive such an understanding. The humdrum effect has to be made an exciting event. The procedural regularities that control in a trial exist to be broken in fiction. Courtroom novels dote on outrage, usually through an element of injustice. Although law as such is not always the villain in fiction, it must be made problematic and somehow an obstruction to a better answer given beyond its bounds.

Three paradigmatic plot situations control the ubiquitous phenomenon of outrage in courtroom fiction. Either the person punished is actually innocent (for example, in Harper Lee's *To Kill a Mockingbird*), the person on trial is punished too heavily (such as in Herman Melville's *Billy Budd* and Bernard Schlink's *The Reader*), or the punishment deserved is questionable (à la John Grisham's *A Time to Kill*). A novel about law succeeds on how unfairness is rendered—on whether or not that unfairness is faced squarely, on whether or not a corresponding fairness, implied or otherwise, reaches its intended audience.

Law and literature analysis easily claims too much for literature. It is not true that novels give "a different way to think about law," nor that novels give law "real world thinking."[17] The even bolder assertion that reading literature makes the absorber of it a more empathetic observer of life is also false.[18] Anyone with experience of departments of literature realizes that the people who work there are not better or more sensitive human beings when it comes to the problems they face or will not face. Is it true that "the border between law and literature has become a bridge"? Maybe so, but it is a farcical leap to use that metaphor to say the bridge will "produce further transformations in both fields."[19]

Imaginative literature may encourage new thought about a specific legal problem, but it does so through the other disciplines that it brings to bear on that problem. Those who claim a separate disciplinary integrity for "law & literature" mistake the enterprise. No one should believe that "extending law and literature studies" to include philosophy and theology "risks dissolving the specificity of the original interdisciplinary undertaking."

Nor does it make sense to celebrate that specificity by claiming "law & literature" "may ultimately lead to a reconfiguration of genres in which 'law' disappears as a distinct discipline."[20]

Law as a distinct discipline is with us for keeps. My work has concentrated on the aspirations against the shortfalls of an American culture that holds extravagant expectations of itself without meeting them. As often as not, law has been the cornerstone of both advance and retreat. Legal thought prides itself on a conservative frame of reference. It proceeds cautiously as one basis of its legitimacy. It thereby holds lines well but misses opportunities for advances in social justice and can retreat by losing track of the things it has accomplished. If its accomplishments are great, law still needs to be reminded of what it does best with those reminders coming from outside of itself.

Each of my previous books on law raised an interdisciplinary question in this form. *Law and Letters in American Culture* asked a historical question with literary implications: how did lawyers seize control of literary production from the clergy in the half century before novelists and poets took over in the 1840s?[21] The answer showed how those same lawyers had the expository facility to secure a form of government that was not only unprecedented in 1787 but virtually unnamed until it was invented. It was also a reminder to the current legal profession about skills in public writing now seemingly lost to it. *The American Enlightenment, 1750–1820* then followed that reminder with a different question: what is the nature of legal facility in letters?[22]

A subsequent book, *The Trial in American Life*, used methodologies in sociology, anthropology, and popular culture as well as historical and literary interpretation to ask yet a different kind of question. Why do certain courtroom events have such a long half-life in communal recognition, and what have been the permanent consequences for American thought?[23] Courtroom decisions frequently exacerbate the larger problems they are forced to address when they solve a particular case. Ideological conflict is the real catalyst of many high-profile trials, and it can inflame communal norms through the embattled hyperbole of advocacy and melodramatic media coverage of it.

Most recently, *Inferno: An Anatomy of American Punishment* turns on a more immediate interdisciplinary question. Why does the United States punish so much more heavily than other liberal democracies?[24] The book has the goal of contributing to a better penal system, and it uses literary texts to illustrate the degradation and pain of the imprisoned when law prefers to look the other way.

The questions asked now in this book again turn on situations where the law, for whatever reason, needs to be reminded of what it does best and what it can do better. Point and counterpoint are both important here. How can literary awareness assist a citizenry to understand law better than it now does? Where can literature, through the showcase of other disciplines, lead law to reform itself or respond to injustices within its purview? The questions in every chapter confront what internalized legal endeavor might not convey or recognize.

For the same reason, these eleven chapters are addressed to a general audience without losing the legal reader. Two of the great problems in contemporary law have been specialization and fragmentation. Long gone are the days when a figure like Oliver Wendell Holmes Jr. could conceive of writing a single book that would summarize the state of law in American culture.[25] Gone as well are the generalists in legal education who prided themselves on teaching all parts of their discipline and held closer to a common language. The arcane nature of legal debate today does not translate easily to public comprehension.

The authority of experts can solve a problem, but it rarely guarantees communal accord.[26] One value of an approach to law through the humanities comes here. How do you join legal and common expectations in shared thought about problems everyone must face? That, too, is an underlying goal of this book. Each chapter opens a path to legal explanation that every citizen should know something about and that every lawyer will gain a more informed point of view about than previously held.

Why are these connections so important? Ronald Dworkin, one of the significant legal theorists of our time, argues that "lawyers are always philosophers."[27] The assertion may be more of an aspiration than a statement of fact, but consider how aspirations become an obligation in thinking about law. Principles of professional behavior still relevant from the time of Justinian more than twenty centuries ago prove the point. The codification of Roman law begins this way: "These are the precepts of the law: live honestly, harm no one, give every person their due."[28]

How does honesty square with the entrenched desire to win in advocacy? Can you engage in legal decision making without hurting anyone?

What is a person's "due"? These are questions that internal legal analysis only begins to solve, and they reach the recipient of law as much as they direct the appliers of it. These questions and others like them indicate that law must reach beyond itself to understand itself. Surely it is right, when we say "the rule of law is a product of the imagination before it is a product of legislative and judicial acts."[29] That act of imagination is special, but it belongs to all of us.

PART 1

Literary Components in the Legal Imagination

LAW, A REACTIVE MODE, MUST translate a problem presented to it into legal terms. Does the client have standing to be in civil court? Has sufficient evidence been found to proceed against an accused in criminal court? The focus is calculatedly narrowing. Everything depends on what law can and wants to undertake. Nevertheless, re-translation back into communal terms remains a necessary part of any decision. Is the matter really worth pursuing? Many a case should not end up with an indictment or in court for reasons beyond the legal focus.

The legal process also tries to leach out the passions from experience that a client brings to it. People enter law in some level of misery, routinely expecting the legal solution to their problem to answer that unhappiness. This expectation is an unreasonable one. Even a successful lawsuit involves a great deal of time, vexation, and money. Winning, while vehemently desired, often leaves clients wondering why they needed law in the first place. Why didn't they simply receive what they already knew they deserved from the get-go?

To protect themselves and to inoculate themselves from the generally dispiriting nature of most legal conflicts, lawyers and judges resort to objectifying language and procedures. Yes, a proper spirit of objectification is an essential aspect of all legal reason in clarifying the problem at stake, but it also keeps everyone's emotions in check, particularly the irrelevant ones, and it has the added effect of lifting law sublimely above the messiness of a specific quarrel.

The vulnerability of the person served by law is thereby doubled. The necessary translation into legal terms satisfies only in part and the happiness quotient expected from judgment will always be less than the hope that led to the courtroom in the first place. Of course, few people seeking a legal remedy ever realize these difficulties, but the realm of fiction about law never forgets them. The courtroom novel or other form of fiction is thus a corrective of sorts, and one of the greatest—and certainly the most direct—in this vein is Stephen Crane's powerful short story, "An Eloquence of Grief," written in 1896 and first published in 1898.[1]

Crane, in this briefest of encompassing narratives, manages to show much of what the legal imagination regularly leaves out but that no one involved in law should forget. His two-page story unfolds through the point of view of onlookers at a preliminary hearing, not seemingly the stuff of high drama. Why is the crowd there? In a variation of the popular injunction, they have come to court not "for charity's sweet sake," but "for curiosity's sweet sake." They are voyeurs after the heartache of those caught in law's web. They wait for "a cry of anguish, some loud painful protestation that would bring the proper thrill to their jaded, world-weary nerves."

The philosophy of naturalism that drives much of Crane's fiction means that no one in this courtroom is really in control even though there is the semblance of control. We are given an assembly line of justice moving rapidly along its mechanical way rather than the enlightened forum of deliberation that we might expect. This is a disappointment that anyone who has ever appeared in traffic court will immediately understand and appreciate.

At the same time, we know that a cry of anguish is in store, and it comes from a sobbing young immigrant servant girl who has been "accused of stealing fifty dollars' worth of silk" from one of two "well-dressed young women" who wait "with the serenity of people who are not concerned as to the interior fittings of a jail." They are accompanied by a similarly well-dressed gentleman who supplies "dignity," which he does "heavily, almost massively," to protect his companions from the unseemliness of having to appear in criminal court.

The odds are already heavily stacked three against one, and when the cry of anguish comes—"I am innocent! Oh, I am innocent!"—the reader's sympathies are naturally on the girl's side. But that is not Crane's real interest; he does not even bother to tell us the outcome. Nor are the invidious class distinctions stressed, although they are there. Three more significant elements hover over this scene, and they all tell us what the law ignores.

First, and most obviously, is the interactive relation of courtroom and community. This event happens the way it happens because a watching community *wants* it to happen. The "spasmodic movement" of the loungers in the wake of the girl's cry is what these otherwise uninvolved onlookers have been waiting for and the public side of law readily accommodates it. How many legal events become high-profile trials because of the people's desire for entertainment?

Second, and more intrinsically important, is the calloused indifference of all aspects of the law to the vulnerability of the accused. There may be no greater public exposure than entering a courtroom under a criminal accusation. As the subject under discussion, an accused person endures the pejorative and rudely steady gaze of everyone else there. The ordinary social defenses of decorum available to make another individual look away in the public sphere are unavailing here against a negatively inclined collective public. Indeed, any such attempt, any visual return by the person in the dock, only intensifies interest and further scrutiny.

Crane gives most of his brief account to this second element in several distinct ways. The contending lawyers enjoy themselves in "preliminary fire-wheels" as formal adversaries in a familiar process. They are earning their pay, and the one earning the most, the lawyer for "the well-dressed contingent," then asks more pointed questions "with the air of a man throwing flower-pots at a stone house." The author gives us a quick but utterly casual—even routine—example of courtroom cruelty, one with shattering consequences for the helpless recipient of it.

To make sure that we do not feel intelligent control over the presumably objective but actually very subjective nature of this process, Crane tells us that the crowd, watching some distance away, "could not always see the judge, although they were able to estimate his location by the tall stands surmounted by white globes that were at either hand of him." When you cannot see the judge in courtroom fiction, justice is also missing. The courtroom lights do not reveal this figure; they are at "either hand." The suggestion is of arbitrary alternatives. Meaningful judicial investment is not apparent; it exists, if at all, in unplumbed shadows.

The story makes more subtle use of a third procedural element. This is a preliminary hearing, but no one has bothered to tell the accused that. She believes that she has been formally judged and found guilty, and her fears are confirmed when "a quick-eyed court officer" clears the way and leads her, now committed for trial, through "an austere arch leading into a stone-paved passage." The implication is of a journey directly to jail, and the policeman is "quick-eyed" and efficient rather than sympathetic in the task. No one, in effect, feels sympathy. We are left instead with the suddenly intrusive voice of the narrator, hidden until now.

The narrator, in the background until this moment, does not want to let this moment go. The panic of this frightened young girl belongs to us all in the experience of life. It occurs when we feel bereft, betrayed, suddenly mortal, or in danger in a world of questionable meaning. The cry of innocence against presumed guilt is "so graphic of grief," it strikes "so universal a tone of the mind, that a man heard expressed some far-off midnight terror of his own thought."

What is ultimately missing in this courtroom is thus another quality: mercy for a suffering person's moment of unnecessary distress. Why is it missing? Law fears gestures of mercy; they imply unequal treatment when offered in some cases but not in others. Strict regularity is more certain and desirable, and that strictness of approach easily extends to all aspects of law. As far as we know, this judge has given no word of explanation to the accused, now a defendant.

Nor are some leading legal theorists at all pleased at the prospect of other disciplines taking a role in such issues.[2] Recently, though, problems in law have led many to question that independent stance. Imaginative literature has assumed a greater role precisely because so many areas of law can no longer be left to the hermetic expertise of the profession, which does make mistakes and does fail to solve serious problems at an alarming rate.

Part 1 takes on three such areas where the study of literature has something more to tell us. Chapter 1, "The U.S. Constitution as Literature," questions the impact of overly narrow, legalistic interpretations of the U.S. Constitution. Should the Constitution be seen as separate provisions "full of contradictions and ambiguities, sources of endless contestation," or as "a general political scheme that is sufficiently just to be taken as settled for reasons of fairness"?[3] Questioners must realize that we lack the skill to write a constitution today that is anywhere near as good as this one from 1787.[4] The Constitution of the United States was written as and remains a unified literary text for the American people to read and abide by, and this chapter, along with recent longer studies, works to recover that more basic understanding.[5]

The second chapter, "The Place of Mercy in Legal Discourse," raises a second problem of growing relevance in the interdisciplinary study of law: the absence of mercy in American law.[6] Why does the United States punish more severely than so many other countries? The intersection of law, philosophy, theology, history, and literature offers the beginning of some answers. Among other things, we see why legal professionals so persistently misinterpret the most famous passage on mercy in English literature, Portia's speech on the subject in William Shakespeare's *The Merchant of Venice*.

Chapter 3, "Immigration Law: An Answer to Intractability," discusses why the United States cannot solve its problem in illegal immigration despite universal recognition that it is a crucial issue demanding immediate answers. The involved texture of the immigrant novel reminds us what it means to enter this country as a person in need of better understanding than is now provided by legal or social discourse. Only an alternative frame of reference can break the political logjam that so consumes and embarrasses the nation today.

1

The U.S. Constitution as Literature

THINKING OF THE CONSTITUTION OF the United States as literature restores the text to the American people beyond its existence as a battleground parsed by experts phrase by phrase. Legal acrimony over the framers' intent and strained understandings of specific language ignore the overall craft that made the document a triumph of collective expression in 1787.

Restoration is admittedly no easy task. Literary, constitutional, and religious frames of reference are all relevant if we are to grasp an eighteenth-century act of extraordinary creativity. The nature of that creativity is important because it remains a potent safeguard. It protects the health of a text that to a remarkable extent defines the country itself, a text that we could not possibly write as well today.

The U.S. Constitution is many things, but it is first words arranged for all to read. Arguments begin when specific integrations of past and present create differences about the scope, intent, and construction of constitutional language. They grow sharp over how to interpret the vitality of language against the meaning of history. In what manner do the statements of 1787 control the modern nation-state? How do original intentions apply to unforeseen consequences or circumstances? Where are the permissions in clauses that are so deliberately circumspect? Can the framers be wrong on certain issues?

We have learned that such questions do not lend themselves to easy legal distinction. Debate turns instead on implicit, often unarticulated assumptions about the nature of constitutional language, and these debates turn on minute phrases in the document rather than on a holistic sense of a uni-fied text. Recovering those unities can also test the underlying assumptions where differences begin.

The nature of constitutional language is a poorly understood subject because it is so seldom examined on its own historical terms despite much talk about the framers' intent. Arguments about the use of given words have stripped phraseology of its place in a larger complexity, the major source of its original vitality. Readers of the Constitution need to remember that writing thrives on a wealth of circumstances and social assumptions beyond claims about authorial purpose.

The writers of the Constitution entered Philadelphia as accomplished eighteenth-century men of letters with a number of specific skills to justify that description. What were those skills and what do they suggest about capacity in the use of language? What did the framers think they could cre-ate in 1787? What was their understanding of the kind of text they strove to make, and how did that understanding change—or develop—across a long summer of debate and documentary exchange?

The real power in language lies in the particulars of perceived possibili-ties and in the manipulations and methodologies of style, tone, genre, and substance that expand those possibilities. These elements are literary skills. They represent a neglected source of the living Constitution. Closer atten-tion to the developing genre of public documents in the Revolutionary Era is thus a necessary corrective, and it can reveal a great deal about the actual craft in such writings.

Philosophically, between 1776 and 1787, the framers became less con-vinced about the self-evidence of truth. The weakness of the system estab-lished by the Articles of Confederation, growing factionalism, Shay's Rebellion, unrest in the western territories, and economic depression—the very facts that brought them to Philadelphia in 1787—made them less certain of agreement and more worried about the textual basis on which agreement might rest.

Even so, an important consistency remains. The writers of both the Declaration of Independence and the Constitution believed in a text as the foundation of agreement, and within this qualified faith, the events of the 1780s brought them together to search for a new aesthetic of control in the writing of the actual Constitution. A major question consists in how these elements come together. We can see the aesthetic at work in Benjamin

Franklin's famous closures when he signs first the Declaration of Independence and then, eleven years later, the new constitution of federal union.

Signing the Declaration, Franklin observes, "We must, indeed, all hang together, or most assuredly we shall all hang separately."[1] The Declaration functions as the artifice behind Franklin's witticism and the artifact of the solemnly sworn policy that he enunciates. The writers of this document not only hang together, they swear to do so in the Declaration. Their concluding oath guarantees the "facts" they submit to "a candid world." Their oath—"we mutually pledge to each other our Lives, our Fortunes, and our sacred Honor"—is then physically figured in the grouped signatures that conclude the document as an open indication of the risks taken. The world is understood as "candid" in the Declaration because it accepts facts as given and hence a right of revolution based on them. Facts are submitted, again in the words of the document, "to prove this."[2]

In 1787, incontestable facts, let alone proofs, were much harder to come by. Placed in the same ceremonial situation at the Constitutional Convention, Franklin achieves a similar certainty in the document being signed but by a far more circuitous route. James Madison describes the event:

> Whilst the last members were signing [the Constitution] Doctr. Franklin looking towards the Presidents Chair, at the back of which a rising sun happened to be painted, observed to a few members near him, that Painters had found it difficult to distinguish in their art a rising from a setting sun. I have, said he, often and often in the course of the Session, and the vicissitudes of my hopes and fears as to its issue, looked at that behind the President without being able to tell whether it was rising or setting: But now at length I have the happiness to know that it is a rising and not a setting Sun.[3]

The world may not have changed much for the always composed Franklin by 1787, but representations within it surely have. Franklin's assumed text in his anecdote, the artist's painting, is hopelessly ambiguous without a larger context: men can and will differ over whether it depicts a rising or a setting sun just as the delegates themselves differed in a final argument over whether the new constitution would mean prosperity and peace for the fledgling union or instead anarchy and civil convulsion.

Franklin had, in fact, taken a central role in these last-minute bickerings, and the substance of his contribution was to raise an unavoidable epistemological uncertainty based on learned ignorance. "For having lived long," he tells the Convention, "I have experienced many instances of being obliged . . . to change opinions even on important subjects, which I once thought right, but found to be otherwise. It is therefore that the older I grow, the more apt ı am to doubt my own judgment" (2:641–42).

The point of this comment is to encourage his divided colleagues to settle for an "apparent unanimity" where "real" accord is impossible and to urge them to incorporate that subterfuge into the Constitution itself (2:643). Knowing that the individual delegates are divided, that they cannot hang together, Franklin proposes that the Constitution be approved "by the unanimous consent *of the States* present," since the majority of each delegation present seems ready to give approval (2:641–47).

In accepting Franklin's "convenient" motion, the framers see, articulate, and welcome its "ambiguous form" (2:643). The unanimity is, of course, a lie. Three leading members of the Convention—Edmund Randolph, Elbridge Gerry, and George Mason—refused to sign the Constitution on the final day of the Convention, and at least three others—Luther Martin, Robert Yates, and John Lansing Jr.—withdrew earlier because of their unhappiness with the emerging document.

The unanimity injected into the language of the Constitution is instead a useful fiction, a myth of glorious harmony that the framers wielded in the ideological struggle to first elicit and then enforce allegiance during ratification. The notion of unanimity can be mobilized without hypocrisy because the text itself has been accepted as an inevitable repository of epistemological ambiguities. Philosophical uncertainty has become a source of political flexibility and literary creativity.

Franklin's strangely useful pessimism might appear idiosyncratic but for the fact that it is shared, even amplified, by a far more important leader of the Convention—James Madison, Father of the Constitution. At issue is how a writer turns a necessarily ambiguous text into an effective tool of ideological conformity within a divided world. The problem of consensus is a vexing one in Madison's writings.

The most famous *Federalist* paper, *No. 10*, argues that disagreement and faction will yield to "the extent and proper structure of the Union," but *Federalist No. 37*, also from Madison's pen, reveals paralyzing philosophical uncertainties that call the entire realm of human agreement into question. Here, in one of the darkest thrusts of the American Enlightenment,

Madison describes three intruding levels of chaos in human existence: "the obscurity arising from the complexity of objects," "the imperfection of the human faculties," and the failure of language itself—"the medium through which the conceptions of men are conveyed to each other adds a fresh embarrassment."[4]

When these elements are compounded in the process of human perception—"indistinctness of the object, imperfection of the organ of conception, inadequateness of the vehicle of ideas"—we are left with a world of impenetrable "gloom." It is one filled with "dark and degraded pictures which display the infirmities and depravities of the human character." This fallen world is so impoverished by its "discordant opinions," "mutual jealousies, . . . factions, contentions, and disappointments" that Madison's "man of candor" regards mere agreement with surprise and the presumed unanimity of the Constitutional Convention with "wonder" and "astonishment." Only "a finger of that Almighty hand" could have supplied such a level of agreed upon understanding in mere men.[5]

The point of *Federalist No. 37* is that real agreement becomes impossible without imposed manipulation and design, a manipulation and design that we can trace to the pen of Madison as easily as he has traced them to the finger of God. The mythic gloss trades on the idea that unanimity in a community of saints comes closest to the will of God and may express a sign of it. Perhaps, but in a religious age, Madison did not emphasize religion himself, cannot be identified by a particular faith, and rarely relied on religious expression in his writings. One has to take his emphasis as a rhetorical device.

The deeper substructure of his position—particularly the metaphor about a guiding finger—suggests how writing the Constitution involved an aesthetic of conscious control, how the document itself depends on questions of craft and even guile, and how thoughts of a waiting but impatient national audience (emphasized everywhere in the Convention as "the People") would take what had been written. The Constitution, to turn one last time to the language of *Federalist No. 37*, is a text where "theoretical propriety" and "extraneous considerations" must meet and where a molding hand resolves the difference.[6]

How are we to know that the Constitution represents a rising and not a setting sun? What is it about the text itself that leads fallible observers to the same conclusion? The rhetoric of the framers urges us to answer these questions by thinking of the Constitution as the expression of a shared truth devised by the elected representatives of an enlightened people. We are urged, in other words, to mystify the text in question. Quite another set of answers comes to mind if we think of the document as a carefully created text, as a manipulated and manipulative work, as the imposed truth of a conscious and philosophically sophisticated elite, as the concrete product of particular writers.

James Madison, Edmund Randolph, James Wilson, and Gouverneur Morris are the four men who actually wrote succeeding drafts of the emerging document from the Virginia Plan of late May, through the Report of the Committee of the Whole in mid-June, to the copy reviewed by the Committee of Detail in early August, to the Constitution as submitted by the Committee of Style in mid-September. Within this authorial focus, three forgotten elements illustrate the original vitality of the Constitution: first, the craft within the writing itself; second, the move from a working paper that all are free to modify toward a public document that will not bear subsequent intrusion; and third, the visual importance of the Constitution as a painting or icon to be viewed in a certain way.

The craft within the document is one of its most ignored features. The Constitution is a miracle of concision, emerging as it does from four months of florid effusion and often bitter debate. It contains just five thousand words of the plainest prose cast in a one-sentence preamble and seven brief articles. Neither verbiage, nor allusion, nor admonition interrupts its prescriptive clarity; there is very little linguistic novelty, almost no philosophic innovation while inventing an entirely new system of government, and minimal elaboration.

These evasions are counterbalanced by a series of more subtle commitments. Brief rather than cryptic, the Constitution confirms a familiar past. Every word belongs to the realm of common understanding in eighteenth-century American experience, and many of them are taken directly from the constitutions of the original thirteen states and from the Articles of Confederation in a reaffirmation of republican principle. In the 1780s the state constitutions were the essential repositories of an American identity. John Adams called them the true history of an emerging republicanism. Drafter in his own right of the Massachusetts Constitution of 1780, Adams thought of his own efforts as "a specimen of that kind of reading and reasoning which produced the American constitutions."[7]

Borrowings from the state constitutions are all the more impressive because the framers were so discriminating. Controversial terms like "national," "republic," and "federal" are barred in the framers' document. The generalities of the Constitution exist within a precise arrangement of tone and structure. The seven articles are ranged in descending order of length, concern, and difficulty. The first three articles—on the legislative, executive, and judicial branches—form the crux of the new government. Each moves from a description of a branch of that government to issues of qualification and selection for office and then to an explicit enumeration of powers and limits.

The final document is strengthened in many subtle ways. Sometime in the rearrangement of twenty-three loose articles into the tightened version of seven (a deliberately chosen cabalistic number), the framers decided that the document should never be completely opened to reinterpretation.[8] The Committee of Style presents the Constitution's ultimate amendment clause with its stipulations on how subsequent changes are to become "part thereof," a phase subsequently changed in the final document to "Part of this Constitution" (2:602). Compare such language with the Articles of Confederation, which allows for "alteration" within the articles themselves.[9]

Amendments to the Constitution are added on to a document that remains intact as a text despite every later revision. The whole discussion of constitutional change takes place amidst the framers' final decisions to reject calls for a second convention and to limit the right of the state ratifying conventions to alter constitutional language (2:629–33). These exchanges leave the people with just two alternatives: "accepting or rejecting [the Constitution] in toto." "Conventions," observes a spokesman for the majority, "are serious things, and ought not to be repeated" (2:646, 632).

Over and over again in the fight for ratification, the framers invoke the uniqueness of the Convention to encircle and seal off the language of their document.[10] The Constitution itself mystifies that language in a literal portrait of the new union. The famous preamble turns the people into the authors of the Constitution by conflating the act of writing with the process of ratification. Contrast "We the People of the United States, in Order to form a more perfect Union . . . do ordain and establish" with the more literal honesty but diminished power of the opening sentence in the Articles of Confederation: "To all to whom these Presents shall come, we the undersigned Delegates of the States affixed to our Names send greeting."[11]

The empowering presence of the people in the Constitution is then joined by the specific articles of government, leading to a conclusion that portrays the union on the face of the document. The signers of the Constitution appear neither in alphabetical order nor by presumed importance of seniority. They are grouped instead by state, with the states themselves appearing in geographical order from north to south, starting with New Hampshire in the north and working in sequence down the east coast to Georgia in the extreme south. The United States thus appear on the page in familiar map form—the perfect icon in answer to Madison's fears about indistinct objects, imperfect perception, and faulty language.

This iconicity becomes more literal in the Constitution makers' image of their work and of themselves as "framing" and "framers." Madison, in *Federalist No. 51*, uses the phrase "framing a government" to evoke the necessary controls, internal and external, that distinguish a government of men from one of angels.[12] The metaphor, a general one in the discourse of the times, conjoins act and object, creation and control, regularity and contrivance, with the overarching notion of order as the ultimate source of many different meanings.

A number of eighteen-century meanings apply here. In Samuel Johnson's *Dictionary of the English Language*, "frame" can mean "to form or fabricate by orderly construction and union of various parts," "to make," "to regulate," "to invent," and, as a noun, "a fabrick, any thing constructed of various parts or members," "any thing made so as to inclose or admit something else," "order; regularity; adjusted series or disposition," "scheme," "contrivance," and "projection."[13] The Constitution, the fabric of union, is all of these things, but most particularly it encloses and thereby creates form in the midst of a nameless chaos. Without the weaver's fabric, the frame signifies only a void.

Alexander Hamilton, no friend to the original plan, turns these characteristics into a rallying call for ratification when he asks, in the question of signing, "Is it possible to deliberate between anarchy and Convulsion on one side, and the chance of good to be expected from the plan on the other[?]" (2:646). The frame, together with the framers' effort, insists upon what might be thought to be missing: recognizable form. It is at once a claim of accomplishment and a rejection of prevalent fears.

The belief in boundaries behind the image of framing eases the three central innovations of the Constitution, all of which involve a chilling open-endedness in conventional eighteenth-century political thought: namely, the amorphous and changeable people as the foundation of all authority, the degree of constitutional separation of powers in government, and the sharing of sovereignty between the nation and its component states. None of these initiatives lent themselves readily to unified form in early American understandings.

Framing is a multifaceted visual aid for an assumed congruity, and the eighty-five *Federalist Papers* build on the premise. These documents argue that the new national fabric is a uniformity woven of apposite parts—not, as others claimed, a weak tissue or, alternatively, a too-powerful contrivance. In the crucial ratification debates, every aspect of the metaphor was important. Madison, for example, would claim that *who the framers are* should count as much as *what has been framed*.[14]

To recapture the conscious manipulation that the writers of the Constitution bring to it is not to question James Madison's famous claim that "there never was an assembly of men, charged with a great and arduous trust, who were more pure in their motives, or more exclusively or anxiously devoted to the object committed to them" (3:551). It does, however, give depth to John Adams's equally famous claim that the Constitution represents "the greatest single effort of national deliberation that the world has ever seen"[15]

We need to see that act of deliberation in its literary sense to recover the full value of the document. National deliberations rarely develop into intellectually impressive events. This one stands out not just because of the oft-noted genius of its participants but because of their practiced talents as men of letters. Between 1776 and 1784, every state except Rhode Island and Connecticut wrote and adopted a new constitution. Seventeen new constitutions in all were written in America during the course of the Revolution, and the very number contains the best key to critical interpretation.

Only in repetition do the possibilities of a genre become apparent. The quantum leap in the quality of language and conception between the Articles of Confederation and the Constitution occurs step by step in state constitutional convention after state constitutional convention, and it has as much to do with developing literary skill and the mastery of a new art form as it does with politics. Skill appears in the framers' shorthand references to various state constitutions during debate on the Convention floor and mastery in a self-confidence rarely lost sight of in every difficulty and disagreement.

Articulations of the difficulty the framers faced illustrate the point perfectly. Madison calls the creating of the Constitution "a task more difficult than can be well conceived by those who were not concerned in the execution of it."[16] Franklin, an avid player of the game, compares it to an infinitely complex game of chess in which every move is contested.[17] John Adams thinks of thirteen clocks striking simultaneously, "a perfection of mechanism, which no artist had ever before effected."[18]

In every case, the fact of difficulty gives way to a metaphoric projection of competence and accomplishment. Madison's executor of a task, Franklin's chess player, and Adams's artist know what to do and how to do it. Thomas Jefferson captures the self-confidence of 1787 when he writes, "It is a part of the American character to consider nothing as desperate; to surmount every difficulty by resolution and contrivance."[19] The combination is illuminating: resolution (an act of will) permits contrivance (the ability to invent order in a crisis).

The framers take the measure of their own ability in the first speech of the Convention. Edmund Randolph begins his criticism of the Articles of Confederation by exonerating the authors of that document for errors made "in the then infancy of the science, of constitutions, & of confederacies" (1:18). He assumes much has been learned in just ten years, since the supposed infancy of 1777, and no one contests the point.

A growing sophistication in the science of constitutions has reduced some of the primal uncertainties. What does it mean to write out a constitution when the ideal model of the British Constitution presumes an unwritten status? To whom does one address such a document amidst raging debates about the locus and feasibility of sovereignty? How and where does fundamental law lie upon a page also dedicated to narrower structural checks and the machinery of modern government?

The many state constitutions that intervene between 1776 and 1787 curb the unfamiliar by placing it within familiar forms. They bring the framers to a greater awareness of genre. The delegates at work in Philadelphia in 1787 remain collectively committed to the sequent toil of successive drafts of the Constitution because they share a series of assumptions about the way narrative, form, and style control unruly content. John Adams observes as much when comparing "the art of lawgiving" to architecture and painting. When he also notes "the fabrication of constitutions will be the occupation or the sport, the tragedy, comedy, or farce, for the entertainment of the world for a century to come," we glimpse the aesthetic behind a major literary achievement, the eighteenth-century American literature of public documents.[20]

Colonial American constitutionalism differs from its English equivalent in its commitment to the written word. The biblical conjunction of sovereignty and the book of law, the need for an artificially imposed order in the American wilderness, and the politics of Anglo-American relations all encouraged the *documentation* of governmental forms as the reference point of communal identity. Colonial Americans responded to the uncertainty and flimsiness of social forms by inscribing fundamental law frequently, even compulsively. Their English counterparts put fundamental law to paper mostly in the form of individual acts and rights and only when faced with an explicit political challenge. Magna Carta and the Bill of Rights of 1689 provide standard examples. In America, the repeated acts of founding wholly new societies turned such political challenges into a social norm. The artifice of colonial charters, pacts, petitions, ordinances, and constitutions represented a perpetual crisis in definition, a steady search for the words that will complete identity.

Documents like the Mayflower Compact of 1620 and the Ordinance and Constitution for Virginia of 1621 create social and political structures as much as they assert individual rights. The desire to "covenant and combine ourselves together into a civil Body Politick" in the first instance and "to settle such a forme of government" in the second requires a psychology of framing. As the Mayflower Compact claims to "enact, constitute, and frame . . . just and equal Laws, Ordinances, Acts, Constitutions, and Officers," so the Ordinance and Constitution for Virginia strives "to make our Entrance, by ordaining & establishing . . . supreame Counsells." Notably, both documents are writing on another writing. Responses in kind to the charters of colonial incorporation from James I of Great Britain, they engender intertextual tensions, operating at once as glosses on the king's grant and extensions of it.[21]

The combinations are important. The psychology of framing, the specific language of ordination and establishment, and the textual mediation of power received and power assumed are touchstones in measuring the evolution of a writerly tradition in early America. The extent of that evolution becomes clear in any comparison of the concise but magisterial language of the U.S. Constitution with the prolix, redundant, anxious, and often unreadable prose of earlier official documents, from the first state constitutions to the Articles of Confederation.

Compare, for example, the preamble of the Constitution with the 1776 Constitution of Virginia:

> We the People of the United States, in Order to form a more perfect Union, establish Justice, insure domestic Tranquility, provide for the common defence, promote the general Welfare, and secure the Blessings of Liberty to ourselves and our Posterity, do ordain and establish this Constitution for the United States of America.[22]

> We therefore, the delegates and representatives of the good people of Virginia, having maturely considered the premises, and viewing with great concern the deplorable conditions to which this once happy country must be reduced, unless some regular, adequate mode of civil polity is speedily adopted, and in compliance with a recommendation of the General Congress, do ordain and declare the future form of government of Virginia to be as followeth.[23]

The difference between these passages is a matter of practice. Every writer struggles through lesser works before a masterpiece becomes possible. Just so the framers prepare themselves in the workshops of congressional and state assemblies. Forty of the fifty-five delegates in Philadelphia had already served in both; half that number had participated directly in the writing of state constitutions and territorial ordinances.[24]

By 1787 many of the writers of the Constitution in Philadelphia understood the deepest workings of such language in ways that we have now forgotten. The hardest lesson, one that the Committee of Detail articulates, requires simplicity in style without losing sight of complexity in purpose. Edmund Randolph and John Rutledge, for the committee, saw the necessity of a scope, style, and tone that ensures a careful encompassing form over detail. In drafting a constitution that will be properly "fundamental," they agreed "to use simple and precise language, and general propositions" and "to insert essential principles only, lest the operations of government should be clogged" (2:137). This spirit of restraint can dominate the writing process because it claims clarity of form as its overriding goal. Randolph and Rutledge distinguished sharply between "the construction of a constitution" and the more open-ended enumeration of mere law; only the former requires "the shortest scheme that can be adopted" (2:137). The accessibility of the framers' document absolutely depends on this point. The federal constitution is twice as clear as its forerunners—the Massachusetts Constitution of 1780, for example—in part because it is less than half as long.

Two other considerations reinforce the literary ability brought to Philadelphia. In 1787, a large majority of Americans embraced the institutional arrangement of a national convention as the appropriate forum for considering national union. The political legitimacy of the Convention ensured the high quality and skill of its participants while reinforcing their self-confidence and mutual awareness.

Benjamin Franklin, George Mason, and James Madison all wrote that they hoped for much from a Convention made up of "the best contribution of talents the States could make for the occasion" (3:21, 32, 37). The special nature of that occasion brought out the best in the best. Virtually every delegate perceived a golden opportunity and worked that much harder to preserve it when troubles mounted. None were paid for their efforts. "It is a miracle that we are now here exercising our tranquil & free deliberations on the subject," Hamilton observes in the most difficult days of late June when differences escalated. "It would be madness to trust to future miracles" (1:467).

The role of the gentleman of letters also suggests a more subtle influence, one that enabled "the best contribution of talents" to understand and thrive upon itself. Much has been made of the framers' adept use of committee structures, their secrecy and restraint before publication, their willingness to suggest solutions without insisting on personal investment, and their ability to compromise over language. These characteristics are what one could hope for in the exemplary writers of the time.

The true gentleman of letters privileges reason over emotion, writes for a small group of social peers, circulates drafts among those peers for correction, avoids publication until agreement is reached, and leaves his work unsigned. In other words, the very qualities that critics cite as weaknesses in early American fiction, poetry, and drama become strengths in the literature of public documents. The retreat to committee arrangements for compromise reveals only the most obvious of these strengths.

Surely the most remarkable trait of the Convention has to do with the delegation of sensitive writing tasks within committees to obviously embattled figures like Edmund Randolph, James Wilson, and Gouverneur Morris. These men took strong stands in debate on the floor of the Convention, yet their colleagues trusted them to express something like the general will in the formal act of writing by assignment. The official selflessness of the man of letters is crucial in this behavior pattern.

Not until the 1830s did Americans learn for certain that the aristocratic, thoroughly conservative Gouverneur Morris penned the final draft of the Constitution. News of his authorship in 1787 would have hurt ratification, but Madison, a sometime opponent, knew that the gentlemanly tradition minimized the danger of publicity, concluding "[a] better choice could not have been made, as the performance of the task proved" (3:499).

The reserved spirit of the man of letters channels authorial identity into a social orientation. Madison captures the essence of that spirit later when he adds, "[The Constitution] was not like the fabled Goddess of Wisdom, the offspring of a single brain. It ought to be regarded as the work of many heads and many hands" (3:533). Art manipulates the familiar to create the extraordinary.

Viewed in this light, the Constitution represents the crystallization of a genre. When "the many heads and many hands" of the Convention were finished, constitutionalism had taken on a different meaning than it had before. By identifying the nature of this transformation, we come closer to understanding the ultimate creativity behind the frequently reiterated concept of "ordain and establish."

John Adams, from hindsight, describes the formative era as "the age of revolutions and constitutions."[25] The phrase contains a vital expectation: that constitutions cap revolutions. By the middle 1780s, early republican leaders assumed that constitutional forms define revolutionary accomplishment and thereby American culture itself. Benjamin Franklin and George Washington, the Fathers among the Fathers, say as much. Franklin's *Information to Those Who Would Remove to America* in 1782 shows just how firmly legitimacy lies in the official word: "Those, who desire to understand the State of Government in America, would do well to read the Constitutions of the several States, and the Articles of Confederation that bind the whole together."[26]

Washington is even more explicit a year later in his farewell to the army, titled the *Circular to the States*. The country's hero warns that "it is yet to be decided, whether the Revolution must ultimately be considered as a blessing or curse." The question remains, he asks, "if we have a disposition to seize the occasion and make it our own" by giving "such a tone to our Federal Government, as will enable it to answer the ends of its institution." The choice, an act of clarification, is whether "to establish or ruin . . . national Character forever." Using history well is not about military glory or even high adventure. It turns on writing down meaning "in the Establishment of our forms of Government."[27]

The same language carries over to the Convention floor four years later. Madison and Hamilton announce they are "digesting a plan which in its operation [will] decide forever the fate of Republican Govt" (1:423–24). Gouverneur Morris sees himself as not just "a Representative of America" but "a Representative of the whole human race; for the whole human race will be affected by the proceedings of this Convention" (1:529).

The framers' rhetoric puts enormous pressure on the plan they prepare. If ordaining and establishing a republican form of government in America at the end of the eighteenth century possesses cosmic significance, then the artifact of ordination and establishment, the document itself, becomes holy writ. Republican virtue resides not in the act of clarification, which was Washington's formulation, but in the clarified result. The Constitution becomes not a symptom of virtue but virtue itself.

John Adams, writing his *Defence of the Constitutions* in the same year, shows the way by insisting that constitutionalism enables virtue, not vice versa. "The best republics will be virtuous, and have been so," he argues, "but we may hazard a conjecture, that the virtues have been the effect of the well-ordered constitution, rather than the cause."[28] Adams and others use their readings in British empirical thought to claim that institutions, rather than the manners and morals of a people, guarantee good government.[29]

But what the framers add on their own in 1787 is the notion that a piece of paper, the text of the Constitution, can be construed as such an institution. The shift involved in this idea is simple but with subtle implications. On the one hand, it legitimates a firmer union; on the other, it creates a lasting tension and potential difficulty. From this moment, the Constitution as process lives in competition with a different notion of the Constitution as artifact, as enclosed institutional form. All subsequent readers face the problem of defining the flexibility of the former within the rigidities of the latter.

The Constitution as artifact entered into the ceremonies of an American civil religion, "a collection of beliefs, symbols, and rituals with respect to sacred things."[30] This happened so quickly because of evangelical strands at work in the period. Powerful religious dimensions embedded in the political culture of early America controlled initial intellectual access to the Constitution in ways now forgotten.[31]

The framers' success became a providential sign, one that dictates acceptance by a republican citizenry in proof of its virtue. When, a month after the Convention, Madison writes that "it is impossible to consider the degree of concord which ultimately prevailed as less than a miracle," he means that events have transcended every rational prediction. Miracles partake of the sacred, and they encourage acceptance over explanation.[32]

As they left the Convention, the framers made acceptance of their miracle of consensus a test of personal and communal salvation. Washington's letter delivering the Constitution from the Convention to Congress plays upon the point in form, style, and content. Sent "by unanimous Order of the Convention," his letter addresses a particularity—"Sir"—from the enlarged perspective of the undifferentiated, first-person plural pronoun: "Sir, . . . in all our deliberations on this subject we kept steadily in our view, that which appears to us the greatest interest of every true American, the consolidation of our Union."(2:666–67)

The litany of pronominal possessives conflates framer and ordinary citizen; "our deliberations" and "our view," referring to the framers' decisions, merge with "our Union," the perspective of every true American. Washington then alludes to differences that might be expected but that never materialize. In his words, "the Constitution, which we now present, is the result of a spirit of amity." Those who would disagree with the document have to know that it is constructed out of "mutual deference and concession" and "is liable to as few exceptions as could reasonably have been expected." All of the acceptable exceptions already have been made! A challenge to any part of the final document violates the communal decorum of amity, forgets "the greatest interest of every true American," and endangers "prosperity, felicity, safety, perhaps our national existence" (2:667).

Agreement with the document looms as the one acceptable interpretation of it. The people share in the act of writing through the related act of ratification. The framers contribute to the sacred text of the Constitution by making it scriptural. It is answerable mainly or rather only through assent.

The Constitution as process and the Constitution as artifact become one. How they apply as one is perhaps the single most important lesson that the continuity of history can teach in constitutional interpretation. The ratification process that engenders the framers' strategy also creates, in debate, a useful tension between process and artifact. The Constitution lives in the dialectic of that tension: in the right of authority to interpret it and in the duty of the citizen to obey it.

Among the framers, Madison does the most to keep the sacred text of the Constitution safely within this spirit of amity. "The citizens of the United States," he writes in 1792, "have peculiar motives to support the energy of their constitutional charters." The complexity of the American system "requires a more than common reverence for the authority which is to preserve order thro' the whole." The "great charters" of government are the worthiest objects of reverence because "as metes and bounds of government, they transcend all other land-marks."[33] The citizen's duty is to protect and preserve "the importance of instruments, every word of which decides a question between power and liberty." Public opinion, Madison concludes, "should guarantee, with a holy zeal, these political scriptures from every attempt to add to or diminish from them."[34]

The amalgamation of political, legal, and religious terminology in Madison's "political scriptures" is significant. His rhetorical stance speaks to a text-oriented culture. From the Bible to the Constitution to the court case, Americans of every century have turned to special writings as the comprehensive and comprehensible units of meaning in thinking about identity and cultural change. A series of agreed-upon texts have contained the spiritual types, political principles, or legal decisions—often all three at once—that define reality and allow an appropriate response when decisions must be made.

Of course, the tensions in such a text-oriented approach to cultural understanding are also real. Every attempt to understand American society has pitted scrutiny of the valorized word against the nature of experience. Resort to a paradigmatic text must answer conflicting demands, including the search for ideals, the need to substitute language for new social forms, and the American compulsion to think that the history of the United States is uniquely ordained. The problem with such an orientation is that it demands a tenacious mastery of the complexities of interpretation as well as a customary reiteration of ideals.

These are not minimal talents to have and hold. They require the knowledge of the historian, the craft of the writer, the available sympathy of the accomplished reader, and the tough-mindedness of the political leader to unite in an act of perception and articulation. Only a balanced awareness of the vitality and integrity of official language can hope to safeguard a knowledge of definition by charter.

An image-oriented culture, one increasingly like our own, may be in danger of losing these capacities by glossing over the complexity of the combinations involved, by taking them for granted, and, most of all, by forgetting the vitality that once drove them. A healthy text-oriented culture must be able to read the Constitution in all of its generic strength, manipulative brilliance, cunning restraint, and practiced eloquence—the primary qualities that made it a unified text for all of its people. When John Adams announced that national virtue comes not from heaven but from the use of reason and the senses in a well-ordered constitution, he added that such a constitution is a very difficult thing to comprehend.[35]

Full awareness of the literary text that is the Constitution of the United States is a necessary task—if just because Americans have lost the capacity to come together and write another constitution anywhere near as effective today. The collaborative skills, the faith in language, the private concealment during debate, the willingness to trust encompassing phraseology, and the generic facility through practice are traits the nation no longer possesses. Does anyone think such a compelling document could be written today? There is every reason for Americans to know better what they have and how they got it if they want to keep it in the way it was meant to be kept.

2

The Place of Mercy in Legal Discourse

LEGAL DISCUSSIONS OF MERCY TEND to be messy even though everyone engaged in them accepts the same definition. Mercy is the suspension or reduction of a punishment that is deserved. Writers from every age debate its relevance, but the basic definition of mercy holds for all and it is simple enough. Nothing is simple, however, the moment the concept is brought into a legal frame for action.

Here are the legal questions over which there is little to no agreement: What is a legitimate legal act of mercy? Is mercy part of justice or not? Is mercy an independent virtue, a dependent virtue, an imperfect virtue, or no virtue at all in law? Whatever its status, if mercy exists in law, under what circumstances does it apply? Why, in fact, is there even a debate? A fundamental premise of law demands like punishments for like crimes. Can either justice or consistency allow different punishments for the same crime?

Light drives these questions, but heat has made debate over them overly contentious. So in order to think about mercy in law with any clarity we must first eliminate several major interdisciplinary confusions on the subject. They are six in number:

1. Legal expounders forget that mercy is a pagan idea as well as a Christian one.
2. Citing early Christian theologians on the subject complicates the problem of origins.
3. Casual use of Shakespeare confuses his understanding of mercy.

4. Pardons, forgiveness, leniency, and release within legal stipulation are not acts of mercy.

5. The conventional theoretical reasons for punishing do not reach the concept of mercy.

6. Mercy on an official legal tongue is almost always a sophistic device.

All six problems also have a common source: law works (or tries to work) through precision, and the difficulty with talk of mercy is that it is so loosely referred to and applied that it lacks functionality except as a rhetorical crutch. For the concept to be a serious doctrinal possibility, it must first be made a technically viable tool.

Confusion over the meaning of punishment also complicates things. Punishment, from the Latin *poenai*, is also the root word for *pain*. Punishment *is* pain, and when inflicted, it robs both punisher and punished of a degree of humanity—so much so that it has taught us to keep punishment limited to legal needs and ends. Yet no one really knows how to measure punishment except in arbitrary ways, and the imposed physicality in it remains a disturbing moral condition. In the graphic words of a long-term criminal, prison is trying to breathe with somebody's fingers up your nose.[1]

Mercy, from the Latin *mercēs* and the Old French *merci*, moderates the unseemliness in punishment through notions of recompense, release, or reward, all of which imply a preferred or perhaps earlier condition. The concept also insists on a felt reciprocity as a counter to the hierarchical or imposed infliction of punishment. It confirms that punishment must be questioned. In the blunt terms just complained of, it asks whether a finger up the nose is necessary.

How can we improve debates over mercy in legal discourse? First we must untangle the confused origins of mercy. That helps lead to a second step: a working definition of legal acts of mercy. With that definition in place, William Shakespeare's dramatic renderings of mercy in *The Merchant of Venice*, *Measure for Measure*, and *The Tempest* allow us to examine the underlying difficulties in the relationship of mercy to law in a way that all can recognize. Current debates on the subject then confirm the difficulty of doing this and leave us with the treatment of law in official legal discourse and the question of how to improve on it.

To begin: validating a pagan concept of mercy does not mean larger approval. Brutality in punishment is a norm everywhere in antiquity. City after city, even whole civilizations, in history have fallen to the sword. Everywhere the weak as well as the guilty suffered appalling cruelty.[2] No one is safe from a terrible end. The most extensive comment on mercy in the classical world, *De Clementia* by Seneca in 55–56 C.E. instructs the most merciless Roman of them all, Emperor Nero, and there is no irony in the seeming discrepancy.[3] The harsher the punishment regime becomes, the greater the need for mercy.

Seneca's idea of mercy, "generosity of mind" (*magnanimitas*), sounds vague until it is fully parsed and understood. He argues for an elevated temperament "shown best on the judge's bench" but available to all.[4] Two words signify mercy in Latin, *misericordia* and *clementia*, but the first invokes "pity," while the second indicates "mildness" and "calmness" as a root meaning.[5] Seneca prefers the second term. He rejects "pity" as a lower emotion that has little to do with "real control of mind." Breadth of vision, accurate sensibility, and visible composure in the face of misfortune are Seneca's terms in a concept that must reach every level of social interaction. In his own words:

> There is a harmony between the virtues, and none of them is better or more honorable than any other, all the same one virtue can be more suited to particular individuals. Generosity of spirit is right for absolutely any mortal, even the lowest of all. After all, what is greater or braver than blunting misfortune?[6]

De Clementia accepts the basic definition of mercy and already answers the main legal objection that so many will advance: "if we say that clemency is 'restraint which offers some remission of a punishment which was deserved and due,' there will be an outcry that no virtue achieves less than what is due for anyone. However, everybody understands that clemency consists of pulling back from what could deservedly be imposed." "Pulling back" refers again to a controlling tranquility or demeanor present in an otherwise savage punisher. Seneca calls it "restraint of the mind when it is able to take revenge."[7] It is also telling that he concentrates on the character of the punisher, not the punished.

Everyone was at risk in Imperial Rome. A tyrannical and mercurial social order had accuser and accused changing places at the whim of an absolute ruler. "How few accusers are free of guilt!" Seneca wryly notes. Only "the ill-informed" could think the opposite of mercy is strictness. "So what then is the antithesis of clemency? It is cruelty, which is precisely barbarousness of the mind in exacting punishment."[8]

Against so many vicissitudes, such uncertainty, and natural vindictiveness, the true magistrate decides for the sake of all and gives priority to leniency. "Whenever he can, he will intercede with Fortune. After all, where will he make better use of his resources and his strength than in restoring the casualties of circumstance?"[9] This last phrase, "casualties of circumstance," is one to which we will return.

For the moment, it is enough to see that the greatest danger in Rome comes from above. Seneca encourages the vicious Nero to empathize more with his people: "Think about this city where the crowd that streams without let-up through its widest streets is crushed if any obstacle slows down its progress, as if it were a swift torrent." Another passage comes closer to home. "A cruel reign is stormy and dark with . . . the people trembling and jumping in terror at any sudden noise." Ruthlessness is its own problem! Unless challenged, brutality flourishes in the commonality of cruelty.[10]

Seneca pleads with Nero on both aesthetic and practical grounds that "it is all the more reasonable for a person who has been put in charge of other people to exercise his power in a gentle spirit and to think about which state of the world is more pleasant to the eye and more attractive." "Think how profoundly lonely and desolate it would be here," Seneca warns in the most poignant passage of De Clementia, "if nothing remained except what a strict judge would acquit." Mercy, in contrast, "is the glory of empires" and, most importantly, "their surest means of protection."[11]

How so? The publicity in mercy furnishes a safeguard through "freedom of decision." Leniency has positive worth. "It forms its judgments not according to the letter of the law but according to what is right and good." It understands in a different way: "The wise man will grant many remissions, and he will save many people whose character is not sound enough but can be made sound." Mercy measures character for alternatives to emerge, as "the wise man will see with which method which character needs to be handled."[12]

Seneca writes on slippery ground and at considerable personal risk. Recall that "blunting misfortune" requires "bravery" as much as "greatness." The writer dares to suggest so much to Nero only by stressing that mercy is hierarchical in form. The figure who has the right—or at least the power—to punish can do so or not as a matter of will. No reader should forget that Seneca writes as a supplicant who knows that Nero will one day take his life as he has taken so many others.[13]

A freer Roman spirit tells us more. Only one emperor wrote about mercy and exercised it on a regular basis. Marcus Aurelius ruled a hundred years after Nero, from 161 to 180 C.E., and like Seneca before him, he adopted the philosophy of stoicism. In his *Meditations*, stoicism means that one must "look things in the face and know them for what they are, remembering that it is your duty to be a good man." What or who is this good man? He appears as "one content with his allotted part in the universe, who seeks only to be just in his doings and charitable in his ways," and yet this same good man must always be on guard against a troubled and troubling world. He must give "scrupulous attention to the day's impressions, lest any of them gain an entrance unverified."[14]

Marcus Aurelius's account of mercy is aphoristic rather than systematic in the mode of *De Clementia*, but the *Meditations* are richer and more knowing for coming from a ruler who openly applies its lessons. As a stoic, Aurelius begins with a check on himself, with "the realization that malice, craftiness, and duplicity are the concomitants of absolute power." The check on others reaches back to the self that punishes: "When men are inhumane, take care not to feel towards them as they do towards other humans." Cruelty is the reflex in a crisis and it must be quelled. Like Seneca, Aurelius accepts an innate brutality in humankind that must be managed with a clear mind. Moderation in judgment becomes "the summit of success" if just because it is so seldom achieved.[15]

The answers to every acrid observation in the *Meditations*, and there are many of those, are kindness, toleration, and leniency. Kindness, in particular, forms a drumbeat throughout the work: "Chief of all features in man's constitution, therefore, is his duty to be kind." Even when a ruler is offended, "kindness is irresistible, so long as it be genuine." There can be "no shrinking from mankind and its vicissitudes," but that insight cannot interfere with the need "to survey and accept all things with a kindly eye." "Impudence," "roguery," "double-dealing," and "culprits" flourish everywhere, but the good ruler will apply "gentleness to meet brutality." The deepest quality in human nature is a positive one ranged against a sea of negativity. "Man is born for deeds of kindness," writes Aurelius, "and when he has done a kindly action, or otherwise served the common welfare, he has done what he was made for."[16]

It is central that the moral framework of the *Meditations* requires no higher being or design for its implementation. The same obligations apply "no matter whether the universe is a confusion of atoms or a natural growth" with a purpose behind it. "We have to stand upright ourselves, not be set up," Aurelius commands. Reason and civic duty serve as guides enough. To look at the world accurately means to "do away with all fancies." There may be nothing but the present to rely upon. One must therefore "limit time to the present" and "learn to recognize every experience for what it is."[17] The world by itself, especially in its negative qualities, teaches Marcus Aurelius to be merciful.

What is the method? "To wish that a rogue would never do wrong is like wishing that fig-trees would never have any sour juice in their fruit, infants never cry, horses never neigh, or any other of life's inevitabilities never come to pass. How, pray, could he act otherwise, with the character he has? If you find it so vexatious, then reform it."[18] You take and use the world that comes to you in all of its malice, indifference, and selfishness, but you do not destroy what you hate; you try to reform it. The gauge, taken from the Greeks, is *epieikeia* or "fair-mindedness," which corrects when "tough standards of justice" apply too severely to "the circumstances of human life."[19]

A summary of this pagan concept of mercy can prepare us for the Christian variant. Classical thought recognizes an innate cruelty in human dealings that must be countered. It accepts that peril and circumstance can dictate human behavior beyond individual control. It insists that public recognition of mercy contributes to communal welfare. It takes a sharp view of the human while never letting go of humanity: *condicio humanae vitae ad colamus humanitatem*. It tries to curb the punisher. Rather than divine sanction, it sticks to a hardheaded appraisal of what the world needs to make human relations bearable.

Christian mercy, whatever its similarities, has a very different orientation. The passions of Christ and the martyrs give new status to suffering; the punished are magnified and the punishers are diminished in a divine plan beyond the inflictor's control. The vicissitudes of fortune and chance disappear. Every circumstance is preordained in a Christian frame of reference. There are no accidental events in a God-filled universe. Intellect tries to fathom the meaning of events, but in search of salvation it looks to the next world rather than the workings of this one. The present is less important than the future. Mercy receives its reward in heaven, not here, and God's mercy exists beyond human ken.

Some of these differences have unique advantages in helping us define mercy as we know it today. Christian theology enriches the hierarchical and supererogatory aspects of mercy. As God (for no other reason than divine will) grants mercy that we do not deserve, so we owe a corresponding mercy to the undeserving under our own control. The prospect of heaven has another virtue. It assigns a specific value to every living soul. God's assumed interest in *every* individual imparts dignity and worth to the low as much as the high, a not insignificant cause of individual consideration in courtrooms today.

Problems emerge, though, when Christian mercy controls legal application. The strain of self-interest in the analogy of divine to human mercy is a first complication. Only those who are merciful receive the bounty of heaven, but mercy is not about what the punisher will receive.[20] Remember, as well, the ascribed polarities in Christian thought: the saved and the damned, the orthodox over the heretical, the good against the legions of evil. Invidious distinctions in the categories of religious regard for human beings do not help a judge spare nonbelievers, wrongdoers, or presumed enemies of the faith.

The stakes in Christianity are also absolute. They make everyone forever responsible for the personal choices they make. Affinities between the expiation of sin and the punishment of crime do not encourage leniency. Neither does the assumption that God will correct human error. Both suppositions give the punisher an unwarranted comfort zone. Even the dignity assigned to the individual soul has pitfalls. Although it signifies absolute worth through shared humanity, dignity can more narrowly identify rank, status, and fungible rights.[21] In this second sense, it leaves the punished vulnerable. A person subject to punishment can lose some or all dignity with demeaning consequences in the eyes of a righteous punisher.

Legal commentators confirm the awkward fit of Christian and legal mercy when they use theology to support or deny the relevance of the concept in law. Recent debate on the subject has turned to religious queries on mercy in the eleventh century by St. Anselm, archbishop of Canterbury. Those who argue this line assume that "St Anselm's two paradoxes of God's mercy are startling in their relevance and even characteristic in contemporary treatments of human mercy."[22]

Modern secular logic does not reach the world of St. Anselm. In writing the *Proslogium* in 1077–78 C.E., Anselm asks God first "how dost thou spare the wicked, if thou art all just and supremely just?" Justice, in this query, rightly assumes the need for balance to be more than a name. "For what is more just than that the good should receive goods, and the evil, evils?" If punishment is to have meaning, how can God grant mercy to the wicked? Anselm's second query is especially pointed: "Why of those who are alike wicked, thou savest some rather than others?" "How, then, is it just that thou shouldst punish the wicked, and at the same time, spare the wicked?"[23] In the all-or-nothing lottery of damnation or salvation, where is the line that condemns some of the wicked to eternal torment while others receive eternal bliss despite similarly evil lives?

Lawyers writing on mercy see Anselm's concerns as the stuff of paradox. They use his words to construe mercy as either a redundancy in law, a disjunctive element, a dangerous adjustment, or an impossibility. The functionalism in legal discourse encourages utility of reference, but Anselm, a Benedictine monk, asks his questions with an eleventh-century mind. Belief, not logic or experience, dictates his understanding. He asks "How do I understand the truth?" He is not interested in "What are we to do?" or "How are we to decide?" He works from a premise already accepted on faith and does not dwell on the adjustment to practical action in this world.[24]

Anselm sees not paradoxes, which resist explanation in a spirit of contradiction, but conundrums, which have answers. He asks his questions only of God, not of other men. He is not assessing analogically but spiritually. He rejects the parallel that requires the logic of God's mercy to be ours. Against the insuperable logic of the questions asked, he is "without contradiction" in the answers he reaches, each of which resists the applications that the legal world would like to assign to it.[25]

The solution to every contradiction lies in an unbridgeable difference: "thy goodness is incomprehensible." A monologue in interrogative mode, the *Proslogium* appreciates more than it reasons. It moves from analysis to prayer and worship for its answers: "O boundless goodness, which does so exceed all understanding, let that compassion come upon me, which proceeds from thy so great abundance."[26]

Yet Anselm grasps what we forget. In one of the most studied passages of the *Proslogium*, he pauses over God's omnipotent powers: "thou art truly sensible (*sensibilis*), omnipotent, compassionate, and passionless, as thou art living, wise, good, blessed, eternal." These thoughts are conventional enough in Christian theology, but real difference comes in a much briefer and more startling negative phrase that finishes the sentence. God, against our mortal misfortune, is "whatever it is better to be than not to be."[27] The emphasis is not on connection but on the enormous gulf between God's ways and our own.

Can pagan and Christian ideas of mercy be brought together? Yes, to some extent. Parsing the diverse origins also prepares us for thinking about what makes a legal act of mercy. The following touchstones are jointly relevant. Worry about rigidity and harshness in punishment. Cultivate humanity in punisher. Use mercy to promote the public welfare. Be aware of larger circumstances. Remember the merit in flexibility. Do not underestimate what worldliness can teach. Accept the ambiguities in human nature. And, not to be forgotten, recognize the presence of cruelty in the norms of a culture.

What are not relevant considerations? Sympathy over the pathos of an individual situation is a dangerous tool in what should be a detached judgment based on a more comprehensive understanding. Analogies to divine will break down. Well beyond doctrinal separations of church and state, religious dogma does not help a sophisticated understanding when the subject is mercy in law. One need not go as far as John Stuart Mill in *On Liberty* (1859) when he suggests that Christian morality falls "far below the best of the ancients" by giving "human morality an essentially selfish character"[28] Still, there is some cause for worry, and that worry raises the character that legal mercy should have.

Every applier must remember that the exercise of mercy in law is an override. It challenges the workings of a legal system by privileging particularity and immediate circumstance. It cannot do this in an arbitrary fashion for no reason or for personal gratification. It must define the exercise as precisely as it is limiting. The functionality of law helps by forcing the problem to a practical level; it asks the idea to become a conceivable act. What, we can begin to ask, should mercy sound like in a courtroom?

Mercy in law should at least be a fulfilled speech act. Using the declarative or imperative mode, a punisher with legal authority utters a statement that is an announcement to a transgressor, an order to the rest of constituted legal authority, and an explanation addressed to a community at large. All must be instructed in what is to be done, why it is to be done, and how it is to be done. The linguistic nature of this order, understood as an action taken, is its delineating characteristic, and J. L. Austin's theory of speech acts enables us to break down its terms into more precise components.

Speech act theory analyzes how words accomplish or fail to accomplish their meaning. Hence, the spoken act of legal mercy does not just say what it thinks; it completes an objective with others. Austin calls this kind of realized statement "a performative utterance" in three parts: a locutionary act (the words said), an illocutionary act (the words rendered in an appropriate circumstance and transparent context), and a perlocutionary act (the impact or understanding of the words delivered).[29] Austin's formula may seem elaborate, but the formal articulation of decisions in law makes it useful in a discussion of legal mercy. Justice so decidedly rearranged requires that everyone—judge, jury, criminal, victim, and community— know the circumstances and the reasoning that bestows a different result. This requirement—full articulation—reaches beyond the people affected. A legal exercise of mercy must reinforce the reliability of law, guard the public welfare, maintain communal safety, and tally with normative perceptions in the surrounding community. Everyone in the rule of law has the right to know why this decision makes sense against a conventionally available solution.

Emphasis on the performative utterance in a legal act of mercy sharpens the focus of our inquiry. It defines the meaning of such an act in a constructive manner, it underlines the restrictions on legal use, and it clarifies the integrity of the philosophical idea in mercy on which it must rely. More immediately, it allows us to distinguish mercy from leniency. Too much loose talk and confusion over such meanings play a major role in the controversies that dominate discussions of legal mercy.

Many of these controversies center on procedures that fall short of the full articulation required. A plea bargain, when a prosecutor arranges for a lesser criminal charge in exchange for information or avoidance of a trial, does not qualify as an act of legal mercy. Neither does a prosecutor's more benign discretionary reduction of a charge, nor do the many unilateral situations in which a legal actor decides to not enforce a law. These measures represent institutional amenities to help the legal process function. They are the oil that lubricates an overworked system.

The law is not without mechanisms of relief—one reason many critics find no need for the concept of mercy in it. When, for example, judges decide to sentence at the lower end of an established penalty spectrum after a conviction, they may exercise compassion and give a full explanation for it, but they still act within the law and need no special justification for what they have done. Decisions of this kind adjust sentencing to a level legally available. Mercy, you will remember, is the suspension or reduction of a punishment that is deserved.

Distinguishing legal acts of mercy so sharply may seem perverse, but it is the only way to see the subject clearly for what it is. At first glance, a parole hearing would seem to be the very stuff of mercy in action. After all, parole grants conditional release from punishment based on the discretion of a parole board that interviews a prisoner after investigating his or her personality, history, adjustment, record, and all submitted information, as well as the prisoner's available attorney, original victims, and any other relevant source.[30]

The word *parole* comes from the French *parol* (meaning "word offered"), and it refers to the exchange of language required when an inmate indicates recognition and acceptance of the conditions set for release and promises to honor them.[31] A successful parole hearing even fulfills the condition of a successful performative utterance, and it has been called in court, with reason, "an act of grace."[32]

Even so, parole does not qualify as a legal act of mercy. It is an extension of punishment. Parole offered is revocable for any infraction, sharply restricts the autonomy of a parolee, and does not count toward time served when revoked, as it frequently is. It remains part of the prison system with a recipient left in suspended animation. Inmates rarely think of parole as an act of mercy. They observe authority taking a further step in control of them, and there is nothing extraordinary or exceptional in that step. The right to a hearing comes in most jail terms and so does the prospect of early release.[33] Parole is a regular, and as currently applied, often futile institutional process.[34]

Related actions also trigger confusion about legal acts of mercy. Forgiveness has parallels to mercy but belongs in a separate category. Forgiveness is not a legal action and it need not include a change in punishment or any act at all. An injured person can forgive and still feel punishment is deserved. No legal officer has a right to forgive an injury inflicted on someone else, and an officer so injured would be disqualified from acting in any legal role involving that defendant.[35]

Pardoning, in contrast to forgiveness, is certainly a legal act, but it, too, is separate from a legal act of mercy even if merciful in intent. A pardon is an executively constituted decision that absolves the need for punishment or further punishment. It need not imply guilt or crime or depend upon a previous register of punishment. It can even be exercised before someone has been officially charged. Pardons require no articulation of the reasons for granting them, nor a reaction in the person receiving one.

Winnowing through so many related possibilities brings us closer to a working definition of our subject. All of the related but distinct forms of proceeding noted lack some aspect of the formally constituted act. As performative utterances in legal terms, each falls into J. L. Austin's "doctrine of the *Infelicities*." An infelicity is a level of misunderstanding or miscommunication or a lack of communication.[36]

The transparency of a legal act of mercy is what separates it from concepts such as forgiveness or pardoning. The act requires sincerity from an appropriate punishing power in granting release from a punishment deserved. It must also take place within a procedural setting that lets everyone, including the relevant community, recognize the action taken. All appropriate participants have the opportunity to understand the circumstances and the relief that is being granted, and the act itself must be articulated in such a way that serves a larger public purpose.

The punisher who would be merciful must somehow balance two close but competing concepts against each other: the human and the humane. An objective perception of deplorable illegality must be held next to a more philosophical perception of the larger situation. But how is that balance to be struck, and when is mercy the appropriate response? There are no easy answers to the balancing needs in these questions, and no one saw the complexity and the dangers in them more clearly than William Shakespeare.

Few legal scholars writing on mercy resist the opportunity to quote and allude to one or more of Shakespeare's three leading plays on the topic:

The Merchant of Venice, *Measure for Measure*, and *The Tempest*.[37] In the first play, legalism kills mercy. In the second, mercy leads to chaos in law. In the third, Shakespeare joins the first two possibilities: crimes deserving punishment seem headed for a harsh response until mercy intervenes with a tinge of chaos thrown in. The plays cover the gamut, each one leaving an unsolved puzzle in line with the author's understanding of a difficult subject.[38]

Shakespeare sees the nexus of law and mercy as a snare. To prove this, he gives the enabling figure in all three plays a questionable trait, one that makes us think all the harder about the nature of mercy that each protagonist offers. Portia, a devious lawyer in disguise, wins her case in *The Merchant of Venice* through ruthless methods. Vincentio, the duke of unhappy Vienna, means well in *Measure for Measure* but turns hypocrite to get his way. Prospero impresses us with his learning and management skills in *The Tempest*, but no amount of knowledge or control validates his domineering manner and his cruelty toward those under his thumb. We regard these figures more than we like them.

The opening of act four in *The Merchant of Venice* gives us the most famous words on mercy in all of English literature and the most fanciful flights about it from the legal profession. Portia's speech urging Shylock to be merciful is quoted whenever the subject comes up, but only a very close reading and attention to context can give us her real meaning.

A brief summary provides that context. The impoverished Venetian nobleman Bassanio has won the hand of wealthy Portia of Belmont, but he has had to borrow the money to court her, money procured for him by his friend the merchant Antonio, who signed a bond with the Jewish moneylender Shylock to finance this courtship. Shylock, seemingly in jest but actually in earnest against the anti-Semitic Antonio, extracts the price of a pound of Antonio's flesh near his heart as the bond on the contract. When Antonio cannot pay, Shylock demands his pound of flesh, and the duke of Venice must grant it until Portia, in disguise as the doctor of laws Balthazar, delivers the argument that rescues Antonio, defeats Shylock, binds Bassanio more tightly to her, and saves her fortune, which had been offered to Shylock.

Controversy over the court scene revolves around the imputed sincerity of Portia's pleas for mercy given Shylock. Does she really give him a chance to change his mind before crushing him, or does she aim to ensnare him from the beginning? Early on, a good actress can answer this debate in either direction. Argument turns on Portia's opening description of mercy:

> The quality of mercy is not strained;
> It droppeth as the gentle rain from heaven
> Upon the place beneath. It is twice blest;
> It blesseth him that gives and him that takes.
> 'Tis mightiest in the mightiest; it becomes
> The throned monarch better than his crown.
> His sceptre shows the force of temporal power,
> The attribute to awe and majesty,
> Wherein doth sit the dread and fear of kings;
> But mercy is above the scept'red sway;
> It is enthroned in the hearts of kings;
> It is an attribute to God himself,
> And earthly power doth then show likest God's
> When mercy seasons justice. Therefore, Jew,
> Though justice be thy plea, consider this:
> That in the course of justice none of us
> Should see salvation. We do pray for mercy,
> And that same prayer doth teach us all to render
> The deeds of mercy. I have spoke thus much
> To mitigate the justice of thy plea,
> Which if thou follow, this strict court of Venice
> Must needs give sentence 'gainst the merchant there.
>
> (4.1.182–202)

The eloquence of this statement is beyond question, but the performative utterance in J. L. Austin's terms is worse than incomplete. The locutionary act of the speaker is deceptive; the illocutionary act of circumstance is not what it appears (much like the speaker); the perlocutionary act, or receptive impact, is deliberately evasive. Portia's statement is false in all three aspects of an attempt at realized communication. Those who quote it in the name of mercy have the words but not the music of its meaning.

How do we know so much? Portia's speech depends on a Christian concept of mercy and Shylock is not a Christian. Any notion of salvation that he might hold differs from what is given here and he would pray differently, but that is not all that is withheld. Portia may be sincere in her belief in mercy but not in her method of conveying it to Shylock. The positive attributes assigned to monarchical or political authority do not hold any meaning for him. All his life he has been treated unjustly by Venetian authority. He cannot look on it with veneration or even respect.

Structurally, the speech also thrives on misdirection. When she reaches for direct address, Portia calls her auditor "Jew," a pejorative term rather than his name, and at this moment in the speech, the axis shifts from the mercy she officially urges to the justice that Shylock demands. From the apostrophe "Therefore, *Jew*" the word *justice*—not *mercy*—dominates Portia's reasoning with the lie that Shylock will have his way if he insists on it. Her closing words—"Must needs give sentence 'gainst the Merchant there"—deliberately secure Shylock's continuing belief in his right to a literal judgment.

All of Portia's subsequent entreaties in this court scene are then calculated for her purposes rather than Shylock's. They seek to discover how far Shylock will go in carrying out his legal act of murder against Antonio so that she can measure the degree of his own coming punishment in violation of a law that any alien who threatens the life of a Venetian citizen is subject to the death penalty. When Portia finally asks if Shylock has provided a doctor to dress Antonio's projected wounds and he answers that he has not, she has the proof she needs in court to claim he means to kill Antonio.

With that proof in hand, Portia springs her trap. Shylock's bond calls for "a pound of flesh," but it allows not for "one drop of Christian blood" (4.1.305–10), and Shylock finds himself confounded by the impossibility.[39] The words cynically carry beyond their immediate import. The legally irrelevant and morally gratuitous addition of the adjective "Christian" to "blood" prefigures how far Shylock will be driven down. Portia stigmatizes the difference of *Jew* from *Christian* in justification of what will be done to him. Shylock loses not only his lands, his money, and his daughter, but, at his mortal enemy Antonio's behest, his faith through a forced conversion to Christianity.

The ruthless nature of this decision brings censure on Portia: "the gulf between her preaching about mercy dropping 'as the gentle rain from heaven' and her vengeful punishment of Shylock is unbridgeably wide."[40] On the other hand, Shakespeare gives her no real choice considering the negative forces all around her and the severity of Venetian law.[41] Every scene in the play underlines cruelty in control of behavior. Portia's choice is either to submit to it or to control it. She mourns the need to control it by answering cruelty for more of it in "naughty times." "If to do were as easy as to know what were good to do," she says, "chapels had been churches and poor men's cottages princes' palaces" (3.2.15; 1.2.12–13).

If mercy does not exist in Venice, what is the purpose of introducing it so vividly in the trial scene? Shakespeare's answer is typically subtle. Knowing one's self, knowing one's world, and knowing one's place in it are essential qualities in gauging the prospect of mercy. Portia alone has that capacity in the fallen world of the play. Not for nothing does Shakespeare give her the legal name "Balthazar" when she examines justice from the safety of disguise. The reference is to one of the three biblical wise men who journey to Bethlehem to witness Christ's birth.[42]

Outwardly, *Measure for Measure* differs sharply from *The Merchant of Venice*. Inwardly, Shakespeare's take on mercy remains much the same. Mercy in this later play is not an aspiration but a reality run wild with turmoil as the result. It is again a difficult concept to work with. A more detailed analysis of *Measure for Measure* appears in the introduction to part 3 of this volume. Here it is enough to know that no balance occurs at any point in the play's vexed juxtaposition of law and mercy.

The two figures who hold the legal power to exercise mercy, Duke Vincentio of Vienna and his designated substitute Angelo, end up using that power for personal purposes in ways that make law less secure in the city. We hear that "thieves for their robbery have authority, when judges steal themselves" (2.2.176–77), and then are made to see it at every social level in the play. Vincentio, who by his own confession has allowed law to degenerate, has gone into hiding to let others solve the problem for him, and we have to agree that "it was a mad, fantastical trick of him to steal from the state" (3.2.89). Authority has not the self-confidence to enforce law on its own terms and can only make things work out by "dark deeds darkly answered" and "craft against vice" (3.2.171, 270). Law has no transparency, an essential condition for the concept of mercy to work as a remedy. The self-knowledge needed to wield mercy is also missing. "That we were all, as some would seem to be, from our faults, as faults from seeming, free," opines the exasperated duke in what is close to double-talk (3.2.37–38).

Even self-knowledge is not enough without a legal framework to clarify what mercy can mean. Shakespeare may have had this problem in mind with *The Tempest*. Prospero, the protagonist of this last play, has the knowledge but not enough of a context to hold himself to account much less others. The play is also so determinedly secular, by comparison to others by Shakespeare, that the emphasis must be deliberate. It takes up the politically dangerous crime of treason, which would normally have had religious implications in Elizabethan England, but Shakespeare does not move in that direction. Magic takes the place of religion, and the result is as close as we come in Shakespeare to a pagan concept of mercy.

The facts are among the plainest in a Shakespearean play. Prospero, the rightful duke of Milan, has been overthrown by his usurping brother, Antonio, in league with King Alonso of Naples, and he is set adrift in a sinking boat with his child Miranda to die at sea. But the two of them miraculously land on an island deserted except for a single native (Caliban) and a host of natural spirits. Father and daughter have survived on the island for twelve years, during which time Prospero gains the knowledge to hold magical sway over the spirit world. As the play opens, a storm and shipwreck have placed Prospero's enemies on the island at his mercy. The action turns on what he will do to them.

For much of *The Tempest*, a name that describes the deposed duke's internal turmoil as much as the external storm, Prospero torments those whom he has some right to punish, and he is very good at it. He has become a consummate torturer through his treatment of Caliban, the native whom he has turned into a slave. As in any slave-ridden society, terror and punishment are the master's means. Magic is the suspect tool Prospero uses to punish Caliban and enslave Ariel, the natural spirit who is made to help him control this new world. Caliban is given physical torments that keep him more or less in line, while Ariel receives vocal threats of brutal treatment to ensure obedience. Together, Prospero and Ariel drive his enemies insane. Prospero watches over all these misfortunes with obvious satisfaction.

The dénouement of the play comes as Prospero and Ariel, his punishing agent, have left the guilty parties imprisoned and gibbering in fear. "At this hour," gloats the duke turned magician, "lies at my mercy all mine enemies" (5.1.12–15). The pleasure in revenge, the reflex in a wronged punisher with vulnerable enemies in hand, dominates in this moment, and it takes Ariel, the pagan, to remind Prospero of the need for mercy: "if you now beheld them, your affections would become tender." Prospero questions this statement: "Dost thou think so, spirit?" Ariel answers with the most moving line of the play, "Mine would, sir, were I human" (5.1.18–20).

To recognize one's humanity is to see the possibility of mercy, but when Prospero eventually heeds this advice, we are left with another puzzle. When should the possibility of mercy remain unavailable? Prospero forgives everyone in the end, including those who deserve severe punishment, and in the process he compromises his own legality as England would then have understood it.

Some criminals only understand punishment. The usurping brother, Antonio, the person Prospero trusted and loved next to Miranda in all the world, is one of Shakespeare's completely amoral villains, much like Iago in *Othello* or Richard III in the play of that name. Antonio has no conscience. "I feel not this deity in my bosom," he boasts when asked (2.1.274–76), and he proves it over and over again. He deposes his own brother to become the duke of Milan, he plans Prospero and Miranda's deaths without a single pang of remorse, he betrays his own city to Naples, and he plots to assassinate the king of Naples with the king's brother Sebastian. Antonio stops at nothing to advance his own career. His ambition is boundless. Guilt is foreign to his very nature.

All the same, universal forgiveness reigns in Shakespeare's reconciliation scene. Prospero knows he is dealing with traitors, the worst of criminals, and he knows they will conspire against him again if given the chance. Nevertheless, he forgives Antonio and Sebastian and will "tell no tales" about their planned act of treason, the narrowly thwarted assassination of King Alonzo (5.1.127–33). In this final scene of forgiveness, Antonio gives no response to Prospero's empty accusation ("most wicked sir!"). He simply bids his time.

By not leveling formal charges, Prospero leaves unrepentant, conspiratorial lawbreakers at large. His failure to reveal their plot amounts to constructive treason, the penalty for which could be a terrible, drawn-out, tortured death in Tudor England.[43] By complicating forgiveness, Shakespeare once again leaves mercy in a problematic relationship with law.

The great advantage of drama in critical inquiry consists in putting all parties knowingly in dialogue with each other where gesture, movement, and expression tell us everything about words spoken or not spoken. The sincerity or falsehood of a performative utterance is there for all to see as well as hear. The importance of these generic qualities in explaining a legal act of mercy, where all must come to a formal understanding, cannot be emphasized enough. Shakespeare joins his art and his knowledge of human nature to convey the complexity of our subject as no other has done.

What does Shakespeare mean to teach us? Experience in authority—knowing oneself and knowing the world around oneself—are essential in any exercise of mercy. Too much mercy belies the name and becomes the wrongdoer's expectation and advantage. Severity in law by itself is not the problem if used to instruct. Problems emerge in the tension between law and mercy. Awareness of how to handle this tension is key. Finally, Shakespeare seems to question the view of Christian mercy noted earlier. The mercy offered by Ariel and accepted by Prospero in *The Tempest* is pagan in form and based on simple humanity. It is also Shakespeare's last word on the subject.

Modern confusion over the nature of legal mercy, far more confused than as construed by Shakespeare, has two major sources and a minor one. Scholars either try to make the concept a relational part of the legal framework, often through specialized vocabulary that others do not want to accept, or they try to exclude it altogether as an inappropriate legal phenomenon. Overt or implied dependence on religious understandings of mercy is the minor impediment, often through overwrought connections between private and legal understandings. Of course, the tension between mercy and justice further complicates each of these problems.

Better far to think of legal mercy as *sui generis*, "of its own kind" and set off. Most legal actions are thought to be compelled; this one is not. Legal mercy, as many point out, is uniquely supererogatory in form—existing beyond expectation or requirement or even duty—and it takes place only as an exceptional remedy. Why not take these words for what they mean? Legal mercy becomes a possibility when the law does what it wants to do rather than what it must do, and in keeping with this act of will, it deserves its own category. Rarely used, it can be utilized only when a number of conditions are absolutely met. It is not even clear that a legal act of mercy should be discussed in terms of punishment given that it stands for the absence or reduction of punishment.

Nevertheless, most debates on mercy in law concentrate on theories of punishment. The seminal essay that guides scholarship is Alwynne Smart's 1968 article "Mercy." There is much to like in this essay, even though Smart's first words set future discussion in stone: "A theory of punishment should give some account of mercy."[44] Smart rightly distinguishes legal acts that should not be considered merciful and dismisses the protest of equal protection (less punishment for one; more for another) by suggesting "some mercy is better than none at all." She adds we are merciful "only when we are *compelled* to be by the claims that other obligations have on us." More specifically, her focus on theories of punishment leads her to argue that only a retributive theory actually justifies mercy.[45]

Too many critics have jumped on Smart's throwaway notion of compulsion in mercy as inconsistent with the supererogatory nature of it.[46] The deeper issue—whether different theories of punishment delineate the uses of mercy with retributive theory in control—has more purchase. Some commentators try to give utilitarianism a better rationale for mercy as closer to the principle of charity. Others challenge Smart's suggestion that benevolence should be the main impulse in exercising mercy. But if most critics differ with Smart over any one of a number of particulars, they generally accept the methodological frame that she establishes. Almost half a century later and counting, most discussions of mercy still turn on theories of punishment in conflict with each other.[47]

A book-length debate between Jeffrie Murphy and Jean Hampton follows this pattern. Murphy, who is against mercy in law, seems to win this argument by getting Hampton, who argues for mercy in law, to agree that "there is a legitimate retributive sentiment" controlling debate over and above notions of compassion and charity. Yet we have to remember that Murphy controls publication of the volume, gives himself first and last word in it, and follows other scholars in too quickly dismissing a utilitarian concept of punishment as too imprecise to be considered as a basis for mercy.[48]

Hampton counters with some valid points of her own. She suggests that hatred with direct affinities to retribution "is another one of those self-defeating strategies for shoring up a shaky sense of one's own worth." Retribution is so close to revenge, she argues, that it lacks a notion of desert and may be no more precise than other theories of punishment. Emotionalism is an often ignored point by retributivists, and allows Hampton to come to a secondary conclusion. Retributive theories do not stand alone. They depend for their purchase on "a variety of non-retributive motives."[49]

Most scholars ignore Hampton's important secondary point. She has urged less debate over differences and more recognition of the interaction in theories of punishment. Ignoring this effort at mediation, most debaters stress the primacy of retribution to remove mercy from legal consideration. At the extremes, we find "a nation confident in its laws and secure in its institutions should be ashamed of the practice of mercy in its criminal justice system"; "by framing the issue as one of mercy rather than of justification, officials and the general public evade their responsibility to reflect upon the law as the official representation of the conventional public morality." More starkly, "a judge has no right to be merciful."[50]

The certainty and blithe dismissal in these and other objections to mercy ignore an available comparative frame of reference. Mercy does have a place in some legal regimes. James Q. Whitman describes "a lasting attachment to the values of mercy" in Europe where a "spirit of mercy pervades Continental justice." "Why," he reasonably asks, "are the values of mercy so much stronger in continental Europe?"[51]

In American law the denials of mercy are categorical; the much rarer affirmations come in highly qualified terms. Mercy becomes "a disjunctive desert" based on "disjunction of penalties."[52] Mercy is "an imperfect virtue."[53] Mercy is "an imperfect duty," "a duty that can only be fulfilled if one has simultaneously embraced a particular end or acted for a particular reason."[54] Few want to give it independent status.

Evasion is another strategy for dealing with this dilemma, and it is one favored by both sides in debate. Why not farm the whole problem out to other institutions? Dan Markel writes in this vein as a firm retributivist. He defines mercy as "leniency granted out of compassion, bias, corruption, or caprice" and uses these pejorative terms to say mercy fails to meet "the democratic difficulty." Acceptable avenues of leniency, such as "constitutional or democratic laws and institutions" or "the presidential pardon or grand jury nullification," are the viable alternatives for Markel. His "retributivist critique of mercy" holds mercy to "the democratic pedigree of criminal laws." Judicial discretion is not an option.[55]

The fact that Robert Misner favors mercy in law does not stop his approach from being remarkably similar to Markel's. He accepts the same catalog of theories of punishment with the language of retribution on top.

With retribution a foregone conclusion, Misner looks away from the legal process for "a legislator, whose personal value system stresses the virtue of mercy." How will this work? "Mercy, carefully used to respect the retributive instincts of the electorate, will permit legislators to move away from the current trend of spiraling incarceration rates with ever-lengthening sentences toward a system that recaptures a semblance of humaneness."[56]

Other arguments for mercy reach for the mystery in spiritual parallels to deal with theoretical difficulties. Christian morality, as we have seen, can support either charitable release or severe punishment. It can function as a rhetorical device for whatever position one wants to argue. "My legislator," Misner announces early in his claim of mercy, "has been influenced in this regard by his own beliefs within the Christian tradition." "My legislator," he concludes, "sees mercy as both a religious and humanitarian imperative."[57]

Markel, arguing the other side, uses the same Christian basis to deny the relevance of mercy.[58] Melissa Beach goes further than either. She writes, "Judges in the United States would do best to emulate God's ways to the best of their abilities."[59] Heidi Hurd traces "the morality of mercy" to "its God-like status."[60] Notions of "cosmic justice," "repentance," "grace," and "benevolence" seem irresistible.[61] Most law review essays on mercy genuflect toward religious sensibilities.

The common ground in these debates is part of the problem. Sometimes what seems obvious is not so obvious if one looks beyond the stock implications that everyone draws from it. What is shared in argument also deserves scrutiny. Ripe for examination is how supporters of a legal act of mercy agree with its severest critics when all emphasize that mercy requires a very tentative act in law. The presumed atypical nature of mercy makes it not only questionable but completely risk adverse.

The all-or-nothing aspect of a legal act of mercy should resist a language of half measures in explanation. As a proceeding that demands risk in the bestower and a deft rationale for all concerned, legal mercy requires full engagement of the imagination. Mercy is a holistic conception, an independent partner alongside justice rather than a subordinated idea or a discrepancy in the system. It cannot be broken down into less than the sum of its parts. Debaters that try to do so miss the point of it. And why shouldn't a concept of mercy be just as tough-minded as a legal concept?

Robert Weisberg in a striking article, "Apology, Legislation, and Mercy," says as much. In his analysis of "the Justice-Mercy Conundrum," he pits scholarship that is "sharply normative" against his own "analytic critique," with the notion of looking at law when it knows it has been too harsh. This allows him to concentrate on what law thinks it is doing instead of dwelling on theorized discrepancies.[62] The shift in focus is especially important because it leads us back to an identifying characteristic of mercy with which this chapter began. A legal act of mercy is not about what law must do but what it wants to do. Weisberg asks us to think about what mercy claims to be in a legal understanding as opposed to whether it should exist, and he is right. It is time to turn to what law actually says about mercy and what it means when it says it.

Many problems here are of a particular nature. The actual law of mercy has most trouble with volition by making that the most worrisome analytical feature. An independent act of will, the grant of mercy reveals and exposes the person offering the benefit more than the one receiving it, and the U.S. Supreme Court's inarticulate, varied, and stumbling approach proves the point. Studies have shown "the Court has no coherent understanding of mercy." It exhibits "basic confusion about the role of mercy" and can never agree on where mercy fits in "the proper balance between rationality and discretion" in assigning punishment.[63]

No one would claim that mercy represents a precise legal concept in Supreme Court doctrine, but it has been a term of art in statute law and court opinion since the 1976 *Gregg v. Georgia* case. *Gregg* made the subject of mercy a frequent topic among law scholars, judges, and practitioners by introducing a separate discretionary penalty phase in death penalty trials with criteria that require new levels of individuation in decisions about punishment.[64]

The stipulation that aggravating factors against mitigating circumstances be considered separately from conviction in death penalty trials has made mercy an unavoidable subject in this aspect of punishment.[65] No one on or off the court has been satisfied with the result. Nor should they be satisfied. Ambivalent use of the term by the highest court in the land—the court that sets the intellectual trajectory of law in America—runs against the precision that legal language customarily demands.

It is easy to see why mercy would be used in loose exchange by a divided court fighting over contrasting interpretations of how aggravation and mitigation apply in deciding punishment of crime. Martha Nussbaum has traced the volatility of Supreme Court debates in this area. Mercy becomes

either a minor ploy or a strategic solution depending on how the evaluations of aggravating factors in crime against mitigating circumstances for a
defendant are conducted. Methodology is part of the problem here. Is the
proper approach a balancing act? A sequential and separate consideration?
Or an emotive enumeration of the element or elements that should count
the most?[66]

Watching the Supreme Court bandy words over mercy reveals ulterior
motives more than a desire for accuracy. In *Walton v. Arizona* (1990), Justices Antonin Scalia and John Paul Stevens spar, without fully recognizing
it, over the meaning of volition in mercy when applied to the bifurcated
investigation of aggravating and mitigating factors of a death penalty case.
The terms used are the conventional ones over judicial discretion, where
the claim of unfettered discretion means arbitrary decisions for Scalia
while the flexibility in discretion grants justice for Stevens. Scalia wants a
balancing test of aggravation and mitigation in the penalty phase. Stevens
asks for more room in the mitigation phase.[67]

Dispute over proper areas of mitigation creates another battleground.
The majority in *Franklin v. Lynaugh* (1988) denies the right of a petitioner
sentenced to death to have the stipulation given to the jury that his disciplinary record during incarceration was without incident. The defense at
trial wanted to prove that their client would not be a danger to others in
prison, a form of evidence that reaches one objection to capital punishment.
Stevens, dissenting, tries to increase the range of merciful consideration.
"Past conduct," he argues, "often provides insights into a person's character
that will evoke a merciful response to a demand for the ultimate punishment
even though it may shed no light on what may happen in the future."[68]

If mercy as a concept now has a recognized role, what it means remains
unclear in the jurisprudence of mercy. In 1985 the United States Court of
Appeals for the Eleventh Circuit held in *Wilson v. Kemp* that a prosecutor
cannot claim that "mercy" describes a sentence of life in prison, but it confirms the need for mercy to be considered: "The Supreme Court, in requiring individual consideration by capital juries and in requiring full play for
mitigating circumstances has demonstrated that mercy has its proper place
in capital sentencing."[69] Well and good, but what is the place of mercy? No
one on any side of these debates knows.

Two years after *Wilson*, in *California v. Brown* (1987), the Supreme
Court quarreled heatedly over the issue. A majority rejects Justice Harry

Blackmun's attempt to define the role of mercy in law more expansively but gives no prevailing definition of its own. The narrowest majority, itself badly fragmented, upholds a conviction on an instruction that asked jurors to ignore "mere sentiment, conjecture, sympathy, passion, prejudice, public opinion, or public feeling" in the penalty phase of a capital case. Dissenting, Blackmun argues that such language denies "sympathy and mercy, human qualities that are undeniably emotional in nature," and he tries to move the concept of mercy to the center in death penalty cases. "The sentencer's ability to respond with mercy towards a defendant has always struck me as a particularly valuable aspect of the capital sentencing procedure."[70]

The Supreme Court has shied away from anything like Blackmun's interpretation or use of mercy even as it has been forced to recognize that the decision to have a separate penalty phase assigns value and use to the concept—a higher value and use than it collectively wants to endorse. As a result, the jurisprudence of mercy wanders in a no-man's land, somewhere between the Court's hesitation and Blackmun's more aggressive and more easily understood insistence that "contemporary values" have made "the sentencer's expression of mercy a distinctive feature of our society that we deeply value."[71]

The Court's hesitation is clearer than its solutions. In 1989, it denied certiorari in *Bertolotti v. Dugger* when acceptance of the case would have forced it to consider "an instruction explicitly authorizing the jury to disregard the trial evidence and to exercise its power of mercy."[72] In *Lusk v. Singletary* from 1992, it again denied certiorari in a case from the same eleventh circuit despite a trial court's statement that "the law of this State does not permit this Court to extend mercy to this Defendant or others convicted of a capital felony." In *Lusk* the word "mercy" seems to mean very little at all. Said the appellate court, in affirming capital punishment, "the trial court's statement that it would not consider 'mercy' was nothing more than an accurate summary of Florida law."[73]

Failure to define mercy divides the Supreme Court down the middle once again in *Johnson v. Texas*. Here, in 1993, a 5 to 4 majority affirms the death sentence of a nineteen-year-old defendant convicted of murder even though insufficient attention is given by the trial court to the mitigating factor of age. Justice Anthony Kennedy, speaking for a slim and divided majority, admits that the facts of the case "compel the jury to make a moral judgment about the severity of the crime and the defendant's culpability."

By the same token, "moral judgment" does not mean "the vagaries of particular jurors' emotional sensibilities."[74] What, then, are the ingredients of moral judgment for the average juror?

The Court in *Johnson* fears the full force of what mercy might entail. "There might have been a juror who, on the basis solely of sympathy or mercy, would have opted against the death penalty had there been a vehicle to do so," Kennedy reasons. Yet the absence of such a vehicle gives no reason to overturn the judgment of the Texas Court of Criminal Appeals because "we have not construed [previous cases] to mean that a jury must be able to dispense mercy on the basis of a sympathetic response to the defendant."[75] The rough equation of mercy with sympathy in Kennedy's language indicates once again that the Court has little interest in a rigorous definition of the concept.

Kansas v. Marsh in 2006, another 5 to 4 decision, appears to give aggravation the edge over mitigation while simultaneously curtailing the range and undefined meaning of mercy in capital punishment cases. The Court reinstates the constitutionality of the death penalty statute of Kansas after the Kansas Supreme Court finds it unconstitutional. The statute "requires the imposition of the death penalty when the sentencing jury determines that aggravating evidence and mitigating evidence are in equipoise." *Marsh* reinstates the law and holds that an equal balance or equipoise leaves a presumption of death not life. The bare majority sustains the concept of mercy as an independent variable within the balancing act but writes to minimize the actual role it might play.[76]

A more recent decision shows how acutely the Supreme Court distrusts its own use of mercy. *Graham v. Florida* (2010) avoids the word while applying aspects of the concept. Without saying so, the opinion restricts formal discussion of mercy to capital punishment. It holds that the cruel and unusual punishment clause of the Eighth Amendment does not permit a juvenile offender to be sentenced automatically to life imprisonment without parole for a crime less than homicide.

Justice Kennedy, once again the swing vote in another slim majority, reverses such a sentence for sixteen-year-old Terrance Jamar Graham as too harsh after Graham violates parole in a second act of armed robbery. Though acknowledging that Graham's punishment is too cruel and implicitly without mercy, Kennedy carefully avoids the volitional attribute that would identify it as an act of mercy. He reaches instead for "a categorical rule" applicable to all minors.[77] It is the tone of Kennedy's language that tells another story.

To decide that Graham's sentence is cruel and unusual, the Court "must look beyond historical conceptions to 'the evolving standards of decency that mark the progress of a maturing society.'" Its decision "necessarily embodies a moral judgment" and "must respect the human attributes even of those who have committed serious crimes." Kennedy compares the severity of sentences in other jurisdictions and finds for Graham, even though "thirty-seven States as well as the District of Columbia permit sentences of life without parole for a juvenile non-homicide offender" and even though Graham's sentence is more common (not "unusual") than other sentencing practices reversed under the Eighth Amendment. The marks of mercy, but not the word, are all over *Graham v. Florida*.[78]

Kennedy's resistance to the core term of what he asserts is tactically brilliant as the swing vote in *Graham*, but that does not keep it from being theoretically foolish. The great irony of walling a still vague and contested notion of mercy entirely within death penalty law should not be missed. Mercy exists in American law precisely where it is least needed! The many grounds for challenging the death penalty have left talk of mercy available but unnecessary even as exaggerated dispute over the term in that context has made it too controversial for use in other areas of legal endeavor.

Obviously, mercy could be a better legal tool than it is, and there are reasons to move in this direction, but it will not happen if current usage and understandings prevail. Expansive references to mercy without proper delineation of the concept is one major handicap. The controversial prominence of mercy as a safety valve in death penalty cases is another. Emotive parallels between mercy in private life and public law make a third. Identification with partially hidden shadowy practices in law is a fourth.

Shakespeare aside, the quality of mercy in law *is* strained, and it should be. Great effort and perspicacity must go into its application. Only the most alert calculation and scrutiny on all sides with a transparent explanation of the reasons for invoking it can justify the use of mercy in law. This kind of rigor is lacking in current understandings of the concept because judges looking to be lenient shy away from effective use of it.

Examples of avoidance of the concept in cases where thoughts of mercy are clearly on the table are easy to find, and they parallel, in their evasions, Kennedy's opinion in *Graham*. Harsh penalties for drug use and distribution have led a number of federal judges to bend over backward to avoid sentencing guidelines while pretending to obey them in spirit. These cases all avoid the word "mercy" for fear of appearing "soft" on crime. They try to be what they are not: hedges and strained qualifications of a law that deserves to be criticized in more general terms.[79]

One must be careful here. No judge can repeatedly flout a law, but a reasoned and objective protest in a particularly relevant case against a law that causes more harm than good might be thought to be part of a judge's duty if mercy can be made more of a working tool. A merciful judgment rendered objectively and pointedly would almost certainly get more notice from the legislative and executive arms of government than current attempts to remain in accordance with a law through indirect challenge.

The pervasive emotionalism of our times may be the most difficult drawback to progress in this area. Glossing mercy with emotion becomes especially dangerous when the law does it to itself. When a figure like Justice Blackmun in *California v. Brown* confuses "humane response" with "sympathy" and calls mercy "undeniably emotional in nature" as part of his opposition to the death penalty, he opens the concept to counterattacks of arbitrariness, impulsiveness, and favoritism.[80]

J. L. Austin's objectifying insistence on performative utterance is valuable as a counterpoint not just because it insists on total comprehension but because it replaces uncertain feeling with the mechanics of a cooler perception. It rationalizes performance and brings calculated method to the understanding of mercy. In using it, a grantor of mercy must scrutinize the sincerity of thought and language used in giving a reduction or release in punishment that is officially deserved. The same words must create transparency in both context and procedure. Finally, they must secure recognition in the receiver of it, full understanding in all relevant legal actors, and communal acceptance through the standards of normative discernment available to it.

Hardest of all, grantors of mercy must authenticate the sincerity expected of them in two additional ways: first, with an admission that a decision to grant mercy gratifies the sentencing system as much as the receiver of it; and second, with a credible claim that the act of mercy still sustains the rule of law. An *admission* means a legal system has been strengthened by the granting of mercy in the preservation of its authority. A *claim* signifies that the rule of law has been sustained because the act of mercy somehow supports communal understanding of obedience to law. These elements are central aspects of a legal act of mercy even though they may be difficult for a grantor to articulate.

Why is this so difficult? The *admission* that the system itself is helped by an act of mercy requires a philosophical adjustment in temperament. Public acknowledgment of the need for mercy strips the punisher of reflexive anger and righteousness in the name of the kindness and institutional vision that Marcus Aurelius requires in one with power over fallen humanity. The generosity in it connects to "freedom of decision" when a punisher chooses "not according to the letter of the law but according to what is right and good." The act of mercy must simultaneously counter any notion of weakness. Mercy, in this sense, secures the legitimacy of a ruler through "conspicuous clemency."[81]

The *claim* that an act of legal mercy preserves the rule of law completes the act and requires an even more difficult rhetorical stance. If admission of benefit adjusts temperament, the claim of congruity demands breadth of vision and rhetorical ingenuity. How can a decision against the letter of the law *support* the rule of law? This is the problem that causes many to doubt— and eventually reject—mercy. Adjustment of mercy to the rule of law must overcome the seeming contradiction.

These two counterintuitive aspects of mercy—admission of legal desirability and claim of congruence with the rule of law—reach to the root of the concept. At issue is a final query: when, exactly, is it appropriate for an act of legal mercy to take place and when is it not appropriate? Three essential but independent conditions allow the prospect of mercy to be considered so long as consideration does not mean action and so long as action respects the integrity of the legal system and more general notions of fairness. If the law in question is too harsh for the particular situation, if proper punishment would cause unwarranted harm beyond the meaning of the stipulated sentence, or if the affected community would benefit more by learning of leniency than by hearing about punishment, then a legal act of mercy can lend itself to the conditions of articulation outlined. All three of these negative conditions exist throughout the United States and at levels of severity that compare unfavorably with justice systems elsewhere.[82]

Mercy is about having the courage to do the right thing openly and for the right reason. The definitions offered here limit its application, but they also turn applications that are appropriate into responsible and accountable action. The ancients gave us the four cardinal virtues, and they often ordered them as follows: justice, wisdom, moderation, and courage. They made courage the fourth virtue, but in a broken world that they continued to break in brutal fashion, they realized that without courage, none of the first three virtues really mattered.

Courage, of course, must have a context in which to operate to be meaningful. A more lucid, carefully articulated concept of mercy in place of the emotional bag of bromides that now exists would be a step in that direction, a small step but nevertheless a step toward recovering a concept now buried in evasion and legal obfuscation. Mercy, properly understood and carefully confined, is a legal tool just waiting to be used.

3

Immigration Law

AN ANSWER TO INTRACTABILITY

THE GREATEST CURRENT CONFLICT IN American understanding involves immigration issues. Everyone knows that law in this area is unfair and a failure with so many examples of injustice that all sides have to acknowledge its pernicious effects yet bitter divisions keep the country from changing the law or dealing with a now massive influx of undocumented entrants. So bitter are these controversies that they begin to question the very fabric of communal understanding.

What it means to be a foreign person on American soil begins to disappear when a member on the floor of Congress generates news cycles by claiming that pregnant women have flown in from the Middle East carrying "terror babies" that will "destroy our way of life."[1] Elected officials equate pregnant immigrants to multiplying rats, compare illegal aliens to the threat of Hitler, and say border agents should "shoot to kill."[2] These are signs of a problem that has grown larger than itself. A country dedicated to the propositions of life, liberty, and the pursuit of happiness cannot allow itself to think this way for long.

What will it take to deal with this issue? An intractable problem remains one not because it lacks answers but because the frustration from internal lines of division polarizes factions and transforms attitudes into extreme versions of concern. An answer must therefore begin outside of the problem as stated, and it begins by unraveling the entrenched cultural, political, and legal divisions. It then turns those lines of force to a different lens, the lens of a story well told. People think differently only if they see differently.

The critic Kenneth Burke expresses this difficulty most succinctly: "A way of seeing is also a way of not seeing."[3]

Anger in fights over the influx of immigration grows out of ideological contradictions at the core of the subject. Etched on the pedestal of the Statue of Liberty are official words from 1886 that greet new arrivals in the harbor of New York City. They read as follows:

> Give me your tired, your poor,
> Your huddled masses yearning to breathe free,
> The wretched refuse of your teeming shore.
> Send these, the homeless, tempest-tost to me,
> I lift my lamp beside the golden door!

These words, placed figuratively in the mouth of the statue, the "Mother of Exiles," come from a solicited sonnet by the poet Emma Lazarus, and they offer an unqualified welcome to all arrivals. Indeed, the more desperate the reader of these words, the more urgently they claim to apply.[4]

When does the assumed right to welcome also imply a power to exclude, and if so, who gets to exclude and why? Subliminal national processes are at work here. In a nation driven by the right to property, no one questions the ability of an owner to protect privately held land from trespass, but how does this idea extend to the assumption that an individual citizen "owns" the country in a way that a new arrival does not? What is it about conceptions that gives anyone the right to challenge an alien on common ground?

The parameters and the size of the situation identify it as an intractable problem. First, you cannot forcibly remove twelve million people living peaceably on American soil without rending the ethos of the United States. Second, a large white but now threatened majority of Americans wishes that people arriving from new ethnicities would go away. Third, an all too human desire to look down on those who are different and less fortunate shapes individual and public opinions.[5] Fourth, hard economic times have increased vocational anxieties and recognition that law and policy have failed to solve a growing problem. Fifth, no one involved in immigration issues trusts an established system filled with contradictions and hypocrisies for all to see.

Against these elements are ignored principles of definition. What has happened to Emma Lazarus's words on the Statue of Liberty? A politics of exclusion has denied the spirit of welcome to countless numbers currently in the land. There now exists a huge and helpless population that cannot, in the words of the "Mother of Exiles," "breathe free" anywhere in the United States. The "golden door" is shut to anyone in this category. Legal regulation has produced its own category of "wretched refuse," and the people in it are treated in ways that are unjust for anyone else in America.

Illegal alien is the derogatory term used to describe the approximately twelve million souls living in limbo in the United States.[6] Pejorative language feeds the prejudice that prevents change, and it has a long history. The end of slavery in 1865 has not reduced bias against black people in part because the language used to describe them does not change. "It is tempting to read into the intersectional war a redirected or displaced aggression against blacks—outcasts before, during, and after the War."[7] Those "outcasts" could be rejected as "an alien black race."[8] Discrimination in a country dedicated to equality depends on the use of such words. To be "outcast" and "alien" justifies otherwise unacceptable levels of negative treatment.[9]

The term *outcast* pushes away. The term *alien* excludes. Taken together, the two clarify the boundaries of an established society. They circumscribe the familiar order, protect the status quo, and encourage nationalistic expression based on omission. Sociologists argue that discrimination answers fear of outsiders by fostering "group identification."[10] When social standing is questioned, "discriminatory behavior is perceived to be instrumental" in status formation.[11] In more anthropological terms, groups stabilize themselves through "rules of pollution" that keep others out. What one is not (and does not want to be) gives form to identity and worth by marking the unworthy.[12]

Pejorative use of these categories influences attitudes toward immigrants and allows prejudice to control barometers in thought. Debate is then based on a false but deeply held conviction: "the pervasive tendency to regard people of different races as essentially different kinds of people," a belief that rarely distinguishes between physical perception and geographical origin.[13] The contending voices grow especially shrill through an added level of confusion and division. Americans can never decide whether homogeneity or difference is the strength of the nation.

The confusion in attitudes has enormous rhetorical significance. As overt expressions of racism become taboo in public life, communal anger, fear, and uncertainty over human difference must find another terminology to express the same innate concerns. The result has been a quantum shift in political discourse. The new term of choice, one that serves conflicting purposes, is the word *alien*. To be alien today signifies more than not belonging. It means something unpleasant enough to convey racial expression without more being said. This is never more so than in debates over immigration where levels of racial toleration fluctuate according to economic need.

Prosperity leads to legal encouragement of immigration, while economic downturns and scarcer employment demand legal discouragement. The institutional history of immigration law clearly reflects these pendulum swings. Congress created the Bureau of Immigration in 1891 and originally placed it under the Department of Commerce and Labor with stimulation of economic growth in mind. The Bureau was then moved to the Department of Labor in 1913 with a more restricted focus on a cheap workforce. In 1940, under the threat of war, the Bureau, by then renamed as the Immigration and Naturalization Service, moved again, this time into the Department of Justice, where legality and restriction became its primary aim.[14]

This negative legal trajectory has increased during the recessions and foreign wars of today. Alien workers continue to be needed but mostly for very restrictive interim work. Reconceived again after the 9/11 terrorist attack on the United States, the Immigration and Naturalization Service was dissolved into three separate units and placed within a conglomerate known as the Department of Homeland Security. Immigration law has now ratified its split personality—welcoming but rejecting—with a new emphasis and terminology. Surveillance against alien forces, the primary mission of Homeland Security, now serves as the *raison d'être* of immigration law.

Here is how a triangulated system in conflict with itself employs "the Aesopian language of the immigration statutes crafted by legislators and bureaucrats." The Bureau of Customs and Border Protection (BCBP) keeps people out. The Bureau of Immigration and Customs Enforcement (BICE) restricts entry to the country to legal immigrants. The Bureau of Citizenship and Immigration Services (BCIS) oversees the transformation from registered legal alien to citizen while keeping illegal aliens where they are. A telling priority controls lines of authority. The BCBP, the BICE, and the BCIS all report to the Department of Homeland Security's Undersecretary for Border and Transportation Services.[15]

The term *illegal alien* identifies a double negative within this legal construct. Original understandings of the word *alien* include "a person hostile to this country," "a native of an unfriendly country," and "an enemy from a foreign land." Each negative possibility is squared into something else when the adjective *illegal* is added. In law, "an alien is a person who is not a citizen." An accepted immigrant is "an alien who comes for permanent settlement—a 'legal permanent resident.'" "An illegal alien is an alien who is unlawfully present . . . or who *otherwise* commits a deportable offense."[16]

The distinction between mere presence and an overt act in conferring illegality disappears, especially when the connotations refer back to "hostile," "unfriendly," "enemy," or "foreign" as definitions of "alien." All illegal aliens thus become criminals at large, a presumed danger to ordinary citizens and a menace to be answered by governmental action and righteous public anger.

Communal hysteria over aliens has popular sources as well. Concepts easily turn virulent in the saturation coverage of an image culture.[17] So it has been with the word *alien*. Since 1979, blockbuster science fiction movies have featured the word in titles and have tied the idea to vicious extraterrestrial and subterranean creatures, beings who destroy whole communities for no reason other than their innately foreign and malicious natures. These imaginary villains are the worst possible "illegal aliens." They move across the screen as serial psychopaths who must be eliminated. They are purged in movie after movie but always with a hidden residue left over to sustain fear in the viewer for the next sequel.[18]

Narrative structure in alien movies thrives on racial claims that comport with the history of discrimination in immigration law.[19] Both frames of reference search for and reject what is too different to accept. It is now forbidden to use racial slurs in public discourse, but parallel terms appear with obsessive frequency in alien movies and in public objections to illegal aliens. In Hollywood cinematic marketing, an alternative life-form lurks somewhere in American society to be rooted out. This horrible being can assume human form, and that form holds audiences in a special way. Viewers can hate "the temporary human" in racial terms unacceptable when used against a real person.

The attraction in alien movies lies in this manipulative use of intersecting vocabulary, which also informs rhetoric in powerful anti-immigration movements in American politics.[20] As racism in public discourse grows increasingly costly to a user of it, condemnations of aliens function as a coded substitute. Movie aliens absorb attention by inhabiting negative American feelings for everything different from the mainstream.

Reality lends a hand by imitating fantasy on immigration issues. In recent years armed quasi-military units along the Mexican border have risen from two thousand to over eleven thousand operatives, equipped with high-tech devices and the latest weaponry. Border Patrols close to Mexico deploy unmanned aerial vehicles named "Predator B" drones to find illegal immigrants crossing the border.[21] Everything about these teams and their weapons implies communal danger.

Not for nothing is the term *illegal alien* central to a national politics of fear and prejudice—so much so that it dominates public discourse even where immigration is not a major presence.[22] Dave Heineman, Governor of Nebraska from 2005 to 2015, made illegal immigration "the defining issue" of his successful election campaigns and legislative agendas even though his state has no border problem, a low unemployment rate, and no population density issue.[23] Pennsylvania legislators warn against the "illegal alien invader."[24] Frequent resort to a language of "invasion" is especially significant; it implies a country losing its identity. Conservative commentators like Pat Buchanan and Lou Dobbs have described the nation as "Mexamerica" on the way to becoming a "Third World country."[25]

Politicians gain political capital through wild exaggerations on the subject. John McCain, seeking reelection to the Senate from Arizona in 2010, claimed that illegal immigrants were "intentionally causing accidents on the freeway." Dwell on that possibility for a moment. Why would fugitives engage in such attention-getting activities? In that same campaign year, the governor of Arizona, Jan Brewer, described "beheadings" and "kidnappings" by illegal immigrants without offering a shred of evidence in support of her allegations.[26]

Demagoguery gains legitimacy through the continued failures and lapses of immigration law. Enforcement has not stopped an estimated 850,000 illegal immigrants from entering the country every year.[27] In identification of the growing problem, the ambiguous meaning of "unlawful"—i.e., mere presence versus an overt criminal act—encourages the pejorative term *illegal alien* to trump the neutral designation *undocumented immigrant*. The second objective phrase says that something needed is missing. The first reflects the desire to keep immigrants from exercising legal rights available to everyone else in America.[28]

Legal doctrine is also stacked against immigrants. Constitutional precedent keeps them from using most legal protections and prevents them from
seeking standing in federal court. Since 1889, the Supreme Court's "plenary
power doctrine" has left all policy and regulation to the political branches of
government (Congress and the President) without the prospect of judicial
oversight.[29] With the judiciary tying its own hands, immigration debates
are highly political and especially hyperbolic during election cycles.[30]

Complicating these negatives are other issues. Immigration law forbids
an illegal alien from seeking legal status much less citizenship, leaving literally millions of people who know only the United States as their home
without conceivable answers to their situation.[31] Sharing the frustration
over federal law from the other direction, a number of states now try to
check undocumented immigrants by denying citizenship to children born
of anyone in this category (so-called *anchor babies*), by denying driving
licenses, by denying access to educational institutions, by denying health
benefits, by denying work, by denying the right to contract, and by authorizing frequent police checks on anyone under "reasonable suspicion."[32]

The insensitivity to basic human needs in such proposals is the reason
for them. By pushing illegal aliens more deeply into "outlaw" status, the
states urge them to "self-deport."[33] The strategies are overt and, beyond the
momentary political leverage they give proposers, the new restrictions are
as misguided as they are heartless. Shouldn't a republican form of government worry about officialdom wielding harassing tactics on any group in its
midst? Once started, where does that stop?

Bullying behavior carried to extremes is also economically unsound.
When Alabama in 2011 passed harsh laws that made the state "hostile territory" for illegal immigrants by demanding proof of citizenship or legal
residency for garbage pickup, school attendance, dog licenses, health
department use, contract reliability, and employment, many farm workers up and went to other states, "leaving rotting crops in fields and critical shortages of labor." From those who stayed came cries from "pregnant
women afraid to go to the hospital, crime victims afraid to go to the police,
and parents afraid to send their children to school."[34] State lawmakers and
executive officers had to admit that their actions had "unintended consequences" and urged each other to "throw out whole sections of the law."[35]

For those who do "self-deport" there is still no answer. Leaving one
state for another does not address the problem for the receiving state, and

most illegal aliens have no other country to go to. "They are Americans in everything but a piece of paper," as one member of Congress averred when recently urging amnesty for illegal immigrants raised in this country.[36] New levels of restriction only compound an already difficult situation.

Whatever people say or try to argue, it is impossible to remove millions of people from the country and it is just as impossible to prevent undocumented immigrants from arriving. The land borders in the lower forty-eight states are simply too extensive. The borders spread across 7,514 miles. It is hardly surprising that enforcement along just the southern border (at a cost of $2 billion a year) has not controlled illegal entry.[37]

Current immigration policies accomplish only one thing: they increase the desperation of the officially unwanted. A new program between federal and state authorities called "Secure Communities," which utilizes a computerized fingerprint database of all entering legal immigrants, turns "every local police department in the country into an arm of Immigration and Customs Enforcement," an institution known by the winning acronym of ICE. Surveillance by ICE uses its information to catch illegal immigrants at higher rates.[38] Despite its name, "Secure Communities" dignifies a politics of fear.

No one can claim success either. Record numbers in deportation do not begin to match the numbers that continue to gain illegal entry every year. Nor do deportation processes reach minimal levels of accepted fairness. Those without counsel have no chance at all. For those who do manage to obtain counsel, immigration judges "offer a scathing assessment of much of the lawyering they have witnessed in their courtrooms."[39]

To personalize the impact of restrictive policies on undocumented immigrants, think about the plight of a person after a minor fender-bender in Gwinnett County, Georgia, in March 2010. Although the accident was the other driver's fault, the blameless immigrant was incarcerated for twelve days for not having a driver's license that the state refused to issue her. Deportation proceedings were started against her even though she had lived in the state for seventeen years as a model employee while raising two children who were American citizens. "If they're here illegally in the United States," insisted the sheriff of Gwinnett County, "they should be deported regardless of the charge." The searches in Gwinnett County include Sunday checks near churches with Hispanic worshippers.[40]

Illegal aliens are not categorically criminals in a meaningful sense, but people who are barred from meaningful employment, who fear surveillance at every moment, who face imprisonment and deportation if recognized, and who can never call on the law for protection—such people have to live beyond ordinary guidelines. When boxed in, human beings resist imposed restrictions.[41] The stringency of current policies turns into a self-fulfilling prophecy. Illegal aliens who disobey laws to survive also become vulnerable to others through blackmail, fraud, and unchecked intimidation.

Current immigration law creates what it wants to correct: crime. The pathos of this situation lies in the mounting numbers and the overall contradiction that no one wants to face. Hope for reform exists only in newsworthy or high-profile cases. You can ignore the contradictions in an abstract category. It is much harder to overlook the plight of an honest person caught by them in front of you.[42] A well-told story can make a difference if it creates viable characters in a welcoming context.

How much difference? Congressional debates in 2010 over the Dream Act, which would have given legal status to illegal immigrants brought to the country at too young an age to be found personally culpable, followed a pattern. Those against the Dream Act spoke in generalities about the will of the American people. Supporters detailed the plight of real individuals caught in the legal net. The act proposing amnesty received majority votes in both Houses, but it was stopped in the Senate by failing to reach the supermajority necessary to overcome a filibuster on the issue.[43]

Experts in legal inquiry agree that those with strong feelings on enforcement often change their minds when faced with an intimate context or when they have more knowledge of a case.[44] Individual cases sometimes work in this way, with controversy leading to a change in law. Unfortunately, the plenary power doctrine keeps even the most poignant story of injustice from being legally told. All significant decisions are left to the political branches of the government where intractability flourishes.

If the personal in the immigration tangle is to succeed, it must reach for public rather than legal cognizance, and this has begun to happen. Individuals at risk are emerging from their legal twilight. Poster illegal aliens, especially young people who have succeeded in America, are proving newsworthy as more people recognize the problem. The stories vary but contain the same message.

Two examples can convey the substance of that message. Isabel Castillo graduated from college *magna cum laude* but finds herself trapped in menial jobs as an illegal alien. She has turned to radio, town-hall meetings, and legislative hearings to challenge the law and "hopes that if people get to see her close up, she will win them over."[45] Maricela Aguilar, who has lived in the United States since the age of three, attends a university on a full scholarship. Describing her "coming out," she says "losing the shame overshadows the fear. I'd much rather clarify to the public that being undocumented is just a circumstance I find myself in."[46]

The appeal of individuals like Isabel Castillo and Maricela Aguilar is direct. They fight for the right to succeed on the terms that American aspirations hold dear—through effort, enterprise, education, public assertion, and achievement. Neither deserves to be classified as a criminal and both argue for all who have been left in limbo despite achievement and skills that should lead to a secure life. In Ms. Aguilar's words, "One day we're going to pass this, don't even worry about it."[47] Actually there is cause for worry. The courage required to come out is real. Both women, and others like them, remain safe only as newsworthy figures, and media coverage gives ephemeral protection at best.

Immigration issues need a longer lasting story, one that a reading public wants to remember. At least once in American history a story has achieved canonical status by answering legal injustice. In *Uncle Tom's Cabin* (1852), the best-selling book in nineteenth-century America after the Bible, Harriet Beecher Stowe describes Senator John Bird, a proposer and complacent supporter of the fugitive slave law. Senator Bird learns to break that unjust law only when a frantic escaping young slave woman and her child arrive on his own doorstep.[48]

Reading about Senator Bird, putting themselves in his situation through the power of story, many in the nation began to change their thinking on slavery. Stowe explains exactly what happened and has to happen. Until this moment in the novel, the senator's "idea of a fugitive slave was only an idea of the letters that spell the word." Stowe's account transforms abstraction into "the magic of the real presence of distress."[49] For most Americans the idea of an "illegal immigrant" remains an abstraction. A more concrete understanding may well depend on the magic in writing, on a story that mesmerizes with the real presence of distress.

Certainly the ability of fiction to influence legal decision making is rare. The tensions between law and the treatment of it by imaginative literature stand in the way. A legal decision drives toward a single goal. An imaginative text mimics its Latin origins. The word *textum* means "web" or "woven fabric," "a framework" made up of joined strands.[50]

The concept of "standing" underlines the differences. To appear before the law, someone must have "sufficient stake in a justiciable controversy to obtain judicial resolution of that controversy." There are hidden variables in this short statement. A litigant must be "adversely affected" in a proper jurisdiction with "a personal stake in the outcome" of "a legally protectable and tangible interest." The personal stake must also involve a "matured or ripened" issue with "sufficient immediacy and reality" in "a controversy worthy of adjudication." Each lockstep development—a clear right in a specific legal conflict before the proper court when the conflict is worthy and ready to be resolved—must be present "to take the initial step that frames legal issues for ultimate adjudication."[51]

Everything, no matter how helter-skelter, has standing in a novel. Conflating fact with fiction, the novelist crafts an artificial conflict that becomes real to a reader. The law declares and answers. Fiction persuades by amusing. When the subject is law, fiction typically persuades through an injustice that law has failed to see, or where it has resisted standing, or when it has found a controversy unripe for decision.

Claims of how literature can help law differ. The connection can provide "a culture of argument" in which justice supplies "translation" between fields of inquiry.[52] It can be "a witness to crisis."[53] It can set a scene of "poetic justice" that "constructs empathy and compassion in ways highly relevant to citizenship" and "public reasoning."[54] It can illuminate "the ideals of impersonality, neutrality, and objectivity that inform the law" with "a template . . . when the legal system breaks down."[55] More dialectically, the relationship between law and literature welcomes "cross-examinations."[56]

All theories on the subject agree, however, on a basic premise. Fiction on a legal issue thrives on what has gone wrong. The connection succeeds when it can make law see a problem that it has not solved or been unwilling to entertain. Senator Bird, the legal agent in *Uncle Tom's Cabin*, comes alive when he accepts his own role in an injustice that should be rectified because it is suddenly in the flesh in front of him. The direct confrontation and the fact that he risks his own life to do the opposite of what he had previously defended drives the account. Nevertheless, the transfer of his realization to a reading public depends on something else. It depends on the power of the story told—the only power that fiction really has.

The mystery in that power needs to be explained. "Story contains, openly or covertly, something useful." "The storyteller is a man who has counsel for his readers," where "counsel woven into the fabric of real life is wisdom." These thoughts distinguish carefully between information ("It lives only in the moment.") and story ("It does not expend itself."). A good story remains permanently available. "It preserves and concentrates its strength and is capable of releasing it even after a long time."[57]

Precisely how a given story transcends time and place is another mystery, and many have tried to explain the phenomenon. Most agree that "one purpose of fiction is to present and reveal character in such a way as to invite moral appraisal" or "to consider moral *character* from a philosophical point of view."[58] Either way, a good story must appeal to a receptive, enduring mentality.

As Harriet Beecher Stowe has already shown us, there is deeper register in a timeless story. Robert Penn Warren—novelist, poet, *and* critic—may come closest to articulating this quality when he asks "why should we, who have the constant and often painful experience of conflict in life and who yearn for inner peace and harmonious relation with the outer world, turn to fiction, which is the image of conflict?" His answer joins the permanence of story to each new reader: "we turn to fiction for some slight hint about the story in the life we live."[59]

With that personal touch in mind, we can return to Stowe's "magic of the real presence." E. L. Doctorow, who blends historical event with fiction in his novels, gives as good an explanation as any. "Complex understandings, indirect, intuitive, and nonverbal, arise from the words of the story, and by a ritual transaction between reader and writer, instructive emotion is generated in the reader from the illusion of suffering an experience not his own."[60] The "ritual transaction" between Harriet Beecher Stowe and her millions of readers turns "illusion" into "reality" through "instructive emotion."

More than transitory understanding is at stake in a story that changes a reader's moral compass. Senator Bird and readers of him in *Uncle Tom's Cabin* see through his eyes a *person*, a young woman on the run from tyrannical but still legal authority. It viscerally helps to know that the escaping slave in Senator Bird's house is Eliza Harris with her little son Harry, and that she has just miraculously crossed the frozen Ohio River from Kentucky on breaking blocks of ice, the most famous scene in the novel. Stowe could bring this figure to life so vividly for herself and her readers by knowing, as many of her contemporaries knew, of an actual incident from 1838 when just such an escaping young slave woman accomplished such a feat, crossing the frozen Ohio River to freedom in the town of Ripley with a child in her arms.[61]

Readers who identify with the fugitive in this scene, or any other scene in which established authority is causing more harm than good, cannot help but feel complicit in that authority. They cannot avoid their own support of a law that hurts an individual in their midst. Whether the person hurt *belongs* in their midst is another question, but that issue disappears in the propinquity of moral sensibility to the injury done by an unfair law. Story, in simpler terms, can awaken readers to a reality and ask them to invest in it. Abraham Lincoln greeted Stowe in November 1862, with this remark: "So you're the little woman who wrote the book that made this great war."[62]

We read a story that touches reality to recognize the problems it contains for us, to find knowledge about ourselves, with an eye for the conflicts that fill our world. These are the timeless qualities that make Henry Roth's 1934 novel a proof text on current issues of immigration. *Call It Sleep* portrays the torments of the most vulnerable of immigrants, a child, and it accomplishes the task with stunning force. We are made to see *the person* at stake, and that person is as innocent as a child brought into the United States by undocumented immigrant parents today. The doubled impact forces a question on its readers: how can we legally add difficulties to the struggles of an innocent child without compromising the dignity and rights that are our own protection and definition?

If, as claimed, "no book in American history molded public opinion more powerfully than *Uncle Tom's Cabin*," it succeeded through its transparency as a novel of sentiment.[63] The same cannot be said of Henry Roth's *Call It Sleep*. No less a critic than Leslie Fiedler said it took him fifty years to fully understand the implications of *Call It Sleep*.[64] Why, then, is a modernist novel laced with structural innovations, sudden breaks, linguistic byplay in other languages, obscure symbolism, gaps in logic, and endless misconnections the best choice for conveying the reality of the immigrant's plight?

The beginning of an answer comes in realization "that every age is dominated by a privileged form, or genre, which seems by its structure the fittest to express its secret truths."[65] Novels of different periods depend on their momentary "generic control of the esthetic response" in the "filter of history." Fiction succeeds when it establishes "an immediate link with the empirical reality familiar to its readers." A reader's investment comes through the pleasure of grasping the unfamiliar within the familiar, "the unknown through the known."[66]

Familiarity in literature in 1934, the year *Call It Sleep* was published, required knowledge of the innovative generic techniques of modernism, a movement committed to "rebellion and innovation in new work which attempts to break with tradition."[67] In the disillusioned decades following World War I, modernism challenged "a botched civilization" with what Ezra Pound famously called "frankness as never before" and "disillusions as never told in the old days."[68] "Secret truths" worth telling had to be told in a new way. The grounded quality and shock value of *Call It Sleep* owe everything to this understanding and to its historical circumstances.

Modernism coincided with the largest influx of new Americans in the first three decades of the twentieth century. Roth's modernist novel captures the greatest moment in that influx, the years 1907 to 1913. The novel is our proof text because it so absolutely invests in the immigrant experience while stylistically using the run-ons and sudden juxtapositions common in modernist technique to cauterize emotion and dramatize confusion without dropping into sentimentality. It finds the familiar within the unfamiliar

Two cohering elements give *Call It Sleep* a spontaneity often lacking in the genre of the immigrant novel, which prefers a retrospective mode. First, Roth insists on stark presentism as his control of the field of perception, and second, his protagonist is a child, and we are held strictly within that child's limited but perceptive point of view. As the first element encourages electrifying juxtapositions of confusion to play across the page through "severe discontinuities," "static simultaneity," "sensory apprehensions of life's surfaces," and "sustained mythic parallels"—all crucial to the heteroglossic mix in modernist narratives—so the second element, the desperation to know of an unknowing and frightened boy, makes childhood the primal scene of immigration.[69]

The boy's very name, David Schearl, bespeaks the fracture that coming to America creates in his existence. "David" means "beloved," a symbol of his mother Genya's obsessive devotion, while the patronymic "Schearl" is Yiddish for "scissors," alluding to the cutting anger of his father Albert. Albert Schearl's frequent rages and violent behavior have two sources in *Call It Sleep*. Arriving two years before his family, he has, like many immigrants, been unable to adapt to life in America. Closer to home, the length of separation from his wife allows him to suspect that his young son might not be his own.

In trying to fathom an adult world that is only half understood by the struggling adults around them, children are the most vulnerable of immigrants. Questions are the dominant mode of a child and David Schearl is filled with them, but unlike other children, he dares not ask those questions in his divided household. He represents the bewilderment of every mind in a new environment. His unspoken questions tumble upon us through stream of consciousness. Roth uses the withheld speech of his frightened child to expose the immigrant experience for what it always is, a familial landscape of ferocious intensity.

All of David's fears are confirmed in the end. The indelible image that he holds of his father is of a raised hammer poised to strike, and it will turn into the truth of the book. In a final cataclysm, Albert loads his misfortunes onto the belief that David is "a goy's get" rather than his own son. "Whirling the whip in his flying hands," he tries to kill the son who is so different from himself and becoming more different in the new land every day.[70]

Commentary has sought to verify Albert's assumption about the paternity of David, but in the momentum of immigration, Albert has no son and certainly not the son he thinks he needs. America, not biology, has taken the son from the father. When introducing the boy to others, Albert objectifies David as "what will pray for me after my death" (29). The phrase bespeaks the Jewish tradition of a son who remembers and prays after his father, but Albert is raising a son who, in trying to adapt to the new world his father cannot fathom, sees only "the face of a foe" (114). The single thing David wants from the angry failure of a father he hates is the physical strength to be free of him (78, 177).

Vortices of fear also define the world beyond the home. The boy's first expressed thoughts are devastating in their portrayal of the immigrant condition: "David again became aware that this world had been created without thought of him" (17). Every immigrant has some experience with this alienation from a new reality. Quick to perceive, David lacks a context for understanding. There may be no greater terror for a keen observer: the need to know up against the knowledge that you cannot learn what is important to know.

The misunderstandings, mistakes, abuse, guilt, and prejudices that guide the immigrant plot toward catastrophe are all heightened by the modernist stream of consciousness that Roth uses to convey the psychology and thought processes of a figure defined entirely by "watchful, frightened eyes" (10, 173). David can find no purchase in a world that appears against him. Lost in the city, he jumbles thought processes in a panic when taken to a police station:

> Trust nothing. Trust nothing. Trust nothing. Wherever you look, never believe. If you played hide'n'-go-seek, it wasn't hide'n'-go-seek, it was something else, something sinister. If you played follow the leader, the world turned upside down and an evil force passed through it. Don't play. . . . Never believe. Never play. Never believe. Not anything. Everything shifted. Everything changed. Even words. . . . Trust nothing. Even sidewalks, even streets, houses, you looked at them. You knew where you were and they turned. You watched them and they turned. That way. Slow, cunning. Trust no'—
>
> (102–3).

These words reveal a desperate insight. The speaker of them must hold himself apart to survive. Alienation carries to every conceivable level of implication; people, words, buildings, even play are all suspect.

From the outset, *Call It Sleep* privileges negative shocks of recognition. The book opens with the symbolic placement of Genya and David arriving "in wonder," gazing at the Statue of Liberty. But this is no "Mother of Exiles." Neither Genya nor her child sees a beckoning beacon of light. "The massive figure" looms ominously above them "charred with shadow"; her halo, "sparks of darkness roweling the air"; her torch "the blackened hilt of a broken sword" (14). Genya's articulation is correspondingly bleak. "Ach!" she cries. "Then here in the new land is the same old poverty" (12).

Roth's stream-of-conscious narrative is horrifying in its capacity to illustrate a fragmenting mind out of control, and at the center is an immigrant being acted upon instead of acting. Here is David late in the novel:

> Only his own face met him, a pale oval, and dark, fear-struck, staring eyes, that slid low among the windows of the stores, snapping from glass to glass, mingled with the enemas, ointment-jars, green globes of the drug-store— snapped off—mingled with the baby clothes, button-heaps, underwear of the drygoods store—snapped off—with the cans of paint, steel tools, frying

pans, clothes-lines of the hardware store—snapped off. A variegated pallor, but pallor always, a motley fear, but fear. Or he was not.

—On the windows how I go. Can see and ain't. Can see and ain't. And when I ain't, where? In between them if I stopped, where? Ain't nobody. No place. Stand here then. BE nobody. Always. Nobody'd see. Nobody'd know. Always. Always No.

(378–79)

The modernist aesthetic of compression and concreteness suggests windows "happen" to the boy instead of receiving his movement across them. The windows "snap off." The shift in agency causes David to dissolve when his reflection does not appear in them. He suffers from disassociations familiar to any new foreign-born resident, but he is more deeply hurt. He thinks the terrain itself is trying to destroy him.

David Schearl comes to us through flashing immediacy. He is the most traumatized immigrant in American fiction—an *immigrant agonistes*, the quintessential alien, alienated even from himself. All of the conventional negatives of the immigrant novel are here but carried to another level, to the extreme: dislocation, vocational despair, confused realities, misunderstanding, language difficulties, discrimination, racism, poverty, generational conflict, domestic strife, fear of authority, and disappointment in America as found.

Today this figure would have a Spanish name, and he would be subject to even deeper uncertainties, fears, discrimination, domestic conflict, and abuse because, as an undocumented immigrant, he would have to live in partial hiding and could never rise to the level of legality. His parents would have much more difficulty finding work. If they found employment at all, they could lose it at any juncture. The slightest encounter over anything could land them in jail. Socially they would endure more intense levels of suspicion, discrimination, and exploitation over their "illegality." Legal surveillance would negate all possibility of meaningful institutional affiliation.

These differences make *Call It Sleep* a precursor. The coming pivotal catalyst for change could be a Latino best-selling novel. Perhaps the generic integrities of today will dictate a movie instead, or a television show, a gigantic blog, a connecting Facebook page, or even a video game, but regardless the theme will be how current legalities have made the immigrant experience much worse than it has ever been.

How close are we to a national crisis involving undocumented immigrants? No one can say for certain, but there is growing concern. Analogies in public discourse between slavery in antebellum America and illegal aliens today suggest some of the dynamics at work. For just as the Fugitive Slave Law of 1850 galvanized heightened controversy, so the severe restrictions that states like Alabama, South Carolina, and Arizona have placed on undocumented immigrants have led to heightened communal scrutiny now.[71] Just as legality over runaway slaves became a focus for public debate, so the decisions that judges now make to uphold or block state laws on undocumented immigrants have led to new alarm over what those laws might mean to the people affected and to surrounding communities.[72] The fact that controversy in both historical moments focuses on legal action suggests an even larger analogy at work.

Uneasiness enters the American rule of law whenever obviously decent people under its province are deprived of fundamental rights. Even as great an avatar of nullification as John C. Calhoun sounds a little queasy when he claims "be [slavery] good or bad, it has grown up with our society and institutions, and is so interwoven with them, that to destroy it would be to destroy us as a people."[73] Calhoun cannot help sounding amiss when he says liberty does not belong to "the undeserving" as "the result of some fixed law." Which fixed law? Why are some "undeserving"? Where can we find Calhoun's "necessary moral qualifications" that say slaves cannot live "under any other than an absolute and despotic government"?[74] A lawyer like Calhoun cannot rely simply on power. He feels compelled to twist the language of law and morality to answer a rule of law that must be normative as well as exacting.[75]

Some of the same queasiness drives legal discussions of undocumented immigrants today, and for the same reason. Two Supreme Court decisions, *Graham v. Richardson* in 1971 and *Mathews v. Diaz* in 1976, symbolize the ambivalence at work.[76] In *Graham*, the Supreme Court will not let "the States favor United States Citizens over aliens in the distribution of welfare benefits" because the phrase "any person" in the constitutional safeguards of life, liberty, and property "encompasses lawfully admitted resident aliens as well as citizens of the United States and entitles both citizens and aliens to the equal protection of the laws of the State in which they reside" (371–72).

Graham restricts the decision to legal or *resident* aliens, but Justice Harry Blackmun, writing for the Court, goes much further when he

announces "classifications based on alienage, like those based on nationality or race, are inherently suspect" and deserve "heightened judicial solicitude" (372–73). Five years later this "solicitude" disappears in *Mathews v.
Diaz*. The Supreme Court holds there "that Congress may condition an
alien's eligibility for participation in a federal medical insurance program"
in a way that "does not deprive aliens of liberty or property without due
process of law" (67).

Curiously, as the Court in *Mathews* backs down from *Graham*, it tries
to limit the distance covered. "Even one whose presence in this country is
unlawful, involuntary or transitory is entitled to that constitutional protection [offered by the Due Process Clause of the Fourteenth Amendment],"
the Court asserts, citing *Graham* and a string of other opinions in support
of immigrant rights (82, 85). This second comment opens the opinion
more than the Court needs by acknowledging the presence of illegal aliens.
Unhappiness over the immigration debate is very much alive here.

If there are entitlements for immigrants, what are they and how far do
they extend? Using the plenary power doctrine that gives regulation of
immigration to "the political branches of the Federal Government," the
Court in *Mathews* shuts the door on a larger solution. "It is obvious that
Congress has no constitutional duty to provide *all aliens* with the welfare
benefits provided to citizens," Justice John Paul Stevens asserts (83), distinguishing *Graham* (applicable to the states) from *Mathews* (applicable to
the federal government) on federalism grounds (85–86). Is it so obvious?
Even here there are tinges of regret and some queasiness. Stevens can't keep
himself from acknowledging that "disparate treatment is 'invidious'" (81)
and subject to charges of "political hypocrisy" (86–87).

The legal minuet in cases like *Graham* and *Mathews* gives hopeful
immigrants the prospect of rights without remedies. It holds all immigrants in place in a no-man's land without elemental protections, recognizing undocumented immigrants while keeping them in their outlaw status
without possibility of meaningful recovery or rectification. The problems,
in other words, remain "intractable" in the eyes of the law. Or can we say
instead that the problems depend on how they will be brought to the law?

Still missing is the right speaker and the right story that might touch
Americans in a different way. For most Americans, undocumented immigrants remain an abstract concept rather than the physical reality of hard-
ships inflicted on individual lives held in suspension. People so held in legal

limbo cannot apply for better jobs. Most communal services are kept from them. They must shun places of worship where they might be identified and they risk exposure and deportation if one of them is placed in an educational institution.

When does it begin to become dangerous to have so many people living without basic rights or possibilities in a country where well-being is defined by the availability of rights and possibilities? Emancipation came only in the violence of civil war, when the slave population had reached almost four million, 12 percent of the total population then in the United States. Illegal immigrants now represent three times that number, and if the estimates of illegal entry remain in excess of deportation rates, the same per capita rate of 12 percent could be reached in a lifetime. That would mean the presence of roughly 40 million souls without rights or expectations in America.[77]

Can the United States find a way to adjust? Again the catalyst of change, if there is to be one, must first come from outside obdurate official channels, and it must tell a story that large numbers will hear and absorb. The form of that story must be as recognizable and powerful as its theme. Whatever its form, it will deliver the message that current immigration law hurts the rule of law more than it helps it. It will be the story of the growing millions of illegal aliens who belong to America because they have been brought up in America and have no other place to go.

PART 2

The Nature of Judgment

THE MOST ADMIRED CIVIL SERVANT in the country serves under a cloud. That would be the judge in an American courtroom: the worthiest of gauges but always a target. Why is there such ambivalence over a figure known everywhere as "Your Honor"? Judges make correct, informed, objective judgments almost all of the time, and for their efforts they are generally taken for granted and then ignored by everyone except those immediately involved.

Trouble comes from elsewhere. It comes in the close call, in those unusual moments when personal will can be thought, often without cause, to determine the outcome of a case. Complaint is understandable, but why do these rare moments of decision making so completely overwhelm the norm? Why does public opinion respond so emphatically with reflexive charges of activism, bias, arbitrary influence, and sometimes with demands for recall or impeachment?

Most complainers do not, in fact, see the real problem. The nature of judgment, not the judge, is the underlying source of difficulty. We have left the important decisions in law to disembodied experts who are asked to remain mysteriously above the fray, and this does not sit well in democratic understandings. Even awareness of the problem seems to compound it. The commentators who actually see the underlying difficulty disagree about its implications and their disputes turn everything back onto the hapless judge criticized in the first place.

The legal academy may be at its most unhelpful on this issue. Some scholars find judges actively "cloaking" immense power through "the presumption among judges and lawyers that practically any political or social question is within their purview." Counterparts more openly proclaim "courts are the capitals of law's empire, and judges are its princes." Even so, most of these differences disappear in a worried consensus, which places "robed power at the center of politics but concealing the subtle judge behind juries, and a quiet inculcation."[1]

A lot of handwringing accompanies these observations of hidden power. "We lack the essentials of a decent apparatus for intelligent and constructive criticism of what our judges do" is a common response. "No department of state is more important than our courts, and none is so thoroughly misunderstood by the governed." Near disaster is a feared consequence. Wherever you look, "popular opinion about judges is a sad affair of empty slogans."[2]

Dignifying the problem while hoping for a better solution is our most knowledgeable commentator on the judicial branch: the Honorable Richard A. Posner, who serves on the United States Court of Appeals of the Seventh Circuit and writes frequently on the issue. Judge Posner does not believe "the nation is ruled by judges rather than by law," but he sees just enough fire beneath that smoke to worry along with the rest. He is similarly struck by "how unrealistic are the conceptions of the judge held by most people, including practicing lawyers and eminent law professors." Correctives are clearly in order.

Although he grants "the secrecy of judicial deliberations is an example of professional mystification," Posner's own answer to such mystification is an elaborate concoction or matrix of "Nine Theories of Judicial Behavior," all of which begin to merge into each other in ways that question the explanatory power of the separate categories other than to imply that the overall problem may be too complicated for most people to understand.[3]

What, then, is the vulnerable but allegedly power-ridden judge to do? In a recent example, the Honorable Thokozile Masipa, serving in the Gauteng Division of the High Court of South Africa, received typically harsh criticism for handling with seeming perfection the high-profile trial of Oscar Pistorius, the renowned handicapped athlete or "blade runner," a national hero who competed in running events of the 2012 Olympics as an amputee who lacked his lower legs. Pistorius was charged in 2013 with the murder of his girlfriend, Reeva Steenkamp, when he shot her four times through a locked bathroom door in the belief that he was accosting a burglar.

In the welter of uncertain evidence about this belief, Judge Masipa found there was enough evidence to convict Pistorius of culpable homicide, but not enough for a conviction of murder. Her verdict was obviously the correct one, yet it led to a barrage of criticism and the need for police protection after threats were made on her life. Here we might remember Masipa's account of what it means to serve as a judge in vexed situations, an account typically given by those who sit on the bench? "You just get on with it."[4]

True enough, but a judge gets on with it by hiding as much as possible. Judge Masipa was largely quiet, even passive, while presiding over the frequent histrionics of the Pistorius trial, but she revealed her total grasp and integrity when the melodramatic defendant claimed during cross-examination that he was making mistakes on the witness stand only because he was tired. The judge immediately intervened. For a fair trial, Pistorius could not be "too tired to proceed," nor did the decision of fairness rest with his willingness to continue despite fatigue. It depended on the court's perception about whether or not it was proper to proceed. The court, and implicitly the world watching the trial on television, needed to be convinced of fairness at work.[5] Very much on her own, Masipa then had to work very hard indeed to convince the world of the rightness of her verdict and judgment.

She succeeded by cleverly justifying her verdict, not through Pistorius's mistakes, but through a nuanced opening account of his darkened house with its open bathroom window on the night of the shooting. Did she manipulate the facts? She did, but that is not the point. Her thick description of the situation made Pistorius's fear of invasion palpable while limiting its significance; we all have to live sensibly with each other in a dangerous world. Pistorius "genuinely, though erroneously, believed his life and that of the deceased was in danger" and "there is nothing in the evidence," runs the judgment, "to suggest that this belief was not honestly entertained." Alas, "there was no intruder." "The toilet door," already carefully designated, "was indeed shut when he fired four shots into it." Accordingly, "there is no doubt that when the accused fired shots through the toilet door he acted unlawfully." No doubt at all.[6]

All of the doubt—communal doubt, that is—remains with the professionally hidden figure of the judge, and here is where imaginative literature can help a lot. Novels declare what is hidden from reality. Ian McEwan, a noted master in rendering professional life, does that for us in his 2014 novel *The Children Act*.[7] How do you make a family judge interesting? Well, first you give her a problem within her own family: a long-time husband suddenly demands an open marriage because the lust has gone from their own. Then you turn the mundane sordid turmoil of domestic quarrels into a life-and-death situation with death as the logical outcome.

You don't stop there because judges are also supposed to be admirable. So you give this one, named Fiona Maye, super intelligence, legal brilliance, the ability of a professional musician, an accomplished voice, and comprehensive knowledge with the quickest perception of great poetry. Finally, since she is a woman who has to suffer, you make all of the men in her life a bit foolish and tedious. Suffice it to say that our judge survives after a slight deviation in decorum, a minor risk that leads to the barest moment of breakdown with the lucky effect of reconfirming her marriage.

The plot of the novel is not, however, our interest. McEwan is exciting because he gets right the figure of the judge in all of its ambiguity. There are hidden costs in performing the judicial function, and he renders them all in dramatic form where we can understand their full implications. And behind them looms an unsolvable puzzle. Judging is a singular practice that forces the decider into studied isolation. The good judge needs independence of character and thought in the solitude that the position demands. The ability to be alone comfortably is therefore a supreme virtue, but it can easily rob the owner of social feeling and engagement.

This happens to Fiona Maye in *The Children Act*. Always perceptive, she has allowed her private life to atrophy in the pursuit of her professional obligations, which admittedly are more interesting and exhausting in their constant demands. Not since James Gould Cozzens's novel *The Just and the Unjust* (1942) have we had a courtroom novel that so accurately conveys the bombardment of obligations, large and small, that beset the profession of law.

Just as naturally, Fiona's practical isolation and ability to pigeonhole events extend to her colleagues on the bench. Not given to sarcasm herself, she is surrounded by the acrid, ironic temperament of fellow judges. These tonal qualities pervade the law through acknowledgment of the mayhem that is its stock and trade, and McEwan shields his protagonist from them while demonstrating their pervasive presence at every level of legal inquiry.

Judges again are special here. They harbor and use irony in excessive doses because they must make decisions that are forced upon them and unpleasant for someone. They also occasionally make mistakes that turn into real injustice. McEwan describes a few of those. Judges loathe admitting such mistakes, and it is always news when one does so in public. Far safer to obscure the mistake in language that means something else. So judges hide a lot, but they cannot get away with it in a novel.

The trajectory of the novel tells us that Judge Maye is going to make a mistake and that she will have to admit it, which she does if only in private; we also intuit that she will have to pay for it emotionally, the weak point in her armor. Such as it is, the mistake does not come from an incorrect judicial opinion. Her decision is the right one, but she has to step a

little out of her role to make it and the effort leads to further adventuring
and risk. As a good family court judge, she does not follow through with
more attention because of the many other cases on her docket and because
in life, another characteristic found in judges, she has been ruled by excessive prudence in the choices she makes. In effect, she misreads "the best
interest of the child" rubric in the legal statute that gives McEwan his title,
The Children Act.

Of course, any lawyer and especially any judge will tell you that "the
best interest of the child" doctrine is a slippery vehicle to wield, manage,
and check later. Was it necessary to check later here? That remains an
open question. The important thing for the novelist is that Fiona Maye's
perceived mistake has opened her up. It simultaneously curbs three minor
vices found in judicial ranks: self-righteousness, over-compartmentaliza-
tion, and a practiced aloofness from all concerned. Fiona has faced a failure of significance and it has made her whole again in the world.

Along the way McEwan gives us judging right down to the dirt under
its fingernails. Just listen to him: "she brought reasonableness to hopeless situations" (5), "a powerful grip on what was conventionally correct"
(7), "the prose needed to be smoothed, as did the respect owed to piety
in order to be proof against an appeal" (9–10), "in pursuit of a look of
constant reproach" (23), "the matter had to be set as a choice of the lesser
evil" (28), "onto the neutral ground, the treeless heath, of other people's
problems" (36), "it was her ideal self she heard" (45), "only a certain style
of banter and irony offered some protection" (50), "her occasional weak
joke fawningly received by counsel for both sides" (63). Something this
informative about actual judicial behavior and its pitfalls appears on virtually every page, but you will not find any of this in legal discourse.

Literary criticism, like fiction, can supply the same illumination.
Each of the three chapters in part 2 reveals a judge hiding in plain sight.
Chapter 4, "Holmes and the Judicial Figure," provides the ideological
building blocks that make the American judge such an admired official
through an overview of the career of Oliver Wendell Holmes Jr. Ralph
Waldo Emerson once said of Henry Thoreau: "As for taking T's arm, I
should as soon take the arm of an elm tree."[8] The same might be said of
Holmes, a cold and rather unpleasant man, and yet the legal profession
has embraced him with excessive adoration as the paradigmatic judicial
figure. Why? And what does that mean?

Chapter 5, "The Opinion as Literary Genre," presents the stylistic conventions in the writing of judicial decisions. We see how the manipulation of these conventions allows judges to appear sure and certain through a rhetoric of inevitability no matter how close the case. The sixth chapter, "*Ulysses* in Government Hands," analyzes the universally admired decision of United States federal judge John M. Woolsey to lift the ban on the publication of James Joyce's most famous novel, but *United States v. One Book Called Ulysses* is a seriously flawed decision that steers obscenity law toward contradictions even though Woolsey has the right result. The chapters in this part collectively show anyone how to read and critique a judicial decision.

4

Holmes and the Judicial Figure

JUDGES, ALONE IN AMERICAN OFFICIALDOM, explain each and every action with a distinct and individual piece of writing, which controls the measure of both performance and personality. They do not win wars, rule parties, run legislatures, or parade themselves in public life. Decisions from the bench, formalized in writing, are how we claim to know them, and the acknowledged master of this craft—so much so that many other judges use his words when they find themselves in an intellectual bind—is Oliver Wendell Holmes Jr., justice of the Supreme Court of the United States from 1902 to 1932.

Holmes could get away with saying things like: "I hate justice," "That is not my job," or "The foundation of jurisdiction is physical power."[1] But why do so many give such a figure first place in the American rule of law? The answer lies not in the legal theorist, but in the writer who captures his times as well as any author who ever wrote.

Holmes's mastery of the judicial opinion has been called unmatched in the twentieth century.[2] More than any other figure, he has shaped the modern concept of the American judge.[3] The man and his writings take on paradigmatic significance not just because of felicity or timeliness or even power of expression. Both the man and his writings respond to the problematic role of the judicial figure in American life and solve the undemocratic nature of the function.[4]

How did Holmes do it? History, literary study, rhetorical analysis, and the visual arts as well as law all become important in deciphering the composite image that Holmes turned into a reality that everyone has accepted.

To understand that reality, we must step outside of law to see inside of it. Even the descriptions of judging by judges confirm the need for understanding through interdisciplinarity.

Listening to judges talk about themselves assumes there is a mystery to be explained. Justice Felix Frankfurter's renowned summary deserves attention in this regard. "A judge," Frankfurter wrote, ". . . should be compounded of the faculties that are demanded of the historian and the philosopher and the prophet." In a sketch of Justice Benjamin Cardozo, he elaborates on the nature of these faculties:

> Immense learning, deep culture, critical detachment, intellectual courage, and unswerving disinterestedness reinforced imagination and native humility, and gave him in rare measure the qualities which are the special requisites for the work of the Court to whose keeping is entrusted no small share of the destiny of the nation.[5]

These almost impossible "special requisites" receive their highest personification in Oliver Wendell Holmes Jr. "He is unsurpassed in the depth of his penetration into the nature of the judicial process and in the originality of its exposition," writes Frankfurter of Holmes's "claim to pre-eminence." "The thinker and artist are superbly fused" in Holmes. "In deciding cases," Frankfurter observes, "his aim was 'to try to strike the jugular.' His opinions appear effortless—birds of brilliant plumage pulled from the magician's sleeves."[6]

The strange juxtaposition of warrior and magician, yet another compound, implies the twofold nature of every judicial decision as much as it celebrates Holmes.[7] The open but deadly blow (philosophical severity in the act of deciding) and the sorcerer's sleight of hand (public justification of the actual decision) require adroit touches. Blood may flow, but it should never spill onto the plumage on display!

The encomiastic mode in such declarations knows no limits. Figures like Cardozo and Holmes emerge not just ideals but existing types. Public officials rarely claim so much for a colleague in modern times. American judges speaking about other judges are the exception; published acts of celebration in this manner are typical. We are in the presence of a distinct genre. Testimonials abound in a hagiographical tradition that supports the judicial figure through two centuries of legal history.[8]

Here is Judge Learned Hand of the United States Court of Appeals for the Second Circuit on the judicial function:

> [A judge's] authority and his immunity depend upon the assumption that he speaks with the mouth of others: the momentum of his utterances must be greater than any which his personal reputation and character can command. . . . He must pose as a kind of oracle, voicing the dictates of a vague divinity—a communion which reaches far beyond the memory of any now living, and has gathered up a prestige beyond that of any single man.[9]

Typical of insider explanations, the passage translates articulation into metaphors of spectacle, and the directions of those metaphors illustrate why judging remains problematic. To "speak with the mouth of others," or to "pose as a kind of oracle," or to "voice the dictates of a vague divinity," or to "reach beyond the memory of any now living," or to enlist "a prestige beyond that of any single man" is, in every case, to enhance authority by hiding it.

Holmes gives his own version of this phenomenon, and it is predictably more concise and memorable. The ideal judge should be a "combination of Justinian, Jesus Christ, and John Marshall."[10] The description works again through discrepancies. It asks the recipient to engage in a game of levels over the capacities assigned to the judicial figure.

Behind the description is Holmes's own complicated act of self-creation, but we need to look more closely first at the exaggerations regarding him within the encomiastic mode. Frankfurter deems Holmes Plato's "philosopher become king," "a significant figure in the history of civilization and not merely a commanding American figure." He "has written himself into the slender volume of the literature of all time." "To quote from Mr. Justice Holmes' opinions is to string pearls." For Learned Hand, Holmes is not just "the example of the accomplished judge" but "the premier knight of his time." In Jerome Frank's construct of law in the modern American mind, Holmes is the one "completely adult jurist."[11]

There is no end to these superlatives. Harold Laski finds in Holmes the equivalent of Chief Justice John Marshall in law and of Edmund Burke and Samuel Johnson in conversation. The popularizer of Holmes's writings, Max Lerner, sees "perhaps the most complete personality in the history of American thought." Dean Acheson, later U.S. secretary of state, is

overwhelmed by "a grandeur and beauty rarely met among men;" "his presence entered a room with him as a pervading force; and left with him, too,
like a strong light put out." Justice Cardozo "always spoke of Holmes as
'the Master,'" as "the profoundest intellect who had ever dispensed Anglo-
American justice," "the great overlord of the law and its philosophy," "the
philosopher and the seer . . . [and] one of the greatest of the ages." "I point
the challenger to Holmes," Cardozo directed. "He gives us glimpses of the
things eternal."[12]

What could possess such men, acknowledged leaders in their worlds, to
go so overboard? To insist on having found and then announcing "a pervasive and intimate national possession"?[13] We have to recognize that the
combinations used to extol Holmes hide some ambiguities. The admirable
features are apparent. They include the cultured legacy and education of
the Boston Brahmin; the already famous name, which passes from father
to son through that legacy; the military record and sacrifice of the thrice-
wounded Civil War hero; the contribution to law of a classic book, *The
Common Law*, in 1881; the extensive correspondence and speeches of the
social figure; and, most of all, a half century of judicial service, extending
all the way to Holmes's ninetieth year, from the Supreme Judicial Court of
Massachusetts to the Supreme Court of the United States.

The features listed reflect virtues: self-confidence, social obligation (or,
more negatively, an aloof sense of caste), great intellectual energy, a love
of ideas (not the same thing), physical courage, stoicism, and, not least, a
survivor's tenacity and acceptance of the concrete, even brutal realities of
experience. Holmes's virtues also point to stances taken in the life: a lasting faith in the military code, support of legal realism, judicial suspicion
of conventional formalisms, intellectual testing of universals against "the
felt necessities of the time," and a commitment to public life that is almost
biblical in its longevity.[14]

The difficulty with a ledger of virtues and of their consistency in practice
is that they still do not explain the level of adulation that the career has
inspired. Adding to the difficulty are relevant criticisms of Holmes and his
achievements.[15] Even the strongest supporters have recognized an important limitation: "rarely has so vast an influence been built upon so slight a
body of legal writing."[16] Today his scholarly writings seem less impressive
than they once appeared. *The Common Law*, while still acknowledged to
be rich in insight, is now "a book at war with itself'" and "a monument

to ... contradiction," the nature of which Holmes never understood.[17] Even the legendary lucidity of the opinions has been questioned. "If clarity, precision, and 'reasoned elaboration' can be said to be the ideals of judicial opinion writing," runs one modern commentary, "Holmes appears to have eschewed these goals in the pursuit of terseness and ambiguity. His opinions have been called as difficult to understand as they are easy to read." Perhaps so, but does it follow, as some have claimed, that "the apotheosis of Holmes defeats understanding"?[18]

The perceived harmonies in his career explain much. The testimonials to Holmes invariably reach for metaphors of completion, connection, and integration. He is the "completely adult jurist," "the most complete personality," the "great example," the one who creates "organic connection" where others find only "discrete instances." "Who else," asks Cardozo," has been able to pack a whole philosophy of legal method into a fragment of a paragraph?"[19]

This excitement over holistic patterns flows from each writer's desire for unities and the ability to find them. Notably, and from the beginning, Holmes himself sees the combinations that must be made to serve, and he uses them to shape an answer to inherent divisions in the judicial figure. The full contours of the career are already there in the Harvard senior's autobiographical sketch from 1861:

> All my three names designate families from which I am descended. ... Some of my ancestors have fought in the Revolution; among the great-grandmothers of the family were Dorothy Quincy and Anne Bradstreet ("the tenth Muse"); and so on. ... The tendencies of the family and of myself have a strong natural bent to literature, etc., at present I am trying for a commission in one of the Massachusetts Regiments, however, and hope to go south before very long. If I survive the war I expect to study law as my profession or at least for a starting point.[20]

The complex tradition of the Boston Brahmin, so casually assumed ("and so on"), the essential appearance of the soldier, the vocational decision for law, and the larger aspiration of the writer all appear in this passage of one who is just twenty years old. Of special interest are three qualifications that the youthful Holmes raises about how the components come together: the soldier's sensible question and prefigured courage about survival; the additional question of whether the law can be more than "a starting point"; and last, the more subtle concern raised in the word "however" over whether a vaguely feminized "bent to literature" can accord with a life of responsible action.

The plotted career develops through careful responses to each uncertainty in the combination of aristocrat, soldier, lawyer, and writer. It succeeds in the ensuing creation of a single image that is true for Holmes in life and then magnified beyond life in others' perception of his ideological importance. The noted justice is the successful soldier, lawyer, and aristocrat, and he can claim much from each experience in his exercise of the judicial function. Yet the ultimate source of cohesion in this complex image always lies in Holmes's definition of himself as a writer fulfilling a writer's duties. Writing is how Holmes thinks of himself. "The thing I have wanted to do and wanted to do is to put as many new ideas into the law as I can, to show how particular solutions involved general theory, and to do it with style." Putting new ideas, showing particular solutions through general theory, and doing so with style are functions of the writing process.

The business of deciding the law is difficult enough, but Holmes finds a greater challenge in the effective and proper use of language. "Ideas are not difficult," he tells one friend. "The trouble is in the words in which they are expressed."[21] Trouble for the writer comes in three forms. First, audiences frequently misunderstand a decision by failing to see a judge's "way of putting in new and remodeling old thought." Holmes therefore refers to his opinions as "preparing small diamonds for people of limited intellectual means." The opinions must sparkle like diamonds if they are to be seen at all.[22]

Second, the best language constantly loses meaning and vitality. Holmes, influenced by Ralph Waldo Emerson, knows that "any idea that has been in the world for twenty years and has not perished has become a platitude although it was a revelation twenty years ago." He also knows that habit and routinization destroy the essence of meaningful thought. "To rest upon a formula," he observes in one of the most important recognitions that any good writer should make, "is a slumber that, prolonged, means death." The judge, no less than the creative writer, must find ways to renew language, and that is harder in the judicial function because a judge must necessarily follow previous writers closely.[23]

Third and last in the writer's difficulties, a language that truly communicates is hard to achieve. "To arrange the thoughts so that one springs naturally from that which precedes it," writes Holmes of his opinions, "and to express them with a singing variety is the devil and all." Merely to report thought in language is to lose it. Holmes assumes the higher duty of making thought "spring" and language "sing." On the bench he "has broken his heart in trying to make every word living and real."[24]

Claims of this sort should not be mistaken for poetic effusions; a famous statement from the presiding judge underlines their philosophical integrity. "The common law is not a brooding omnipresence in the sky," writes Holmes in *Southern Pacific Co. v. Jensen*, "but the articulate voice of some sovereign or quasi-sovereign that can be identified."[25] Reducing the law to human scale places burdens on the language of the lawgiver. The conditions within Holmes's assertion—an articulate voice and a sovereign that can be identified—foreshadow the writer's task, the need to create voice and identity in a claim of authority.

Holmes's ability to convert the writer's difficulties into strengths is the true source of his genius. He turns a personal search for voice into an expression of the times. This accomplishment, as Frankfurter explains, moves beyond "a coherent judicial philosophy, expressed with pungency and brilliance" to one "reinforced by the Zeitgeist, which in good part was itself a reflection of that philosophy."[26] Brilliance and coherence join in something larger than themselves: the creation of a representative figure.

The possibilities first emerge in the successful soldier. The gentleman officer, like the Union itself, is proud of his endurance and survival in the field; they reinforce a superior sense of place, not to mention a certain contempt for the common in life.[27] Others have demonstrated how the Civil War reinforced a patrician stoicism and the belief that "the struggle for life is the order of the world," or that "[man's] destiny is battle."[28] Holmes uses this frame to picture himself in the boldest terms. When a cousin who remains a civilian jokingly asks how Holmes grows a thicker mustache, the latter's response is without humor and often repeated: "Mine was nourished in blood." The oversized mustache, a conventional symbol of manly visibility and assertion, proves what Holmes called "the bloody birthright of heroic days."[29]

The soldier's experience has dimensions in a writerly point of view. The war is always there for the judicial figure. Holmes worked in a room with two crossed swords hung high on the wall: his own, carried in the Civil War, and that of his great grandfather from the French and Indian War.

Experience in war initiated a "disassociation between mind and feeling," a "deadening of sympathetic feelings" referred to as "Olympian aloofness" in him. Holmes values "the spectator view," one which stands at a "distance from the world." The returning soldier does not see less, but his "way of looking" is high above. The perspective is not of men fighting so much as the battle fought.[30]

Commentators trace the same traits in the "austerely solitary life" of the judge, and Holmes openly welcomes "the secret isolated joy of the thinker . . . the subtle rapture of a postponed power . . . more real than that which commands an army."[31] The military comparison, a frequent one in Holmes, is telling here. He prefers detached intellectuality, a stance that the judge will use to mediate conflict.

The undemocratic nature of these preferences in perspective could hardly have bothered the aristocrat, but the judge wields them as strategies with supreme self-confidence, even impunity, because of the soldier's earlier experience. The problematic judicial figure falls back on the man of action who risked everything for his country. He thinks of judicial controversy as "the rolling fire of the front" and finds his own position "on the fire line."[32]

The war concurrently frees Holmes from any anxiety of influence regarding the literary reputation of Oliver Wendell Holmes Sr. It reverses the patriarchal norm. The son uses his experience in the army to claim ascendancy over his eminent father. "I have better chances of judging than you," writes Holmes in their exchanges over the war effort. "I think you are hopeful because (excuse me) you are ignorant." Ironically, Holmes Sr. gives a more accurate account of respective military strengths than the soldier in the front lines. Notice, as well, that the son's parenthetical pretense of politeness is actually rudeness. The soldier's right to speak, his right to be the authoritative teller, relegates the father to silence.[33]

We see this much and more in Holmes Sr.'s ambivalent description of the soldier when home on furlough and surrounded by admiring female visitors: "I envy my white Othello, with a semicircle of young Desdemonas about him listening to the often told story which they will have over again." Though freighted with acknowledged jealousy, the passage is more complex than that. It conveys how completely Holmes Sr., has been cut off from his natural function as the vaunted leader of discussion. The greatest conversationalist of antebellum culture has lost his audience to his son.[34]

Think about this shift in audience. The son's repeated story receives more interest than the father's spontaneous wit, with permanent implications. The reversal allows Holmes to adjust to changing definitions of the writer. Holmes Sr. is famous for *The Autocrat of the Breakfast Table* (1858). He is a mid-nineteenth-century man of letters who questions, satirizes, punctures, and amuses from an assumed social framework. He cultivates with intellectual interplay and his vehicles are the light essay, romance, and occasional poem. The son, writing in suddenly different times, looks elsewhere and is happy to do so.[35]

Mere *belletrism* is a source of derision in the soldier's war journals. "The 20th [Holmes's regiment] have no poetry in a fight," the son proudly reports to his father. "It's very well [for you]," he adds, "to recommend theoretical pourings over Bible & Homer—One's time is better spent with Regulations & the like." Later Holmes would criticize the lack of cohesiveness and force in Holmes Sr.'s writings: "he contented himself too much with sporadic aperçus—the time for which, as I used to say when I wanted to be disagreeable, had gone by."[36] At no point in life does Oliver Wendell Holmes Jr. seem to have difficulty in being disagreeable when he wants to be disagreeable!

The son's criticisms of the father carry a double message. Holmes rejects the paternal legacy, but he lives within the encompassing tradition. Father and son differ over the nature of literature, not its importance. The greatest sustained intellectual effort of Holmes's life, his book *The Common Law*, is the work of a Boston Brahmin succeeding in the 1870s and 1880s. The difference lies in the son's insistence upon "a single subject" and his need to bring overarching order to the writing process. As the writer of *The Common Law* puts these matters himself:

> My articles though fragmentary in form and accidental in order are part
> of what lies as a whole in my mind—my scheme being to analyze what
> seem to me the fundamental notions and principles of our substantive law,
> putting them in an order which is a part of or results from the fundamental
> conceptions.[37]

Holmes handles the seeming circularity of this "scheme" through his search for order. But something else is also at work. The writer's thirst for connection matches the yearning of his times. His late-nineteenth-century readers are receptive to his kind of answer. "The remoter and more general aspects of the law are those which give it universal interest," Holmes convinces one of his law school audiences. "It is through them that you not only become a great master in your calling, but connect your subject with the universe."[38]

The soldier-judge forges literary unities where others find only complication in postbellum America. War plunges Holmes into realist notions that will dominate discussions of literary endeavor for his lifetime. He knows he must create his own sense of consistency amid the indifferent forces and apparent chaos of a dangerous world. On the other hand, the proliferation and democratization of magazines and newspapers, also by-products of the war, have lowered the social caste of a writer for journals.

To remain the writer as a gentleman, as a Boston Brahmin, the younger Holmes must reach for "the higher journalism." He self-consciously insists on a coherent level of commentary beyond mere observation and critical insight. Instinctively, he makes another right decision. He resists the aesthetic strictures in conventional poetry and fiction, generally known as "the genteel tradition," that are forcing polite literature (and the socially prominent writer) away from harsher realities and common experience.[39]

The effect is to leave Holmes somewhere between Carlyle's hero as the man of letters and the hero as political leader and "missionary of Order," as described in *On Heroes, Hero-Worship, and the Heroic in History* (1841). Holmes must write—it is the worthiest human enterprise he knows—but he must do so as "the man of intellect at the top of affairs."[40] While many writers of the postbellum period falter creatively under these tensions, Holmes thrives on them. The life of the judge supplies every answer.

Two popular writings from the middle of his career—"The Path of the Law" (1897) and "Law and the Court" (1913)—reveal Holmes in full appreciation of the judge's literary powers. Thematically, the first essay argues for empirical standards and legal realism, but Holmes's rhetorical emphasis has a more celebratory agenda. "The Path of the Law" begins with assertions of judicial importance: "the whole power of the state will be put forth, if necessary, to carry out their judgments and decrees."[41] Judges, when they consult and write about reports, treatises, and statutes, serve as oracular figures. They gather "the scattered prophecies of the past" from "sibylline leaves." Their duty, "nearly the whole meaning," is "to make these prophecies more precise, and to generalize them into a thoroughly connected system." "The prophecies of what the courts will do in fact, and nothing more pretentious, are what I mean by the law." Here is the expository function of the judicial figure, although Holmes's statement about it *is* pretentious. He leaves out the panoply of state and federal executive and legislative powers that also inform exercise of law in American polity and culture.[42]

The argument of "The Path of the Law" rests in Holmes's conviction that judges clarify the system. Judges make the "body of law . . . more rational and more civilized." They refer every rule "articulately and definitely to an end which it subserves." Two premises turn this mechanical task into a literary adventure of heroic proportions. Holmes believes law can be "reduced to a system" through the right expression of "first principles," and if law is "a business," its power lies in "the command of ideas."[43]

The presumed command of ideas controls matters and makes law exciting to an age confused by the fragmentation in modernity: "the law may keep its every-day character and yet be an object of understanding wonder and a field for the lightning of genius."[44] The fact that Holmes often refers to judicial restraint should not blind anyone to a larger act of creation. In Holmesian rhetoric, judicial figures are the mediating forces between mundane fact and extraordinary possibilities. They are the source of genius in the republic of laws.

His later "Law and the Court" offers one of many creative accounts of this genius. The essay is instructive because it appears in response to criticisms of judicial wisdom at a time when scholars agree that "judicial interpretations . . . were major obstructions to the adaptation of law to the needs of the weaker segments of the community in an urban and industrial society."[45] Holmes replies that "attacks upon the Court are merely an expression of the unrest that seems to wonder vaguely whether law and order pay." The real need is "for us to grow more civilized," and he is more than ready to show the way.[46]

The conclusion to "Law and the Court," where Holmes appears as the calm and authoritative representative of civilization, is worth quoting in its entirety because of its answer to "the unrest" bothering everyone:

> And so beyond the vision of battling races and an impoverished earth I catch a dreaming glimpse of peace. The other day my dream was pictured to my mind. It was evening. I was walking homeward on Pennsylvania Avenue

near the Treasury, as I looked beyond Sherman's Statue to the west the sky was aflame with scarlet and crimson from the setting sun. But, like the note of downfall in Wagner's opera, below the sky line there came from little globes the pallid discord of the electric lights. And I thought to myself the Gotterdammerung will end, and from those globes clustered like evil eggs will come the new masters of the sky. It is like the time in which we live. But then I remembered the faith that I partly have expressed, faith in the universe not measured by our fears, a universe that has thought and more than thought inside of it, and as I gazed, after the sunset and above the electric lights, there shone the stars.[47]

Holmes, a cultural symbol speaking at one of many dinners before gathered luminaries, can depend upon the associations in the passage to carry beyond themselves. The vested authority of official position in Pennsylvania Avenue near the Treasury Building, the encapsulation of the Civil War in Sherman's statue, the extended reference to Wagner by the cultivated man of letters, the entitlement to closure in the aging judge as he walks homeward into a setting sun (Holmes is then seventy-one years old)— these elements resonate in a claim of cultural standing. They also respond to cultural fears by handling "the pallid discord" of change and the potential disaster of a coming Götterdämmerung.

This is what is meant by putting oneself on the page. We recognize the carefully entrenched and reinforced figure in part because of its many-sided insistence upon itself but also because of primal unities and a consistency of tone. The language used by Holmes in this passage borrows from established patterns of ideological confirmation in American culture. When critics refer to a public voice in American literature that is "aristocratic, legalistic, encyclopedic, forensic, habitually expressing itself in the mode of an eloquent wisdom," they could describe Oliver Wendell Holmes Jr. as well as Jefferson and Lincoln.[48]

We can see the act of self-creation more clearly in a literal rendition of the judicial figure. When Charles Hopkinson painted Holmes's portrait in 1929 (figure 4.1), Holmes's complex reactions show how carefully he thinks about himself as judge. Judicial portraits are a formal genre and hang in many law schools. As an established medium, they enable another kind of examination of the judicial figure and a test of critical implications. An iconography of appropriate images is part of legal perception.

FIGURE 4.1 Charles Hopkinson, *Oliver Wendell Holmes* (1929). Oil on canvas, 95" × 59.5." From the Legal Portrait Collection, Harvard Law School. Reproduced by permission of the Harvard Law Art Collection

Holmes, in fact, often uses painterly images in his writings; the power of portraiture to capture life is a recurring theme.[49] He particularly admires the portrait by Hopkinson, painted during Holmes's eighty-ninth year. "As I see the result emerging I am very glad, for [Hopkinson] not only has made an admirable likeness but a very vivid one." Two days later he is, if anything, more enthusiastic: "Hopkinson has a gift for catching a likeness and for vividness I think—and I am quite proud of his results." Still later, the finished product "pleased me mightily." Holmes knows the portrait will hang "as the pendant to one of Marshall" in the reading room of Harvard Law School, "the handsomest compliment that they could pay."[50]

Then Holmes says something far more interesting. "That isn't me," he says of the finished portrait, "but it's a damn good thing for people to think it is."[51] The comment reveals an acute understanding of the judicial figure as symbol. "We live by symbols," he explains in his own literary portrait of John Marshall, "and what shall be symbolized by any image of the sight depends upon the mind of him who sees it."[52]

There is more to this theory of representation. "It is most idle to take a man apart from the circumstances which, in fact, were his," Holmes observes. People will see what circumstance allows them to see. A celebration of someone like Marshall must incorporate the multifaceted life into a single figure that all can accept despite each separate understanding. "It is all a symbol, if you like," Holmes concludes, "but so is the flag." A powerful, familiar, unifying identification can override every difference.[53]

Holmes readily accepts a likeness that "isn't me" because more people will "think it is." Turning to the portrait itself, we can see how well Hopkinson has brought together the different elements of Holmes's career in a unifying, artistic statement of the judicial function. Holmes has been placed well above the viewer's perspective in judicial robes that open to reveal the morning suit, winged collar, watch chain, and rosette or lapel pin of the aristocratic gentleman. The thick mustache, an enduring badge of military service, is now white. Holmes's left hand rests, though not for support, upon the back of a chair that is partially obscured and that faces away from view into an unseen inner chamber. The right hand holds a document of legal size. Both artifacts suggest a zone of reflection.

Holmes emerges from his chambers with judicial opinion in hand. He appears in the moment of transition from the privacy of a decision reached to the publicity of a decision to be announced. To underscore the theatricality in that transition, Hopkinson frames his subject in curtains and places Holmes astride a divide in the carpet that separates inner and outer rooms. Legal document, watch chain, lapel pin, and the left epaulette of the judicial robe form a continuous curve that points back to private chambers, but the figure counters by facing directly out of the painting and blocking all thought of another's entrance into his domain. The left foot moves forward in a rejection of inward invitation.

Everything about the painting conveys the certainty and superiority of a decision reached. Holmes carries no pen for emendations and the expression with which he greets the viewer is free of solicitation. His mind is made up on the subject at and in hand. Judgment is secure and Holmes needs no assistance in making it. Significant artistic shadings modulate these themes. Hopkinson, wrapping the body of Holmes in a nimbus of light, adds a negative halo or darkened circle for the head to contrast with the white of hair and collar. The general effect is to elicit reverence for a secular figure.

The painting itself is dark with little color to relieve the proper gravity and officialdom of theme and subject. Contrasting light from an undisclosed source floods the foreground to Holmes's right, bathing that side of his face and the legal document in that hand. A viewing of the painting begins with this lighted emphasis upon the jurist's head and text. The device creates a first impression in which the intellectuality of the judge's undertaking confirms the legality of his writing.

Spatially, Holmes enters into the lighted area to deliver judgment. The same device leaves the left side of his face—the side closest to the mystery of the inner chamber—in shadow. The contrast might have troubled its subject but for the artist's compensatory deployment of the strongest of all judicial metaphors. Hopkinson mutes the tensions that he has raised in a series of balances: the prominent hands at each side indicate symmetry, and the left leg, slightly forward, receives the same illumination as the right side of the face. Holmes is in perfect equilibrium, the necessary posture for forensic wisdom.

Basic distortions contribute to vividness. Hopkinson's canvas is extremely large, virtually five by eight feet. Even so, and making every allowance for scale, the body of the figure in the painting is enormous. The artist arranges the flowing judicial robe to suggest a more impressive physique than Holmes could possibly possess in his eighty-ninth year. This magnification serves several purposes. Holmes liked to emphasize that force "is the *ultima ratio*."

"The foundation of jurisdiction is physical power," he announces in court."[54] Hopkinson's massive figure literalizes this side of the judge's philosophy.

Holmes can only be pleased by a representation that looks as if it could enforce its own decrees. There is, however, a more subtle dynamic also at work in the image. Power and authority can either coordinate or contend in the judicial function. Coordination involves a complex interplay and requires what Holmes thinks of as "this double view of life," the real source of intellectual or judicial balance.[55] Appropriately, intellectuality and the authoritative text are radiant with light in Hopkinson's painting, but they are also extensions of the darker strength in the robed figure.

A second distortion shapes the head of the portrait. Minimal lines, a slight extension of the jaw, and the highlighted vigor of mustache and eyebrows combine to suggest a man who is old but not elderly; the face is eternal rather than aged. Nor is the conceit an entirely fanciful one. Holmes in maturity encompasses the whole telling of the republican experience. From the young soldier whose grandmother remembers the evacuation of Boston at the beginning of the Revolution to the old judge who advises President Franklin D. Roosevelt, he is the true American witness.

Holmes regards his longevity with pride and goes to some pains to record it.[56] When Hopkinson captures the same elements visually, he harnesses them to the rhetoric of Anglo-American law. The figure on the canvas embodies a long line of legal reference that likes to place law in time out of memory.[57]

Not surprisingly, the artist's tools and techniques for presenting the formal figure are themselves conventions within the genre of the judicial portrait—conventions that everyone, including the artist's subject, knows and exploits. The luminous foreground against a somber subject, the studious accoutrements (book, desk, or chair), the prominent hands and rich carpeting—all appear in the companion portrait of John Marshall painted by Chester Harding in 1829.[58] But Hopkinson, exactly a hundred years later, understands that conventions are to be used and not just followed. His variations—the hidden study, the written opinion, the divided carpet, the complex lighting—are significant. They capture the carefully created figure that Holmes has made of himself as judge.

The portraitist can turn idea into image so successfully because it has been one all along. Hopkinson is only the last of many, starting and ending with Holmes himself, to articulate his value in spectatorial terms.

In 1919 Holmes writes, "I now look forward to what impressed my childhood as most wonderful—to being carried in a civic procession as a survivor." In the same year, Acheson converts Holmesian "grandeur" and "presence" into "strong light" and "pervading force."[59] The survivor whose strength and official identity are enhanced by light is already familiar and confirmed here.

Needless to say, these strategies of self-creation have their real significance in courtroom decisions. Three Supreme Court opinions in particular— *Lochner v. New York* (1904), *Frank v. Mangum* (1915), and *Abrams v. United States* (1919)—illustrate the range of the writer's craft and self-image. Although all involve a minority view, each refigures the judicial image in a different claim of authority, and the power of these claims clarifies a gift for dissent that continues to puzzle students of judicial philosophy. How does a judge who rejects many of the philosophical implications of dissent create such a "power of constructive negation?"[60]

If Holmes is most memorable in dissent, it is because his customary ability to see himself and put it on the page works through the primary requisite of the genre. The dissent in *Lochner v. New York* has been called "the most famous opinion of our most famous judge" and "the greatest judicial opinion of the last hundred years."[61] Holmes disagrees with the majority's use of the Fourteenth Amendment to invalidate a New York statute that limits the working day in bakeries to ten hours or less. His difficulty is that of every dissenting judge: he must find a way to privilege language that lacks authority.

Holmes solves this problem by creating an independent persona to speak for him as the one true judge. His opening sentence, set off by itself, refers to himself no less than five times: "I regret sincerely that I am unable to agree with the judgment in this case, and that I think it my duty to express my dissent." There is, of course, no regret here. Nor is there any hesitation to contradict, though it is done with great finesse. The continuing parade of first-person pronouns and possessives in the next paragraph— seven more in two sentences—contrasts with a topical assertion in objective terms ("This case is decided upon an economic theory which a large part of the country does not entertain.")[62]

The opinion, written in fewer than six hundred words, does not elaborate on either claim or theory. Instead it juxtaposes both against the higher wisdom of the created persona, the "I" of the opinion. The scholar who once thought the lawyer of the future "is the man of statistics and the master of economics" turns his back on both.[63] He rises above such details: "my agreement or disagreement has nothing to do with the right of a majority to embody their opinions in law." What bothers him is that the judges in the majority opinion have been partisans who "share" or "embody" convictions or prejudices" to "enact Mr. Herbert Spencer's Social Statics."[64] Holmes lectures his colleagues from high above them:

> A constitution is not intended to embody a particular economic theory. . . . And the accident of our finding certain opinions natural and familiar or novel and even shocking ought not to conclude our judgment upon the question whether statutes embodying them conflict with the Constitution of the United States.

The verb "to embody" beats like a drum through this section of the opinion, and Holmes uses it, in a play on words, to warn that "every opinion tends to become a law." Judges, through their opinions, are the embodiment of the law. Holmes closes with a quick review of the issues in *Lochner*, one that goes through an increasingly problematic series of reliable observers. We move from the "rational and fair man," to the "reasonable man," to "men whom I certainly could not pronounce unreasonable."

There is wit in this studied declension. Holmes uses it to depict the difficulty of decisions in a fallen world. A judge does not just weigh "the natural outcome of a dominant opinion" through propositions. The complexity of concrete cases requires more than that. In the most ignored aspect of this famous opinion, Holmes responds with a one-sentence summary of the true judge at work. "The decision," he writes, "will depend on a judgment or intuition more subtle than any articulate major premise." The subtlety claimed displays the master craftsman in action.

Frank v. Mangum evokes a different set of talents.[65] The trial and subsequent murder of Leo Frank comprise one of the most notorious miscarriages of justice in the history of the country. Frank, a young New Yorker who manages his uncle's pencil factory in Atlanta, Georgia, is tried and convicted of the murder of a fourteen-year old employee, Mary Phagan, on the flimsiest of evidence amidst public tumult. His appeals are turned down on the ground that due process has been complied with. When a firm majority of the Supreme Court refuses to look beyond the lower courts' rulings, Holmes dissents.

Reaching beyond the Court's formalism to substance, in this case communal hostility at trial, Holmes argues that procedure here has been "an empty form," "an empty shell." Proof of his disagreement with the majority comes swiftly and tragically. Four months after Holmes's dissent, Leo Frank falls to illegal means because legal remedies have failed him. On August 17, 1915, he is dragged from prison, tortured, and lynched by a town mob.[66]

Holmes's dissent lets the facts of Frank's trial speak for themselves. Since these facts are what the majority refuses to consider, Holmes adopts the role of storyteller. He opens with a scene of utter intimidation "in a court packed with spectators and surrounded by a crowd outside, all strongly hostile to the petitioner," with the "stamping of feet and clapping of hands" and frequent "roar of applause." All later readers find themselves held by Holmes's conclusion: "We are not speaking of mere disorder, or mere irregularities in procedure, but of a case where the processes of justice are actually subverted."

The art of this language transcends legal strategy. "The storyteller is the figure in which the righteous man encounters himself."[67] Holmes gives the event literary power through dramatic self-inclusion, substituting judge for defendant and expert for victim. The shifts let him enter his own story:

> We must look facts in the face. Any judge who has sat with juries knows that in spite of forms they are extremely likely to be impregnated by the environing atmosphere. And when we find the judgment of the expert on the spot—of the judge whose business it was to preserve not only form but substance—to have been that if one juryman yielded to the reasonable doubt that he himself later expressed in court as the result of most anxious deliberation, neither prisoner nor counsel would be safe from the rage of the crowd, we think the presumption overwhelming that the jury responded to the passions of the mob.[68]

The failure of the trial judge to maintain proper order is an error in performance that other judges can see and correct. As that judge, Holmes is the next "expert on the spot" as well as the storyteller's righteous man. He has both the knowledge and the craft to correct what had been done in Atlanta.

Holmes's dissent in *Abrams v. United States* carries the writer as judge to yet another level, within the generic confines of the judicial dissent, and so it has been read. The opinion changed the history of free speech in America.[69] Charles Wyzanski, federal judge for the District of

Massachusetts, thought this contribution to free speech made it more than an "immortal opinion"—it was "haunting poetry." He places it on par with just two other speeches in history, Pericles's Funeral Oration and Lincoln's Gettysburg Address.[70] Most readers concentrate on the final paragraph in Holmes's opinion:

> When men have realized that time has upset many fighting faiths, they may come to believe even more than they believe the very foundations of their own conduct that the ultimate good desired is better reached by free trade in ideas—that the best test of truth is the power of the thought to get itself accepted in the competition of the market, and that truth is the only ground upon which their wishes safely can be carried out. That at any rate is the theory of our Constitution.[71]

The passage builds on familiar rhetoric in American politics.[72] But as a peroration, it transcends all politics. It unfolds within other disciplinary considerations that are the real source of its power. Holmes's concerns in *Abrams* are profoundly literary in scope, and he assumes the guise of critic to make his argument.

The opinion relies on the presumed ability to separate language that matters from language that does not. The majority in *Abrams* decides that five political activists (sentenced under espionage and sedition acts for distributing leaflets against the decision to send American troops into Russia after the Revolution of 1917) have not been deprived of their freedom of speech under the Constitution.[73]

Holmes, dissenting, asks two straightforward legal questions about the language at issue. Did the defendants intend their language to hinder the American war effort against Germany, as the Espionage Act of 1917 would require? Next, did that language give rise to a clear and present danger that this unlawful objective would be accomplished, as *Schenck v. United States*—the test for limiting free speech—stipulates?[74] By clever arrangement, Holmes's answers thrive on a looser rhetorical claim. On a variety of levels, Holmes decides to prove that the defendants' words simply do not count in the scheme of things.

The efficacy of language as theme permits a strange and, in the end, poignant reversal. The opening pages of the dissent are given over to the defendants' pamphlets. Holmes's purpose is to trivialize their meaning and importance. His tones humorously deflate the brag and bounce of radical pamphleteering. Selected passages from the defendants' writings suffer in that contrast. In Holmes's account, these excerpts are really just ridiculous "pronunciamentos" when they are not "usual tall talk."[75]

These and other phrases dismiss the problem outright. The first of the two pamphlets in question is "a silly leaflet by an unknown man"; both, says Holmes, are by "poor and puny anonymities" who avow "a creed that I believe to be the creed of ignorance and immaturity when honestly held." The peroration in *Abrams* further marginalizes the defendants as literary incompetents. The country can safely leave these defendants to participate in the "free trade in ideas" because their ignorance will fail in "the competition of the market."

Eloquence notwithstanding, there is a catch to this logic that Holmes turns to magical use. Seeing himself with his usual clarity, Holmes has to accept that his own words have failed in the free marketplace of ideas. Seven colleagues, the overwhelming majority of the Court, have just rejected the suasion and fluency of his opinion, and this requires an affecting admission: "I regret that I cannot put into more impressive words my belief that in their conviction upon this indictment the defendants were deprived of their rights under the Constitution of the United States."

The words do more than call attention to his function. They restore the dignity of the defendants he has just traduced. The closure in *Abrams* invests everything with new meaning. The trivialized defendants receive status as communal members unjustly punished for their beliefs. The judge's truest moment has come in his recognition and response to defeat. If he is right— and Holmes thinks that he is—he has not been eloquent enough. By accepting the power of thought as the best test of truth, he commits himself to an incessant search for more impressive language when language fails.

Holmes's integrity lives in this definition of the judge as wordsmith. As he argues in another case, "a word is not a crystal, transparent and unchanged, it is the skin of a living thought and may vary greatly in color and content according to the circumstances and the time in which it is used."[76] Solace after the defeat in *Abrams* lies in this love of language. The ideal writer should be able to reach those who currently remain unconvinced with a better effort next time. It is all part of "the main excitement of life," "the gradual weaving of one's contribution into the practical system of the law."[77]

Holmes, as always, welcomes the difficulty with the promise that he will overcome it. "A thousand times I have thought that I was hopelessly stupid," he writes late in life, "and as many have found that when I got hold of the language there was no such thing as a difficult case."[78] Tenacity of a special sort is required. Anything less than "the eternal pursuit of the more exact" is "intellectual indolence or weakness."[79]

The tough-minded Holmes, the spirit he liked to wrap around himself and make the world see and acknowledge, is unavoidable here, but it is not the key to understanding either the man or the judge who sat on the bench. Sustaining everything he ever did is a loftier virtue and belief that every writer should hold dear. "Every living sentence which shows a mind at work for itself," he tells us, "is to be welcomed."[80]

5

The Opinion as Literary Genre

THE APPELLATE JUDICIAL DECISION SEEKS a public audience, but wrapped in legal paraphernalia it remains mysterious to most readers. Genre theory can be a useful corrective here. Form in any published product is a significant key to meaning. Writers create with established forms in mind, and the content they offer depends on that previous act of recognition.[1] Judges are especially reliant in this regard. They must consider more than a single established form in the opinions they write. They have to depend on the forms, substance, and expressions of specific previous courtroom opinions. We can, in consequence, expect more involved generic recognitions to play a role in their efforts.

To test this hypothesis and to understand more about the generic implications of judicial opinion writing, the flag salute cases of the early 1940s provide ideal testing ground. Although the selections are arbitrary, the two Supreme Court cases in question, *Minersville School District v. Gobitis* (1940) and *West Virginia State Board of Education v. Barnette* (1943), are unmistakably good choices.[2] The most important trials in the thirty-one Jehovah's Witnesses cases that figure in the sixteen civil liberties opinions of the Supreme Court between 1938 and 1944, these two are familiar to scholars and at least by implication to general audiences. The symbolic importance of the flag and of the salute keep them in the public eye.

Other factors support an analysis of *Gobitis* and *Barnette*. Examining a controversy from the past removes the heat but not the importance at stake. The issue in these cases—the enforcement of the flag salute and the pledge of allegiance in the nation's schools—remains a volatile issue at moments in

American thought.[3] *Gobitis* and *Barnette* also represent those rare instances when the Supreme Court reverses itself in a short time period. We have in these cases judicial language at its most engaged. Circumstance, ideological difference, institutional authority, public disagreement, and political explosiveness make the language still memorable.

The central dynamic at work is easily conveyed. The Court in *Minersville School District v. Gobitis* decided by an 8–1 margin, with Justice Felix Frankfurter writing the opinion and Justice Harlan Stone dissenting, that the rights of a pupil who refuses to salute and pledge allegiance to the flag in a public school are not infringed by a requirement for all students to participate. Such a pupil also cannot claim violations of due process of law and religious liberty under the Fourteenth Amendment.

Writing for a 6–3 majority just three years later, Justice Robert Jackson overruled *Gobitis* in *West Virginia State Board of Education v. Barnette*. His opinion held that West Virginian regulations enforcing a compulsory flag salute in public schools were unconstitutional. As such, *Barnette* represents the Court's first clear-cut commitment to strict review of legislation challenged under the First Amendment (either directly or as incorporated into the Fourteenth Amendment) and the decision has fueled debate ever since over the meaning of restraint and activism in judicial thought.[4]

Summary of the two cases suggests a final source of power in the examples chosen: we are in the presence of literary masters of their craft. All of the vital opinions in both flag salute cases were drafted by major talents on the Court: Frankfurter, Stone, Jackson, Hugo Black, and William Douglas. *Gobitis* and *Barnette* supply the best in judicial thought and language under maximal pressure and in competition with each other. Along the way, they present and test generic integrities through the strain and expression of intelligent and deeply felt differences in legal thought.

What can we learn from these two cases about the judicial opinion as a literary genre? Notions about deliberative oratory, the formula of facts stated, decisions rendered, and the psychologies of precedent are clearly available. Never mind them. Put these obvious elements to one side. They are the identifications easily made, and their very easiness blocks awareness of deeper structures at work in the judicial opinion.[5]

Current genre theory cares less about issues of classification and definition than it does about principles of construction and interpretation. Critics think not about surface traits but about the driving impulses in the writing under examination.[6] Four primary elements mark the modern judicial opinion, and they are elements that do not classify so much as they convey tonal, methodological, and rhetorical energy in this kind of writing. They are, in the order to be taken up here: the monologic voice, the interrogative mode, the declarative tone, and the rhetoric of inevitability in judicial writing.

Consider first "the enormous significance of the motif of the speaking person ... [in] legal thought and discourse," a recognition that comes most forcefully and knowingly not from a judge, practitioner, or legal scholar, but from a literary critic.[7] The current electronic availability of court records should not disguise the fact that attorneys, defendants, witnesses, experts, and judges speak their words in court. Courtroom advocacy and judicial control privilege the voice even when its owner uses pen, pencil, or computer. The appellate decisions of our highest courts are written as if read aloud in a courtroom where adversaries and other interested parties meet to accept a determination.[8]

A judge, like a lawyer, is a mouthpiece as well as a wordsmith, and the first element in the genre of the judicial opinion has to do with that intrinsic combination. A speaking judge in the act of judgment is profoundly monologic in voice and rhetorical thrust. When Felix Frankfurter delivers his opinion in *Gobitis*, he speaks for seven other justices as well, but only Frankfurter actually speaks. The language and tone are his own, and his personal investment becomes clear from the anger and stridency of his subsequent dissent in *Barnette*.

The monologic quality in the judicial opinion has several subsidiary characteristics. Most noticeably, the judicial voice works to appropriate other voices into its own monologue. The goal of judgment is to subsume difference in an act of explanation and a moment of decision. In both *Gobitis* and *Barnette*, alternative views are raised within the controlling voice of the judicial speaker and with the foreknowledge that these voiced alternatives will submit to that speaker's authorial intentions. The rhetorical subtleties in this movement are many, but the essential act of expropriation should be clear. In a majority judicial opinion, differences from the speaking voice are raised only to be answered by it.[9]

Because the monologic voice must speak entirely for and through itself, it is self-dramatizing. It has no other choice. Judges often solve this difficulty by stressing the importance of a decision that only they can make.

Frankfurter, for example, opens his *Gobitis* opinion with the phrase "a grave responsibility confronts this Court," and this solemnity carries into the enticing promise that "judicial conscience is put to its severest test" in "the present controversy."[10]

The thrust of self-dramatization reverses what one normally finds in the dramatic monologue of imaginative literature.[11] While the dramatic monologue works to distinguish the characterized speaker's meaning from that of poet and poem, the monologic voice of the judicial opinion seeks identification between speaker and text.

The need for that identification of speaker and text can be seen in more subtle stratagems of self-dramatization. The monologic voice sometimes seeks its own embodiment by projecting a visible judicial persona into the frame of the opinion. Again, Frankfurter provides the best (though not the only) example in the cases at hand. In *Gobitis* and *Barnette*, he distinguishes "my purely personal attitude" from his Jewish identity (speaking as "one who belongs to the most vilified and persecuted minority in history") while he carefully adds that "the duty as a judge . . . is not that of the ordinary person."[12] History always matters. The year is 1940 and the enforced diaspora and execution of millions of European Jews for nothing more than their ordinary identities is in progress.

Writing from the opposite side, in *Barnette*, Justice Jackson has his own way of putting the judicial figure on the page. He creates an image of judicial legitimacy by insisting on "the oversimplification so handy in political debate" against "the precision necessary to postulates of judicial reasoning."[13] Justice Frank Murphy's concurrence thrives on a more visionary image of office: "Reflection has convinced me that as a judge I have no loftier duty of responsibility than to uphold . . . spiritual freedom to its farthest reaches."[14]

Judicial self-fashioning is a complicated phenomenon while remaining a conventional art form.[15] Its many variations serve essentially two purposes within the genre of the judicial decision. Most fundamentally, image and voice reassure each other and the listener-reader of a level of virtue above and beyond ordinary human behavior. The more difficult the case, the more important this personification of ideal power becomes. The judicial figure resembles Walter Benjamin's storyteller: both are narrators whose tellings must convey sincerity, meaning, and some level of truth. And in both, acceptance by a listener-reader depends on appraisal of character and integrity beyond narrative.[16]

Character aside, judicial self-fashioning serves a second central purpose in the judicial opinion. Frankfurter's language of obligations, Jackson's precision in judicial reasoning, Murphy's loftier duty—all point to a claim of compelled performance. The one thing a judge never admits in the moment of decision is freedom of choice. The monologic voice of the opinion never presumes to act on its own.

The judicial voice must appear as if it were forced to its conclusion by the logic of the situation and the duties of office, which together eliminate all thought of an unfettered hand. *Gobitis* and *Barnette* both insist on the strict boundedness of judicial decision making. "When the issue demands judicial determination," runs a typical Frankfurter warning, "it is not the personal notion of judges ... which must prevail." Or, again, "it can never be emphasized too much that one's own opinion about the wisdom or evil of a law should be excluded altogether when one is doing one's duty on the bench."[17]

The quotations point to an inversion. Utterly free from direct interference, the monologic voice nonetheless assumes a persona that is enmeshed within a corporate machinery of decision making. The voice speaks alone. The persona behind it accepts and moves on a stage of perceived boundaries, compelled narratives, and inevitable decisions. The tension here is intrinsic to judicial performance; the more self-conscious the monologue, the greater the speaker's claim of a chorus in the background.

A further distinction should be drawn here. "Doing one's duty on the bench" does not mean personal removal as Frankfurter characterizes it ("one's own opinion about the wisdom or evil of a law should be excluded"); it instead depends on the presumption of a collective personality of right-thinking figures, all of whom reach the same decision because they have thought correctly through a mutual concept of duty. Self-consciousness, of this sort, guards against a particular vulnerability.

The judicial monologic voice needs all of that collective authority behind it to blunt its non-majoritarian status in a democratic republic.[18] Unelected and largely unaccountable, a federal judge, in the act of speaking, must respond to the seeming inconsistency of imposing separate or unrepublican authority on democratic processes. That seeming inconsistency also explains why judicial formalisms of all kinds continue to thrive long after the loss of professional consensus on objective decision making.[19]

Somewhere in every judicial decision a belief in neutral judgment deflects criticism. The presumed removal of personal predilections allows all parties to accept a compelled decision, one that every fair judge would presumably reach despite differences in style and approach. Hidden in the presumption is a strategy of management. Assertion of a neutral decision is the easiest way—some would say the only way—to convince a democratic society that independent judges believe in justice for all.

The importance of this point cannot be overstated. Judicial formalism is not just a legal philosophy that can be put aside or an intellectual residue in the history of ideas. It is an innate psychological impulse at work in judicial performance. Helping that formalism along are the claimed objective but actually subjective ways that judges raise questions in writing a formal opinion.

The real creativity in a judicial decision thus comes through the interrogative mode, our second controlling generic impulse. Questions are peculiar as well as central to opinion writing—so peculiar and so central as to make the interrogative mode the methodological anchor of judicial rhetoric. Every reader should scrutinize the questions that judges ask, especially if they answer those questions themselves immediately. Asking a question a certain way dictates a logical answer, a maneuver identified in classical rhetoric as *hypophora*. Left for the reader to decide is whether the device guides perusal or manipulates discourse by confuting a position not held by the writer.[20] Judicial prose is inordinately fond of the second strategy.

Every court makes a fundamental decision about the question before it, and the wording in that first decision controls all others. Practice before the Supreme Court literalizes this inclination. The first page of a legal brief submitted to the Court consists of one thing: the question presented by a litigant in a manner that will lead to the answer wanted. Legal counsel spend hours on this one page in order to lead the Court toward just the right formulation of the issue in their client's interest. They understand what an earlier member of the profession, Francis Bacon, observed four centuries ago: the questions we ask shape our knowledge far more than do the theories we propose.[21]

Generic considerations in the judicial opinion magnify Bacon's observation a hundredfold. In *Crowds and Power*, Elias Canetti observes that power adheres to the questioner who is answered and that in judicial examinations "questioning gives the questioner . . . a retrospective omniscience."[22]

The power of a judge consists in the right to ask the first and the last questions—and to answer both, usually with the first leading directly to the last. All questions in the deciding opinion of a court are slanted in rhetorical scope because they are asked with an answer already in mind. The calculated march from questions to answers controls the routinized ceremony of judgment.

Symptoms of the interrogative mode are readily apparent in the majority decision of *Gobitis*.[23] Frankfurter asks four versions of the same question, each a successive refinement of the previous one that in sequent toil precludes disagreement. "We must decide," he begins, "whether the requirement of participation in [the pledge of allegiance], exacted from a child who refuses upon sincere religious grounds, infringes without due process of law the liberty guaranteed by the Fourteenth Amendment."[24] Within three paragraphs the question has begun to shift from a theory of rights toward a justification of authority. "When does the constitutional guarantee [of religious freedom]," asks Frankfurter, "compel exemption from doing what society thinks necessary for the promotion of some great common end?"[25]

A progression toward certainty follows. Two pages later the version of the question has hardened into a justification of authority for the sake of unity: "the question remains whether school children, like the Gobitis children, must be excused from conduct required of all the other children in the promotion of national cohesion." By the end of the opinion, Frankfurter has again transformed the question: "the precise issue, then, for us to decide is whether the legislatures of the various states and the authorities in a thousand counties and school districts of this country are barred from determining the appropriateness of various means to evoke that unifying sentiment without which there can ultimately be no liberties, civil or religious."[26] How can anyone object to such a threat to the democratic process?

The questions that Frankfurter decides to ask are the keys to the judgment that he wants to reach (in this case, a rejection of the claim that a compulsory flag salute violates the constitutional rights of the Gobitis children). Each shift in the interrogative mode incorporates more listener-readers into coded national identifications. Each demands a greater primal allegiance, which makes the ability to stand against it harder and harder. Remember that the question before the court has to do with allegiance.

Elsewhere Justice Benjamin Cardozo summarizes the strategy at hand: "The common denominator silences and satisfies." "We glide into acquiescence when negation seems to question our kinship with the crowd."[27]

In the dynamic of power exercised, the interrogative mode joins the monologic voice. Mikhail Bakhtin writes that "all rhetorical forms, monologic in their compositional structure, are oriented toward the listener and his answer."[28] The power of American judges can be gauged almost entirely through their ability to frame the question that courtroom litigants and the American people must receive on a court's terms.

We can illustrate that power perfectly by seeing how easily *Barnette* overrules *Gobitis* by recasting the dilemma. Faced with the need to change its mind, the Court responds by asking a different question! In the words of Justice Jackson for the Court in *Barnette*: "the *Gobitis* decision . . . assumed . . . that power exists in the State to impose the flag salute discipline upon school children in general. . . . We examine rather than assume existence of this power and, against this broader definition of issues in this case, reexamine specific grounds assigned for the *Gobitis* decision."[29] Well, not exactly. *Gobitis* does examine state power and closely at that. Jackson simply declares otherwise.

If the courtroom opinion as literary genre is rooted in the interrogative mode, it ultimately convinces through a third characteristic, the declarative tone. The only fully sincere questions in opinions—sincere in the sense that they ask for answers beyond the ken of the interrogator—appear in dissents. To appreciate this difference, compare Frankfurter's bland orchestration of questions and set responses for the majority in *Gobitis* with his more penetrating, worried, open-ended, and angry queries in his *Barnette* dissent. A thoroughly aroused Frankfurter pummels the majority in *Barnette* with question after question, ones that still haunt the Court today more than seventy years after they were asked.

Listen to him. "The real question is, who is to make such accommodations [for individual beliefs], the courts or the legislature?" "Is this Court to enter the old controversy between science and religion by unduly defining the limits within which a state may experiment with its school curricula?" "What of the claims for equality of treatment of those parents, who, because of religious scruples, cannot send their children to public schools?" "Is it really a fair construction of such a fundamental concept as the right freely to exercise one's religion that a state cannot . . . compel all children to attend public school to listen to the King James Version although it may offend the consciences of their parents?" As Frankfurter observes in his unhappiness with the answers the majority offers in *Barnette*, "these questions are not lightly stirred." They have, in fact, been stirred again and again every decade since.[30]

Dissents, like this one by Frankfurter, unsettle by design and ask difficult questions in hope of redress the next time. In tonal contrast, a controlling opinion uses questions to establish agreed-upon solutions. In its insistence upon an answer now, it resists mystery, complexity, revelation, and even exploration. The selling of an affirmation—namely, judgment—foists a language of certainties on the genre.

How does the controlling opinion work toward its need for certitude? It typically raises complexities only to dismiss them in the act of judgment. Jackson, worrying in *Barnette* about the shifting sands of constitutional language, still concludes that "much of the vagueness of the due process clause disappears when the specific prohibitions of the First [Amendment] become its standard." Really? Admitting that "changed conditions often deprive precedents of reliability and cast us more than we would choose upon our own judgment," he answers "but we act in these matters not by authority of our competence but by force of our commissions."[31] These responses are tonal in content rather than logical. They announce more than they explain the Court's decision.

The declarative tone succeeds because of a series of implicit assumptions about the complexity and meaning of event in a judicial decision. The single most useful rhetorical tool of judicial certitude conflates the actual world with the world represented in the text.[32] The courtroom, as a forum, takes that complexity—the original and often messy disruption that provokes legal action in the first place—and transfers those elements of contest and uncertainty into a linear narrative with a set direction.

The judicial opinion molds the conflicts of a trial transcript into a cohesive narrative of judgment, turning social problem into legal incident. Stepped stages of intellectual articulation transpose the scene of conflict into a figuration of collective life.[33] Each step requires linguistic simplification, no matter how complicated the actual decision turns out to be. Judgment reduces deviance to a definition of acceptable behavior. This is its mission, and everything welcomes the declarative tones that make it possible.

We see some of these elements in the original circumstances leading to the flag salute cases—circumstances that the judicial opinions present only in altered form. For example, there is no real legislative enactment in the events that precede the *Gobitis* case except for a Minersville Board of Education requirement passed hastily after the controversy in the school first developed. Yet Frankfurter assumes in *Gobitis* that the "case before us must be viewed *as though* the legislature of Pennsylvania had itself formally directed the flag-salute." Frankfurter creates the inference of a legislative determination and uses it to warn against a result that will "stigmatize legislative judgment." These and other improvisations simplify the narrative of judgment that he wishes to impose upon a multifaceted situation.[34]

It is also relevant that *Gobitis* comes at the high-water mark of American fears over the Nazi peril.[35] These communal fears are not raised directly, but phrases like "authority to safeguard the nation's fellowship," "the promotion of national cohesion," "national unity is the basis of national security," "the binding tie of cohesive sentiment," "the seeds of sanction for obeisance to a leader," "the deepest patriotism," "a comprehending loyalty," and "the kind of ordered society which is summarized by our flag" all address a nation under global threat.[36]

In a combination that often figures in the genre of the judicial decision, a specific conflict has been influenced by barely mentioned external considerations. Judicial opinions try to reflect the will of the people—people who are caught in their own webs of implication. Specific standing and immediate conflict may drive *Gobitis*, but communal anxieties dictate judicial rhetoric well above those schoolchildren in Minersville, Pennsylvania. Much of this changes by 1943. Jackson, for the *Barnette* majority, can rely on a different communal posture: "the fast failing efforts of our present totalitarian enemies" pose much less of a threat to national unity.[37]

The *Barnette* Court, without ever directly acknowledging the fact, faces a different political situation. Fear of invasion has evolved into the happier psychological realm of prospective victory, and we see as much in Jackson's finding that "the action of local authorities . . . invades the sphere of intellect and spirit which it is the purpose of the First Amendment to our Constitution to reserve from all official control."[38] With officialdom more safely guarded and secure, it can afford to be more generous.

By 1943 the nine Supreme Court justices have also realized an unforeseen cost of their decision in *Gobitis*. The Court's rejection of the Jehovah's

Witnesses' position in 1940 branded the sect as an unpatriotic group deserving of punishment. The decision identified an unacceptable otherness that unleashed wartime persecutions against members of the sect. Across America in the early 1940s, starting within weeks of the Court's decision, Jehovah's Witnesses were fired from their jobs, stricken from relief rolls, burned out of their churches, driven from their homes, forced to migrate in groups, assaulted individually, mobbed, stoned, jailed as Nazi agents, incarcerated for their own safety, and, in one instance, castrated.[39]

An oblique acknowledgment in *Barnette* reveals how cluttered events can be absorbed and processed into a different clarity of judgment in a courtroom. In their concurring opinion, Justices Douglas and Black observe, somewhat gratuitously, "the devoutness of [the Jehovah's Witnesses'] belief is evidenced by their willingness to suffer persecution and punishment, rather than make the pledge."[40] These words transform shameful and largely forgotten communal persecution into a shining example of steadfastness and courage to be esteemed by everyone. All thought of deviance has been erased. In its place, appreciation of the Jehovah's Witnesses' admirable behavior has made them, once more, thoroughly and commendably American.

The nature of this transformation again has generic significance. The language of affirmation and tonal certainty in the typical judicial opinion encompasses and includes. Tonal detachment replaces a zone of inquiry and brings everyone into the fold. Certitude, assertion, and abstraction are essential strategies in the declarative tone as it reaches down from above to be accepted from below. No significant Supreme Court decision is without these qualities.

Nor can any of the separate qualities that achieve generic significance be understood in isolation. Textual awareness is not a matter of adding up singular traits. Everything depends on how strategies of communication come together to promote holistic reception, and even that level of appreciation can be a problem. Quick acceptance of a text can get in the way of detection. By design, the combinations in effective judicial communication cloak how reception actually works.

The elements already noted in the judicial opinion—the monologic voice, the interrogative mode, and the declarative tone—are separate strategies, but they come together to form a rhetoric of inevitability.[41] In the juxtaposition of positions taken, in the friction of nationalisms claimed, in the dissents registered, and especially in the reversal of decisions made, *Gobitis* and *Barnette* produce alternative answers that are *not* inevitable but must be made to appear so. Competition in the opinions makes the rhetoric of inevitability a central device rather than just a peripheral asset in a foregone conclusion. Disagreement between the justices accentuates the compulsions in narrative and the manufactured nature of closure.

We can clarify the concept of inevitability through the critic Kenneth Burke's use of the term. Burke sees present and future things in terms of a now fixed past; legal precedents establish just such a relationship by creating an "immutable scene . . . of 'eternal truth, equity, and justice.' "[42] For further clarification, refer to the most famous literary discussion of determinism in modern times: Leo Tolstoy's epilogue to *War and Peace*, where "history," "reason," and "form" are the hallmarks of inevitability in life.

For Tolstoy, "the more remote in history the object of our observation[,] . . . the more manifest becomes the law of necessity." "Reason gives expression to this law of necessity." "Freedom is the thing examined, Necessity is the examiner. Freedom is the content. Necessity is the form."[43] The same three factors—history, reason, and form strained through the judicial freedom to define the law of necessity—identify the methodological preoccupations and tools in judicial decision making.

A court opinion uses reason and a belief in measured form to articulate and justify the hold of the past over the present. The philosophical affinities come out of the common law tradition, from time out of memory, and receive their most vivid Anglo-American expression in the writings of Edmund Burke.[44] The importance of the Burkean framework in modern American law explains a great deal in judicial patterns. "We find our visions of good and evil and the denominations we compute where Burke told us to look, in the experience of the past, in our tradition, in the secular religion of the American republic. . . . This is not, as Holmes once remarked, a duty, it is a necessity."[45]

When judges "deliver the opinion of the Court," as Frankfurter and Jackson do in *Gobitis* and *Barnette*, they impose a view of history to secure a decision in the present. They act as keepers of the past in order to safeguard the present. Precedent, experience, and the long history of the Court make judicial "duty" everyone's "necessity." "Experience," "the past," "our tradition," "the present," and the decision to be reached come together in Kenneth Burke's "immutable scene."

One way of thinking about the rhetoric of inevitability is to realize how compulsively judges associate their own views with a presumed correct course in history. Even more than historians who tell or interpret a story instead of making legal decisions, judges need to find themselves on the victorious side of history. Tied to precedent, their natural recourse is the example, which pares history down to manageable doses. Judgment is not a record of the past; it *uses* the past selectively to assess normality and prescribe normalization.[46] What *was* and what *is* come together in the ruling expectation of what *must be*.

The problem, of course, is that the complexity of the past can justify a variety of conclusions. "History" authenticates every position taken in *Gobitis* and *Barnette*. In *Gobitis*, Frankfurter refers to the "centuries of strife" that provide "a guarantee for religious freedom in the Bill of Rights" and to "the judicial enforcement of religious freedom" as "a historic concept," but he concludes that "it mocks reason and denies our whole history to find in the allowance of a requirement to salute our flag on fitting occasions the seeds of sanction for obeisance to a leader."[47]

The same "whole history" belongs to Justice Stone but in dissent. He complains that "the law which is thus sustained is unique in the history of Anglo-American legislation" and warns that "history teaches us that there have been but few infringements of personal liberty by the state which have not been justified, as they are here, in the name of righteousness and the public good."[48]

History is thus a judicial battleground when a court disagrees with itself. For Jackson in *Barnette*, "history" condemns "officially disciplined uniformity" of the kind involved in a compulsory pledge and "authenticates . . . the function of this court" through the majority's decision.[49] None of this keeps Frankfurter from feeling "fortified in my view of this case by the history of the flag salute controversy in this Court." Nor does it assuage his fear that the majority has forgotten how to "decide this case with due regard for what went before and no less regard for what may come after."[50]

Reverence for the Constitution means that the fiercest battles over history in judicial language take place over the original intent of the founders. The lengthy and tangled writing careers of Thomas Jefferson, James Madison, John Adams, Benjamin Franklin, and Abraham Lincoln serve many different purposes in *Gobitis* and *Barnette*. Contesting Justices Frankfurter,

Stone, Jackson, and Murphy prove equally adept in calling upon renowned forebears in support of their positions.[51]

Frankfurter at least acknowledges the dangers in this patriarchal search when, in *Barnette*, he recognizes "too tempting a basis for finding in one's personal views the purposes of the Founders."[52] Even so—and this is the significant point—Frankfurter's act of recognition does not prevent him from citing those same founders more frequently than any other justice in the flag salute controversy.

Intentionalist arguments persist, despite occasional judicial glimmerings of their limitations, because the judicial rhetoric of inevitability requires a directed and selective use of history to be effective. The founders do not appear in these opinions as sources of remedial wisdom. They are icons out of a glorious past that is assumed to be "correct," "providential," "victorious," or "clear."[53]

Cast in these terms, intentionalism, like judicial formalism, is a device that no court can resist. Both—a faith in origins still evident, on the one hand, and a belief in objective judgment, on the other—reinforce a rhetoric of inevitability that translates into a language of obedience. "[Law] rests in large measure upon compulsion," writes Frankfurter in *Barnette*, and he recognizes that compulsion in a free society depends less on force than on a common understanding, on what he has designated in *Gobitis* to be "the binding tie of cohesive sentiment."[54] The task of the judicial decision is to transform common understanding into a legal tie that binds.

Study of the generic form shows how this need to bind works for good and ill. A better grasp of the skills and creativity in such writing should and can bring awareness of manipulations in language that need to be watched and sometimes curbed. Greater concentration on the nature and development of questions asked, sharper scrutiny of uses and abuses of history, some notice of judicial self-fashioning, more awareness of the projected assumptions in decision making, and a deeper concern for hidden perspectives and projected certitudes in the judicial voice are the keys to a better understanding of the rhetoric of inevitability.

The knowing reader or auditor must not accept automatic consignment to any of the places that judicial language relegates its audiences: that of the interested parties who must obey, that of the working practitioner who must accept, that of the concerned citizen who has no immediate recourse, and even that of other judges who must apply the language given in future cases. A qualified skepticism, what one literary scholar terms "methodical quizzicality towards language," is an effective tool for gauging plausibility against mere ingenuity in the judicial opinion.[55]

Skepticism, so understood, means perception, not cynicism or fatalism. Analysis of law from outside of it is one way to insure its correctness. Awareness of the strategies that instill conviction, recognition of the rhetorical means, and knowledge of the possibilities in generic practice supply necessary tools of evaluation that should apply to judicial decisions.

There is a growing importance in mastering these tools of perception. Acrimony is on the rise in American understandings of the judicial function and in the function itself. If critics as well as participants in judicial performance are to clarify increasing philosophical differences, they must come to grips with a difficulty that is primarily literary in scope and implication. Some within the legal profession even call for a "new form of activist law-talk," one that will "construct a new language . . . responsive to the distinctive demands imposed upon legal discourse by the rise of an activist state."[56]

There is a better way to make this point. Many simple forms of critical inquiry apply here. "Books," Henry David Thoreau noted, "must be read as deliberately and reservedly as they were written."[57] Judicial opinions deserve that kind of consideration from all who read them. Courts use words to secure shared explanations and identifications; they also use them as weapons of control. External scrutiny makes the combinations of welcoming words and hidden manipulations safer ones to use. Appreciation of the integrity in language is, after all, the first safeguard in a republic of laws.

6

Ulysses in Government Hands

DISTRICT JUDGE JOHN M. WOOLSEY'S decision in *United States v. One Book Called "Ulysses"* lifted the ban on publication of James Joyce's novel in the United States, and it remains one of the most famous and widely read judicial opinions in American history.[1] Of course, the decision, delivered on December 6, 1933, may still be remembered because the triumphant publishers printed it in the front of every Random House and Bodley Head edition of the novel for years on end.

There is, nonetheless, more to this. The controversy over *Ulysses* receives credit for changing the law of obscenity and for originating a field of legal inquiry known as "law and literature."[2] The irony in these widely held assumptions is rich. Obscenity law starts down a hopeless path with Woolsey's decision, and literary celebration, though certainly understandable, has obscured a lot of sleight of hand in Woolsey's arguments.

In purely analytical circles the opinion is known to be defective. Critics have said the opinion is "palpably false," full of "well-intentioned lies," and "not recognizable as law."[3] Woolsey was not overturned, but he was soon corrected on appeal in an appellate decision by Circuit Judges Augustus N. Hand and Learned Hand, both of whom were more renowned jurists than Woolsey.[4] Nevertheless, it is Woolsey's decision that we remember. Why we remember it reveals something about communal notions of judicial performance and even more about connections between law and literature.

Should we be surprised that Judge Woolsey stretched the truth instead of telling it whole, as a witness would be required to do in court? The answer to this question depends on how much the truth has been stretched. Judges emphasize given facts while ignoring others in writing opinions, and they reshape doctrinal understandings without admitting a difference in legal consequences. Judge Woolsey has done both in lifting the ban on *Ulysses*, but if so, what possible excuse can a judge give for deserting the demand for accuracy and precision that should dominate formal legal proceedings?

The question is important because Woolsey's opinion is typical of many judicial performances in high-profile cases. The devices that shape those performances should be better understood by a reading public. We also need to know what makes Woolsey so convincing, even inspiring, despite questions about his tactics from legal critics and despite even sharper divisions and problems over the definition of obscenity. To the extent that Woolsey departs from the standards of precision required at trial, what are the justifications for it, and what do they tell us about how to read a judicial opinion?

Woolsey may have followed the advice of one of the most revered judicial figures of his day. "There is an accuracy that defeats itself by the overemphasis of details," writes Benjamin Cardozo in a 1931 essay on judicial opinions. "I often say that one must permit oneself, and that quite advisedly and deliberately, a certain margin of misstatement."[5] Cardozo was chief judge of the New York Court of Appeals at the time, and he writes in a source known to everyone in the profession.

If anything, Cardozo's influence is even greater two years later. During the trial of *Ulysses* in 1933, Cardozo sits on the Supreme Court of the United States as its newest and most celebrated associate justice, and he has taken his seat on the court with unprecedented levels of acclaim, including a rare bipartisan nomination process with a quick and unanimous Senate confirmation.[6] Not to be forgotten, Cardozo actively practices the loose use of facts that he preaches. In writing his own opinions, most famously in *Palsgraf v. Long Island Railroad Co.* (1928), he ignores crucial facts to reach the result he wants.[7]

Four controlling elements in judicial writing can help us to understand what is at stake when a judge deviates from literal accuracy. These elements should also aid scrutiny of judicial opinions in general. What are the rules to be followed? Do Judge Woolsey's deviations from fact and doctrine represent an acceptable use of his authority or a more questionable method in *United States v. One Book Called "Ulysses"*? Woolsey has clearly decided, before the case, that he wants to change the direction of obscenity law. When, to put the question another way, do the ends justify the means in a judicial opinion?

Aristotle stipulates the first element in judicial writing. In *On Rhetoric* he distinguishes between political and judicial performances. A speaker in politics must "show that circumstances are as the speaker says," but in a judicial decision "this is not enough; rather, it is first serviceable to gain over the hearer."[8] Cicero, following Aristotle, clarifies the idea. An orator need only please (*delectare*) while a judicial decision-maker has the higher obligation to "move" (*movere*) or "gain over" understanding.[9]

The need for persuasion is so intense in a judicial opinion because the contending hearers in court are formally divided with at least one reluctant auditor and probably more disappointed on one side. The ideal judicial opinion must decide the case while covering some of the distance between winners and losers. The language used should be circumspect as well as declarative in tone—not the easiest combination.

A judicial opinion exists because a serious dispute or doctrinal issue cannot be resolved in any other way. Two passionately held positions have remained in conflict; otherwise, the problem would have been handled earlier and in a simpler fashion. The official decision in response to such intransigence must be convincing to such an extent that all of those who are seriously interested in the outcome, including the community beyond the courtroom, accept the decision that has been made. Just as adversarial argument at trial is heated, polarized, and hyperbolic, so the judicial explanation must quell anger and division through overruling calm, the Aristotelian notion of *praünsis*. Judges seek a renewal of normalcy, "a settling down" in the name of difficulty resolved.[10]

The second controlling element in judicial rhetoric seeks clarity beyond the immediate decision. Judges speak to reinforce *stare decisis*, the understanding that like cases will be decided in like manner through precedent. The outcome of the case should agree with previous decisions and should inform future cases if based on comparable facts. The efficiency in this arrangement leads judges to generalize certain particulars over others. Again it is Benjamin Cardozo who articulates the importance of this strategy.

Somewhat disingenuously, Cardozo puts his thoughts in the mouth of that authority all judges love to cite, Justice Oliver Wendell Holmes Jr. Quoting Holmes "from uncertain and perhaps inaccurate memory,"

Cardozo confirms a crucial manipulation in a judge's arsenal: "to philoso-phize is to generalize, and to generalize is to omit."[11] Holmes generalized all of the time. He got away with it because he knew how to do it extremely well while seeming to be practical about it.

These first two rhetorical elements—the need to move understanding toward common acceptance and the goal of encompassing like matters through controlled similarity—lend themselves to a third occasionally devious stance in opinion writing. No judge can afford to come before disputing parties with an arbitrary or even an uncertain decision. A judge cannot say "I could have decided this case either way, but I have chosen for the moment to decide it this way rather than the other way."

No matter how close a case may have been, a judge tends to assume a fatalistic tone in writing out a seemingly foreordained conclusion.[12] As Jus-tice Hugo Black once explained to his new colleague Justice Harry Black-mun: "Harry, never display agony in public, in an opinion. Never display agony. Never say this is an agonizing, difficult decision. Always write as though it's clear as crystal."[13]

Black's warning indicates the fourth, more hidden rhetorical problem in judicial opinions: how can one appear clear when one is not? The boldest answer to this question comes from Judge Richard A. Posner, "probably America's greatest living jurist" and its most distinguished scholar on the mechanics of jurisprudence.[14] In *How Judges Think* (2008), Posner divides judges into two camps: legalists and pragmatists. Legalists follow prec-edent and statutory interpretation while pragmatists decide on the basis of consequences.

Posner admits "most American judges are legalists in some cases and pragmatists in others," but what if neither approach responds adequately to the need? Sometimes "legalist techniques run out" and sometimes the "consequences of a decision are unknown." Sometimes "a strong moral or emotional reaction (maybe indignation aroused by the conduct of one of the parties) overrides both a legalistic response and a concern with conse-quences." Worse, "the application of a rule to facts is problematic when the facts are incurably uncertain." The answer to these dilemmas, although few judges will admit it, requires an act of imagination, "the exercise of legisla-tive-like judicial discretion."[15]

Woolsey decides *United States v. One Book Called "Ulysses"* within this zone of uncertainty over consequences. Without saying so, he gives free range to Posner's exercise of legislative-like judicial discretion. The problems are several. What are the rules for judicial discretion, a controversial concept at best in American law? Does it apply only when nothing else will do? How much transparency should appear in the exercise of a power associated with judicial discretion? Can it simply evade existing law as Woolsey seems to have done?

Technical expertise must meet common understanding in a successful judicial opinion. How this is to be done and with what balances remain unclear, and current rhetorical theory (with its stress on relativism) complicates aspects of this coordination. The trajectory of theory has discounted the universal frame that Aristotle has given to all of rhetoric. "Field-dependence" is the new basis of correct persuasion, and legal scholars have used the theme of disciplinary separation to say that "truth in law is a matter of the forms of legal argument, not the conditions that make propositions of law true."[16]

Can truth in a judicial opinion be hermetically sealed? Should a decision for the common good be "field-invariant" instead of "field-dependent"?[17] Both levels of articulation, the professional and the common, must connect to yield convincing truth. Success lies in the coherence supplied over and above the separate levels of conception addressing a problem.[18]

Judicial truth thus becomes a variable in tension with itself and in search of holistic relation. Legitimacy in the higher coherence sought depends on the connections drawn between truth as legal form and truth as common accuracy and sincerity.[19] Woolsey in *United States v. One Book Called "Ulysses"* plays loosely but cleverly with these connections, and we can use his example to look for guidelines that apply to the writing and comprehension of judicial opinions. Cleverness in truth is part of the strength of an opinion; looseness is not if the opinion is to be durable, and it must be as law.

Truth in law may have its difficulties, but it is a compelled ingredient in every judicial decision at two levels, truth (an objective basis) and truthfulness (accuracy and sincerity in the word spoken).[20] How much and what kind of truth is required when a judge knows that a controversial decision will continue to remain controversial no matter what is said? What level of exigency frees a judge to enter the realm of discretion to create legal truth, and what recognitions should go with the crossing of that professional Rubicon?

The stakes in *United States v. One Book Called "Ulysses"* seem starkly one-sided today when put in the interrogative form that Woolsey faced in 1933. Should James Joyce's novel *Ulysses*—now recognized as one of the greatest novels, perhaps even *the* greatest written in English in the twentieth century—be cleared for publication in America where many want to read it, or should the copy imported from France in an arranged test of obscenity law be seized and destroyed by the government of the United States as a violation of section 1305(a) of the Tariff Act of 1930?[21] When the question is asked this way, Woolsey appears on the side of the angels with an easy decision to make.

The doctrinal issues seem just as clear-cut from hindsight. Woolsey and other judges in America objected to the rigid state of obscenity law in the 1930s. The law in most jurisdictions was as imprecise as it was harsh, and consistent application of its terms would have condemned many major works in the literary canon, including scores of works from classical antiquity and even sections of the Bible.

The dominant strand in decision making in the United States through the first third of the twentieth century follows *Regina v. Hicklin* (1868) from the Queen's Bench in England. *Hicklin* established the test for obscenity at "whether the tendency of the matter charged as obscenity is to deprave and corrupt those whose minds are open to such immoral influences, and into whose hands a publication of this sort may fall." So worded, the *Hicklin* standard was vague as a doctrine and arbitrary in application.[22]

The Queen's Bench in *Hicklin* also insisted that decisions about obscenity be left to the triers of fact rather than to cumulative expertise and ruled that any part of a text found to be obscene condemned the whole work. Good law in parts of the United States as late as 1957, *Hicklin* came to be known in modern parlance as "the pervert's veto." All a jury or judge (as trier of fact) had to decide was whether *anyone* out there, whether of good or bad character, would be open to immoral influences by the mere availability of the material in question.[23]

By these lights, *United States v. One Book Called "Ulysses"* seems like the perfect case for overturning bad doctrine, particularly for a judge like John Woolsey, a well-educated, extremely well-read man well-known in literary circles with his own collection of first editions of rare books. Why, then, does Woolsey complain from the bench that "this isn't an easy case to decide?" Why spend time worrying aloud about "his extremely difficult position in being required to pass on a book that for ten years had evoked the most violent denunciations and praise from all manner of learned men and women"?[24]

The contradiction between this seemingly easy case and Woolsey's difficulties in deciding it raises often ignored problems in judicial rhetoric. There may be progress in ideas, but ultimately no era is more enlightened than any other. Every era has its blind spots or taboo subjects in control of communal discourse, and crime as a subject is particularly vulnerable to stereotypical thinking. Judicial decisions are time-specific to conventional sensibilities of the moment, held to locality by the form of articulation they must take, and bound by extant legal proscription and background.

Each of these three pressure points plays a role in Woolsey's initial hesitation and later language. Taken in order, the rigid moral sensibilities on display become clear when, against all logic, the prosecution weakens its own case by refusing to read passages from *Ulysses* aloud with women present in the courtroom.[25] Nor can the pressures of local knowledge be forgotten in this trial; few courtrooms decide a case against a surrounding community, and many people in Woolsey's world objected to the content of *Ulysses*.[26] Third, precedent often controls understanding beyond logic; a doctrine like the *Hicklin* standard may be imperfect, but it had achieved longevity in the United States for a reason.

Woolsey had to deal with these difficulties and others. No matter how you read *Ulysses*, some language in it is obscene by the communal standards of the 1930s, and the government could argue that much of the novel qualified.[27] How much obscene language is enough? Finding *some* obscene language—indeed, *any* obscene language—proves the government's case under *Hicklin*. Court precedent and, by implication, the Tariff Act of 1930 also condemn the whole work if *any part of it* is found to be obscene.[28] Woolsey knew he was engaged in a high-profile trial where communal pressures would remain intense. He also recognized that the decision would have a permanent effect on his reputation either way.[29]

Legal proscription, the third pressure point on judicial performance, gives Woolsey a more subtle quandary. He must ask himself, if not *Hicklin*, what then? What standard against obscenity should take its place? The questions are important to consider because Woolsey's answer in *United States v. One Book Called "Ulysses"* sets law down a path where nothing written can easily be declared obscene. No one today knows quite where to draw the line between obscene and acceptable material. Is a standard that finds too much material obscene (the *Hicklin* standard) worse than finding nothing obscene despite extant law on the books to punish it?[30]

Woolsey leans in favor of the novel. Two years prior to *United States v. One Book Called "Ulysses*," he dismissed obscenity charges against nonfiction books on married love and contraception.[31] Even so, *Ulysses* presents real difficulties. Joyce's novel is renowned or notorious in a clash of opinions. It is also luxuriant in its use of profanity, overt sexuality, deviant sex for the times, and voyeuristic scenes of lust in action.

Woolsey's questions of counsel from the bench show what he wants to do. He values literary enterprise, and we cannot be surprised if that influences his personal inclinations. Objectivity may be the aspiration in judicial thought, but current theorists of jurisprudence tend to be legal realists on this subject. Few deny "that preconceptions play a role in rational thought" or "that the nonlegalist influences on a judge are likely to operate subliminally."[32]

The issues before us are therefore not about the decision to be made. They are about how Woolsey manages his decision, how he resists the charge of obscenity against difficulties in his solution, and how he guards the means as well as the ends in an inevitably controversial decision. When a court challenges even an ambiguous legal presumption like *Hicklin*, the rhetorical skill of a judge becomes twice as important and possibly twice as dangerous. We can test Woolsey's skill in these matters through three accepted dimensions in classical rhetoric: *arrangement* (the ordering of argument), *ethos* (the disposition of character through control of point of view), and *audience* (ideal reception).

Judicial opinions are never mystery stories. The major revelation comes first with the decision reached, and Woolsey dutifully opens by "dismissing" the government's case.[33] The last words of an opinion are similarly prescribed. They confirm the decision in as affirmative a tone as possible, and Woolsey's final words follow that part of the pattern too: "'Ulysses' may, therefore, be admitted to the United States" (185). Left in between are the explanations as to why the decision was made. Woolsey's problems and ours lie in this middle dimension.

Generic constrictions can be a strength. Woolsey turns the *fait accompli* of the decision and the final stamp of approval into bookends that reveal another recognizable form of argument. The opinion is short, just three full pages in the *Federal Supplement*. Nevertheless, Woolsey divides the body of his opinion into six separate parts, each brief section topped with a roman numeral. The effect, for anyone who attended high school in America in the twentieth century, is instantaneous. Woolsey has made his opinion a geometry proof; it moves from one axiom to the next in *quod erat demonstrandum*.

The geometric structure is important because it allows Woolsey to obscure the difficulty he has with extant law. We do not even get to any real discussion of law until section 6, Woolsey's last, and there is method in his reliance on a presumed theorem. Long before the final section, with its brisk treatment of the law, anyone reading the opinion would have already been swept along by a cultural proof. We have so much earlier support for Woolsey's decision that no other answer seems possible. Law is not the answer in lifting the ban on *Ulysses* so much as the capstone to a judgment already presumed by other means.

Follow the ordering of the six sections of the opinion for what they accomplish rhetorically in Woolsey's logic:

1. Section 1 sets procedural limits (182–83). It takes the decision away from the normal trier of fact—a jury—and places it in Woolsey's hands because *Ulysses* would be too difficult for jurors to handle.

2. Section 2 (183) confirms Woolsey as the trier of fact. The study of *Ulysses* has been "a heavy task." Woolsey is qualified by "many weeks" of study. The trier of fact is suddenly an expert witness!

3. Section 3 (183) has this expert witness using his authority as trier of fact to find no pornographic intent. "I do not detect anywhere the leer of the sensualist."

4. Section 4 (183–84) then connects the absence of salacious intent to the "astonishing success" of "a sincere and honest book."

5. Section 5 (184) sees "each word of the book" as part of a "mosaic," so no "dirt for dirt's sake" can be found in this completed "picture." No law or "more objective standard" can be found here as well.

6. Section 6 (184–85), finally provides a definition of obscenity—"tending to stir the sex impulses or to lead to sexually impure and lustful thoughts"— and *Ulysses* is not obscene because "it is only with the normal person that the law is concerned." Woolsey, after all, has not been stirred!

Woolsey, as the self-assumed trier of fact turned critical expert, argues that *Ulysses* is a sincere and honest book with no pornographic intent because Joyce has remained true to his method in tracking modern theories of the human mind. Whatever seems unacceptable in part turns into a contribution to the whole. Ergo, since informed readers will appreciate Joyce's method as normal people (Woolsey's standard for the law), nothing in the novel is obscene.

The tonal qualities that control this decision are ingratiating, placating, conversational, sometimes witty, and at times sly, but their driving force comes through a claimed erudition that is never absent—an erudition traceable to the literary criticism Woolsey has been surreptitiously fed by defense counsel.[34] The tenor, if not the fact, is also judicial. The tones of the early sections cancel the heat in controversy. Every word insists that a calm view will find no problem with the decision made.

Woolsey soothes those who think *Ulysses* might corrupt the morals of women by admitting Joyce's words can "lead to what many think is a too poignant preoccupation with sex in the thoughts of his characters." Too poignant? "The words which are criticized as dirty are old Saxon words known to almost all men and, I venture, to many women" (183–84). Profanity becomes a worthy tradition! Woolsey makes his readers good, agreeing English descendants either by birth or literary cultivation.

For those who worry that America's youth might yield to the sordid practices described in the novel, Woolsey moves the debate to foreign territory. In faintly anti-Irish registers, he speaks of "types of folk" from "the lower middle class in a European city." Of Joyce, Woolsey confides, "it must always be remembered that his locale was Celtic and his season Spring" (184). The condescension in these remarks moves in two directions. It diminishes Joyce's foreign and lower-class characters as potential influences on the American elite that might read *Ulysses*, and it more subtly derides the officious propriety of those he addresses who seem to be objecting to the novel.

The middle ground of the critic at work in the first five sections of Woolsey's opinion has something for all sides. "'Ulysses' is an amazing *tour de force*" reads the opening sentence of section 5; "it seems to me to be disgusting" is then said later in the same paragraph (184). For the squeamish, "if one does not wish to associate with such folk as Joyce describes, that is one's choice" and "quite understandable" (184). Yet in the very next sentence

Joyce offers a rousing question for the high-spirited and intellectually adventurous: "when such a great artist in words, as Joyce undoubtedly is, seeks a true picture of the lower middle class in a European city, ought it to be impossible for the American public legally to see that picture?" (184). What thoughtful person can say "no" to such a question?

Woolsey brings this early discussion of *Ulysses* down to "a matter of taste on which disagreement or argument is futile," and arguing to impose a standard besides that of taste seems "little short of absurd" (184). Taste thereby moves to the side of *Ulysses*, and Woolsey's conclusion is archly sophisticated on this score. He decides "that whilst in many places the effect of 'Ulysses' on the reader is somewhat emetic, nowhere does it tend to be an aphrodisiac" (185). To parse this language in down-to-earth terms, the novel might make you vomit but it will not lead to lustful thoughts. There is genius in the juxtaposition. No one feels lust while nauseous.

There is another touch of rhetorical genius in this conclusion. Woolsey, with the same subtle condescension, quietly fuses the role of judge to that of the expert critic in a parting shot. He grants " 'Ulysses' is a rather strong draught to ask some sensitive, though normal, persons to take" (185). But what kind of peril is this? The metaphor equates reading the novel to drinking a glass of beer! Much closer to home, what auditor will confess to a normalcy that is overly sensitive?

If you want to disagree with Woolsey—accomplished critic, proven man of letters, and urbane judge—you turn yourself into a fuddy-duddy on moral matters. The threat is gently delivered but real, and it is leveled against the self-conscious social circles that Woolsey knows so well. His opinion plays on the insecurities of the *cognoscenti* in society. Woolsey tells all would-be sophisticates how they should think if they wish to retain their identity in this nebulous but exacting category.

Is the threat necessary? Consider for a moment the fault lines in Woolsey's argument. Even James Joyce thought that parts of his novel "exploit obscenity." Notorious obscene works and references to them appear regularly in the pages of *Ulysses*. Joyce owned a large collection of pornographic material himself, maintained a "lively interest in pornographic writing," and remained personally obsessed with the varieties of sensual display in sexuality.[35] No less a critic than Leslie Fiedler concludes that "of all the popular modes porn is most central to *Ulysses*."[36]

As for the inner workings of the novel, a "sensual leer" (from several different directions) controls the Nausicaa section of *Ulysses*. Joyce's protagonist, Leonard Bloom, masturbates in public while gazing at the virginal Gerty MacDowell's deliberately exposed underwear; a description of fireworks parallels the sexual act in a way that no one can mistake. The same charge might be made of Molly Bloom's orgasmic soliloquy at novel's end.[37] The author's prose is openly voyeuristic in a lustful way. Women in sexual activity appear as objects in a male fantasy rather than subjects.[38] Much like *The Odyssey* on which it is loosely based, *Ulysses* is a tale of male adventure.

If Woolsey did spend weeks reading *Ulysses* and researching works about it, he decided to avoid pertinent facts available to him. To find *no* pornographic intent and *no* obscene passages in *Ulysses* more than ignores facts; it falsifies them against the standards of law. The appellate decision qualifying Woolsey's decision hits out at this failure hardest and first. "We may discount the laudation of *Ulysses* by some of its admirers," Augustus Hand writes for himself and Learned Hand in oblique reference to Woolsey's stance as the self-styled literary critic in the lower court.[39]

Hand also faces the main issue directly. "That numerous long passages in Ulysses contain matter that is obscene under any fair definition of the word cannot be gainsaid," he notes. The appellate court halves the difference between itself and Woolsey's lower court decision. Yes, there is obscene material, but Hand agrees with Woolsey that Joyce's "erotic matter is not introduced to promote lust." The proper test should be "whether a publication taken as a whole has a libidinous effect." In saying so, Hand more honestly takes on *Hicklin* and distinguishes it.[40]

Woolsey's understanding of the legal standard that he employs is also suspect. When he finally gets down to the law in section 6 of his opinion, he says "it is only with the normal person that the law is concerned" (185). What can he mean by such an assertion? The normal or "good person," as Oliver Wendell Holmes Jr. demonstrates in his essay "The Path of the Law," rarely falls afoul of the law. Morality usually holds this figure in place. Law depends instead on a "bad man" theory. "If you want to know the law, and nothing else," Holmes reasons, "you must look at it as a bad man who cares only for the material consequences."[41]

The "pervert veto" of *Hicklin* may be an absurdly rigid gauge for obscenity law as an exclusive standard, but is the mythical "normal person" as a gauge much better? Woolsey, it should be recalled, spends the first two sections of his opinion explaining why twelve such normal persons should *not* serve as jurors in deciding the issue of obscenity in *Ulysses*. Why, then, should the decision be made by a judge, who then adds two presumably normal friends of his own to help him?

These weaknesses do not stand out in Woolsey's opinion as much as they might. One answer lies in the persona that John Woolsey inserts into his opinion. Like any accomplished performer, Woolsey manages his argument through *ethos*, the disposition and manipulation of the speaking character in his decision.[42] He is believable on the page, a necessary trait in a judge explaining a crucial decision. By controlling point of view, where point of view is both a tool of persuasion and the means of fortifying identity in the persuader, he is master of the single greatest asset a judge has in appearing to a reader. Manipulation of both is the ultimate source of power in Woolsey's opinion.

The novelist Henry James was the first to understand the multifaceted complexity in point of view and its attachment to identity when he spoke of "the spreading field of perception" and its relation to "the posted presence of the watcher."[43] More recent scholarship attaches point of view to five levels of interaction in a text. There is always an overarching worldview that controls what the text can be, an authorial view within that worldview, the separate view of the narrator of that text, the view of figures embedded within the text, and finally the point of view of the reader.[44] Persuasion in a text or performance depends on how well these separate but related views come together in a credible narrative.

Woolsey orchestrates separate points of view to make his own procedural needs appear as if they come from other directions when in fact they reflect his personal preference. Early in section 1, he notes that the parties in conflict have "waived their right to a jury trial." Buried in this section is Woolsey's admission that the waiver comes from a "suggestion made by me." Are anxious litigants going to challenge a judge's suggestion? Likely not. Woolsey then implies he was the last to agree with the idea: "it seems to me that a procedure of this kind is highly appropriate" (182–83).

Section 2, where Woolsey explains "the study of 'Ulysses'" follows a similar strategy. This is the shortest section in the opinion—just two brief paragraphs, five sentences in all. But these five sentences are more than enough to create a vivid presence in the narrating persona. The first paragraph of two sentences is dominated by no less than five first-person pronominal forms as Woolsey makes much of the burden he has shouldered: "for many weeks," he somberly relates, "my spare time has been devoted to the consideration of the decision which my duty would require me to make in this matter" (183).

The shift in point of view in the second short paragraph of section 2 is then abrupt. Composed entirely in the third-person or neutral voice, it invokes the arduous labor that reading *Ulysses* would place on *anyone*: it is "a heavy task" (183). The image that emerges is of a remarkably conscientious, objective, and cultured judge, an acknowledged savant equal to the problem at hand. But acknowledged by whom? By the judge himself! The shifts in view help us to forget that Woolsey has crafted this flattering self-image.

In section 3, the established image of the erudite critic as judge legitimizes Woolsey's announcement that Joyce has no pornographic intent. No evidence of any kind is presented for this claim. Woolsey relies instead on "the reputation of 'Ulysses' in the literary world" and dismisses those who might object to Joyce's "unusual frankness." As a member of the literary elite and in securing that status in his own text, he is equally frank in rejecting untoward intent in Joyce. Only later do we learn that this is an irrelevant concern. The content of a book, not the author's intent, truly determines the question of obscenity.

This third section again confirms the narrator's authority by conflating points of view. The image of the erudite judge gains an utterly decisive voice by mounting the platform of authority constructed for him in section 2. This time first-person singular pronouns, entirely absent just before, come hard and fast at the end of the section: "I do not detect anywhere the leer of the sensualist. I hold, therefore, that it is not pornographic" (183).

Section 4 then again submerges this first-person speaker, this time into a series of parenthetical references until the end, when we hear "I hold that 'Ulysses' is a sincere and honest book." Woolsey gets to this conclusion by dragging the reader's point of view into the worldview that Joyce "has been loyal" to present. The blockbuster sentence that controls the section is worth quoting in full:

> Joyce has attempted—it seems to me, with astonishing success—to show how the screen of consciousness with its ever-shifting kaleidoscopic impressions carries as it were on a plastic palimpsest, not only what is in the focus of each man's observation of the actual things about him, but also in a penumbral zone residua of past impressions, some recent and some drawn up by association from the domain of the subconscious.
>
> (183)

The always familiar ("each man's observation of the actual things about him") connects with the newly relevant ("the screen of consciousness") in this passage. Woolsey is giving instruction in modern theories of the mind and tells his auditors to recognize themselves through it. The language used is browbeating and stocked with specialized vocabulary.

Next, to legitimize "the screen of consciousness" at a more popular level, Woolsey offers a vehicle familiar to all. "What he [Joyce] seeks to get," he observes, "is not unlike the result of a double or, if that is possible, a multiple exposure on a cinema film which would give a clear foreground with a background visible but somewhat blurred and out of focus in varying degrees" (183). Anyone who has entered a movie theater grasps the nature of this parallel. The cultural logic for *Ulysses* is complete at this moment. Woolsey signals as much: "I think the criticisms of it are entirely disposed of by its rationale" (184).

Section 5 is largely repetitive, but it has a special purpose in mind. *Ulysses* is "an amazing *tour de force*," but praise is nimbly interspersed with first-person pronominal sentences of negative admission. The book is "not easy," "disgusting," and "contains . . . words generally considered dirty." These sentences come in the narrator's own confidential voice. Woolsey is following the time-honored judicial practice of giving the losing side its due. (184)

The promised objectivity of Woolsey's legal conclusion continues for three more paragraphs before turning into a festival of personal commentary. The shift turns point of view into an overt theme. In the opening paragraphs of section 6, we hear from the speaking subject passively to indicate again his duty: "I am, therefore, only required to determine whether 'Ulysses' is obscene within the legal definition of that word" (184).

For the first time, the narrator also moves to the first-person plural subject pronoun to describe what "we are here concerned" to decide. When a judge moves from the singular to the first-person plural subject pronominal form without explanation, one possible goal is to welcome more participants into the argument. Woolsey is a solitary judge making a decision, but through the language of "we" a gathered collectivity are now all part of the process of a decision that all should welcome. (184).

The move to a more personal finale is elaborate. Returning to the concept of the trier of fact, Woolsey introduces two of his friends as fellow triers under the rubric of *l'homme moyen sensuel* (the average feeling man.) They fill "the same role of hypothetical reagent as does 'the reasonable man' in the law of torts." Is anyone surprised that these two anonymous friends, whom Woolsey identifies as "literary assessors," agree with his decision when asked for an independent judgment? (184–85).

One of these friends "with average sex instincts" turns out to be Henry Seidel Canby, editor of the *Saturday Review of Literature* and peripherally connected to the case despite Woolsey's disclaimer. The other, Charles E. Merrill, is a wealthy financier and socialite known popularly as "Good Time Charlie" from regular appearances in newspaper gossip columns.[45] He also happens to be the cofounder of Merrill & Lynch. Neither man, ostensibly from different directions, has any trouble deciding *Ulysses* is not obscene.

Woolsey introduces these figures to make the trier of fact seem "more objective" and to guard against charges of a decision based on "his own idiosyncrasies" (184). The insertion of the device is important for another reason. It supports Woolsey's naked assertion: "it is only with the normal person that the law is concerned." Why "the normal person," whatever that means, should be the ideal gauge for understanding pornography is left unplumbed. Woolsey wants to refute the "pervert veto" of the *Hicklin* standard without saying so, and here once more Augustus Hand's appellate decision faces the issue more directly. For Hand, *Hicklin* and its progeny no longer "represent the law."[46]

The great advantage that John Woolsey has over the stodgier, if more precise Augustus Hand lies in the persona he has crafted to preside over his decision. He refers to himself in personal pronominal forms no less than twenty times in the final ten sentences before judgment. He and his two friends, "men whose opinion on literature and on life I value most highly," join hands and minds. Woolsey observes, "I was interested to find that they both agreed with my opinion" (184). Do we hear from them if they do not agree?

The image that the reader accepts is of a careful decision-maker who leaves no stone unturned. Trust in the speaker (*ethos*) will always move the right audience (*pathos*).[47] Woolsey succeeds brilliantly in this regard. But what *is* the right audience for this decision? Those interested in a judicial opinion extend from the parties involved, to law enforcement mechanisms, to legal reporting and venues (not limited to an appeal process), to those attending in a courtroom, to media outlets, and on to the wider public. A high-profile trial can complicate concentricity by pitting different audiences against each other.

Woolsey, aware of these tensions, writes for the interested public and, within that public, for *literati* most concerned. His urbane tones, arch vocabulary, critical analysis, and aesthetic sallies ("it must always be remembered that his locale was Celtic and his season Spring") all suggest a literary audience. When controversy involves an idea more than a real crime, addressing the audience most concerned with the idea would seem appropriate. The conflict over *Ulysses* unfolds as an arranged event by both sides to test an idea and the criminal to be punished if found guilty is a book. A book facing the death penalty!

Even if all of this is true, is Woolsey's focus the correct one? Is the literary elite the primary audience, among many, that should receive the rhetorical focus of attention? The appellate court responds with strictly legal implications in mind, understandable in an appeal of law. Augustus Hand resists the stylistic flair so apparent in the lower court decision. Is that the better model? One might argue that each court does its own job well, but there are troubling tendencies in Woolsey's opinion and they have to do with the audience that he has decided to target for major consideration.

In several places Woolsey's argument ignores the law or actually leads away from it. The removal of the test of obscenity from a common jury to a presumably more sophisticated judicial figure brings automatic relief to any writer composing on the edge of what might be considered obscene subjects, but it confuses the whole notion of "the normal person" as the gauge for making a decision that is offered later. If the measure of obscenity is its damage to a community, a jury is that community. The whole of section 2, on whether or not Joyce has pornographic intent in writing *Ulysses*, is irrelevant as law, although an obvious boon to those who would like to test the limits of obscenity law. Woolsey throws a bone to creative writers in this section of the opinion more than he details legal implication. The charade of objectivity in Woolsey's selection "of two friends of mine" as "hypothetical reagent[s]" also falls apart the moment we learn the withheld identity of these two figures.

Woolsey encounters a hidden and sometimes insidious characteristic of audience in these acts of persuasion. When a judge in a high-profile case faces a sector of a community that is culturally powerful and heavily invested in a particular conclusion, the tendency to address that sector more particularly is strong. That part of the audience cares so much about the conclusion to be reached that any argument in favor of its position is welcome, whether the argument is legally relevant or not. The result in *United States v. One Book Called "Ulysses"* is disquieting on two counts.

A judicial opinion is flawed when the logic offered makes it more difficult to accept an internal argument than the conclusion reached.[48] Law as articulated from the bench is all about what justifies a decision. Weak reasoning opens the door to uncertainty and bad precedent. The anonymity of Woolsey's "two friends" sharing his decision is similarly problematic. Transparency is a virtue in a judicial decision. The figure on the bench needs it to secure the connection between law and public understanding. When secrecy resists transparency, it is inappropriate.[49]

In a celebrated essay entitled "How to Make Our Ideas Clear," the philosopher Charles Sanders Peirce contends that "a clear idea is defined as one which is so apprehended that it will be recognized wherever it is met with, and so that no other will be mistaken for it."[50] If sincerity is one of the twin virtues of truth, it requires transparency, and Woolsey has not really been candid with his audience. If authenticity is the other virtue of truth, Woolsey flunks the two aspects that sustain it: integrity in "the investigator's will" and in "the methods that the investigator uses."[51] The opinion, putting the decision to one side, does not stand up in an investigation of the facts that support it.

At the same time, any serious discussion of truth must contend with a paradox in postmodern thought. A majority of observers will admit that lies and deceit abound in contemporary life, and yet many of the same observers have difficulty admitting there is such a thing as "truth."[52] Can one have a notion of falsehood without an idea of truth? The most that can be said today is that most commentators believe truth is somehow relational.

Available common ground is limited but important. The analytical philosopher and logician Bertrand Russell decides that "truth consists in some form of correspondence between belief and fact."[53] The pragmatist William James concurs but only to the extent that truth, "a property of certain of our ideas," means "the agreement" of these ideas with "reality" so long as "reality is taken as something for our ideas to agree with." James concludes that "true ideas are those that we can assimilate, validate, corroborate, and verify." Logically, "false ideas are those that we can not."[54]

The more contemporary philosopher Charles Taylor adds that no man is an island when it comes to understanding reality. The human mind "is in this sense not 'monological,' not something each accomplishes on his or her own, but dialogical." Mutual exploration allows truth to emerge; it requires "properties, common or complementary which are of value" and depends on a shared "horizon of significance."[55] The transcendentalist Henry David Thoreau addresses the subject more epigrammatically but still in relational mode: "It takes two to speak the truth—one to speak and another to hear."[56]

Taylor notes a second complication on the question of truth, and he does it in a way that explains a feature of Woolsey's understanding in *United States v. One Book Called "Ulysses."* He argues that modern historical contingencies create "subjectivation" in approaches to reality. "Things that were once settled by some external reality—traditional law, say, or nature—are now referred to our choice." In defining authenticity, "orders of meaning" give way to "a language of articulated sensibility."[57]

The implications in Taylor's comments are vast for how a judicial decision might be made. If one no longer follows a model or looks for correspondences to an objective reality, but instead seeks to *create* an understanding, the tools for resolving a problem have changed. In *Regina v. Hicklin*, decided in 1868, the mere presence of certain descriptions was sufficient external evidence to find obscenity. By *United States v. One Book Called "Ulysses"* in 1933, the sensibility of a trier of fact becomes the key to a determination.

Looked at in this way, Judge John Woolsey modifies communal understanding through his decision-making skills, a modification that leaves him free of personal blame. The same modification explains why Woolsey's visible presence on the page becomes doubly important. If a speaker's sensibilities have become the test of truth, we want to know as much as possible about the person behind those sensibilities. Yet even so, can we assume truth through the context, authority, and consensus claimed by a judicial decision?

Legal truth, much like the definition of truth given by William James, exists when it has been validated, corroborated, and verified where the gauge of truth is "behavior appropriate to its context."[58] Pragmatists like James, legal experts posit "a practical truth" that is "less a correspondence between statement and reality than a relation between speaker and hearer." Truth then depends on "a *trustworthy* speaker, a *cogent* argument, and a *convinced* audience" to be worthy of the name.[59] So far so good, but authority *requiring* agreement can hardly be called dialogical truth. "If they were to understand properly how they came to hold this belief," the philosopher

Bernard Williams asks of those who nod in the presence of authority, "would they give it up?"[60]

The need for the transfer of *all* information from speaker to listener for a meaningful agreement becomes clear from yet another test of relational truth. "What it means for a statement to be true," Raymond Geuss writes, "is that it would be the one on which all agents would agree if they were to discuss all of human experience in absolutely free and uncoerced circumstances for an indefinite period of time."[61] If this standard demands too much, it reaffirms the primacy of the speaker to listener relationship in the search for truth. Geuss, Thoreau, William James, and by extension Charles Taylor, with his insistence on "the dialogical in human life" and "reasoning in transitions," all demand the canniest and most attuned of listeners in response to a speaker. They want the kind of listener who shares enough with the speaker to be able to answer back.[62]

The engaged citizen in a republic of laws can never just trust authority.[63] Transparency in explanation is always necessary. "That the legal system often fails to yield correct results because the basic facts are not reliably discovered is a highly significant truth."[64] The ultimate question becomes whether or not a judicial decision aids or deflects the exchange demanded, and at the last we are left with something like Henry James's "posted presence of the watcher" as the control on dialogical truth.[65]

PART | 3

The Public Uses of Legal Eloquence

ELOQUENCE IS IN THE EAR of the auditor. No speaker succeeds without an appreciative audience. Of course, appreciation is notoriously hard to quantify, but it begins in the established authority of a speaker, and the variables in that authority are specific in legal eloquence.

People obey law, which always confines behavior in some way, only if four aspects in the authority of the speaker's communication persuade the receivers of it. The difference in expression between the right thing and the wrong thing to do must be obvious. The logic or reason behind the legal assertion must be distinct. Association in what has been said with an established order must be readily apparent and, lastly, the consequences for disobedience must be available and credible enough to deter willful disregard. Permeating all four characteristics—in fact, central to all of them—is one more absolutely crucial virtue: clarity, in both tone and expression, is essential.

We typically take these elements of authority for granted in a country where the rule of law is strong, but challenges to them can be especially violent in a country where so many are armed and eager to use weapons capable of reaching far beyond themselves. For this and other reasons, it helps to determine how legal eloquence supplies the upper hand in a democratic society where consent depends so heavily on belief, and for our purposes, imaginative literature is especially attuned to the issue of authority through convincing speech.

Novelists and playwrights, in their need of conflict, use performative utterance to convey the imaginative settings that society cannot safely tolerate in reality. The best speeches and dialogues in the works we read again and again evoke communal fears to test the limits of human behavior. Nowhere do we see this tendency more powerfully than in *Measure for Measure*, a play in which law has lost its voice.[1]

Measure for Measure is generally regarded as Shakespeare's darkest "problem play," a work "so savagely bitter as to be unmatched in this regard."[2] The greatest critic of the early nineteenth century, Samuel Taylor Coleridge, even called it "the most painful—say rather the only painful—part of his genuine works."[3] There are, in fact, many problems in the play—sexual, political, moral, communal, institutional, and characterological—and all of them go unresolved in Shakespeare's deliberately unsatisfying conclusion. Still, the overriding problem is the failure of law and the difficulties that authority encounters in trying to recover it.

Vincentio, duke of Vienna, ostensibly through leniency but really through neglect, has allowed the law to be "more mock'd than fear'd." Constables no longer enforce regulations. They lack respect, are easily avoided when they try to act, and have become imbecilic. Licentiousness and corruption reign in the city. "Liberty plucks Justice by the nose" and "quite athwart goes all decorum."[4] Law has become just a "scarecrow" that the inhabitants use as "their perch, and not their terror." [5] To answer this problem, Vincentio puts the overly strict Angelo in charge with the established justice, Escalus (the name means "balance" or "scale"), as his subordinate, while the duke pretends to travel and goes into hiding as a friar to watch proceedings.

The unpracticed and rigid Angelo is the first of many to fail. Handed the novelty of legal power, he uses it first on an honest couple, Claudio and Juliet, who are affianced to marry. The charge is "fornication," and under strict Viennese law it means a death sentence for Claudio. When Claudio's sister, the virtuous Isabella, asks for mercy for Claudio, her plea arouses the puritanical Angelo through her purity and he harasses her, saying he will not only kill Claudio but torture him to death if she will not sleep with him. The Duke, after much difficulty, thwarts these crimes by breaking his own laws. He substitutes Angelo's wronged fiancée Mariana for Isabella through a bed trick, exposes Angelo's treachery, and then pardons everyone, all while forcing the relevant parties to marry in ways that make any real happiness in their future lives hard to imagine.

Not the Duke but a lying, oath-breaking, perjuring snitch and rogue named Lucio oversees most of these proceedings. "I am a kind of burr, I shall stick," he declares, and indeed he does to everyone and everything (4.3.177). "Lucio" means "light," but in one vital sense Shakespeare's label is not ironic. Lucio is the fish that swims well in these polluted waters, and it makes him the one person who actually understands himself in a debased society. All of the other characters function as strangers to their inner selves and pretend to be what they are not; there is no balancing social and legal order in Shakespeare's Vienna to stabilize their identities.

The knowing Lucio thereby enables the one sincere and powerful example of eloquence in the play when he goads the passion of the repressed Isabella to the surface in her effort to save Claudio from Angelo. Even so, and despite its power, Isabella's effort at persuasion fails. Here, as everywhere, inspiration (from Lucio) is separate from sincerity (in Isabella). It does not, however, stop her from delivering the central message of the play:

> But man, proud man,
> Dress'd in a little brief authority,
> Most ignorant of what he's most assur'd—
> His glassy essence—like an angry ape
> Plays such fantastic tricks before high heaven
> As makes angels weep; who with our spleens,
> Would all themselves laugh mortal.
>
>   (2.2.118–24)

If we do not know ourselves—our glassy essence—we rise above ourselves only in unacceptable forms of self-righteousness. Instead of becoming like angels, we fall beneath our best human selves. Angelo has ignored his true essence—*nosce te ipsum* in its Latin origins—and when challenged, it robs him of identity and the ability to speak as he once did. "What dost thou," Angelo asks himself at the end of this scene, "or what are thou, Angelo?" (2.2.173).

The importance of the play for us lies here. In *Measure for Measure*, those who have the authority never say the right thing and those who say the right thing never have the authority to back it up. The Duke, in disguise as a friar, delivers one of Shakespeare's greatest speeches. It contains lines never to be forgotten: "Thou hast nor youth, nor age, but as it were, an after-dinner's sleep dreaming on both" (3.1.32–34). Even so, the Duke's language fails to persuade Claudio to accept death. It is couched in a stoicism more pagan than Christian, and it is a fabrication to boot. It belongs to Vincentio's manipulation of events as an assumed member of a holy order. The Duke may mean what he says personally, but it is not a sincere communication in the context in which it is given, and predictably Claudio is not convinced by it.

By extension, law repeatedly fails in the play because it lacks a grounding in articulated belief. We see it most clearly when Vincentio, still in disguise, needs a dead body (or actually a severed head) to assure Angelo that Claudio has been executed against the bargain that Angelo has made with Isabella. Barnardine, a prisoner condemned to death for nine years who has managed to avoid execution through the neglect of the Duke, is supposed to supply that need, but when the combined forces of law (the Provost), religion (the Friar), politics (the Duke), and institutional wherewithal (the Executioner) demand that the "careless, reckless, and fearless" Barnardine put his head on the block, he simply refuses. "I swear I will not die today for any man's persuasion." No authority, the Duke notes in exasperation, can "persuade this rude wretch willingly to die" (4.2.141–42; 4.3.59, 80).

Persuasion wanting is everything in this play. The Duke succeeds only through the weakest of all clarifying claims on legal eloquence: fear of the consequences for criminal activity. He intimidates everyone, most egregiously the innocent Isabella. He falsely accuses her of lying, falsely sends her to jail for telling the truth that he knows to be the truth, and falsely pardons her on her release for doing nothing wrong. He then adds that he has saved her brother from death after, again falsely, convincing her that Claudio is dead. All of these maneuvers seek to make Isabella grateful and pliable to his coming proposal of marriage.

Shakespeare surely means it when he carefully keeps Isabella from answering the Duke's marriage proposal, which comes to her in tonal registers somewhere between an unfair question and an unfairer command, oiled by revelations of all that he has done for her. Isabella is the only sincerely eloquent figure in this drama. She uniquely "hath prosperous art ... with reason and discourse" and "a prone and speechless dialect such as move men" (1.3.172–75). Nonetheless, Shakespeare resists the opening for a final burst of fluency. He purposefully leaves Isabella silent for the last eighty-five lines of the play.

That purpose is about the failure of eloquence in *Measure for Measure*. Shakespeare signals this lack through the characters most capable of noting its absence. Early on in the play, Escalus, who has the best judgment in Vienna as the most experienced and active figure on the bench, rues his helplessness when robbed of the authority to proceed effectively. He asks "which is the wiser here, Justice or Iniquity?" (2.1.169–70). Vienna is not arranged or governed with enough law or wisdom to give a meaningful answer to this question.

Vincentio, "duke of dark corners," has similarly negative insights after witnessing all of the play's events while in disguise as a friar. As "a looker-on in Vienna" instead of the ruler over it, he sees "corruption boil and bubble till it o'errun the stew: laws for all faults, but faults so countenanc'd that the strong statutes stand ... as much in mock as mark" (4.3.156; 5.1.315–19).

The state exists in worse shape than he previously imagined. "There is scarce truth enough to make societies secure," he despairs, even while accepting this realization as "the wisdom of the world" (3.2.220–25).

Yet, and this seems to be a salient point in the play, Vincentio's fatalism and his ultimate pardon of everyone, including the out-and-out villains Angelo and Lucio, leaves Vienna as legally unmoored as when he first left it. There is no reason to expect better behavior or legal recognition from anyone who has previously misbehaved.

Fear of punishment is never enough to secure a legal regime. *Measure for Measure* has many other dimensions, but first and foremost it establishes that authority is wrong to place whole trust in the "strict statutes and most biting laws, the needful bits and curbs to headstrong jades" (1.3.19–20). Law must speak itself into the belief of a people. Citizens must *want* to obey law as a matter of well-being. A society that lacks this interactive quality of legal health will descend into something unpleasant and unacceptable, as Shakespeare's Vienna has done.

Missing is the eloquence of both form and articulation in legal expression. The importance of its presence in a variety of forms is the theme of this section on the interdisciplinary value of law, literature, rhetoric, and speech theory. Law, it turns out, depends on a whole variety of articulated forms and circumstances to get its message across.

In chapter 7, "Lawyer Lincoln and the Making of Eloquence," our most accomplished presidential speaker uses classical forms of oratory to lay out the connection between law and religion in his most important communications to the American people. An autodidact further tempered by the horrors of the Civil War, Abraham Lincoln uses the traditional patterns in rhetoric to control the expectations of a suffering and divided citizenry. We overlook how important regular courtroom performance was to the evolution of this speaker, one who literally redefined the nation as it moved from a confederated republic into a democratic modern nation-state.

Chapter 8, "Memorialization in the Spirit of Law," takes the problem of legal eloquence into the realm of physical representation. Memorials are often overlooked as an expression of law, but they remind us of who we legally are and, often enough, of what we have done wrong. One of many memorials to the Holocaust, the relatively simple one in New York City's Riverside Park, accomplishes both objectives through the starkest of designs arranged around a few engraved words. The conflict in who we are and in what we want to be is palpable in this symbolic manifestation of inhumanity at a level that no one should be allowed to forget. The question that this memorial implicitly asks? How will we keep ourselves from ever allowing this level of criminality to happen again?

Concision, after all, is one of the ignored virtues in eloquence. The ninth chapter, "Precision in Persuasion," takes us to the most articulate current judicial figure in the country, the Honorable Richard A. Posner, who sits on the Seventh Circuit of the United States Court of Appeals and who is also the most cited legal scholar of the twentieth century and into the twenty-first. We find him here using an easy court case, though one very artfully described, to make a much larger legal point. He gives us judicial activism at its most responsible by using the case and the law behind it, but not the decision itself, to suggest that the legislative branch reconsider misguided definitions in the law of homicide. Eloquence can be many things. In Posner's decision, it is a rhetorical call for reform that you know is right and is also a pleasure to read.

7

Lawyer Lincoln

THE MAKING OF ELOQUENCE

ABRAHAM LINCOLN WAS A COURTHOUSE litigator and spent more time speaking in the courtroom than any other president of the United States. To appreciate his eloquence, the gold standard in American political discourse, one has to understand what it meant to be a lawyer in antebellum America. What Lincoln said in court shapes his great oratorical performances of 1861 to 1865.

In tracing Lincoln's eloquence it may be just as well that no videotapes exist of him speaking. He had a high, less than pleasant voice; he moved awkwardly; he spoke with a twang that annoyed many in the Eastern establishment when they did not make fun of it. We marvel at the great speeches today when we read them, automatically granting them hallowed status, but to fully appreciate their worth we must recover the oral craft behind them. A better grasp of how "our most eloquent president" spoke is also timely. We live in an age when eloquence in public speech has become a source of political controversy—enough of a controversy that we might ask "what is eloquence?"[1]

The disembodied words of Lincoln hold us today, and that already tells us something. Eloquence comes out of time, circumstance, and knowing performance, but it reaches beyond its original components. Although Lincoln, speaking in the crucible of the Civil War, saw just how to convey sacrifice during the greatest blood-letting the country has ever seen, much more was actually at work in his words than thematic power. What interested citizen has not intoned Lincoln's opening benediction to his second inaugural speech? "With malice toward none; with charity for all; with firmness in the right, as God gives us to see the right, let us strive on to finish the work we are in."[2]

There is plenty of method behind the way we hear and say these words. But why have the words themselves remained so important in American speech? The best expressions in language are the ones we want to remember, and attention to the details of Lincoln's mastery can help to explain how they reach toward permanence, the ultimate requirement of eloquence. Cutting across the details is the fact that Lincoln was an autodidact, a self-taught man who was secretive about it, and this sense of mystery has produced a tangled web of implications over the nature of his accomplishments.[3]

The recent turn in interpretation has been toward the soulful tones in Lincoln's words as manifestations of personal distress. The dark side of the man's psyche competes with the oft-told tales of his political genius.[4] One of Lincoln's most compelling traits has compounded these differences in interpretation; our sixteenth president exhibited a remarkable capacity for intellectual growth at every stage of experience. "There was probably no year of his life," wrote Horace Greeley, not always an admirer, "when he was not a wiser, cooler, and better man than he had been the year preceding."[5]

There is, despite these difficulties, one vital area of common ground in all approaches to Lincoln. Every interpretation recognizes the centrality of speech in his rise to political prominence and, eventually, the presidency. Until 1856 Lincoln was a lesser, one-term congressman known for unwisely opposing the Mexican War on the floor of the House of Representatives in 1848. One speech on May 29, 1856—his condemnation of slavery before Free Soilers at the birthplace of the Republican Party in Bloomington, Illinois—would catapult him into national prominence.

More formative speeches followed. On June 16, 1858, Lincoln's "House Divided" speech as the Republican nominee for the Senate from Illinois and the ensuing Lincoln–Douglas debates made him the leading Republican of the West. Less than two years later, on February 27, 1860, the Cooper Institute address in New York shifted the Republican nomination for president away from the clear frontrunner in that state, Governor William Seward, to Lincoln. All of these triumphs came to a man who had held no significant public office for thirteen years and who had lost twice in seeking one.

The speaker's platform used successively for ever more strident objections to slavery launched a major career. Lincoln spoke, as was the tradition, for well over an hour at a time, and he drew huge attentive audiences on each of these occasions. Much earlier, he left a clue to the nature of the influence that public speaking could have. "Extemporaneous speaking should be practiced and cultivated," he wrote to beginning lawyers in 1850. "It is the lawyer's avenue to the public. However able and faithful he may be in other respects, people are slow to bring him business if he cannot make a speech" (2:81).

Recognition of Lincoln's creativity and greatness thus depends on what it meant to "make a speech" in America in the mid-nineteenth century. With that in mind, we approach Lincoln's originality through an established mode that happened to be the major literary genre of its time and the most dramatic source of national formation for a country in danger of falling apart. Not by accident was the man praising "extemporaneous speech" a practicing lawyer talking to other lawyers. They were the crown princes of an oratorical age. They dominated literary as well as political sources of explanation throughout the antebellum era. Lincoln rose as the final dominating figure within that configuration; he was simultaneously of his time and unique within it.[6]

If running for the state legislature from New Salem in Sangamon County at the age of twenty-two counts, the politician predates the lawyer, but Lincoln's twin pursuits—politics and law—were shaped by previous experience. What little formal education Lincoln received, less than a year in all, came from a "blab school" near Pigeon Creek, Indiana. The slang expression bespeaks its main characteristic. Pupils read aloud while a schoolmaster measured progress by walking the room and listening to each charge's voice amidst the din of all.

The method is noteworthy because Lincoln would later claim that he could not understand fully the things he read unless he read aloud, thereby hearing along with seeing the words on the page.[7] Here is our first clue to Lincoln's eloquence. The ear, not the voice, is the key to his reception and to reception of him. At times the musicality and metrics of his prose come close to poetry. Everything reads better than it was originally spoken. The same auditory quality made Lincoln an excellent listener of others, a talent that helps to explain his capacity for continuous growth through the absorption of what was useful around him.

Both traits are evident in his tenure as president. Lincoln had the knack of taking advice from his cabinet advisers while always seeming to improve upon it. A famous example, often cited, includes Lincoln's reworking of suggestions in language given to him for his first inaugural address by his rather presumptuous new secretary of state, William Seward. "Lincoln's literary skill," the historian Don E. Fehrenbacher notes, "is most readily observable in those instances when he took someone else's prose and molded it to his own use." Seward was no mean orator, but in every instance of many changes in his "First Inaugural Address," Lincoln's language shows greater felicity and power.[8]

Where did these skills come from? Lincoln was deeply rather than widely read. His primary sources as a young man were the Bible, Shakespeare, William Scott's *Lessons in Elocution* (along with various books on grammar), and Sir William Blackstone. The first three sources were central to a bible culture that privileged pulpit oratory. All four were part and parcel of the times and can be found everywhere in Lincoln's prose, but the fourth source, Blackstone's *Commentaries on the Laws of England*, gave most to Lincoln's confidence in speaking and writing.

"Blackstone lawyer" was a popular epithet of the times, and the *Commentaries* ranked second only to the Bible in importance as a literary and intellectual influence on the early history of American thought and institutions. Blackstone's four volumes, published in England between 1765 and 1769, sold many more copies in America than in his homeland. Among other things, it asserted that proper structure in language could sustain a concept of country even in difficult times and over the most insignificant of places. Blackstone called his work "a general map of the law marking out the shape of the country." In the still evolving United States, this belief in law as the shaper of countries gave structure to the states, meaning to the uncertain territories, and possibility to the uncharted wilderness beyond both.[9]

Lincoln, who in 1809 was born and raised in that wilderness and who escaped from it as soon as he could, used language to control "the frontier line" where "the panther's scream, filled night with fear / And bears preyed on the swine" (1:386). An unwilling hunter in an environment where everyone hunted (4:62), he was an avid reader as far back as he could remember and the best writer in his neighborhood as a boy. His first political statement of note, "Communication to the People of Sangamon County" on

March 9, 1832, stressed "the public utility of internal improvements" for "the poorest and most thinly populated countries," and it named "education," an area in which he knew himself to be "defective," as "the most important subject which we as a people can be engaged in" (1:5–8; 2:459; 3:511).[10]

The Enlightenment ideal that one could impose reason over chaos counted for much in Lincoln's approach to his own situation and to his thinking about the country at large. Blackstone's version of the idea was a practical application. In reading the *Commentaries*, Lincoln later said "[I] never read anything which so profoundly interested and thrilled me" and "never in my whole life was my mind so thoroughly absorbed."[11] The imposition of law over undefined space fed ambition as well as the need for order; it gave Lincoln the lifelong belief that the right words could define a nation and mold its destiny.

Early on Lincoln made it clear that the right shaping words would have a legal connotation. "Let reverence for the laws be breathed by every American mother, to the lisping babe, that prattles on her lap," he declaimed before the Springfield Young Men's Lyceum in 1838. "Let it be taught in schools, in seminaries, and in colleges;—let it be written in Primmers, spelling books, and in Almanacs;—let it be preached in the pulpit, proclaimed in legislative halls, and enforced in courts of justice. And, in short, let it become the *political religion* of the nation." Even "bad laws" should be "religiously observed" until they could be reformed (1:112). The words are noteworthy far beyond themselves. They prefigure a philosophy as well as a strategy in reforming the divided nation of the 1860s.

Long-term vocation molds thought in certain ways, and contemporaries noted how hard Lincoln worked at his.[12] "The leading rule for the lawyer . . . is diligence," he once wrote, so it is hardly surprising that his own efforts as a courtroom lawyer perfected a speaking style that would carry from law into politics (2:81). Forensic debate refined four essential sources of rhetorical power: first, equanimity in the face of conflict; second, an instinct for the root of a matter that tended to concede nonessentials; third, a gift for plain expression, as opposed to the ornate style required of nineteenth-century orators; and fourth, a legal identity that enabled religious thought away from the dogmatisms of his day.

Each of these elements is worth a closer look as a speaking tool in the later president. Combat in courtrooms turns many a lawyer into an aggressive "mouthpiece." Lincoln avoided conflict whenever it was unnecessary, but he relished debate on a vital issue. The combination meant he knew when to challenge, when not to, and when to simplify. As he advised a fellow lawyer, "it is good policy to never plead what you need not, lest you oblige yourself to prove what you cannot." "Billy, don't shoot too high," he told his law partner William Herndon. "Aim lower and the common people will understand you." Colleagues all noted Lincoln's homespun ways and his tactic of yielding peripheral points while being "as hard to beat in a closely contested case as any lawyer I ever met."[13]

The first three legal prongs of Lincoln's rhetorical prowess—equanimity in conflict, concession of nonessentials for a central concern, and simplicity of expression—are most easily found in the prolonged Lincoln–Douglas debates of 1858. Here is where the politician faced the most negative pressure in an oral contest. Lincoln's initial defensiveness is clear, and it backfired with humorous reactions in the press when he saw himself as "*a living dog* against *a dead lion*" or a lion "*caged* and *toothless*," improbable references to Senator Stephen A. Douglas, the popular incumbent and powerful standard-bearer of the Democratic Party (2:467).[14]

"The Little Giant," as Douglas was called, had the upper hand. He accused his more obscure opponent of "dangerous radicalism." Lincoln was a "Black Republican" who would abolish slavery, welcome racial mixing, and disobey the Supreme Court, which in its 1857 *Dred Scott* decision ruled that Negroes had no inherent legal rights in the United States. Lincoln's famous declaration that "a house divided against itself cannot stand," a metaphor advisers urged him not to use, gave Douglas another opening; a house *undivided* meant Lincoln would destroy states' rights by imposing national uniformity everywhere. Lincoln's use of the Declaration of Independence ("all men are created equal") also hurt him. Racial prejudice was the trump card that Douglas used to persuade a white electorate.[15]

Any one of these accusations, if widely believed, would defeat Lincoln, and he calmly answered by conceding the legality of slavery in the Southern states, conceding the social inequality of the black race, conceding the lawfulness of the Supreme Court's ruling in *Dred Scott* (while seeking its legal reversal), and backing away from negative implications of "the house divided" metaphor. The real issues between him and Douglas, he insisted, were simpler. They entailed *the expansion* of slavery into the territories and the moral status of slavery as a reprehensible institution that had to be curtailed. All of the complexities came down to "the eternal struggle between these two principles—right and wrong." Put more colloquially, "You work and toil and earn bread, and I'll eat it" (3:315).[16]

But if Lincoln's down-to-earth, figurative wording of the normative problem in slavery contained the nub of his argument, it was the sophisticated lawyer who really bothered Douglas. The dilemma that Lincoln forced upon Douglas, after extracting a procedural understanding that they would answer each other's queries directly (3:39–42), came in a crafted legal question. "Can the people of a United States Territory, in any lawful way, against the wish of any citizen of the United States," Lincoln asked, "exclude slavery from its limits prior to the formation of a State Constitution?"(3:43)

The question was an impossible one for Douglas to answer on political *and* legal grounds. "The Little Giant" had argued that slaves were merely physical property, but if so, by what right could a public vote strip a man of his personal property?[17] When Douglas reluctantly had to answer that such a vote could free a slave in the territory, he sacrificed philosophical coherence as well as his party's future support in the Southern states, losses that would cost him the presidential election in 1860.

Fully aware of the import of Douglas's admission, Lincoln described his loss to Douglas in the senatorial election of 1858 as "a slip and not a fall."[18] The same shrewdness, the same marriage of subtlety and common touch, would characterize his presidency. Lincoln as president would handle conflict within his contentious cabinet with remarkable equanimity, outmaneuvering his political rivals there at every turn.[19] His parallel reliance on an exaggerated spirit of concession, often in colloquial terms, appears in almost every public statement. He used these devices to search for and explain common ground but even more adroitly to redefine the nature of that ground.

Lincoln's response to a challenge from the most influential media figure of the age, Horace Greeley, aptly illustrates these strategies. The Confiscation Act passed by Congress on July 17, 1862, freed the slaves of all declared rebels when under Union control, and Greeley, a leading abolitionist, used his newspaper, the *New York Tribune*, to demand that Lincoln enforce the law. On August 20, 1862, Greeley wrote "what an immense majority of the loyal millions of your countrymen require of you is a frank, declared, unqualified, ungrudging execution of the laws of the land, more especially the Confiscation Act."[20]

Greeley's letter created a media firestorm in the darkest moments of the war, but Lincoln dealt with it in a single stroke that earned "universal approval."[21] In an unprecedented move for a sitting president, he responded to Greeley's challenge with a newspaper letter of his own in Washington, D.C.'s *National Intelligencer*. This letter, printed just three days after Greeley's letter, asserts that Lincoln will save the Union "the shortest way under the Constitution," the document that he has sworn to preserve, protect, and defend. "If I could save the Union without freeing *any* slave I would do it," Lincoln writes, pointing to the constraints the Constitution places on him, "and if I could save it by freeing *all* the slaves, I would do it; and if I could save it by freeing some and leaving others alone, I would also do that" (5:388).

Despite its simplicity, this language pulls rank even as it subsumes it by juxtaposing Lincoln's "view of *official* duty" to warmer affinities with Greeley ("my oft-expressed *personal* wish that all men everywhere could be free"). As president, the "paramount object" was "to save the Union," a claim that lifts Lincoln apart and above. The tone of these words objectifies the writer as the staunch though burdened oath taker of union, an exalted or at least separating status that Lincoln frequently invoked.[22] Yet all potential offense in this aloof stance has already been removed by a genial series of epistolary concessions to one "whose heart I have always supposed to be right." Lincoln refuses to quarrel with the powerful newspaper editor about facts or combat Greeley's "impatient and dictatorial tone." The president waives them all "in deference to an old friend" (5:388–89).

The fourth prong of Lincoln's legally inflected powers of persuasion, his unique brand of religiosity, is harder to explain even though it dominates the late speeches of the wartime president. Of importance here is the independence of the sixteenth president's spiritual understanding from denominational controls and, hence, his unhampered creativity when speaking on the subject from secular platforms.

Legal training helped to give Lincoln that independence of thought. In Western culture, coming out of the secular Enlightenment, legal theorists curbed the totalizing framework of religious thought by separating church and state and promoting religious toleration. They did so by borrowing from religious thought with correspondences for legal use, which enabled translations from the voice of God to the voice of the people.[23]

A certain kind of legal mentality welcomed these translations. An ardent reader of the Bible, Lincoln never joined a Christian church, and that failure came up in election politics—most dramatically when he ran for Congress in 1846 against the circuit-riding Methodist minister and fervent evangelist Peter Cartwright. Cartwright argued that Lincoln's religious irregularity made him "an infidel" unfit for public office on religious grounds, a contention still made in political contests today but of particular moment for Lincoln campaigning in the Bible Belt of rural Illinois.

Lincoln's response is illuminating on several levels. He took the charge seriously enough to respond with a "Handbill Replying to Charges of Infidelity." He had "never denied the truth of the Scriptures" and had "never spoken with intentional disrespect of religion in general, or of any denomination of Christians in particular." He was no "open enemy of, and scoffer at, religion" but rather believed "the higher matter of eternal consequences" to be a private matter best left to individuals and their "Maker" (1:382).

The negatives quite clearly outweigh the positives in this explanation. The writer of it admits to no specific belief or practice or even a Christian faith. Given the scurrilous nature of Cartwright's attack, Lincoln's response is temperate, controlled, and, above all, distant in its own assurances and the way they are offered.

This same distance appears in a curious exchange during the White House years. When on September 13, 1862, ministers presented memorials calling for emancipation based upon a public meeting in Chicago, Lincoln responded that same day with a letter that quickly found its way into the *Chicago Tribune*. Noting that he has been approached by many religious men with opposite opinions "who are equally certain that they represent the Divine will," Lincoln observes, "I hope it will not be irreverent for me to say that if it is probable that God would reveal his will to others, on a point so connected with my duty, it might be supposed he would reveal it directly to me" (5:420).

The wry humor in this passage should not disguise that Lincoln increasingly saw himself as an instrument of divine will. His belief owed something to earlier Puritan or Calvinist traditions still prevalent in America; his God was inscrutable but wholly immanent in human history. "The will of God prevails," Lincoln wrote in a private meditation on the war just two weeks before his meeting with the Chicago ministers, and this deity operated through "human instrumentalities" as "the best adaptation to effect

His purpose." There is, however, a warmer nineteenth-century strand in Lincoln's framework beyond Calvinist rigor. His version of providence welcomes human progress. In keeping with his profession, he also looks with favor on the normative development of human law (5:403–4).

Heaven in nineteenth-century thought accepted a benevolent link to natural law, which in most treatments of the subject denied the validity of slavery. God therefore could be said to prefer freedom and equality. Lincoln reasoned "God can not be *for* and *against* the same thing at the same time." "Meditation on the Divine Will" leaves it unsaid, but how could God be *for* slavery? Corralled by Lincoln's reason, "God wills this contest, and wills that it shall not end yet." Like Zeus in Homer's *Iliad*, Lincoln's God holds the scales of good and evil balancing over the horrors of the Civil War, even though "He could have either *saved* or *destroyed* the Union without a human contest."

There is an underlying theme in "Meditation on the Divine Will." Lincoln's pledge to save the Union would ultimately require the deaths of an estimated 623,000 Americans, and each ensuing major battle was bloodier than the last. At Gettysburg, in just the first three days of July 1863, fifty thousand men out of 170,000 engaged were lost in one way or another. In the Union Army alone, one in nine died during the Civil War, a ratio that exceeds the draconian punishment inflicted on the Roman legions, where as a punishment one in every ten soldiers would be executed if a unit retreated without an order to do so.

The appalling numbers of the war dead weighed heavily on Lincoln. He openly despaired over them, and it is natural to find him sharing the burden with belief in a God who wanted the war to take place and willed that it continue amidst unprecedented carnage. The comfort Lincoln received was not unlike the advocate performing before a higher authority who has ultimate responsibility for decisions made.

Half of the presidents of the United States have been lawyers. If Abraham Lincoln presents a special case among them as a speaker, it is because he honed his professional skills in a time when oratorical delivery before a jury was the crucial ingredient of a successful practice.[24] Lincoln handled more than five thousand cases across a legal career spanning twenty-four years. He appeared before the Illinois Supreme Court more than 333 times.[25] Steeped in courtroom advocacy, he instinctively adopted similar patterns of address in the White House—a point overshadowed by his more obvious gift for language and the ability it gave him to refashion the presidential genres in which he spoke and wrote.

The list of possibilities for analysis is long. His "First Inaugural Address," with its balancing of constitutional priorities, its use of contract theory through the "fundamental law" and "universal law" of national formation, its frequent resort to "strict legal right" in federal action, its sophistication in maintaining "all constitutional rights," its precise reading of legal "affirmations and negations, guaranties, and prohibitions," its astute and accommodating lawyerly reduction of slavery to "dry legal obligation," and its calls on "the mystic chords of memory" and "the better angels of our nature" is a masterful act in its deployment of the honed elements of law into oratorical eloquence. (4:262–71). Horace Greeley called it "worthy the charge of a Chief Justice to a jury, and containing more sound law than is often found in charges twenty times its length."[26]

Consider another address. Lincoln's first message to Congress on July 4, 1861, offers one of the best legal justifications of union ever written: "that form and substance of government, whose leading object is, to elevate the condition of men—to lift artificial weights from all shoulders—to clear the paths of laudable pursuit for all—to afford all an unfettered start and a fair chance, in the race of life" (4:438). Moving on, who can resist the "Second Annual Message" of December 1, 1862, where Lincoln wrote of his generation's inability to escape its legal obligations and, hence, the coming judgment of history. "We shall nobly save, or meanly lose, the last best hope of earth" (5:537).[27]

The Emancipation Proclamation of January 1, 1863, is most literally the work of a legal mind. Lincoln worried about his official right to emancipate the slaves of the rebellious South against specific language supporting slavery in the Constitution, and his language in the Proclamation is especially legalistic in consequence. Only the Thirteenth Amendment, once rejected but finally passed by Congress, eased the earlier writer's worries. "A question might be raised whether the proclamation was legally valid," Lincoln admitted with relief on the day of hard-won passage. "But this amendment is a King's cure for all the evils" (8:254).

However rich each of these possibilities are in legal lore for analysis, they can be placed to one side. The truest defense of the speaking lawyer in President Lincoln should rest on his most memorable words, and the subject of eloquence automatically privileges two late efforts. No two speeches in

American history have been more frequently or closely interpreted than the Gettysburg Address on November 19, 1863, and the "Second Inaugural Address" on March 4, 1865. Whole books have been written about the 271 words in the first speech and the 701 words in the second.[28]

The words themselves have been so widely accepted as the most expressive the nation has produced that all efforts to explain them fall somewhere beneath them. Twenty-first century absorption in the sound bite as the unit in public speaking has made it that much harder to appreciate the studied intellectual dimensions in Lincoln's prose. Nineteenth-century speeches tended to last several hours, and we have lost sight of the established forms of anticipation in oral performance on which they depended for reception. Lincoln never forgot these forms, even in his shortest and most concise efforts.

While Lincoln packs plenty of feeling into his most condensed prose masterpieces, a calculated professional distance in his use of emotion is the fuel of eloquence in him.[29] Structure, control, and rigor are important aspects of Lincoln's style, and the oft-noted brevity of his "Address Delivered at the Dedication of the Cemetery at Gettysburg" gives perhaps the clearest view of these virtues. Lincoln always spoke slowly. Even so, it took him less than three minutes to deliver his words. Here they are in full:

> Four score and seven years ago our fathers brought forth on this continent, a new nation, conceived in Liberty, and dedicated to the proposition that all men are created equal.
>
> Now we are engaged in a great civil war, testing whether that nation, or any nation so conceived and so dedicated, can long endure. We are met on a great battlefield of that war. We have come to dedicate a portion of that field, as a final resting place for those who here gave their lives that that nation might live. It is altogether fitting and proper that we should do this.
>
> But, in a larger sense, we can not dedicate—we can not consecrate—we can not hallow—this ground. The brave men, living and dead, who struggled here, have consecrated it, far above our poor power to add or detract. The world will little note, nor long remember what we say here, but it can never forget what they did here. It is for us the living, rather, to be dedicated here to the unfinished work which they who fought here have thus far so nobly advanced. It is rather for us to be here dedicated to the great task remaining before us—that from these honored dead we take increased devotion to that

cause for which they gave the last full measure of devotion—that we here
highly resolve that these dead shall not have died in vain—that this nation,
under God, shall have a new birth of freedom—and that government of the
people, by the people, for the people, shall not perish from the earth.

(7:23)

Others have written of Lincoln's march through time sequences from
the past (in the first paragraph), to the present (in the second paragraph),
to the future (in the third),[30] but no one has noticed how closely this projection follows the natural bent of courtroom oratory, where the task is
to explain first what happened, then what it means in court, and finally
what should be done about it in the future through punishment, reward,
or rectification.[31]

In a similar analogy to legal argument, the Gettysburg Address presents a dispute that must be dealt with through right proceeding, and the
movement toward right proceeding is triggered, as in legal argument,
through the interrogative mode. The burning question raised at the outset is a close one in 1863: "Can" the nation "long endure," or will the horrors of civil war overwhelm it? To this institutional question Lincoln
adds a related one that applies directly to his audience. Will those who
fought at Gettysburg "have died in vain"? If so, if the Union is not saved,
then the responsibility for disaster becomes more intimate. The living
who have not saved the Union will have committed a crime of omission
against "these honored dead."

Lincoln obliquely recognizes an intolerable alternative in dedicating
the cemetery of the war dead: the possibility of meaningless slaughter.
He resists that prospect by tying the living to the dead through the concept
of dedication and by insisting through it that "this nation . . . shall not
perish from the earth." The rhetorical shift from *testing* whether the nation
"can long endure" to *resolving* that it "shall not perish" relies on the lawyer's
oratorical device of redefining a key term through related iterations.

The speaker's first five uses of the word "dedication" move temporally
from the original dedication of the country by the fathers of it, to the continued dedication by intervening generations, to the dedication of those
who fought at Gettysburg that the "nation might live," to the problem
of dedication in the moment, to the actual dedication at the battlefield.
Lincoln uses the continuum to create a sequent progression.

Lincoln's words move inexorably toward a sixth level of dedication to come, and the new level will be that "of the people" dedicated to "a new birth of freedom" for all Americans, not just, as it has been, for some Americans. This "increased devotion" comes through allegiance to the "honored dead" who "gave the last full measure of devotion" to this cause. The variations of the term march in pairs: from dedication to principle ("conceived and so dedicated), to dedication to the dead (the field and hallowed ground), to dedication of the unfinished work of the dead (for us, the living) in confirmation of temporal movement through the address.

These words work through Lincoln's ability to remove himself from the page while retaining the sincerity of voice and the embodiment of principle required.[32] Not coincidentally, the same tactic applies to courtroom advocacy. Every manual on the subject reminds lawyers that they are not the subject or even the object of debate, and the fact that Lincoln frequently adopted strategies of self-effacement in legal practice is a matter of record.[33] At Gettysburg, he followed suit. He kept his client, in this case the United States of America, as the focus of concern and resisted persistent efforts to extract a more personal speech during his two days in and around the battlefield.

Many aspects of Lincoln's gift for language in the address, all found in the earlier lawyer, have been described: the measured tones, the biblical phraseology, the sixty-one repetitions, the parataxis of balanced terms, the grammatical inversions, the use of antithesis, the assignation of a turning point through self-correction, the short sentences balanced against a long one, the frame of simple language (four of every five words are of one syllable) juxtaposed against technical terms like "proposition," and finally, the comprehensiveness that includes both sides in the conflict without speaking down to either.[34] Despite the colossal bloodletting at Gettysburg, there are no enemies in Lincoln's speech. His use of "they" refers to "these honored dead" without differentiation between Blue and Gray.

There is, however, a driving argument beyond commemoration in Lincoln's speech. The Gettysburg Address is a meditation about how things have gone wrong for *all* parties, leading to a closing directive that *all* must somehow answer that wrong. As in legal discourse, Lincoln's words move toward a solution and his jury this time is the nation. Pronominal forms in the first-person plural, the emblem of national cohesion, direct this solution by incorporating every available listener. Expansive uses of "we," "our," and "us" receive constant reiteration—fifteen times in the three short paragraphs offered. Lincoln grasps, as theorists would later argue, that "the crucial question relating to national identity is how the national 'we' is constructed and what is meant by that construction."[35]

The move toward inclusiveness was natural as well as good policy. Courtroom orators in the nineteenth century reached for scope across concentric audiences—from judge, to jury, to spectators, and on to the community at large. Lincoln physically speaks at Gettysburg but is really speaking beyond it. Notice, for example, that he never uses the name in the actual address. "Gettysburg," four months after the bloodiest battle of the war, stood for unprecedented butchery and continuing bitterness on November 19, 1865. Lincoln's address changes that by welcoming all Americans, North *and* South, to the possibility of "a new birth" out of the original birth in which all retained ideological stock. From the first sentence, every American is summoned through the figuratively mutual category of "our fathers," the forebears who "brought forth on this continent, a new nation" in which all now share.

Yet for all of its inclusiveness, the Gettysburg Address is not without distinguishing bite—a bite controlled by traditional structure in presentation. As innovative as the address appears, it relies on conventional notions of delivery to ease reception of a new idea. That new idea, presented in embryonic form during the Lincoln–Douglas debates, turns on the Declaration of Independence, which can no longer be said to favor slavery while simultaneously claiming that "all men are created equal." As others have explained, Lincoln at Gettysburg turns the Declaration into the fundamental document of foundation in order to correct the Constitution on slavery without overthrowing it.[36]

Lincoln himself prefigures this privileging of the Declaration in 1859 by declaring "all honor to Jefferson—to the man who, in the concrete pressure of a struggle for national independence of a single people, had the coolness, forecast, and capacity to introduce into a merely revolutionary document, an abstract truth, applicable to all men and all times, and so to embalm it there, that to-day, and in all coming days, it shall be a rebuke and a stumbling block to the very harbingers of re-appearing tyranny and oppression" (3:376). These are the words of an accomplished wordsmith, one whose use reveals his own inclination and ability to transform a central document by filtering coolness, forecast, and capacity through the power found in abstract truth. The forgotten intricacy of Lincoln's effort at Gettysburg is all about the capacity to change thought through form, arrangement, and projection toward a better future.

The forgotten refinement of the Gettysburg Address is crucial in convincing nineteenth-century Americans of an idea that they would not have entertained in cruder form. Although he was self-taught, Lincoln studied the form and use of language intensely, memorizing long sections of manuals on grammar and elocution as well as speeches of all kinds. Perhaps by instinct but just as likely through long practice, he gave his words at Gettysburg the classical arrangement of oratory followed in Lincoln's time and popularized by copy after copy of Hugh Blair's *Lectures on Rhetoric and Belles Lettres* (1784).[37]

Six standard requirements of correct rhetorical arrangement guide Lincoln's thoughts to a receptive reader. They are, in order, *exordium* (catching the audience's attention); *narration* (setting forth the facts); *division* (distinguishing points stipulated from points to be contested); *proof* (supporting the case); *refutation* (confuting opposing arguments); and *peroration* (a summation that stirs the audience). As brief as it is, the Gettysburg Address" follows this pattern in an era attuned to these rhythms in oratorical performance. Some contemporaries recognized as much by calling it "a model speech."[38]

Lincoln's *exordium*, the high-sounding opening sentence, gives us "a new nation, conceived in Liberty, and dedicated to the proposition that all men are created equal." The timing, "four score and seven years ago," reaches boldly back to establish the Declaration of Independence as the formative document rather than the Constitution as its primary guide, and in doing so, it legally demolishes the premise of secession by positing a *single* nation tied to the proposition of equality instead of a collection of separate states sharing very limited powers and understandings. Lincoln shrewdly underlines the point by setting this opening sentence off as its own paragraph. Meanwhile, patriotic phraseology—"our fathers brought forth on this continent"—diffuses protest over the deeper meaning.[39]

The *narration*, or statement of facts, is similarly brief, consuming the short second paragraph. Lincoln identifies the Civil War, the gathered meeting on a battlefield of that war, the reason for being there, the act of commemoration, and the propriety in doing so. Welded to these facts is the higher drama of another fact. The endangered Union is in a struggle for survival, "conceived" as it is "in Liberty." A good lawyer always uses the facts for more than context, and Lincoln doesn't miss the opportunity. The "altogether fitting and proper" act of commemoration confirms the decorum of the occasion and echoes legal and constitutional import by deciding what can and cannot be done, all while insisting that the struggle continue so "that nation might live."[40]

Division follows immediately in the opening of the long third paragraph. Despite what has been just said, the gathering *cannot* dedicate, consecrate, or hallow ground already more profoundly sanctified by "the brave men, living and dead" who furthered the struggle for their country. The ceremonial gathering becomes a redundancy at this moment in Lincoln's argument, and the *division* becomes serious when he adds "the world will little note, nor long remember what we say here."

Proof, riding quickly to the rescue, answers this potential frustration by indicating the living *do* have vital tasks to perform both here and elsewhere. On the present battlefield, the living must "highly resolve" that "these dead shall not have died in vain." Once resolved, they must prove their resolution on other battlefields in dedication to "the unfinished work" and "the great task remaining before us." Only the living can *prove* the validity of the founding fathers' original "proposition," here referring to Euclid's technical requirement of something in need of proof.[41] The living have not only a duty but an opportunity when they guarantee that their nation, "so conceived and so dedicated," will endure.

Tied to these several assignments, in a subtle linguistic stroke, Lincoln allows a faint aura of *refutation* to hover over his last two sentences; the device works through reiteration of the single word "rather." "It is for us the living, *rather*, to be dedicated here to the unfinished work," and in a slight inversion, "it is *rather* for us to be here dedicated to the great task remaining before us." The setting off of the first use with commas is quietly smoothed away in the second, which leads into the final long sentence of Lincoln's *peroration*, "that government of the people, by the people, for the people, shall not perish from the earth."

These last words are so moving because they give final assurance against the naked fear expressed earlier that the nation might not "long endure." The *narration* in the second paragraph of the Gettysburg Address could only recount the danger in the dark days of 1863. Lincoln's *peroration* responds by reaching beyond time and overcoming all fear in the rolling reiteration of a *continuing* people's government.

Like all truly crafted narrative, the Gettysburg Address does more than resolve. It circles back on itself in its quest for thematic extension. It confirms, but it also ends on a new plane, a higher level of equilibrium, one that mirrors the way a closing argument in court would end with the decision required.[42] At the outset of the war, Lincoln told Congress, "This is essentially a People's contest" (4:438). Now, in new and more confident phrasing, without the qualifying adverb "essentially," he delivers not just his answer but the government itself into the hands of a people who have sacrificed for it and who, as a reward for their continuing sacrifice, will receive "a new birth of freedom."

Lincoln's "Second Inaugural Address" has less to do with a people's freedom in its concentration on communal sin and the need for penance. "The address sounded more like a sermon than a state paper," Frederick Douglass observed in the audience on March 4, 1865, and there is evidence to support the claim.[43] Only one other president in the eighteen inaugural addresses delivered before Lincoln's addresses had taken words directly from the Bible and even then the speaker, John Quincy Adams, used a single neutral passage.[44] Lincoln, breaking the mold once again as a speaking president, quotes or paraphrases from four separate passages after naming the Bible directly. He invokes prayer three times and God fourteen times in the second shortest inaugural by an American president.[45]

The admittedly profound religious orientation takes attention away from the lawyer who is speaking. Lincoln's "Second Inaugural" is a canny political document arranged against a legal crisis of unknown dimensions. It is the work of a man reaching for an acceptable concept of judgment. Where is the justice in six hundred thousand war dead and the related misery of millions more? Lincoln, burdened by his own role in producing those mountains of misery, needs a legal answer beyond himself, and he accomplishes this by translating his pain into civic terms. He needs a commensurate theory of punishment and finds it in a sanitized version of the *lex talionis*, "eye for eye, tooth for tooth, hand for hand, foot for foot."[46]

As before, a proper understanding of Lincoln's speech requires that we concentrate on the structure that Lincoln gave it in four tonally different paragraphs of unequal length. It is so much easier to understand what is at stake by "seeing" the words as Lincoln would have in writing them out.

The complete "Second Inaugural Address," too often quoted only in part, reads as follows:

At this second appearing to take the oath of the presidential office, there is less occasion for an extended address than there was at the first. Then a statement, somewhat in detail, of a course to be pursued, seemed fitting and proper. Now, at the expiration of four years, during which public declarations have been constantly called forth on every point and phase of the great contest which still absorbs the attention, and engrosses the energies of the nation, little that is new could be presented. The progress of our arms, upon which all else chiefly depends, is as well known to the public as to myself, and it is, I trust, reasonably satisfactory and encouraging to all. With high hope for the future, no prediction in regard to it is ventured.

On the occasion corresponding to this four years ago, all thoughts were anxiously directed to an impending civil-war. All dreaded it—all sought to avert it. While the inaugural address was being delivered from this place, devoted altogether to *saving* the Union without war, insurgent agents were in the city seeking to *destroy* it without war—seeking to dissolve the Union, and divide effects, by negotiation. Both parties deprecated war; but one would *make* war rather than let the nation survive; and the other would *accept* war rather than let it perish. And the war came.

One-eighth of the whole population were colored slaves, not distributed generally over the Union, but localized in the Southern part of it. These slaves constituted a peculiar and powerful interest. All knew that this interest was, somehow, the cause of the war. To strengthen, perpetuate, and extend this interest was the object of which the insurgents would rend the Union, even by war; while the government claimed no right to do more than to restrict the territorial enlargement of it. Neither party expected for the war, the magnitude, or the duration, which it has already attained. Neither anticipated that the *cause* of the conflict might cease with, or even before, the conflict itself should cease. Each looked for an easier triumph, and a result less fundamental and astounding. Both read the same Bible, and pray to the same God; and each invokes His aid against the other. It may seem strange that any men should dare to ask a just God's assistance in wringing their bread from the sweat of other men's faces; but let us judge not that we be not judged. The prayers of both could not be answered; that of neither has been answered fully. The Almighty has His own purposes. "Woe unto the world because of offences! For it must needs be that offences come; but woe to that man by whom the offence cometh!" If we shall suppose that American Slavery is one of those offences which, in the providence of God, must needs come, but which, having continued through His appointed time, He now wills to remove, and that He gives to both North and South, this terrible war, as the woe due to those by whom the offence came, shall we discern therein any departure from those divine attributes, which the believers in a Living God always ascribe to Him? Fondly do we hope—fervently do we pray—that this mighty scourge of war may speedily pass away. Yet, if God wills that it continue, until all the wealth piled by the bond-man's two hundred and fifty years of unrequited toil shall be sunk, and until every drop of blood drawn with the lash, shall be paid by another drawn with the sword, as was said three thousand years ago, so still it must be said "the judgments of the Lord, are true and righteous altogether."

With malice toward none; with charity for all; with firmness in the right, as God gives us to see the right; let us strive on to finish the work we are in; to bind up the nation's wounds; to care for him who shall have borne the battle, and for his widow, and his orphan—to do all which may achieve and cherish a just, and a lasting peace, among ourselves, and with all nations.

(8:332–33)

The seemingly perfunctory opening paragraph and the clumsy structure, with its immensely long third paragraph, are what a reader first notices when looking at the entire "Second Inaugural" instead of hearing parts of it. Remarkably, the whole first paragraph dwells on what the speaker will *not* talk about ("little that is new could be presented"). Typically, Lincoln removes himself as a persona from the scene ("there is less occasion for an extended address than there was at the first") and, once again, the legal language of procedural notification, "fitting and proper," supplies the hook of arrangement.

The thing not to be dwelt upon because previous "public declarations have been constantly called forth on every point and phase" is euphemistically rendered as "the great contest." Lincoln can afford to talk in these abstract terms because, despite the fact that "no prediction in regard to it is ventured," the conflict itself moves toward a successful conclusion. He signals that direction when he says "the progress of our arms" has been "reasonably satisfactory and encouraging to all." Although never announced, this success is the problem the renewed president now faces. One of Lincoln's greatest talents is knowing what *not* to talk about. Once again, he follows his own earlier legal advice: "it is good policy to never plead what you need not, lest you oblige yourself to prove what you cannot."[47]

Still in indirect terms about the real problem, the second paragraph returns to the physical conflict, but now the voice is dramatic in comparison to the cooler opening. Lincoln's abstract "contest" metastasizes into an animated, driving, brutal force beyond human reckoning. The negative word withheld in the first paragraph is "war," yet it comes wildly alive here in a litany of seven repetitions within five short sentences.

What "all dreaded" and all continued to misunderstand has arrived. Enfolding dread in a monosyllabic closure of just four words, Lincoln ends this paragraph with the words "And the war came." No one wanted war, but still it came in all of its horror. Fear and ruin dominate the paragraph: "anxiously," "impending," "dreaded," "avert," "insurgent," "*destroy*," "dissolve," "divide," "deprecated," "survive," and "perish."

Nor did anyone anticipate "the magnitude, or the duration" of war once it came. In delusion, all Americans on every side expected "an easier triumph, and a result less fundamental and astounding." With universal misapprehension in play, the beginning of the long third paragraph takes up the failure of all to understand what war would do to them. This section expounds on the degeneration of everything and everyone in the face of war. Earlier, on October 5, 1863, Lincoln had written out his own view on the subject in a monody of disgust that is worth paying attention to in this context:

> At once sincerity is questioned, and motives are assailed. Actual war coming, blood grows hot, and blood is spilled. Thought is forced from old channels into confusion. Deception breeds and thrives. Confidence dies, and universal suspicion reigns. Each man feels an impulse to kill his neighbor, lest he be first killed by him. Revenge and retaliation follow. But this is not all. Every foul bird comes abroad, and every dirty reptile rises up. These add crime to confusion. Strong measures, deemed indispensable but harsh at best, such men make worse by mal-administration.
>
> (6:500)

The real objective of Lincoln's "Second Inaugural," still offered indirectly, lies in answer to these ills. His words strive to prevent the insincerity, the malice, the confusion, the deception, the delusions, the revenge, the retaliation, the harshness, the crimes, and the maladministration of "this mighty scourge of war" from overflowing and polluting the peace that must follow. Lincoln's unstated problem as the first second-term president since Andrew Jackson is not the war, but the peace. It is a misnomer to think he speaks to pacify the South; he speaks to make the North relinquish the emotions and distortions of war once it becomes possible to restore the South to full membership in the Union.

Congress had tried to wrest control of the war effort from Lincoln on several occasions, and in further anger in 1865 it wanted "to take the process of reconstruction out of the president's hands."[48]Lincoln's assassination would give his political enemies the means to maintain a warlike mentality against the vanquished. Even so, even if the words of the fallen president would come to mean nothing in the rages of Reconstruction, the words themselves were as cunning as anything Lincoln ever delivered, and his calculated touch contributes to their higher eloquence instead of detracting from it.

To see as much, we must first understand that slavery was always the second issue for Lincoln despite its prominence in the "Second Inaugural." The unified, constitutionally-protected destiny of the Union was always his first priority. Early in the third paragraph, Lincoln makes all sides acknowledge that slavery "was, somehow, the cause of the war," but with emancipation accomplished he can reasonably add "Neither [side] anticipated the *cause* of the conflict might cease with, or even before, the conflict itself should cease." Hence, with slavery at an end, there is no need for the moral self-righteousness of further division, an aspect of delusion that is the very child of war.

Lincoln steadies this argument with two countervailing paraphrases from the Bible. Drawing on Genesis 3:19, he wonders how Southerners "should dare to ask a just God's assistance in wringing their bread from the sweat of other men's faces," but he immediately counters with "let us judge not that we not be judged" from Matthew 7:1. The juxtaposition of biblical passages works to strip all sides of their pretensions to knowledge over the course of war that all have stumbled into.

There are two tactical moves at work in this strategy, one epistemological and legal and the other theological. In the first, Lincoln diminishes the anger-inducing, normative distance between North and South by forcing a recognition that opposing sides, whether on the battlefield or in a courtroom, will each believe in a right answer through separate understandings of justice. This insistence parallels Kant's influential notion of how legal positivism must work, but Lincoln came to the same conclusion by arguing legal cases where each side passionately held a different truth. If both sides can claim to be right, then accommodation requires thinking together about the problem in the mediating way a court of law proceeds.[49]

In the second and more obvious theological move, Lincoln uses scripture to prepare the nation for a daring transition. He holds to what was still a bible culture in 1865. For if humanity has been groping in the dark, Lincoln says "the Almighty has His own purposes," which are distinct and inscrutable but part of an overarching design. Once recognized, God's purposes dictate that meaningful anger must pass from human agency to Him. God therefore exists as the appropriate punisher of transgressions in which all have shared. "Woe unto the world because of offences!" says God. Lincoln finds these words in Matthew 18:7, but he translates them into civic terms with another favorite literary text as a rhetorical backdrop.

God enters as a mediating higher judge into the destiny of the Union in order to answer and punish communal "offences" that have distorted the body politic and society. The humbling assertion is a daring stroke in the face of Union audiences already flushed with the prospect of victory, and Lincoln may have been led to it by another source on "offences." Shakespeare's similarly disjointed society in *Hamlet, Prince of Denmark* contains a passage that Lincoln had memorized. In act 3 of the play, King Claudius falls to his knees in recognition of the hollow success he has won. His place on the throne has only come through the brother he has murdered.

Victory, in other words, is not everything. Claudius, too, speaks of an "offence" that "smells to heaven." "To confront the visage of offence" is to realize that "Offence's gilded hand" cannot escape divine justice, whatever it might seem to accomplish "in the corrupted currents of this world." The thrust, if not the result, of Claudius's speech, parallels the "Second Inaugural": God must punish, and it is right that He do so.[50]

With God in place, the longest sentence in the "Second Inaugural" follows. Its seventy-eight words fill over 10 percent of the whole document, and they form a question that lawyers frequently use in argument: *hypophora*, or asking the question in a way that allows you to answer as you desire.[51] Lincoln uses this mode to reduce the national problem to manageable terms. To paraphrase, what American citizen can possibly question the divine attributes ascribed to the living God for using the Civil War to punish the nation for the offence of slavery? In answer, "as was said three thousand years ago, so still it must be said 'the judgments of the Lord are true and righteous altogether.'"

The inner quotation in this fourth and last biblical reference comes from the ninth verse of Psalm 19, and the phrases just before it carry a dual message: "the commandment of the Lord *is* pure, enlightening the eyes" and "fear of the Lord is clean." Only God's way can purify and enlighten the republic. Only fear of Him can make us clean again, and the significant element in this cleansing design is God's presumed exactitude in punishment.

Lincoln offers the plausibility that "every drop of blood drawn with the lash, shall be paid by another drawn with the sword." And if so, nothing will be left over. No added punishment by former combatants becomes necessary. So compelling is this distancing anger for absorbing the unclean blood of the Civil War that Lincoln proposes to his cabinet that an amendment be prepared to insert God into the Constitution.[52]

The "Second Inaugural" does not end here. It continues in Lincoln's peroration, the last and shortest paragraph of his speech, and it gives the normative words most memorably associated with his name: "With malice toward none; with charity for all; with firmness in the right, as God gives us to see the right." The point to remember, however, is the structure that gives these final words their extraordinary power. Lincoln has siphoned off the anger, confusion, and hatred of war by giving it all to God, allowing a return to humanity and a new path for combatants away from their warlike traits.

Although the normative weight in this strategy of reconciliation is remarkable on its own, it has its mundane equivalent in the earlier lawyer. Lincoln "settled" wherever he could. "Discourage litigation," he advised. "Persuade your neighbors to compromise whenever you can. Point out to them how the nominal winner is often a real loser. . . . As a peacemaker the lawyer has a superior opportunity of being a good man" (2:81). The rhetorical strategy of *ethos*, establishing sincerity and credibility in performance as the "good man," was important to the lawyer known as "Honest Abe."[53] The same "good man," as president, secures his sincerity in the last words of this speech as clever as they are moving.

A thousand questions were on the table in March 1865. How were the Southern states to be reincorporated? What was to be done with the leaders of the Confederacy when captured? How far down the hierarchy of command would treason apply? Who or what kind of government would rule in Southern state capitals? Lincoln wrote that "one-eighth of the whole population were colored slaves." How was this huge, utterly impoverished, totally uneducated group to be cared for and habilitated as free citizens? Lincoln ignored all of these puzzles even though they were on the tip of every American's tongue.

Instead the speaker devotes his last words to a framework of visible caring through the concept of charity. The traditional language of care for the downtrodden is so abstracted and familiar that the personal becomes general. Lincoln carefully offers only the solutions that were immediately possible and uncontroversial. Who could disagree with the need to "bind up the nation's wounds," or to care for the figures in that metaphor, the wounded or dying veteran, "his widow, and his orphan"? To a nation crying for it, Lincoln offered "a just and lasting peace." The mixture of abstract premise, synecdoche, and example works for Lincoln's time and every other, and Lincoln knew it.

The speaker commented on his performance to the seasoned New York politician and journalist Thurlow Weed, and he assumed Weed would convey to others "a truth which I thought needed to be told." "I expect [the Inaugural Address] to wear as well as—perhaps better than—anything I have produced," Lincoln wrote, revealing the rhetorical shelter that calling upon God had given him. "Men are not flattered by being shown that there is a difference of purpose between the Almighty and them," he explained. "To deny it, however, in this case, is to deny that there is a God governing the world" (8:356). The roles of accomplished orator, spiritual leader, shrewd politician, and conjurer of juries are hived as one in the "Second Inaugural Address," and every role appears in these short sentences of explanation.

Abraham Lincoln is so useful in approaches to the subject of eloquence not just because he is good at it. His innovative interest in concision from the platform alongside reliance on established oratorical strategies is strikingly unusual in the nineteenth century. He seems, in consequence, almost as modern as he is traditional. His prose allows us to read him now as he desired to be read then.

Even if we concentrate on individual passages in Lincoln's oeuvre today, the forms of his performances—far more calculated than he is generally given credit for—lift his efforts above those of other speakers. "With malice toward none" is not memorable in the absence of the argument that goes before it. Lincoln's famous triptych—"government of the people, by the people, for the people"—would simply paraphrase Daniel Webster's "Second Reply to Hayne" if we haven't first digested the redefinition of the people that precedes it in the body of the Gettysburg Address.

Form, in this sense, bespeaks completion, an essential feature of successful public reason. "The significance of completeness," writes the philosopher John Rawls on this subject, "lies in the fact that unless a political conception is complete, it is not an adequate framework of thought in the light of which the discussion of fundamental political questions can be carried out."[54] Eloquence depends on unfolding form to convey thought. It supplies the means by which an audience is prepared to receive a conception or argument through a realized frame of reference and familiar structure.

Lincoln understands that you can only change people's thinking through the forms available to them. True eloquence is rare because real thought, a requirement in eloquence, is equally rare at all times in all ages. New ideas never receive a quick hearing. Most people fear original thought and even regret a different version of familiar thought. The true orator must couch thought in an identifiable form that will lift an audience out of its comfort zone of conventional perception while directing it in a fresh way. Lincoln, who repeatedly broke new ground as a speaking president, had this ability. He knew how to organize an audience's perceptions. He understood how to be heard anew.

All of Lincoln's best efforts solved this formidable difficulty by making audiences part of the solution to a clearly identified circumstance and the problem it presented. One additional effort, his now largely forgotten "Second Annual Message to Congress," on December 1, 1862, provides a final, illuminating example of this craft at work. Most have forgotten its importance. Here the sitting president managed to turn the mundane genre of the Annual Message (now referred to as the State of the Union Address) into an art form. The "Second Annual Message" is, in the words of one scholar, "a paradigm of rhetorical leadership."[55]

In the last month of 1862, the war is going badly and negative results in the elections a month earlier have led many to declare a "want of confidence" in presidential leadership.[56] Lincoln begins by listing the gathering ills around him. How many leaders would do this? The nation is "unhappily distracted," the economy has "radically changed," the social condition is "disturbed," international relations are "less than gratifying," financial "fluctuations" need "diligent consideration," and Indian "hostilities" plague the West. Infecting all are "the folly and evils of disunion" and "the fiery trial through which we pass" (5:518–31). None of this is good for the man in the White House.

Nonetheless, the writer faces these issues directly, giving an objective description of each. This tactic—along with the calmest of tones in delivering so many manifest ills—proves sincerity and determination in the writer. So positioned, the embattled president turns to two larger claims, one positive and the other negative, to cast a rhetorical net over the country's problems. For the first, the writer employs *pathos*, or emotional assertion; for the second and more threatening, he turns to *logos*, or reason; both are then subsumed in *ethos*, the integrity of the presenter with purposes in mind.

The positive, more emotional element is the country itself, the lay of the land fully and movingly described. Lincoln offers his belief in a unified territory to insist that geographically "the national homestead" cannot be split asunder; it is "the home of one national family." "Physically speaking, we cannot separate. We cannot remove our respective sections from each other, nor build an impassable wall between them. . . . There is no line, straight or crooked, suitable for national boundary, upon which to divide."

The great negative element is, of course, slavery, and it dominates the rest of Lincoln's message to Congress. It also rather cleverly provides the emotional center of every other national difficulty. Therefore, it must be dealt with through reason rather than emotion. "Our national strife springs not from our permanent part; not from the land we inhabit," Lincoln declares, reaching back to his holistic vision of country. Instead, it comes from the human aberration of slavery. "Our strife," he concludes, "pertains to ourselves—to the passing generations of men; and it can, without convulsion, be hushed forever with the passing of one generation." The generations connect the negative of slavery to the positive of the land; rhetorically, this reaches back to a quotation from Ecclesiastes that Lincoln uses to introduce his geographical encomium to country: "the earth abideth forever."[57]

Three carefully reasoned, proposed amendments to end slavery follow immediately after the assertion that "our strife pertains to ourselves." The rest of the "Second Annual Message" wrestles with the "great diversity, of sentiment, and of policy, with regard to slavery" through an analysis of each amendment. All of the alternatives from perpetuation of slavery as "a dry legal obligation" to colonization, "compensated emancipation" for some, or full emancipation for all are given in this section.

Lincoln's emphasis is on collectively solving the problem that can solve all other problems. "Because of these diversities, we waste much strength to struggles among ourselves," he reasons, and his ready answer becomes obvious. "By mutual concessions we should harmonize, and act together." What if they cannot? Lincoln presents an implied threat that comes again in his peroration: "In times like the present, men should utter nothing for which they would not willingly be responsible through time and in eternity."

The whole problem comes down to a question of human temperament in response to a specific dilemma that challenges nature itself in two ways: slavery, the owning of a human being as property, and rebellion, the result of slavery in dividing the American land. Both are equally unnatural acts in Lincoln's account.

The turn toward a new kind of rationality is then triggered by a question, which again Lincoln answers to his own advantage in legal fashion: "It is not 'Can *any* of us *imagine* better?' but 'Can we *all* do better?'" Imagination is no longer a singular quality for "any of us"; it becomes a collective necessity that must pull *all* together in the knowledge that "the dogmas of the quiet past, are inadequate to the stormy present."

Novelty in temperament and thought are the requirements of the hour to solve the problem of slavery, and Lincoln does not disappoint. "As our case is new so we must think anew," he declares. "We must disenthrall ourselves, and then we shall save our country" (5:537). The sound bite of its day—"We must disenthrall ourselves"—controls through Lincoln's frank narrative about the issues to be overcome.

Lincoln has been narrating a story. The citizenry of the United States has grown askew and confused by controversy and the turmoil of war. Americans have given up what they rightfully possess—a bountiful land— through contention over a significant but limited distinction in the body politic. They have been wrongly enthralled, "held spellbound" by acrimony over slavery and the violent course of events flowing there from. The counter offered by Lincoln has the virtue of simplicity in difficulty. Equanimity comes with his call for a more proper spirit of reflection and the strange word "disenthrall" conveys that need.

The root word *thrall*, or *thral*, signifies "slave" or "slavery." "To enthrall" has two meanings: "to spellbind" but also "to enslave" or "bring into bondage." Lincoln's reliance on "disenthrall" ("to set free from enthrallment or bondage, to liberate from bondage") introduces a double meaning of powerful import.[58] The writer of the "Second Annual Message" has joined the vexed issue of freeing slaves to a general call for citizens to free *themselves* from bondage to the convention-ridden and now discarded past.

Although the controversy over emancipation may be great, it melts into the broader communal need for a better collective understanding. Whatever happens, the people must adjust to the alarms and disruption of war that are making them so uncomfortable. They must stop and think instead of simply reacting. Lincoln uses the word "disenthrall" to orchestrate the necessary pause. Drawn to the pivotal word by its peculiarity, we are held by its strange meanings. "Disenthrall" reinforces the writer's decision, answers troubled times, and raises the level of recognition in the moment of reception.

This is eloquence.

8

Memorialization and the Spirit of Law

ONLY LAW STANDS BETWEEN CIVILIZATION and the natural cruelty in human behavior when left to itself. So when law fails, the event in question has a long half-life in cultural memory. When law fails egregiously, civilization collapses into something too awful for any recovery to remember as clearly as it should. Knowing that, a community cannot allow itself to forget what it has done, even though in its shame it does not really want to remember the details. One recourse, a predictably ambiguous one, comes through visual memorialization, a token gesture to be sure, but a realization nonetheless that "Hell is—other people."[1]

To capture communal trauma in artistic form is never easy and the iconography will be incomplete. Its creators rarely tolerate the full ambiguity of complicity in what took place. Aesthetically, no one ever wants to visualize awfulness accurately. Memorials try to be beautiful, or at least tasteful, and this raises an issue in proportionality. The architect or painter—and also likely a committee that controls both with its own wishes and money—must portray an absence, the inability of law to prevent the event that must be remembered.

There are other problems. The memory of failure, with the shame that a community feels from it, resists the visualization of blame. Why did law fail? "The spirit of the laws"—an enlightened acceptance of law beyond enforcement—disappears in the trauma of such events, and it does not appear well in memorialization.[2] How do you depict the death of spirit? The memorialist who recognizes the loss has a predicament. Can you represent the ephemeral concept of communal will, much less the loss of it, in the size, shape, and form required? The invocation of sadness is a frequent remedy, but is it sufficient?

Scenes of memorialization can be large or small, intricate or simple. Even so, all share the same difficulty in trying to capture the contingencies that have made the situation to be addressed so permanently disappointing. The allure in a memorial depends on this level of disappointment being realized but perhaps not to its full extent by the viewers who decide to attend. As members of the human race, we are fascinated in horror when we realize what we are capable of doing to each other. That horror grows if law—the protection we often regret when it confines us—stands aside, vanishes, or, so much more painfully, aids the worst in us.[3]

Fascination is indeed the response of a visitor to one of these shrines; there are, of course, no permanent residents, only caretakers. Along with shame, voyeurism, concern, awe, anger, regret, and condemnation all vie with commemoration. Some places are tourist attractions, a slightly off-putting aspect depending on the cause. Survivors and the progeny of survivors are also there. The exact posture, demeanor, or decorum called for on these occasions no one knows quite how to solve. Some memorials are famous and even sources of communal cohesion; others are way stations stumbled upon.

Examples abound and with a great variety of concern and purpose. Take an odd one. The *State of Tennessee v. John Thomas Scopes*, the controversial monkey trial of 1925 testing theories of evolution, was one of the great failures in law as well as a comedy of errors at the time. The trial put science and religion on a collision course in the history of ideas of the United States; it rewarded anti-intellectualism in its judgment, it limited educational possibilities for many generations, and it left the city of Nashville embarrassed by the world's accusations of backwardness.

Why would one want to remember this event accurately? A large and brilliant mural, *The Scopes Trial*, proudly graces the lobby of the Vanderbilt University Law School today, where it is one of the city's great attractions. The painting is a commemoration and has its own appeal, but does it attract so many viewers because over 40 percent of Americans still question the theory of evolution?[4] Is it there to encourage law students to realize that the wrong side won that case or to direct future cases as a cautionary tale in law? After all, the United States still contests the issue of evolution in courtrooms across the country.

In comparable fashion, two paintings of John Brown, the harbinger of the greatest cataclysm in American history, are popular attractions in the Metropolitan Museum of Art in New York City.[5] *The Last Moments of John Brown* (1884), by Thomas Hovenden, depicts the famous abolitionist on the way to his execution with the rope already around his neck. It presents Brown as a benign martyr still dispensing love to the African Americans that he sought to free. An alternative vision, John Stuart Curry's *John Brown* (1939) gives us "Mad John Brown," a maniacally staring, wild-haired, gesticulating, furious figure presented in front of an approaching tornado. It takes two paintings to convey the ambiguity of Brown's historical meaning, and both draw crowds who surely experience different reactions in front of each portrayal.[6]

We reach for definition and measure through the calamities that befall us, and the reach is somehow different when law, without the spirit, authorizes disaster. Most people agree on the absolute worst overall failure of law in modern times. The Holocaust, with the active complicity of legal decision making in country after country, led to the extermination of over six million Jews in Europe during World War II.[7]

Virtually every country in the war shares some responsibility for genocide in this case, including the United States, which turned a blind eye to "The Final Solution" and used immigration law to keep away fleeing Jewish people seeking asylum on its shores. Each country, in expiation, has then answered for itself by building some kind of commemoration as a reminder of what was done.

In recognition of those needs and just behind the majestic spires of the Notre Dame Cathedral reaching high into the sky in Paris, there is a small but countering concave structure. The Mémorial des Martyrs de la Déportation sinks into the ground at the very eastern tip of the Ile de la Cité, the island in the middle of the Seine. The claustrophobic bunker of narrow halls and underground prison cells that make up the Mémorial des Martyrs creates a modern catacomb, though one without actual bodies. It is a symbolic burial ground for the two hundred thousand Jews *legally* deported from Vichy France to the Nazi concentration camps in Germany and Eastern Europe.

As you descend into the memorial you find cut into the rough stone of the floor of this chamber a circular plaque with a moving inscription. It obliquely indicates how easily humanity can lose itself against itself.

The words read: "They descended into the mouth of the earth and they did not return." Blame is masked, but not altogether. As you leave the memorial you encounter another inscription, one that is more hopeful. It calls on the need for two states of mind. It asks you to "Forgive but Never Forget." Both hopes are clearly important, but how do they register against a rising tide of anti-Semitism in twenty-first century Europe?

Serious injustice of this kind is painfully local yet reaches for universal significance, one way to handle blame. An effective memorial about injustice strives to project both dimensions, local and universal, through a warning. Whatever you think about the possibility of progress in history, the warning says "beware: this can happen anywhere and at any time." When the spirit of law dissolves and law becomes whatever the strong dictate, injustice rises quickly and few there are who want to recognize its sudden presence. Only law, kept and protected, stands in the way of the hatred that humanity reserves for the parts of itself that it differs with.

A local and altogether small memorial, closer to a way station than a famous site, can stand for the complexity, the meaning, and the appeal of all such sites. Its passive singularity adds to its poignancy. Not many people bother to stop for it. It is easily overlooked although never forgotten by some.

In New York City at the southern end of a promenade in Riverside Park, just below Eighty-Third Street overlooking the Hudson River, there is a circular space enclosed by a wrought iron fence fourteen feet in diameter. Just inside the curved edge of the fence, in a semicircle facing north, are a series of planted rhododendrons, which are calculated to flower in April and wither in May. Everything in and around this structure is circular except for a single slab of square white granite placed in the center of the stone floor of the enclosure with words carved in bas-relief.

The objects noted form the Warsaw Ghetto Memorial Plaza, dedicated on October 19, 1947. The inscription on the granite slab reads as follows:

This is the site for the American memorial to the heroes of the Warsaw Ghetto battle, April–May 1943, and to the six million Jews of Europe martyred in the cause of human liberty.

These words are assertions, but they simultaneously bespeak historical uncertainties among the horrified survivors of 1947 who arranged for the memorial. Would there be a more extensive memorial on this site in the future? There would not be one, though one was planned as the words "this is the site for" indicate. Funds were lacking and so, markedly, was the general will of the surrounding populace and officialdom.

A deeper and more painful uncertainty is also carved in the words of the bas-relief. Must the fighting dead be distinguished from the merely dead with that second longer prepositional phrase and its implied separation? "*And to* the six million Jews martyred"? Why not the simpler, more welcoming, encompassing phrase "*and* the six million Jews martyred"? Why not one unified recognition instead of two since they are so intimately connected?

Some were in a position to fight; most were not. What would you personally have at hand if an armed force invaded your home today? Much larger questions are relevant here. If you didn't fight, were you less worthy? How hard must one fight for one's rights to be found legally sound? Only later would the world learn of heroic sacrifices among those six million slain and of the terrible price that those who did resist had to pay.[8]

The flowering rhododendrons in April of the Memorial Plaza are carefully chosen. They celebrate the resistance of those people who fought to the end against heavily armed Nazi SS storm troopers; they wither in May just as those who fought were slaughtered in that month while the world watched. Altogether four hundred thousand people perished after quarantine in the Warsaw Ghetto, whether through illness from confinement in such tight quarters, through deportation to concentration camps, through direct murderous attack, or through torture.

The memorial has two opposing meanings: the celebration of the human spirit and the recognition of what humanity is capable of inflicting upon itself. A separate sign on a wooden post near the memorial explains the acts of shining courage that we would all like to be capable of mounting when challenging hopeless odds. Peculiarly, though, on at least one occasion and maybe more, the same sign has exhibited the darker second meaning as well: gratuitous cruelty beyond reason or explanation.

Again in April, in an act as timely as the flowering rhododendrons, the sign was severely mutilated in 2008 with dark purple gobs of slathered graffiti. Nothing else in the plaza was damaged on this occasion; it was the meaning of the plaza that the defacer meant so explicitly to attack—one more proof, if proof be needed, that humanity is *always* capable of destroying itself, *always* capable of unhinging hatred of others, *always* willing to show malice without the slightest pang of guilt.

Standing in the way of these negative propensities are the laws of the land that assign guilt. Anti-Graffiti legislation—in the form of the New York City Administrative Code, Title 10 (Public Safety), §10–117 to §10–117.2 and New York State Penal Law §145 and §145.05—make such acts of defacement illegal as criminal mischief in the third degree. Anyone who sprays paint on a public sign can expect to be punished and will be punished if properly identified, charged, and convicted.

For legal mechanisms to work, there must be communal objection when pain is inflicted unjustly on others, and the largest shame of the Holocaust lies here. All of Europe was directly and legally complicit in the deportation and massacre of Jews.[9] Country after country allowed the Third Reich to distort the meaning of law until it became unrecognizable. "Justice as fairness" disappeared. In its place arose the most pernicious quality in all of human nature, the superiority complex endemic to social life. Everyone likes to have someone to look down upon, whether through race, status, ability, class, ancestry, association, ownership, vocation, intelligence, or fortune.[10]

Not by accident, properties of social distinction are the ones that philosopher John Rawls eliminates to create justice in his "original position" for its most fashionable legal form—"the veil of ignorance," a formulation that encourages the claims of liberty and equality for all through reciprocity. Unfortunately or fortunately, depending on your perspective, the Rawlsian construct depends on a rational world. The philosopher signals that himself by quoting Hegel: "When we look at the world rationally, the world looks rationally back."[11]

All of law, at least in a republic of laws, tries to insist on this point. The reason of law cannot explain the hatreds alive in humanity; all it can do is control them through the force of its will wrapped in what must be benevolent power. That benevolence also depends on the support of a surrounding community willing to ascertain what is just and to complain when it finds injustice in its midst.

Exactly how this exercise in control is to be managed afresh remains a vital question in the twenty-first century. A particularly eloquent writer on the superiority complex, James Baldwin, offers one of the sharpest views of the problem. "That men," he writes, "have an enormous need to debase other men—and only because they are *men*—is a truth which history forbids us to labor." This insight allows another. Baldwin approaches the legal predicament when he adds, "If one really wishes to know how justice is administered in a country, one does not question the policemen, the lawyers, the judges, or the protected members of the middle class. One goes to the unprotected—those, precisely, who need the law's protection most!"[12]

The Jews of Europe were left unprotected and then made absolutely vulnerable. This was done very publicly through law and whole peoples did nothing to stop it. Many, in fact, encouraged the suddenly inflicted nonlegal status of Jewish people out of prejudice or self-interest. Very few helped those so thoroughly disenfranchised. The Jews of Europe became a people without legal standing or recourse. They were legally dead long before they perished, but they perished all the easier because they were publicly known to be legally dead.

It all seems so predictable today. What if law and the legally minded had agreed to stand in the way in the 1930s instead of yielding to Nazi propaganda? When exactly does passive injustice become active injustice? How much really bad law will make the system illegal in the minds of a people? The inability to draw easy lines of distinction in answer to these questions underlines the primal purpose in memorials already identified: this kind of awfulness can happen anywhere at any time, and no one is above it.

It follows that an even higher purpose of memorialization has to be an awareness of *where* it might happen again and *why*. Where today are people unprotected by law and therefore absolutely vulnerable? The ultimate goal in all of the marble, concrete, copper, bronze, inscriptions, and paint on canvas in memorialization has to be prevention. These structures and images occupy public space in order to prevent future memorials to future terrible events from being necessary.

Unfortunately, one does not have to look far to inform such a search. Unprotected and vulnerable! To be unprotected and vulnerable in an electronically connected global world is as frightening as it has ever been, but the ability to compare exacerbates the situation in new ways. For perhaps the first time in history, the legions of unprotected people can now see the leisured security of the legally protected, and their recognition through telecommunications is a major source of tension in struggles all over the world today.

Consider the situation for what it is! To have nothing and to have no means of getting anything while seeing what others have and that you might have! For some, and perhaps a growing number, this recognition means that their most valued possession will be a weapon to take what the world is blocking them from having. Alternatively, that weapon can be held to destroy what others possess in ideological anger over the values of a consumer culture.

We are beginning to see violent events of this kind every day, and the weapons are now immeasurably more powerful, disguisable, and movable than ever before. The terrorist bomb, the handheld missile, the chemical attack, the repeating firearm, the nuclear device, the aerial assault, and the myriad forms of technological invasion—all allow devastating strikes from afar, suddenly, and often in secret. Together they have made the world unsafe everywhere for those who have something to lose.

The legal challenge of the twenty-first century is as old as Aristotle and still unresolved. Retributive justice must find its corollary in greater forms of distributive justice.[13] Of course, for this to happen communal wherewithal must join legal stipulation in the "Spirit of the Laws." Justice in its broadest sense is more than a corrective of wrongdoing. It assumes the common humanity that all memorials strive to portray. How many more memorials, filled with the sadness of legal failure, will the world have to build?

9

Precision in Persuasion

FOR A NUMBER OF YEARS I taught a joint seminar for third-year law students and advanced Ph.D. students in literature. We examined legal transcripts, judicial decisions, and related essays about legal events. The law students were quicker in finding essential language, the root of the matter. The students in literature were more adept at critiquing that language once it was found. These differences in approach were not absolute ones, but they were always noticeable and they held even after they were pointed out.

You find in language what you are looking for. The law students were searching for holdings and their relation to other holdings. The students in literature were more concerned about what the language in this particular holding might mean as opposed to what it declared. They closely analyzed the words themselves and the historical context of when the legal event had taken place. Both approaches were valuable in discussion, but crossover skills appeared only if the student in literature was thinking about law school.

Disciplinary skills, as important as they are, can turn into familiar talents on display. If one is not careful, they limit inquiry as much as they enable it. There are drawbacks, as well as advantages, in each disciplinary inclination that need to be faced. Law students are ready to rest once they find what seems to be the answer to the problem addressed. Students in literature are sometimes too eager to get on to other questions before basic issues have been settled, and they are overly critical of how a problem has been solved without considering the controlling nature of the problem addressed.

Academic enterprise is simultaneously useful *and* obstructionist when it gives—or pretends to give—the mercurial aspects of language a fixed level of precision about what has been written. The act of reading instills an overwhelming desire to know, and this compulsion encourages disciplinary claims of precision. Bringing the disciplines together creatively on this issue of precision, without allowing them to get in the way of each other, is an objective more easily articulated than accomplished.

The language of law is prescriptive, authoritative, directed, and fixed in its insistence on decisions.[1] The language of literary criticism is evocative, penetrating, suggestive, harmonizing, and, at its best, a marriage of concrete and theoretical analyses of a text assumed to be ambiguous. Legal and literary interpretation also maintain different standards of what counts as evidence for making an argument, how to ask questions about that evidence, and which test of time to apply in reaching an answer.[2]

Legal language is defined by its presumed clarity and the observed importance of the speaker or writer supporting it. Clarity and reason give certainty to understanding and permanence to the solution if presented by the right speaker.[3] These are major linguistic assets in law, and they are supported all of the way down the line in legal manuals and law school classrooms. The first "fundamental principles of legal writing" are "brevity and clarity," "simplicity of structure," and "issue by issue arrangement . . . so that structure reveals the sequence of thinking or the merit of the points under discussion."[4]

The test of time is a little different in literary understandings. The aesthetic value of a literary text and its continuing relevance to general readers control assigned worth. The claim on clarity is also a little harder to pin down although it is not without merit. Certain differences from legal understanding remain more obvious. The famous line "I have measured out my life with coffee spoons" may furnish a definitive grasp of themes in T. S. Eliot's "The Love Song of J. Alfred Prufrock," but no one would call it the holding of the poem. The name "Prufrock," however instructive it might be, does not turn the speaker into the controlling authority who provides the meaning of the poem.[5]

A favorite expression of precision in language in literature comes from Mark Twain, in whose writing timing and tone are more important than "issue by issue arrangement." "The difference between the right word and the almost right word," wrote Twain, "is the difference between lightning and a lightning bug."[6] The literary sentence, with very different norma-tive registers at stake than in legal thought, insists that only the finest word will do, but what is the nature of that finest word and how should one look for it?

Twain, the realist as humorist, and many other writers in imaginative literature believe that the right language should reflect the values, thought, and tone of the setting described. The right word comes out of intuitive reservoirs as much as reason. It does not emerge from mere calculation, as it might in law. Nor do the writers of it have much interest in presenting a decision to the world. They show why that world thought and acted the way it did.

No judge or lawyer is likely to agree with the poet Eliot when he delivers his utter frustration over the use of language:

> Because one has only learnt to get the better of words
> For the thing one no longer has to say, or the way in which
> One is no longer disposed to say it. And so each venture
> Is a new beginning, a raid on the inarticulate.[7]

A different grasp of precision in language applies in the poet's under-standing, and the question is whether or not law has anything at all to learn from it.

So unalike are these settled differences that they raise a larger question. Why not leave law to do what it does best and literature to do what it does best, and the same for philosophy, sociology, theology, anthropology, and the visual arts? The answer in this book has been that law cannot do best just by doing what it thinks it does best.

Paul Kahn summarizes the need for an external perspective on law in *The Cultural Study of Law*: "We cannot grasp the law as an object of study if the conceptual tools we bring to the inquiry are nothing but the self-replication of legal practice itself." The rationale for a separate point of view lies in "the intersection of reason and will, which are thought to be the twin sources of a legitimate legal order." Reason comes from legal thought while the general will to support it comes from the people. Key to this "intersec-tion" is the clarifying nature of language that law and the people share.[8]

Commonality in language usage, joining the people and law, becomes paramount for the intersection of understandings or what others call

"transactional associations" to work. That is why legal philosophers uni-
formly demand a high level of common language in defining a rule of law.[9]
Well beyond the common parlance used in all law, the language of the law
must be open and publicly available. It must be known to a community,
and it must be clearly stated for the interaction that a meaningful rule of
law requires.[10]

Problems with clarity and open publication develop when law speaks
only to itself or when the use of reason becomes intricate to the point of
abstruseness when addressing a difficult problem. Even then, translation
that reaches a general audience would seem to be necessary, but here, in its
starkest form, is the dilemma between common understanding and professional expertise. Some would even say the difference is a yawning gap that
cannot be overcome.

One result has been a brand of intellectual fatalism. It encourages "selective transmission" of language by distinguishing between "conduct rules,
which are addressed to the general public and are designed to guide its
behavior," and "decision rules, which are directed to the officials who apply
conduct rules." In other words, it might be acceptable if the internal business and duties of the law are not conveyed to public understanding.[11]

When should a professional language enjoy seclusion of reference?
Maybe in some professions—medicine, for example—but not in law despite
its admitted complexity, and this would seem to be particularly relevant at
a time when public confidence in governmental regulation has fallen to an
all-time low. The most hallowed national decision-making institution in
law, the Supreme Court of the United States, receives a measly 30 percent
approval rating today.[12]

To let law speak only to itself on any level is the beginning of the end
of a rule of law. Why would anyone think such an arrangement should be
allowed to exist? It assumes that legal language can reach levels of objectivity that guarantee its safe use while protecting those to whom it might not
be immediately available, but the notion that legal decisions are exercises in
objectivity and neutrality has long been exploded.

What remains in its stead is faith in a correct use of clarifying language.
The shift in explanation is from the presumed objectivity of the law to the
assumed precision conceivable in legal language.[13] Still we are left with the
essential question: In what does the idea of precision in legal language con-
sist? If we assume, as we have, the difficulty in agreeing over the slipperiness

of language in general, what is it that makes legal language different, and if that difference holds up, is that one reason why law students in a joint seminar could feel comfortable in stopping with discovery of the holding of a case?

Already the first legal realists who first discounted belief in judicial objectivity in the 1930s make these questions hard to answer. As Felix Cohen so neatly put it, "anyone who offers guides for decision making, in the guise of facts, for instance, is really participating in the market place of ethics (justice) by supplying another set of premises from which to choose."[14] Ethical premises, not objectivity, drive judicial decisions, and legal realism wants to insure that those premises be in the open. Cohen argued for close analysis of words actually used as the right test of sincerity in a judicial decision.[15]

We are then thrown back on the sincerity of the speaker, the stature of that speaker, and the openness with which that speaker declares the choices that have been made or need to be made. Surely one aspect in these priorities, returning to Cohen's insistence on the sincerity of the words used, involves parsing the difference between lightning and the lightning bug. But maybe not! The judge who favors "painstaking analysis" as the source of clarity in legal decision making—something that no one could possibly disagree with—also argues that "pursuit of literary techniques is more likely to undermine than to reinforce the success of the opinion in meeting its judicial obligations."[16]

A challenge to the independence of legal discourse must be careful about what it is not. It need not dispute the calculated differences in legal discourse from common language in the name of what linguists call understanding through "group cohesion."[17] The idiosyncrasy of wordiness can also be left undisturbed. Some redundancy is necessary; it helps the law to safeguard its meanings from evasion. The challenge is therefore not to the odd use of binomial expressions ("any and all," "null and void"); nor to passive voice ("the cases are consolidated," "it is affirmed"); nor to nominalizations (from "infringe" to "infringement"); nor even to a certain amount of linguistic creativity ("the poison pill" in the law of mergers, or "hedonic damages" in tort law for loss of enjoyment of life).

These devices—harmless in themselves except as surreptitious claims of authority—contribute to professional trust in the objectivity of legal language, and they aid legal language to be distinct, but they are not the underlying problem that generates so much belief in that objectivity. Of far greater significance is professional confidence that law can fix language in place not just in the moment of its expression but well into the future.

Language does not really work that way. Why should legal proponents of its use feel that they are exempt from a volatility that keeps language on the move?[18] The assumption is all the more problematic since law must take up diverse situations in its decision-making capacities while using the same linguistic tools.[19] Precision in language does not lend itself to the presumed ability to keep it fixed.

Yes, fixed language is forced on the legal profession in many guises. Decisions must abide by legislative statutes even when those statutes seem unhelpful. The obligations of legal precedent and established doctrine force a return to the same language over and over, though often enough in a new context. One response has been to encourage fixed language through what are known as "terms of art." A term of art in law is a phrase understood to "have a relatively precise meaning."[20]

Relatively precise? The wiggle word, the adverb in the definition, is revealing. Legal terms of art allow changes in meaning while claiming that the real signification remains fixed through the same language. They instill the exact opposite of precision in language by casting a broad umbrella over many meanings and applications. A quick example can prove the point. A fixed phrase like "restraint of trade" in the Sherman Anti-Trust Act of 1890 has long required reinterpretation as "a term of art" to cover a variety of situations.[21]

For perhaps the most famous example of inexcusable fixation in doctrinal and precedential terms, consider the notorious "Rule in Shelley's Case." The original case from the middle of the fourteenth century closed a tax loophole in the inheritance practices of feudalism. With the end of feudalism, the fixed term of "art" soon allowed law to bilk many modern heirs out of rightful estates. The difference in conveyancing between "from A to B and his heirs" as opposed to the antiquated tax dodge, "from A to B for life and then to his heirs," required a fully trained and remunerated professional eye to escape the mistake, one reason the rule was retained for centuries to the distress of legatees left without standing to receive.[22]

Fixed legal terminology can also lose its original meaning without losing its power to influence a result. Law can even forget the basis of the language it has created while sustaining or even requiring its use.[23]

These problems are acute when "fixed" is understood to mean "precise." How far does "heirs at law" as a term of art extend given the intent of a testator who has indicated her twenty-five first cousins should share equally in the estate when "heirs at law," despite its plural form, refers in law to a single maternal aunt? Answer: not far enough. The twenty-five cousins are left in the lurch. Extrinsic evidence, even if explicit, does not count when a beneficiary can be identified on the face of a will.[24]

The tort law of negligence is full of such obfuscation. The concept of "proximate cause" to establish negligence seems to mean whatever a judge wants to think it means. A favorite confirmation of this floating signifier, one often cited, is that of Benjamin Cardozo in *Palsgraf v. Long Island Railroad* when how close an innocent injured bystander stood to an explosion determined whether damages could be awarded.[25] In response to this case and others like it, most commentators recognize that proximate cause is "a notoriously flexible and theoretically inconsistent concept."[26]

Law ventures into troubled waters when it borrows professional terms from another discipline. Take, for instance, its distinction between parody and satire, where parody is a defense against copyright infringement but satire under its "fair-use" doctrine is not. Says the Supreme Court, parody must "mimic an original to make its point, and so has some claim to use the creation of its victim's (or collective victims') imagination, whereas satire can stand on its own two feet and so requires justification for the very act of borrowing." The Court seems to act on the impression that satire is the sharper weapon.[27]

Literary critics will have none of this. *Gulliver's Travels* is at once a parody of travel literature *and* a satire of English culture. All parody satirizes the work or thing it addresses, and parody, to the extent that it is different, is much easier to inflict than satire. Why should the Court give parody legal leverage to what in literary terms is "a parasitic mode, necessarily coming after the host text which it imitates or feeds upon"? The distinction simply does not hold up against literary practice.[28] When the Supreme Court distinguishes parody from satire by arguing that parody resembles "comment or criticism," as though satire does not, critical theorists can only shrug.[29]

Courts decide, but in deciding they should keep their faith in abstract formalism and their trust in legal language from "creating the illusion of certainty in a world of uncertainty." Explanations of law belong close to the ground.[30] Even the Supreme Court is often criticized for its "woeful disregard for how language operates in real life situations."[31]

We are left again with the problem of defining precision in practical terms. Judges are accomplished wordsmiths, so what is lacking when critics say judicial language does not reach real-life situations? A literary sensibility can help to solve this problem. Writers of fiction and even of poetry and drama must secure an aspect of their work in reality to be believed. Twain, in his concern for the right word, seeks the believability of language through a reader's visceral perception of it. Eliot, in his "raid on the inarticulate," hopes for a similar perception by striving for the right voice to make a point in a new way.

Judges, in order to be authoritative, must define the world before them in more mundane terms and through an issue already given a setting. Unlike a writer in imaginative literature, they cannot rely on evocative language to surround the subject. The two traditional requirements in formal definition—"the requirement of *non-creativity* and that of *eliminability*"— hold judges to the sticking point. For a definition to be credible, it does not summon novelty in language to what it elucidates; the old must define the new. The thing being defined needs an equivalent statement not containing its own terms; the definition fixes the subject being defined, it does not reflect it.[32]

If we accept that definition is central to the judicial opinion, then we must also accept the literal restraints just noted. There is, however, a silver lining in literary terms. The best definition of a term demands linguistic imagination within the precision called for. To fix terminology correctly is also what we expect of a judge who keeps pragmatic realities in view, who uses an identifiable voice to achieve the right declarative tone, and who penetrates the thickets of the law with the general integrity of language in mind.

A close reading of a concrete example can clarify these abstract aspirations, and for that purpose we turn to the American judge who has done the most to define the nature of judicial thought and to reform current judicial uses of language. Richard A. Posner, legal theorist as well as judge on the United States Court of Appeals for the Seventh Circuit, has written many books on the subject, including but not limited to *The Problems of Jurisprudence* (1990), *How Judges Think* (2008), and *Reflections on Judging* (2013). The most cited legal scholar of the twentieth century, Posner is particularly useful for immediate purposes. He can also claim expertise in the connection of literature to law through yet another book that has gone through many editions, *Law & Literature: A Misunder-stood Relation* (1988).[33]

Creativity in law, not always stressed for good reasons, requires recognition of the opportunity presented, which in turn requires "self-awareness," a trait Posner often finds missing in others who sit on the bench.[34] The opportunity in *United States v. Daniel L. Delaney* (2013) was a peculiar one, and Posner had to be just as peculiarly aware of the stature he holds within the profession in order to seize it.[35] The case itself is a deceptively simple one and could have been handled in a few sentences instead of fourteen pages. Why does Posner give it such extended treatment? The facts, immediately below, appear to have been conclusive with the lower court's decision.

Delaney, a federal prisoner serving a term for unarmed robbery, strangled his cellmate to death after beating him severely with both his fists and the victim's cane before tying him up and finally killing him. Convicted by a jury of first-degree murder and sentenced to life in prison, the defendant appealed. The jury should have found him guilty of voluntary manslaughter for killing in "the heat of passion." Delaney said he had learned that his victim was a child abuser and that he had broken into a sudden rage as an abused child himself. Posner answers as we would expect given the situation and the defendant's case: "since the jury had solid grounds for finding murder rather than manslaughter, the judgment is AFFIRMED" (13).

The opportunity for Posner lies not in these facts, nor in the appellee's purposes on appeal. Delaney does not seek a reduction from first-degree murder to second-degree murder because both would keep him in prison for life; only a finding of manslaughter would yield a shorter maximum sentence of fifteen years in prison. Even so, Posner's interest is over distinctions between degrees of murder and in the language used to define them because he knows that the terminology used is often confused in court decisions.

Posner's account of the facts is spare but telling in the details that he decides to convey about "the single issue presented," the possibility of manslaughter on appeal (1). The tone is casual but direct. Neither the killer nor the man killed is ever identified by name in a singularly bloodless description of a horribly prolonged, tortured death. Brevity is everything here. The horrific crime is not how the writer wants to hold our interest, although he doesn't want us to forget it either.

Here is what we get from the literary realm of story: "late one night, as a guard walked past the defendant's cell, the defendant told him that he had to be moved to a new cell" because his cellmate "had [had] to go. He was a child molester." We learn that the victim, "a substantially older and weaker man than the defendant[,] . . . had apparently put up no resistance to the defendant's assaults"; that the defendant had told an FBI agent that he attacked the cellmate only "after some thought"; and that the defendant said he "didn't really intend nothing. . . . I want[ed] to, like, beat him up, you know?" (2).

Every one of these incursions points toward murder and not manslaughter: the objectified and thoroughly unsympathetic defendant, the off-the-cuff language to the guard proving that the defendant knows his victim is dead or dying with no intention of helping him, the lack of provocation or resistance from the victim, the substantial premeditation in the attack, and even the poor grammar ("didn't really intend nothing") and direct admission ("beat him up"). Everything says murder, and the unnamed defendant has already been found doubly dangerous before the attack. He is a convicted robber and had been placed in "the prison's segregation unit because of a fight he had with another inmate" (1). Not given but easily intuited is the likelihood that the nonviolent victim had been placed in the segregation unit precisely because he was a convicted child abuser and needed protection from other inmates.

Notice that no further attention is given to the guard who "walked past the defendant's cell" or to other forms of responsibility by authority that might have saved the victim's life. The attack on the cellmate has to have been prolonged and at times noisy beyond the cell, yet penal obligation has no place in this account. That again is not the writer's interest. Structurally, Posner's description of the facts ends with the defendant saying that he "didn't really intend nothing" except to "beat him up, you know?". The words are strategically placed. They show violence was intended (2).

Nothing described disturbs or overturns the transparent finding of murder. At issue for Posner is not the appeal but the language of the law and the need to clarify it. For the same reason, he quietly dismisses the idea that "murder of a sexual molester is a common reaction of a person who has been sexually molested" (11).

With the case so tepidly and briefly handled in less than a page and a half, page 3 of *United States v. Delaney* launches into elaborate statutory distinctions between first- and second-degree murder in the federal criminal code. The terms "malice aforethought," "willful, deliberate malicious, and premeditated killing," and "maliciously to effect the death of any human being" set off the first designation (3). The only real difference between first-degree and second-degree murder turns on the possibility of a death sentence for the former, but that distinction is not on the table in this case. Delaney has been sentenced to life in prison, and it would apply in either degree. So why talk about it?

Posner quarrels with the law not the case. He can do so without risking reversal, confusion, or even major controversy over his decision because the case itself is a lead-pipe cinch. Opportunity knocks in his recognition of an easy decision that nonetheless has dramatic appeal. He has an interested audience, which has been drawn in by the horrifying facts of the case, and he uses that attention to highlight his concern that the language for murder in the federal statute is "abstract and archaic" and traceable to lost "medieval origins." So archaic is this terminology that "laypersons, including jurors" and even judges are confused by it (5).

That confusion is Posner's key. Rubbing salt in the federal wound, Posner next demonstrates that Illinois's criminal code and the American Law Institute both have jury instructions "written in plain language" that avoid most of these difficulties. The current federal language is bad not only because it is confusing but also because it encourages "linguistic ineptitude" and "barbarism" in language through such misconstrued constructions as "malice of forethought." The very word " 'malice' has no consistent meaning in law." Indeed, the lower-court judge has apparently misunderstood the terminology herself. So strained is current statutory language that semantic misperception comes dangerously close to "erasing the distinction between first- and second-degree murder" (5–8).

Other puzzles with additional lower-court confusion quickly materialize. The interpretation of "heat of passion" required to reach a designation of manslaughter was mishandled when the trial judge expected the standard to apply to "an *ordinary* person—that thus would *naturally* cause a *reasonable* person in the passion of the moment to lose self-control." What, Posner wants to know, is the average or ordinary or reasonable person in "the subset consisting of past victims of child sexual abuse?" (9–10). In the foreground of this question is the evidence we already have of a thoroughly depraved and previously violent inmate to whom such terms as "ordinary" and "reasonable" hardly seem to apply.

Here, too, the Model Penal Code of the American Law, often cited in the opinion "for thoughtful advice," proves to be much better. "It defines a heat-of-passion killing, more clearly than the judge's instructions in this case." One might think further criticism of the trial judge amounts to over-kill in the light of an offhand admission. "No matter; our defendant doesn't quarrel with the heat-of-passion instruction" (11). Again, why bother? Because Posner is troubled by a "seeming oddity." He worries that the government must bear "the burden of proving absence of heat of passion beyond a reasonable doubt" after the defense has given the claim "some evidentiary base" (12). The clincher arrives a page later: "Probably 'heat of passion' shouldn't be thought a defense" (13).

Who should be listening to all of this? The answer is "everyone." A leading appellate judge in the country is doing his job by pointing to problems and inconsistencies in established law that might make a big difference in other cases, and he is indicating with all the eloquence that precision can bring exactly how the law might be improved through adoption of language in the Model Penal Code. The fact that these problems and inconsistencies make no difference in *this* case is crucial. The case does not get in the way. Instead it provides an objective platform for discussing the state of the law in anticipation of future cases where life and death could well be under consideration.

Judges above and below Posner and Congress have been asked to take heed. New and more careful law is needed here. This is where creativity in the judicial function should be found. Is it on the edge of what should be allowed? Apparently so. At least Posner's concurring colleague on the Seventh Circuit, William J. Bauer, thinks so. Pointing to his own "suspense until the last minute" of Posner's opinion, Bauer adds one brief oblique sentence, "I'm not sure it provides a clear trail for future prosecutions but I sign on because the result is in keeping with the evidence" (14).

Missing in Judge Bauer's comment are several basic recognitions. There is no suspense in Posner's opinion that a close reading does not dispel. The initial description of the case makes his intentions clear. More seriously absent in Bauer is recognition of the creativity called for in a reform-minded judge. Where else should we expect knowledgeable concern about problems in established law and recommendations to come from than from an appellate judge with life tenure in the federal system?

Judge Posner is an exemplum of that reform-minded phenomenon, and there is clear literary sensibility behind his concern and his ability to voice it through the history and particularity of language. Posner has long been on record that "literary analysis of opinions is highly promising"; that "judicial opinions . . . are unavoidably rhetorical, and in much the same way as literature is"; that literature is central to general "knowledge" and "belief" beyond its emotional satisfactions; that the study of rhetoric is important in a judicial style because "many questions cannot be resolved by logical or empirical demonstration"; that ignoring a literary under-standing of rhetoric "has retarded the application of specifically literary insights to the study of judicial opinions"; and that "the benefits of litera-ture for judges . . . must be sought in the craft values displayed in works of literature, notably *impartiality* (detachment, empathy, balance, perspec-tive, a complex of the possibility of other perspectives than the writer's own), *scrupulousness* and *concreteness*."[36]

Properly understood and used, these characteristics can produce the precision in language that is called for and needed in legal writing. There is no single solution. A dozen skills based on wide reading must come together. Tactical crafts in writing must interlace with knowledge and belief. The list Posner has given—detachment, empathy, balance, awareness of other per-spectives, scrupulousness and concreteness— is a good one for the literary awareness behind it. Only widely imbibed reading skills will join detachment *and* empathy in a balanced awareness of other perspectives with continuing attention to the concrete and the scrupulous.

That said, we can add one more quality implied by all of the rest on Posner's list. Precision in judicial writing is necessarily tough-minded in the way we find it in *United States v. Delaney*. Clarity is tough-mindedness here. The opinion takes up only what it has to take up to be clear about its objectives. Precision reigns through the deliberate, careful focus away from the emotionalism that might detract attention from the legal prob-lem of interest. An accurate appreciation of the tools of analysis in liter-ary enterprise encourages a detached level of scrutiny, what might also be called canniness in address.

The hardest thing in thought is to get beyond habitual thinking. The major accomplishment in *United States v. Delaney* comes through

Posner's desire and ability to challenge reflexive use of unhelpful but familiar terminology. Who has not heard the expression "malice afore-thought"? Yet hearing it, no matter how often, does not make it accurate. Mark Twain again summarizes the essential problem: "Habit is habit, and not to be flung out of the window by any man, but coaxed down-stairs a step at a time."[37]

"Technical legal terms," heavily censured in *United States v. Delaney*, promote habitual thinking and can cause mistakes in legal determination. Technicality is necessary to an understanding of detail but not as linguistic formalism floating high above the conflict at issue. Posner rejects the technical in the name of "plain language" (5). Why is plain language such a safeguard? It is the language of communication.

Literature is the gift that keeps giving. Worthiness in language holds a voluntary audience in imaginative literature. Judges can rely on an obligatory audience, but they should not depend on it in what they write for a public audience, which means every judicial opinion they pen. Remember the earlier claim of *concreteness*. Reading widely and deeply catches the earthbound language of the realm. Its vigor and natural plainness are guards against habit and stimulate the reader's own thoughts.

Here, after all, is the real test of time. In a famous phrase, we are urged on as readers to get "to know, on all the matters which most concern us, the best which has been thought and said in the world." The best is never habitual. Getting to know the best that has been thought and said turns "a stream of fresh and free thought upon our stock notions and habits, which we now follow staunchly but mechanically."[38] Literary awareness can protect law from mechanical applications, which sooner or later lose their precision and go wrong when up against the variety in human experience. Predictability, a virtue in law, can also be its Achilles' heel. Routine expectations welcome habitual reference.

Two literary masters indicate how the precision in writing must counter the idleness in conformity. Samuel Johnson, when he calls language "the dress of thought," attacks both carelessness in composition and failure to rise to the occasion through the usual minutia of application. "Some false-hoods are continued by traditions," he observes, "because they supply commodious allusions."[39] Ruthless in his own attack on allusions, Ezra Pound urges "language charged with meaning to the utmost possible degree." The goal is to be heard. "Literature is news that *stays* news."[40]

The vitality of law is not contingent on everyone reading and understanding it, but it does require that anyone who wants to read and understand should have a clear path to do so, and that is particularly important when the law *is* news. Making legal prose the dress of thought and striving for meaning in language to the utmost degree are good places to ensure that this happens when it should happen. The public uses of legal eloquence depend on it, and they will die without it.

PART 4

When Law Fails

FAILURE IN LAW OPENS A path to chaos. The gloomy Arthur Schopenhauer may have said it most vividly: "Man is at bottom a savage, horrible
beast. . . . Wherever and whenever the locks and chains of law and order
fall off and give place to anarchy, he shows himself for what he is."[1] Even
small failures can become a problem. People everywhere take advantage of
lapses in accountability, so much so that the officials responsible try not to
articulate failure when it occurs.

These same officials will also blink under too much pressure and when
under the gaze of alternative forms of order—whether political, religious,
or military in posture—and in blinking they encourage that part of a content citizenry to blink with them. Imaginative literature, a protest medium,
responds by countering these secretive tendencies. It tries to open the eyes
that officialdom would prefer to keep and find closed. Literature succeeds
when its expressions remind everyone of the true basis in a rule of law:
namely, the communicated confidence between governor and governed.
Only that confidence gives the constitutive relationship of culture and
legality meaning and integrity.[2]

Too much failure in law will destroy any confidence, and in this sense a
rule of law is always vulnerable to unfairness in the legal process. Nor is it an
accident that the most powerful renditions of this vulnerability have reached
formal expression in the Latin American novel and essay, with vivid perceptions and dramatic depictions of lawlessness in country after country.

Simón Bolívar, the hero of Latin American independence, captured the
essence of the regional plight early in the nineteenth century. "He who
fights for freedom in Latin America ploughs in the sea," Bolívar observed,
and the best calculations of this mournful declaration continue to come
from the world of fiction rather than law, with the best known coming
from Gabriel García Márquez's massive *One Hundred Years of Solitude*
(1967) and his subsequent novella *Chronicle of a Death Foretold* (1982).[3]

The much shorter *Chronicle of a Death Foretold* can serve as a quick proof
text.[4] García Márquez gives us a small village without a name, one that
thereby epitomizes the fragility of the rule of law in all of Latin America.
The entire population of this village is complicit in the murder of an innocent man. A chronicle is normally a historical record, and García Márquez
builds his story around an actual event although with artful twists of his
own. Part mystery, part parable of instruction, this novella is a remorseless
account of how the enemies in thought and action trump the law.

The most beautiful girl in the village, Angela Vicario, is returned to her parents on the night of her wedding when her new husband discovers that she is not a virgin. Beaten by her mother and then forced to divulge her seducer, she names a notorious rake, Santiago Nasar. Angela's twin brothers, Pablo and Pedro, then brutally murder Nasar the next morning. Most of the village watches the act after the brothers tell everyone that they are going to do it. Everyone knows what is going to happen, but no one warns Nasar even though "no one believed it had really been Santiago Nasar." Yes, "he went about . . . nipping the bud of any wayward virgin," but there is no evidence that he did so on this occasion (89–90). Soon after, a visiting magistrate, again tellingly without a name, clears the brothers of any crime for "homicide in legitimate defense of honor," and he does so even though he cannot find "a single clue, not even the most improbable, that Santiago Nasar had been the cause of the wrong" (48, 98–99).

Our interest is less in the intricacies of this plot than in the five related failures in law that it depicts. When does honor trump law? How does it overwhelm law in a clear case of murder under legal scrutiny? Why does honorable vindication of the crime destroy so many other lives beyond that of Santiago Nasar? Which problems keep the village from solving the solvable mystery behind this crime? And what does the acknowledged failure of law do to the village and, by extension, to a Latin American understanding of the rule of law?

The code of honor relies on a different value system than law: status comes through an ascending order of assumed rights on the surface of things. Meaning is established through external or social opinion, correctness through personality, merit through prowess, and authority through expectations. In a combination of all of the above, behavior is defined by personal obligation when facing a challenge. Law, in contrast, applies equal rights for status, investigation for meaning, performance for correctness, process for finding merit, expertise for authority, and, in a combination of all of the above, it demands institutional wherewithal for determining behavior when facing a challenge.

In García Márquez's fictional village the code works through a covert gender war in which men are defined by indulgence, sexual mastery, subjective levels of freedom, and formal possession of the village. Women are held instead to rigid standards of sexual purity, social passivity, domestic limitation, and obedient objectification. They also accept a masculine right to rule the home with honor. Even so, women abiding by this code of honor get their own back by controlling male behavior subversively when they can.[5] In the leading example, Angela, forced to name her seducer, "looked for it in the shadows, found it at first sight among the many, many easily confused names from this world and the other, and she nailed it to the wall with her well-aimed dart, like a butterfly whose sentence has already been written. 'Santiago Nasar,' she said." (47).

Separate possibilities explain Angela's decision. Either she thinks her brothers will not dare attack the wealthy, formidable, and usually armed Nasar or she acts in resentment over the arrogance of a man who is "too haughty to have noticed her," who ignores her beauty and disparages her in public as a "ninny" and "the booby" (32, 89–90). Either way, all external clues point away from Nasar as the seducer and toward the Vicario household itself as the source of the problem.

Although the narrator thinks the mystery of the seducer "will never be cleared up," the reader realizes it was not seduction but incest that has robbed Angela of her virginity (89). Her father, Poncio Vicario, raped her, almost certainly in childhood when she could not defend herself. The only real mystery turns on how many in the Vicario household are aware of the abuse beyond Poncio and Angela herself.[6] We cannot know this last point because no one in the family is willing to talk about it.

A public disgrace that cannot be addressed creates unbearable conflict in a code of honor, and for that reason, a more acceptable or conventional answer—that of Santiago Nasar as the seducer—must be found and enforced. The real answer, that of the father who has sexually abused his daughter, creates too many levels of additional disgrace to be tolerated. Under the code, that secret must be kept. Nonetheless, public reparation remains the highest priority. Honor must be vindicated in some way.

But vindication is not the same as understanding. However logical to the village, the answer accepted by it—the killing of Santiago Nasar—does not get to the root of the matter. Everyone knows Nasar is not guilty, and the lie in killing him prevents other truths from emerging. It simultaneously heaps new levels of disgrace on all other potential sources of explanation, including the religious, political, and legal alternatives, all of which are savagely parodied in *Chronicle of a Death Foretold*. The result is a complete loss of collective conceptual integrity, with devastation for all who have made Santiago Nasar their scapegoat.

The village has given itself "an open wound," one that will not heal. "We couldn't talk about anything else," the narrator reveals, and yet "none of us could go on living without an exact knowledge of the place and the mission assigned to us by fate" (96–98). In the aftermath, in their compulsive need for evasion, the villagers never agree about anything that took place, including the simplest matters, like the nature of the weather on the day of the murder. Communal cohesion needs law, and those closest to Nasar are destroyed by the lawlessness that they have accepted . . . with one notable exception.

The exception, the only person with the normative stature to investigate the event with any accuracy, is the narrator, a close companion of Nasar and, more crucially, a member of the one family in the village that had nothing to do with the murder. Being absolved of the crime means being able to think through law. That said, it takes the narrator, also unnamed, twenty-seven years before he can bear to return "to this forgotten village, trying to put the broken mirror of memory back together from so many shattered shards" (6).

The forgotten village is, of course, not forgotten, but it is shattered. It represents every society where civic understanding has been undone by the failure of law. A legitimate legal process might not have exposed the taboo of incest in García Márquez's village, but it would have cleared Santiago Nasar of the accusation and it would have brought resolution and some communal expiation by convicting and punishing his murderers. Something much worse has also happened. An already fragile rule of law has been broken.

No one will assume these extremes for the rule of law in the United States, but there should be concern when the state ignores its own insistence on legality, and that now occurs with some frequency through regular governmental invocations of "national security." This is an ostensibly peace-loving nation that has been at war since 1941, well over half a century and counting. War, especially much war, changes civic understandings. It gives sanctity and unusual privileges to extraordinary state action.[7]

The last part of this book uses literary analysis to explore the dangers when arguments of national security override legal explanation. In the first real inklings of this rhetorical evasion, "The *Somers* Mutiny and the American Ship of State," we see how a still weak military establishment in 1842 uses patriotic fervor and a politics of fear to justify illegal action.

Questions about that action produce one of the great novellas in American literature.

The final chapter, "Invading Panama: The Power of Circumstance and the Rule of Law," carries these concerns up to the present and into the military juggernaut that characterizes the modern nation-state today. The invasion of Panama by executive order against international law in December 1989 was widely accepted by the American people and prepared the way for subsequent decades of military adventurism in Iraq, Afghanistan, and other less publicized locations. Time and again, the consequence has been illegal action disguised and acknowledged only long after the fact through a generally hesitant literature of journalism.[8]

Every illegal act that goes unrecognized threatens the rule of law. The obligation of a community under law is to raise awareness of that danger wherever it appears by connecting legal obligation to the alternative forms of discourse that a community needs to recognize itself and react to changes in governmental understanding. If the rule of law remains strong in the United States, it still depends on the confidence that the governed must feel in the legal integrity of the governor, and it should give some pause that so many Americans today are eager to distrust and challenge the authority over them. The connection of law and literature is thus always more than an academic enterprise. It is one of the heartbeats in a healthy body politic.

10

The *Somers* Mutiny and the American Ship of State

HIGH-PROFILE TRIALS GAIN SPECIAL ATTENTION when the question before the court does not settle concerns triggered by perceptions of the event. That happened in the *Somers* mutiny affair of 1842 and 1843. In one of the first trials using national security to justify illegal governmental action, the court martial proceeding of Captain Alexander Slidell Mackenzie divided the country over national fears.

The central event, which led the captain of an American naval vessel to execute three of his crew while at sea, comes to most readers today through an aside in Herman Melville's last great masterpiece, the unfinished novella *Billy Budd, Sailor (An Inside Narrative)*. At the time, the captain's action mesmerized the nation. Two legal procedures, a court of inquiry and then a court martial against Captain Mackenzie, divided antebellum Americans, and the deepest source of conflict remains with us today. When claims of national security intervene in the legal process everyone should take notice, one reason why history books and articles continue to explore the *Somers* affair.[1]

Melville had an intimate reason for being interested in the case. His cousin was a central figure as second-in-command aboard the *Somers*. Half a century later, transforming the *Somers* affair into fiction, he was more interested in the philosophical source of conflict.[2] Always concerned as a former sailor about the abuse of seamen, Melville wrote instead of the plight of the punishers, of "that harassed frame of mind," "the urgency felt, well-warranted or otherwise," of the officers on the *Somers* who feared a mutiny in progress and punished preemptively to avoid it.[3]

Billy Budd as story accentuates the unbounded nature of the punishers' fears, and it makes the mutiny a villain's lie rather than a discovered plot. The nature of authority is its real subject. In orchestrating the execution of Billy Budd, "the Honorable Edward Fairfax Vere," captain of the ship, puts the dilemma of his drumhead court in interrogatory form: "How can we adjudge to summary and shameful death a fellow creature innocent before God and whom we feel to be so?—Does that state it aright?"[4] Well, does it?

The condemned men aboard the *Somers* were not as popular or innocent in temperament as Melville makes his "Handsome Sailor." Billy Budd strikes a spontaneous but fatal physical blow when falsely accused of plotting a mutiny by a petty officer "in whom was the mania of an evil nature."[5] Even so, the same problem applies to the events of 1842 and 1843, and Melville's interest in the ambiguities of the *Somers* affair—"the urgency felt, well-warranted or otherwise"—contains a veiled question that still vexes communal understanding.

Why did the conclusion of the original legal case, an acquittal of the captain, not end the matter? Several reasons apply, but the most important one reaches far beyond the trial. The *Somers* affair produced the first sustained version of a national uncertainty best stated again in question form: when in a democratic culture should a claim of national security be allowed to override an accusation of crime against a government official? High-profile trials remain of interest when their resolutions leave an unanswered question on the table. The *Somers* trial did more than that; it raised an unanswerable question, one that has come up with increasing frequency in the modern nation-state.

Although any claim of national security, as in the *Somers* courtroom, will be openly political, such trials are weakly characterized as political events. Every trial is political. The state, along with the accused, is scrutinized for the fairness of its proceeding, but famous courtroom events raise more than that. They are best understood through the characteristics that sustain interest: first, a *spread of conflict* (beyond the original legal issue into common parlance); second, *cultural surprise* (a shock that reverberates); and third, *iconographic significance* (a sustaining visual element through the personalities involved).[6] The *Somers* trials feature all three elements with an intensity that deserves explanation.

The *spread of conflict* in the *Somers* court of inquiry and court martial was extraordinary even for a high-profile trial. Why did these events lead to such heated and seemingly extraneous debate among the public intellectuals of that day? Why did so much of that debate turn on a familial narrative fixated on mothers when the episode occurred on the high seas entirely among men? Why did leading commentators take such counterintuitive ideological stances in exchange with each other?

Surprise and *iconographic significance* also apply. The *Somers* affair shocked everyone as the first claimed mutiny to take place in the United States Navy, and the central mutineer was none other than the son of the sitting U.S. secretary of war. Excitement over these elements forged a third iconographic focal point. The captain of the *Somers* came to epitomize either strong or weak governmental authority depending on whether one believed the executions had been legally justified or not. Disputes over him grew fierce. Commentators weighed his strength or weakness in parallel with what they thought were the nation's problems and how they thought those problems should be solved.

The United States of the 1840s were still discussed in plural form. They were regionally committed, separate states dealing with sectional strife, threats of disunion, weak national leadership, a growing slavery issue, and grave economic uncertainty after the devastating panic of 1837. How did one think of the still fragile union? Were the states—with new and different entities across the continent clamoring for admission—a loose confederation or a unified state? These questions dominated discourse, and the *Somers* affair gave them context and urgency. Instead of a proud "ship of state," the metonymy for nationhood in nineteenth-century thought, the *Somers* had come apart on the open sea.

What happened aboard the *Somers*? What went wrong there? The first question is one of fact. The second, misunderstood even at trial, raised the nebulous realm of circumstance. Procedurally, these questions should be separated at trial and then brought together for a court to act. The necessity of an early coming together in the *Somers* case caused controversy to flourish. The facts received broad agreement. Why they happened depended on circumstance and that was hotly disputed.

Fact and circumstance diverged over whether or not the Captain Alexander Slidell Mackenzie of the *Somers* had erred in summarily hanging aboard ship Midshipman Philip Spencer and two crewmen, Samuel Cromwell and Elisha Small, after accusing them of mutinous behavior. The legal stakes in an overreaction were high. If Mackenzie made his decision to execute the accused beyond the necessity of his situation, he could be held criminally liable for murder in either a military or a civil court. If you wanted him punished, you wanted him removed from military understanding, where officers might protect their own. Opponents of Mackenzie fought for trial in a civil jurisdiction.

The undisputed details are these.[7] The *Somers*, a small brig but one of the fastest ships on the sea, was on a training mission for young sailors, on a mission from New York to the coast of Africa and back. The ship was over-crowded as it left port on September 13, 1841. Built for a maximum crew of ninety, the *Somers* sailed with 120. Just twelve men aboard were officers. Of the 120 on the *Somers*, only 25 percent were out of their teens. Two of the twelve officers were just sixteen years of age with several others almost as young; eight officers, counting the captain, were experienced enough to train younger protégés.

One particularly significant detail is often overlooked. Overcrowding meant that the usual contingent of marines, the ultimate keepers of order aboard a naval vessel, had been left behind. The ship was also too congested to maintain the customary physical separations between officers and men. Command structure had to rely on strict naval decorum to sustain order through lines of authority, and breakdown began here.

Although it was not a fighting ship in the most powerful sense, the *Somers* was a well-gunned force on the open seas capable of outrunning bigger ships and devastating smaller ones. It was designed to catch and punish slave ships and tariff-breaking commercial vehicles, which were part of a black market in human cargo and goods. There was, nonetheless, more to the *Somers* as a naval ship on an official mission. In the age of sailing ships, military standing came through the number and quality of ocean vessels a nation possessed. Everyone agreed (whether from a legal, naval, or political perspective) on two assumptions: the *Somers* represented American honor as well as an international gauge in the balance of power. It would be a national disgrace as well as a serious danger if the ship fell into the wrong hands.

A little over two months into its mission and on its way back across the Atlantic, after a stop at the island paradise of Madeira, the *Somers* experienced a noticeable drop in crew discipline. Some of the difficulties were traceable to the disruptive behavior of Samuel Cromwell, chief bo'sun's mate in charge of administering punishment to sailors, and Acting Midshipman Philip Spencer, who fraternized openly with the sailors against orders and gave them forbidden tobacco, liquor, and money. Both transgressors spoke with disdain of Captain Mackenzie and flaunted rules of ship conduct. Both had been admonished but not punished.

In this deteriorating atmosphere and on the evening of November 25, 1842, Philip Spencer secretly approached the ship's steward, J. W. Wales, with a detailed plan of mutiny that he claimed had the backing of a number of the ship's company. He meant to convert the *Somers* into a pirate ship at the first opportunity. The amazed Wales, threatened with immediate death if he divulged the plot, listened for two hours while Spencer spelled out the conspiracy in enough detail to make it credible. It is relevant that Wales felt himself under close surveillance by Spencer and a sailor that Spencer had claimed to be part of the conspiracy, Elisha Small, for the rest of that evening and night.

When Wales, afraid for his life, managed to get unobserved to a senior officer early the next day, that officer reported the conversation between Wales and Spencer through ship's hierarchy to the *Somers*'s captain. Captain Mackenzie pondered the matter for the better part of November 26 while asking his second-in-command, Lieutenant Guert Gansevoort, to watch Spencer and the crew for suspicious behavior. Gansevoort did notice signs of insubordination and unfriendliness in Spencer, Cromwell, and some of the crew and reported what he had seen. Mackenzie, who had meanwhile reviewed a long history of infractions by Spencer prior to the voyage and aboard ship, decided to face the issue directly after first receiving that report from Gansevoort.

On that same evening, with his leading officers armed and mustered around him on the quarterdeck, Mackenzie challenged Spencer over the meaning of his meeting with J. W. Wales. When Spencer admitted having the conversation but declared "it was in joke," Mackenzie responded, "This, sir, is joking on a forbidden subject. This joke may cost you your life." He had Spencer arrested and put in irons on the quarterdeck, there being no secure place aboard the overcrowded *Somers* that might serve as a prison.[8]

The language used in this opening interview is instructive. Mackenzie was already contemplating drastic action, a fact substantiated by a witness.

He ordered that Spencer be put to death if he attempted by word or sign to communicate with other crew members. The captain's suspicions would develop into certainty when a search of Spencer's locker disclosed a ciphered message in Greek that, when decoded, listed members of the ship's crew for a clandestine venture where some appeared under the heading "The Certain," some under a separate heading "The Doubtful," and still others under a third heading "To Be Kept Whether They Would or Not." The remainder, including all of the officers, was to be thrown overboard, Wales would testify. The lists and some of the names on them corroborated what Wales heard the previous day. (197–98).

The arrest and ironing of Midshipman Spencer in plain sight naturally attracted crew interest, and attraction became alarm when on November 27—with less evidence except for a questionable accident to the top-gallant mast—Samuel Cromwell and Elisha Small were also arrested and put in irons and two other sailors were flogged for infractions that had led Mackenzie to fear a general breakdown in discipline. In further response, on November 28, the captain gathered his crew to warn them that a mutiny had been contemplated and that he "was in the possession of the names of those who were implicated" (199).

Mackenzie meant for his speech to quell unrest. It had the opposite effect, a twist in events that led many to question the captain's judgment as a leader. Officers and crew alike would later agree that alarm and disorder among the crew became acute at this point, and it was easy to see why. Who would be next to be accused? By November 30, four other crewmen—Daniel McKinley, Alexander McKee, Charles Wilson, and Benjamin Green—were in irons as well. In Mackenzie's own words, "each new arrest of prisoners seemed to bring a fresh set of conspirators forward," and he asked himself a question that showed the depth of his apprehensions: "If the most deeply implicated were ironed, would all the dangerous be in custody?" Fearing loss of control of his ship while still several weeks from home port, he ordered his seven senior officers to meet together to advise their captain on what should be done with the main conspirators (200–201).

Meeting that day and on the next morning, December 1, the senior officers of the *Somers* unanimously reported that Spencer, Cromwell, and Small "have been guilty of a full and determined intention to commit a mutiny on board of this vessel," and recommended they be "put to death, in a manner best calculated as an example to make a beneficial impression upon the disaffected." They at no point questioned or cross-examined the three accused men. The three, each at first protesting in his own way, were then hanged on Mackenzie's order with the armed officers ordered to cut down any sailor who failed to pull on the ropes that executed their condemned crewmates (203, 206–7).

In the aftermath, there would be one last element of consensus on the facts. Order aboard the *Somers* seems to have improved following the executions as the *Somers* made its way back to New York, enforced by round-the-clock vigilance of the fully armed and by then thoroughly exhausted, sleep-deprived officers of the ship. But why was there better order? The question leads back to circumstances aboard ship.

Circumstance molds the facts at trial on the all-important issues of intent, justification, and blame. Controversy during the naval inquiries centered on these contextual issues. There was no question about what Mackenzie did; there were plenty of questions about why he had done it and if it could be justified. Curiously, among all of the questions raised, one relevant aspect of circumstance remained off limits.

The experiment in educating new sailors aboard the *Somers* had clearly failed. It had been benighted to believe that beginners in sea life as young as thirteen could learn the integrity of their craft from hard-bitten older sailors and distant officers, some of whom were barely older than their charges. The navy would solve this problem of policy very quietly. It established the United States Naval Academy at Annapolis, Maryland, in 1845.[9] Naval education would henceforth be a formal undertaking begun on land.

What is *not* expressed at trial in a forum where all things tend to be exposed is always of interest and a comment on the times. Some of what happened aboard the *Somers* came from misguided naval policy. Organizationally, and beyond Captain Mackenzie's control, the ship had been vulnerable to corruption of authority. Why, then, did no one speak of it? Institutions protect themselves first. Blame of official policy would have implicated the high command of the United States Navy, and none of the senior officers who ran inquiries in the *Somers* affair were about to raise that issue. The navy was managing a scandal that already touched everyone in the service and saw no point in making matters worse.

The willed obliviousness of the naval inquirers shows what trials can do and what they cannot do. If circumstance explains events, individuals, not circumstance, are put on trial. Procedurally, the officers of the naval inquiry and court martial proceedings could limit the scope of their investigations by narrowing their questions to the circumstances of the moment and calling them facts. Did specific conditions aboard the *Somers*, on December 1, 1842, justify Alexander Slidell Mackenzie's decision to execute three of his own crew in response to a conspiracy of mutiny that threatened his ship? In the words of the judge advocate, who confused fact with circumstance in prosecuting the court martial, "whatever may have been the impressions and motives of the commander at the time cannot affect the question of fact, as to whether the necessity did in truth or not exist." (257–58).

Turning circumstances into facts appears most frequently in questions over the uncertainties involved. Could an extended joke about a conspiracy to commit mutiny, if a joke it was, allow a captain to designate "three ringleaders" and declare them "three principal criminals" guilty of mutiny and subject to immediate execution in peacetime? (202–3). When does a ciphered list of names that supports indirect oral evidence of a mutiny constitute an act of mutiny? Did approaching the ship's steward, a petty officer, with a plan of mutiny under a threat of death constitute such an act? Were Cromwell and Small executed through guilt by association?

This last question was a particularly difficult one. Hard evidence against Cromwell and Small, evidence beyond the observation of their friendly contact with Spencer and minor insubordination, did not exist as to their guilt. Spencer had even said, in what he thought would be his "last words," that Cromwell was innocent and Cromwell would insist on it right up to the moment of his execution (203).

Worse, were the two sailors hanged with Spencer because, as Mackenzie observed, "the three chief conspirators alone were capable of navigating and sailing" the *Somers* without officers (203, 74–75, 143)? Could you hang three men to show the rest of a suspected crew that they no longer had the means to carry out a successful mutiny? Worse still, how sure could the captain be that unrest in the crew had anything to do with mutiny when it was just as logical for that unrest to be keyed to their anxiety over loose accusations coming in their direction? As more and more people were arrested and placed in irons on circumstantial evidence, wouldn't the average uneducated sailor fear that he might share the same fate as the first three, and then others, who had been placed in irons?

The questions continue. What was one to make of Philip Spencer, the nineteen-year-old boy/man at the root of the problem? Captain Mackenzie did not help his case by admitting on the record that he told the doomed midshipman "it was not in nature that his father [Secretary of War John Canfield Spencer] should not have interfered to save him" if the *Somers* took the conspirators into port. Amazingly, Mackenzie then added words repeated at trial and all across America: "For those who have friends or money in America there was no punishment for the worst of crimes"; hence "the best and only service he [Philip Spencer] could do his father was to die" (204).

At trial the hanged midshipman would figure either as a man or an errant boy, depending on whether one stood for or against Mackenzie. Either way, the subject was a melodramatic one. Spencer had previously committed acts that amounted to conduct unbecoming an officer, including physical run-ins with other military officers, alcoholism, and breaches of duty in which he was the clear instigator, all of which would have led to severe reprimands and maybe even expulsion from the navy but for the quiescence of higher authorities intimidated by having to answer to the notoriously irascible secretary of war. Mackenzie had been impolitic but not wrong on this issue. John Canfield Spencer knew no limits in his support of his wayward son and would throw all official propriety aside in seeking to prosecute Mackenzie in civil court for the murder of his son.

Philip Spencer had failed to progress in two different colleges, had been in and out of a series of drunken public scrapes, and had even stolen money and other items from his own family. Forever saved from his transgressions, he had no idea or compunction about where bad behavior must stop. Today, he might be classified as a juvenile delinquent who might grow out of adolescent difficulties. In 1842, he was an officer and a gentleman expected to behave as one with expected penalties levied if he did not.

But if the divide between man and boy worked well at sea, it became less clear on shore, in court, and in hindsight over the extremity of the penalty inflicted. At least one subsequent account would refer to "the murder" of "the high-bred boy." Philip Spencer, according to William H. Seward, then governor of New York, must have been innocent of serious wrongdoing: "I should as soon have expected a deer to ravage a sheepfold." Seward relied on how "friends know our children."[10] What could these words mean against so much evidence of Spencer's bad conduct? It helps to realize that the United States of the 1840s was on the cusp of changes in its thinking about how to raise its young.

The shift, slow but inexorable, inched away from the hardheaded vocational apprenticeship of young children at an early age toward a domestic concept of nurtured development in the home, not in the workforce.
The plan to educate juveniles through long sea voyages bespoke the earlier
vocational orientation, but the U.S. Navy had little interest in dwelling on
that educational policy following the *Somers* affair. Commentary about the
trial would therefore emphasize a more sympathetic, tender, familial side in
favor of Philip Spencer with help coming, oddly enough, from Mackenzie
himself.[11] The reasons for that help are complicated and turn on a literary
phenomenon with national implications.

Not least amidst transformations about childrearing was a growing belief that the safety of the nation itself might be in danger from the
changing times. Would the young be ready to guide a country that seemed
headed in less exalted directions than its earlier history? Story, sermon, and
essay raised these problems with metronomic regularity during the antebellum period.[12] Much, it was believed, depended on the proper education
and normative formation of new generations that had less knowledge of
republican foundations. It was imperative that a virtuous country produce
a virtuous progeny.

Was that happening? Everyone in America worried about the answer.
The behavior of Philip Spencer, whether illegal or not, underlined the question. He was the son of an important national leader. Where, if not from
such an exalted source, was new leadership to come? Mackenzie would not
be alone in raising these questions through familial discourse. But could
one take Mackenzie at his word when it turned into so many words and
self-serving ones at that?

Here it is telling that Mackenzie's rise in the navy had been aided by an
ancillary rise. He was a well-known author of naval history and travel books,
and these publications won him gratifying friendships with such leading
writers as Washington Irving and Henry Wadsworth Longfellow. From the
other side of the lists, they made him a formidable enemy in James Fenimore
Cooper, another literary titan. The two men had clashed earlier over their
accounts of the Battle of Lake Erie in the War of 1812. Recognitions within
these lofty circles clearly mattered to the captain of the *Somers*. Events would
show they mattered at least as much to Mackenzie as his naval rank.

The charges against the accused were serious ones. Still, Mackenzie could
not keep himself from taking advantage of the literary opportunity before

him. As soon as he arrived on shore, he wrote out a passionate, highly sentimental account of mutiny aboard the *Somers* with his own agony as the
centerpiece of concern. The mutiny became a melodrama in his hands, and
we need to understand why. The controlling example before this eager storyteller was a greater melodrama known to all who thought about ships:
the famous British mutiny of the *Bounty* in 1789. In popular lore, that
mutiny had been provoked by behavior of the notorious Captain William
Bligh. Mackenzie wrote at such length to prove he was no Captain Bligh!

Thirteen thousand heartrending words would pour from Mackenzie's
pen recounting his own personal distress aboard the *Somers*. All of them
were part of the court record, and they would lead his own counsel, Theodore Sedgwick, to lament every one of them. Sedgwick recognized "a dia-
bolical document" when he saw one. He knew it would cause no end of
legal difficulty, and it did for both lawyer and client.[13]

From another perspective, however, that of the relation of courtroom
to community in antebellum America, Mackenzie's account is a culturally
grounded text of significance. His reliance on the literary impulses of his
day opens into the emotional registers of the time and into the shape that
legal conflict would take.

The extraneous words of a defendant at trial have artifactual significance
for both sides in a dispute, and this defendant's overly expedient account
of a presumed mutiny lent itself to diametrically opposite conclusions.
Was Mackenzie the kindly, caring leader who sacrificed himself for flag and
country as he represented himself, or was he something of a fool, an incom-
petent captain, a poor educator, and an inadequate parental surrogate who
lost control of a ship full of youngsters?

Either story would attract attention. Both fascinated a magazine readership steeped in combinations of patriotic discourse and domestic melodrama. Competing stories make a high-profile trial. They occupy mutually
exclusive discursive space in advocacy. Only one story can win, but in their
conflict both must intrigue for a community to fight over them with the
prolonged enthusiasm that defines a high-profile trial. That happened in
the *Somers* affair and continued long after legal closure.

Mackenzie's account wallowed in stereotypical thinking to explain his
situation, and the power of the impulses he tapped would dominate the
legal narrative in public understanding. In play were an obvious national
narrative, a bizarre familial narrative, and a prescient abolitionist narrative.

The priorities given to each would divide social, intellectual, and political elites from Boston to the nation's capital, with New York City at the epicenter. Some of that expansive range in commentary was Mackenzie's fault, but not all. Everyone, it seemed, needed an external understanding to decide on the law. The nineteenth-century understandings available were the ones that Mackenzie had tapped.

Adding to confusion and cross-purposes, the legal narrative would empower the extraneous narratives that overtook it, and for that reason, we begin with it. The court of inquiry and court martial faced special difficulties on strictly legal grounds. Neither legal proceeding could rely on strictly statutory terms or case precedent. Mackenzie had clearly broken military law when he hanged Spencer, Cromwell, and Small. The relevant legal articles of the naval code called for a formal court martial proceeding before anyone accused of mutiny could be put to death.

Mackenzie's actions, based on the sought recommendation of his hastily convened senior officers aboard ship, did not meet the level of procedural integrity required by law, and that was particularly true in peacetime.[14] Mackenzie realized as much himself when he wrote "in the necessities of my position I found my law" (203). Claims of necessity are, of course, the very stuff of story.

The questions that the initial inquiry and court martial had to answer were twofold, and both turned on a dimension of necessity that made them speculate beyond the law. Was Mackenzie justified in hanging his crewmen? If so, and backtracking in ways that implied some procedural confusion, what could justification mean when killing others beyond established law? Mackenzie answered these questions by wrapping his actions in patriotic discourse. "Their lives were justly forfeited to the country which they had betrayed, and the interests of that country, and the honor and security of its flag, required that the sacrifice, however painful, should be made" (203).

Easily said, but was wrapping oneself in the flag sufficient? Even Mackenzie worried about the answer. The sentence just before his justification of necessity raised prospects meant to alarm the court and the public beyond the court. The *Somers*, if commandeered and turned a pirate ship, would have roamed the seas bent on mayhem and plunder. Fear of piracy dogged the period, and Mackenzie knew how to give that fear maximal effect. In earlier language, he had warned that the conspirators, if they gained control of the *Somers*, had planned to attack commercial shipping as a pirate ship. They would as part of their plan "destroy every vestige of the captured vessels, after having removed what was useful" (203, 195).

The "useful" tag in this statement contained a salacious detail. Most crew and passengers of a captured vessel, like the loyal members of the *Somers* crew, would be murdered directly or made to walk the plank, but not all! The conspirators intended "to select such of the female passengers as were suitable and after they had used them sufficiently to dispose of them" (195, 11). "Used them sufficiently"? Not for the last time, women, nowhere in evidence aboard ship, occupied a position of prominence in debates over the *Somers* affair.

In the face of these horrendous details, could Mackenzie *think* these things could happen or did he *know* they were *about* to happen? Those for Mackenzie assumed the first standard of proof, while those against demanded the latter, but neither standard lent itself to a straight legal answer. J. W. Wales's account of his two-hour conversation with Spencer, relayed through the purser, Mr. H. M. Heiskill, then to Lieutenant Gansevoort, and on to the captain was hardly evidence of an imminent mutiny, but it was evidence of the possibility. The message in code found in Spencer's locker was more evidence, but how definitive was that evidence and worthy of what reliance?

Alternative forms of explanation beyond law were needed by both the prosecution and the defense to explain the difference between an overreaction and justified punishment. Did the captain and his officers panic by making a mountain out of a molehill or, badly outnumbered by an increasingly recalcitrant crew, did they stop a mutiny that had begun to take place? A last fact, one of geography, made the question doubly important.

The *Somers* had been more than five hundred miles from its home port, more than two-weeks sail away, at the time of the executions, but the ship had been close to an English port on the Caribbean island of St. Thomas, where the *Somers* would dock for a matter of hours in the night just three days after the hangings. Mackenzie did not seek to make the port in St. Thomas before executing the so-called conspirators. Nor did he ask for help from British authorities after arriving there in what he still conceived to be a dangerous situation aboard ship during his brief stop. Why not?

The law could not answer such a question. Left to itself, though, the military court could draw the conclusion that Mackenzie and his officers had misconstrued the degree of necessity and might be found culpable. Why had they acted so precipitously just three days from available assistance? There had to be answers to this question to counter the naval legal code with its insistence on an official trial instead of a summary sentence. "The law of necessity" covered only part of the distance to St. Thomas.

There were three possible answers at trial over why St. Thomas could not provide available succor, and all pushed the court into further realms of speculation. On the basis of very little evidence, Mackenzie and his officers claimed first that the conspirators had chosen the days right before the scheduled arrival at St. Thomas to launch their mutiny (42, 65). Second, and related to the first, the officers repeatedly insisted that the ship could not possibly have made port before the mutiny took place.[15] All well and good as claims of sincerity, but these replies basically repeated already questioned beliefs about a mutiny in progress.

Something more was needed, and the need took the officers of the *Somers* further and further afield from law. Their third answer opened into a national narrative where all could participate on their own terms without expertise in law. The honor of the navy was in question, and it extended easily to the honor of the nation.

Court proceedings made all of this clear. "Why did you say you would sooner go overboard than seek protection in St. Thomas?" the prosecution asked acting Master Lieutenant Matthew Perry. Part of Perry's answer reached back to the first two answers offered: "[because of the conspiracy] it would be an impossibility to take the vessel into any port." The rest of it reached wildly beyond the situation. He responded, "Because I thought it would be a disgrace to the United States, the navy, and particularly the officers of this brig; my reasons were that if an American man-of-war could not protect herself, no use in having any" (66).

Such extreme logic led to correspondingly extreme replies. The naval judges on the court were just as quick to raise the ideal of honor. "After the discovery of the intended mutiny, and before the execution of the ringleaders," asked one judge, in a question that assumed what the court was supposed to prove, "was the *Somers* in a state to sustain the honor of the American flag, on the event of her going into action?" The answer? "She was not" (56). These comments and others like them, offered first by Mackenzie, sold well enough in military court.[16] Elsewhere they raised doubts.

A code of honor is never really law. Praise for the honor of officers, ship, and nation did not sound quite right against the sacrificed lives of three citizens. Nor was that all. Too much talk of naval honor suggested a military court protecting its own and itself.[17] How far could a national narrative go in giving a credible explanation of events in court? Certainly Mackenzie was not above unseemly use of it. Moments after the execution, with some of the crew in tears and with the warm bodies still swaying above him, Mackenzie demanded that all aboard "cheer the ship." "I gave the order, 'Stand by, to give three hearty cheers for the flag of our country;' never were three heartier cheers given," the captain testified (207).

Today, citizens save their highest respect for powerful military services when thinking about governmental authority. In the antebellum period, most Americans still feared standing armies, military bustle, and a Caesar who could subvert the republic.[18] The desire for civilian control in a libertarian legal tradition remained strong, and it led to calls for a civilian federal or state court to try Mackenzie. Those calls would become action when John Canfield Spencer and Samuel Cromwell's widow, Margaret Cromwell, tried to have Mackenzie charged with murder in federal and state courts. They failed, but not before enormous amounts of energy were spent on the controversy in and out of courts of law.[19]

Even now newspaper furor over jurisdictional conflict arises when a military officer is charged with conduct outside of prescribed military law.[20] Back then, it would pull the leading judicial figures of the nation into the fray. Justice Joseph Story of the Supreme Court, the most eminent legal figure in the country in the early 1840s, thought "the circumstances would form a complete defence for a homicide on shore, in the view of an enlightened civil tribune; *a fortiori*, they would at sea, on shipboard, and under the stern laws of war."[21] Story's only challenger for preeminence agreed with him. The chancellor of New York, James Kent, "delivered an elaborate opinion that the circuit court of the United States for New York cannot lawfully take cognizance of the case."[22]

Executive authority, by comparison, remained eerily quiet. The overt antagonism between two powerful cabinet members, with an especially weak president presiding over them, made silence the official policy. Enraged over the death of his son, the splenetic Secretary of War John Canfield Spencer fought repeatedly with Abel Parker Upshur, secretary of the navy, who was in charge of the proceedings in the inquiry and court martial of Mackenzie. Ostensibly over them, John Tyler, the tenth president, proved incapable of mediating this conflict.

Tyler, it has to be remembered, was the first vice president to succeed to the nation's highest office through the death of an incumbent president, William Henry Harrison. He was known by the withering epithet, "His Accidency." "A calculating and devious politician," one always "positioning himself to avoid political minefields," Tyler had been a Democrat who opportunistically switched parties and joined the Whig ticket to run with Harrison, a war hero, on the winning campaign slogan, "Tippecanoe and Tyler Too." An afterthought to balance the ticket and a party renegade, Tyler was also a slaveholding Virginia aristocrat who had temporized on slavery and everything else to get where he was. He pleased no one in the high office that he had so assiduously sought.[23]

Connections were easily and loosely drawn in the national narrative. Tyler symbolized weak leadership in a country that felt itself without a strong hand in control of the ship of state. The nation, like the *Somers*, seemed without direction. Although political parallels to Mackenzie's management of his ship played well for those who wanted to find him guilty, they inserted heat rather than light into the debate. The national narrative each side deployed resembled the legal narrative that each side used. Both were loudly invoked, but neither brought satisfaction or explanation to a puzzled nation. Enter a familial narrative that no longer seems bizarre when attached to the vexed question of leadership lost or gained.

During these events and debate over them, mothers figured with astonishing frequency aboard a ship without mothers anywhere in sight. The key to the discrepancy between language and fact came first in an aside in Mackenzie's narrative of events. "I have no respect for a base son of an honored father—on the contrary, I consider that he, who by misconduct sullies the lustre of an honorable name, is more culpable than the unfriended individual whose disgrace falls only on himself" (196). How far did Midshipman Spencer's disgrace reach beyond him and to whom? "The circumstance of Mr. Spencer being a son of a high officer of the government" had the effect of "enhancing his baseness" in Mackenzie's estimation (196). Honor falling into disgrace and culpability identifying baseness became touchstones in a familial narrative that carried well to the issue of leadership. Philip Spencer's behavior and the reasons for it were the ultimate puzzles to be solved in the *Somers* affair.

Mackenzie's words forced this issue back on the Spencer family. If the honored but famously tough-minded father and busy secretary of war could not be held responsible for his son's "baseness," what of the despairing mother who might die when she heard what happened? About to be executed, Spencer invoked her in these terms: "This will kill my poor mother." As the controlling melodramatist, Mackenzie falls away in stunned silence before this sudden knowledge. "I was not before aware that he had a mother" (204).

Really? Mackenzie knew full well of the honored father, and Elizabeth Spencer was an accomplished socialite and energetic hostess on the Washington scene as the wife of a leader in President Tyler's cabinet. Yet, in keeping with the familial narrative, Mackenzie staggers back and recovers slowly "from the pain of this announcement" (204). Devastation of a mother always sells a sentimental tale. Alongside Spencer, we also have the forlorn Elisha Small, who greeted the news of his sentence with similar sentiments in Mackenzie's account: "I have nobody to care for me but my poor old mother, and I would rather that she should not know how I have died" (204).

Mothers in these and other passages are dangerously frail but mysteriously empowered. The feminine ruler of the domestic sphere was fixed and ascendant in American understanding by 1842, even if the paradigmatic text that summarized its full impact on leadership came later in 1847 with Horace Bushnell's "Views of Christian Virtue." Bushnell's essay contained a message already delivered many times from the pulpit.

Bushnell, "probably the most influential American religious thinker of the nineteenth century," summarized what the nation had come to feel. He wrote of "domesticity of character," where the parent—and especially the mother—presided over "those humble, daily, hourly duties, where the spirit we breathe shall be a perpetual element of power and love bathing the life of childhood." He saw "the house, having a domestic Spirit of grace dwelling in it"; it was "the church of childhood."[24]

Mothers, spiritualized in the cult of domesticity, were the natural keepers of that first church in the home. So how had Elizabeth Spencer failed this her youngest child? Aboard ship and therefore by her role in the earlier life of Philip Spencer, she represented shame and despair in the face of her husband's lost honor. In the realm of Mackenzie's story, her fate resided in his use of the words of her son. Implicitly but logically, Mrs. Spencer would be undone by the knowledge of having failed to nurture Philip Spencer in the Christian path of virtue that could have made him the leader he deserved to be.

The epigraph to Bushnell's "Views of Christian Virtue" comes from Ephesians 6:4: "Bring them up in the nature and admonition of the Lord." Then this: "But suppose there is really no trace or seed of holy principle in your children. . . . Have you nothing to blame in yourselves, no lack of faithfulness, no indiscretion of manner, or of temper, no mistake of duty, which with a better and more cultivated piety, you would have been able to avoid?" Against this nightmare in childrearing, Bushnell posited an organic concentricity of engagement and responsibility; it moved from the family, the church, and the school toward the state, an organism propelled from the start by "the moral agency of the parent."[25]

Mackenzie underlined his own version of this familial narrative with an accusation of Spencer, which he tied to the national narrative: "I informed Mr. Spencer that when he had been about to take my life, and dishonor me as an officer[,] . . . it had been his intention to remove me suddenly from the world in the darkness of the night . . . without a moment to utter one murmur of affection to my wife and children, one prayer for their welfare." Full orchestration of the familial narrative came with the execution. Spencer's life "was now forfeited to his country," but he would have the opportunity not given to Mackenzie in Spencer's plan of mutiny. "If there yet remained to him one feeling true to nature," Spencer would be allowed to leave a proper word for his parents (203).[26]

What should that message to the parents be? Coming in his final hour to an acceptance of Christian virtue that had been encouraged by Mackenzie, and only after forgiveness had been procured all around, Philip Spencer intoned, "I feel sincerely penitent, and my only fear of death is that my repentance may be too late." When urged by Mackenzie "to send some words of consolation in so great an affliction," especially words "for any one whom he had injured to whom he could yet make reparation," Spencer completed the familial narrative: "I have wronged many persons, but chiefly my parents" (204).

Captain Mackenzie, the punisher, transforms himself in these prolonged moments into guiding pastor, priestly confessor, evangelical converter, and surrogate parent. In seeking the forgiveness of all concerned, he went even further. Of Small, the least of the conspirators, if serious conspirator he had been, Mackenzie wrote, "I felt that it was yet necessary to my comfort to receive the assurance from his own lips" (206). Against such emotionalism, he also realized a sentimental tale works best by what is left out. The actual execution of the conspirators interrupts Mackenzie's emotional familial version of events for just the briefest of sentences couched in passive and objective voice: "The word was accordingly given, and the execution took place" (207).

One goal in this narrative would prove futile. Mackenzie sought to propitiate Spencer's "honored parents," particularly the "distinguished father, whose talents and character had raised him to one of the highest stations in the land." Mackenzie never knew when to stop. Using the example of the now dead midshipman, he added a cautionary tale before the crew again in the record. "I spoke of the distinguished social position to which this young man had been born; of the advantages of every sort that attended the outset of his career, and of the professional honors to which a long, steady, and faithful perseverance in the course of duty, might have raised him" (207).

The familial narrative explains the absence of leadership in Philip Spencer, but it ends in shame, regret, and implied blame for the family above him. There was, however, a nuance in all of this excess. Did Mackenzie realize how cleverly this ploy helped the uncomfortable naval officers who, in overseeing the charges against him, were seeking to contain a naval scandal? The embarrassing question of a failed policy in naval education for new sailors could be subsumed. It could be pushed back to the earliest period of character formation, back to Bushnell's "plastic nature of childhood."[27]

Watching all of these narratives unfold, sometimes sitting on the bench alongside the military judges who invited him to join them, the renowned New York diarist Philip Hone saw another story at work. In one of the shrewdest comments on the case, he wrote "there is no middle ground in this business; it was altogether right or altogether wrong."[28] These words recognize the rhetorical polarities in adversarial argument despite middle ground in actual circumstances. Mackenzie had to be either right or wrong. But Hone knew the same polarities dominated another vein in the parlance of the times. Another strict normative divide challenged the nation itself, and it too was alive in the *Somers* affair. Abolitionist thought relied on the same bifurcations.

The Missouri Compromise of 1820 created a brief middle ground over slavery while the nation argued over whether its peculiar institution was altogether right or altogether wrong. The compromise prohibited slavery north of the 36° 30' parallel except for the boundaries of the proposed state of Missouri. No one really accepted the artificiality involved. It left the country nervously half slave and half free. Soon enough, the ideological hypocrisies in the arrangement would come apart. A temporary solution, a running sore in the body politic, the Missouri Compromise made sectional strife fester into the 1840s, and that strife took the form of growing abolitionist opposition to slavery in the North.

The political instability explains one of the real puzzles in the *Somers* affair. Figures like Charles Sumner and Richard Henry Dana Jr. normally would have been thought to side with the sailors in such a case. Both antislavery men drew analogies between the treatment of sailors and slaves, and Dana, in *Two Years Before the Mast* (1840), had published a mesmerizing account of the misery of common sailors under the absolute sway of sea captains. The practice of flogging sailors automatically called to mind the same punishment in slavery. Yet both men were among the staunchest supporters of Captain Mackenzie despite his use of flogging as a form of discipline aboard the *Somers*.

Sumner and Dana insisted that Mackenzie had been justified in his actions, and they rose to his defense. Dana's experience and knowledge of sea life made him an especially forceful and popular advocate in discussions of the case. Several factors explain their support and that of other noted antislavery figures, such as Mackenzie's lawyer Theodore Sedgwick and Sedgwick's more famous relation Catharine Sedgwick, a popular novelist who wrote of republican motherhood in the domestic sphere.[29]

Like Mackenzie, many members of the social and intellectual elite thought Philip Spencer had deserted his class through the "baseness" that Mackenzie had identified. Spencer, they felt, deserved the punishment he had received. "Among the educated people, in the professions, and in what we call in America, the upper classes," Dana wrote Mackenzie, "you were (you must excuse me the indelicacy of a direct compliment to a stranger) a hero, and not a hero of the sword, but the hero of moral conflict."[30]

The move from martial to normative identifications in these words is instructive. If there was no social excuse for Philip Spencer in falling so far below the behavior expected of his class, a broader accusation clinched the elite's opposition on moral grounds. Spencer was more than a gentleman turned pirate. He had planned to use the *Somers* to profit from the slave trade. He meant to subvert the very purpose of a ship created to prevent that illegal trade.

Nothing could justify these motives in abolitionist thought. Again and again, in recognition of a class opprobrium that also reached the issue of slavery, Mackenzie and his officers overrode the objections of the prosecution in their effort to connect the charge of mutiny to the conspirators' interest in slavery.[31] The power of this tactic in a trial that reached a national audience can hardly be overemphasized.

Slavery was *the* forbidden governmental subject, the thing to be avoided in political office whenever possible. Congress had received over 130,000 petitions calling for the end of slavery in the 1830s, and the divided House of Representatives responded by barring discussion of such petitions in session after session with renewals of the prohibition into the 1840s. These "gag rules" made trial cases important by default. Courts of law, unlike legislatures and executives, had no choice but to treat the issue. They had to deal with slavery as cases came before them. The contradiction of owning human beings in a country governed by democratic rule of law took hold here. Fugitive slave trials would fuel abolitionist thought until the very different trial of John Brown made it a potent political cause throughout the northern states.[32]

Here, in essence, was the third and most compelling reason for support of Mackenzie among the abolitionist elite. The unwelcome compromise and general paralysis of Congress, alongside a weak and detested slave-owning president, caused figures like Sumner and Dana to deplore the lack of authority and action in the federal government. Those against slavery had no reason to expect state-level action against the institution anywhere in the South, and they rightly feared its spread into the Western territories. Hope lay in a stronger federal executive. Only a constitutional amendment guided by a firm president would bring down slavery and, in their view, save the union. Not until 1865 would that happen.[33]

In this frame of reference, swift action by Captain Mackenzie may have saved the *Somers*, and if so, he represented the kind of federal authority needed to save a ship of state foundering under the taint and divisions of slavery. The moral fiber of the republic was at stake aboard the *Somers* and in the nation. The threatened rebellion aboard ship had its parallel in the threatened secession of the South over slavery.

Abolitionists, like nationalists and the naval officers in court, could couple their own theme to the honor of the flag. Everyone for Mackenzie needed a normative claim that could rise above the suspect argument of necessity. Dana was one of many who saw the vital importance of establishing Mackenzie as a moral and intellectual force beyond his feckless actions and the sentimental story he told the court: "He has every mark of a calm, self-possessed, clear-minded man, entirely free from that dashing, off-hand or assuming manner which sometimes attends the military button.... He is more noted for conscientiousness, order and thoroughness, than for imagination or enthusiasm."[34]

A rather different captain of the *Somers* emerges in this description, and "if the officers were morally certain of an outbreak," they had to act. Primacy belonged to "their solemn duty as public officers, at all hazards to prevent this vessel's becoming a pirate, in the hands of men who would have the power and the will to commit the most dreadful atrocities of which we can form any imagination." As in abolitionist thought, moral certainty justified action.[35]

Charles Sumner wrote in a similar vein: "It is sufficient, if it be shown that the Commander, in taking the steps that he did towards the suppression of the mutiny, acted in good faith, even supposing subsequent knowledge may have made it evident that he erred in judgment." Mackenzie *thought* he was right, so the "*actual* guilt of each one of the three persons executed" did not have to be found. "It seems to us, most clearly," wrote Sumner, "that this is not essential to his justification in any point of view; certainly it is not requisite to his legal justification." Most clearly? Certainly?[36]

An *apprehension* of mutiny on the part of Mackenzie sufficed, legally invested as he was, in "sudden and indefinite powers to meet a peculiar emergency." The extent of power claimed here is staggering unless one remembers the abolitionist context. So certain is Sumner that "we have forborne all inquiry into the guilt of Spencer, Cromwell, and Small, believing that it is irrelevant to the determination of the merits of the defence."[37] How could mere unsubstantiated belief by the captain of a ship justify the execution of three men? The answer came in many paragraphs, but it could be summarized in two words: national security.[38]

Sumner's version of American vulnerabilities, like so many others, sought to scare a citizenry into passive acceptance of the power needed to strengthen the state. It culminated in a nightmare vision of the *Somers* as pirate ship. "Like a baleful meteor, it shoots over the troubled ocean, with unwonted fears perplexing the navigation of the world. . . . It arrests the commerce of the country, floating on every sea." Arrest accomplished, it destroys everything in sight. "It fastens upon one of those stately ships . . . the gentle vessel, gay with the beautiful and the cherished of the land, bearing to foreign shores wives in the fresh morning of a husband's love, and maidens the light and joy of happy household hearths." All become "the pirate's prey."[39]

This particular fusion of national and familial narratives worked well, appearing as it did in the prestigious *North American Review*. The urgency of its message becomes clear by analogy. Sumner's "baleful meteor" of a pirate ship precedes similar tactics of raised apprehension often used in the twenty-first century. Mutiny aboard the *Somers* worked on the public mind much like potential terrorist hijackings of airplanes or thefts of intercontinental ballistic missiles or nuclear weapons do today.

People of very different persuasions can be brought together through fear of the unknown. Inventive projection of threats render the unknown too terrible to resist. Consider again Richard Henry Dana Jr.'s description of the possibilities aboard the *Somers*: "men who would have the power and the will to commit the most dreadful atrocities of which we can form any imagination."[40] Against such inchoate uncertainty, the claim of national security can carry all before it, including basic notions of legality.

Nineteenth-century Americans looked for answers depending on their gauge of the dangers facing the country, and gauges differed. Then as now, a fundamental question divided attitudes and responses: where was the line to be drawn between a citizen's rights and protecting the citizenry at large from real or, some thought, imagined dangers? What strikes a reader today is how both supporters and detractors of Captain Mackenzie could so passionately claim they were right amidst so many unknowns aboard the *Somers*.

Rhetoricians explain the vehemence in conflict by "the field-dependence of our standards." Opponents argue from established cultural positions and get stuck away from the actual interests that dictate their positions.[41] To reduce conflict one must "focus on interests, not positions." Reconciliation, if it is to happen, occurs through a deeper level of perception. It comes "not in conflicting positions," but through attention to "each side's needs, desires, concerns, and fears" and adapting accordingly.[42]

Why did that spirit of reconciliation fail in the *Somers* affair? The narratives employed—legal, national, familial, and abolitionist—competed with each other even as they came together in numerous, changeable combinations. The variations in these combinations led proponents to disagree with each other vehemently, and that vehemence moved them away from a larger similarity of interests.

Everyone's main concern was arguably the same. Americans shared an anxiety over the validity and future course of the United States of America. How to express that anxiety diverged. Disputants fought over what the country meant to them as opposed to what it was supposed to become without quite realizing how the failure to distinguish between these two levels of concern intensified debate. Differences were really uncertainties. Filtered through legal controversy, these doubts could be transformed into certainties through annoyance and then anger over competing interests in the legal decision.

The symbolic importance of the *Somers* served both sides. Something had gone terribly wrong aboard the ship. No one could deny that much. Terms like "honor," "the flag," and "sacrifice" implied a disgrace that had to be met. Where was blame for the shame in mutiny to be assigned? The need to find fault brought everyone back to the meaning of the country and the country's perceived danger. Had established authority failed or had the rising new generation of Americans run amok? There was no commensurate answer to questions from different expressions of the same national anxiety, and the disparities took discussion toward a more frustrating level. Should national honor and security triumph over legal form?

High-profile trials rarely ease this kind of challenge. The law demands a narrow answer and often gives one, but the spread of conflict frequently defies at least part of that answer by raising unsettled issues in the body politic. That is what happened in the *Somers* affair, and therein lies a cautionary tale.

High-profile trials will always be measures of communal thought. They also shape it in ways that deserve attention. The efforts in the 1840s to make national security a trump card in the legal process seem simple enough today, but they make the *Somers* trial a prism for examining the rhetoric of national security and for thinking about how the same trump card applies in a modern nation-state with vastly greater power and equally vaster security worries and arrangements. It should worry everyone that the same rhetoric of fear is now used to keep results away from full public consideration.

Invading Panama

CIRCUMSTANCE AND THE RULE OF LAW

THE UNITED STATES HAS BEEN at war, though often undeclared, since 1941, and unprecedented military action can shape the identity of a country in unforeseen respects. Such an event took place during the winter holiday season of 1989 when the United States invaded Panama. The invasion was unprecedented in two ways: first, it had the goal of capturing and punishing General Manuel Antonio Noriega, the acknowledged head of another sovereign state against international law; second, it led to a successful trial of that deposed foreign leader as a common criminal under domestic law in a U.S. district court against previous legal policy and doctrine.

Virtually every commentator at the time recognized these novelties, but most approved of U.S. action with minor reservations, and few addressed the implications of what had happened. One of the few that did was Arthur Schlesinger Jr., and it is relevant that he addressed the subject as a historian of the United States, not as a lawyer or political operative. Disciplinary focus counts when people disagree. Schlesinger put his realization as a question: "Does no one give a damn when an American president goes to war on his own as if American foreign policy were his private property?"[1] Why did "no one gave a damn" in 1989, and what has that indifference meant in American understandings when military power is involved?

The invasion of Panama set the table for more complicated invasions of Afghanistan and Iraq a little over thirteen years later. In 1989, then Secretary of Defense Dick Cheney organized the attack in Panama under the name "Operation Just Cause."[2] It was a self-validating label bolstered by five justifications, each of which would have its later parallel in the invasions of Afghanistan and Iraq when he served as vice president under George W. Bush.[3]

The five reasons given for invading Panama, in descending order of specificity, were as follows:

1. General Noriega, ruling in Panama, had conspired with the illegal Medellín Cartel in Colombia to subvert the American "war on drugs," and this made him a security threat as well as a criminal that had to be brought to justice through the unilateral power of the United States.
2. The invasion was necessary because Noriega threatened the Panama Canal.
3. The invasion was "just" because it would make Panama "safe for democracy."
4. The invasion would be "just" because the Panamanian people would welcome American soldiers as liberators.
5. The invasion was a commensurate response to Noriega's own declaration of war against the United States.

Each reason given was suspect at the time as a legal rationale for invasion, and the second, third, fourth, and fifth would soon prove to be factually insupportable; only the first would be tested in court.[4] Nevertheless, military success would overwhelm all questions about the legality of the invasion, and the rapidity of that success would give then President George H. W. Bush a notable and needed boost in domestic popularity and political clout. By a margin of six to one, or over 80 percent, the American people, ignoring widespread criticism from the international community, gave enthusiastic support to President Bush's decision "to invade Panama and overthrow Noriega."[5]

By itself, domestic popularity is never enough to confirm unprecedented governmental action under a rule of law. Legitimation—especially of unprecedented military action at the behest of executive authority— requires legal validation at some point, and validation in this case would center on what to do with Manuel Noriega after he was captured and brought under military guard to the United States. In many ways, Noriega's legal situation would become the numerator to the denominator of invasion. The Panamanian leader's conviction in 1992 would give public form to the larger issue.

What was to be done with Noriega? His presence as a captive on American soil raised new questions of law. Was Noriega, "the Chief Executive

Officer" of Panama from 1983 to 1989, a prisoner of war with certain rights? Did the Geneva Conventions apply to him? Could the head of another sovereign state who had been brought by force into the United States by a president acting in his capacity as commander in chief be tried as a common criminal on domestic charges in an American courtroom?

James Madison in *Federalist No. 37* discusses the problem when lines of authority between "the three great provinces—legislative, executive, and judiciary" raise new questions. "All new laws," he writes, ". . . are considered as more or less obscure and equivocal, until their meaning be liquidated and ascertained by a series of particular discussions and adjudications."[6] More than a little was "new" in the Panamanian adventure. What did illegality in *international* law mean in a *national* adjudication? Could making Noriega "a common criminal" answer the uncommon resort of invasion to get him?

The particularity of adjudication in the Noriega case would be considered in the U.S. District Court for the Southern District of Florida under Judge William Hoeveler. The legal conclusion of that adjudication— Noriega's guilt—would then dominate received history and obscure what actually happened in and to the United States between December 20, 1989 (the day of the unprecedented invasion) and April 9, 1992 (the equally unprecedented moment when Manuel Noriega was found guilty and became the first foreign head of state in the nation's history to receive a verdict from an American jury.).

The interface of law, politics, and history leading to *United States of America v. Manuel Antonio Noriega, et al.* gives less confirmation to these events and encourages examination on broader methodological grounds. For if legal decisions at trial (in this case, the conviction of Noriega) supply closure to transgressive events, the applications of law in courtrooms do not always give the best interpretation of the events they have to entertain, and that was true here. In the Panama affair, a wider perspective tells a different story, one with concerns reaching far beyond the Noriega case.

Legal decision-makers try to answer such concerns by claiming their decisions are piecemeal and exact. The functionalism in legal endeavor orders the meaning of events through a human record in lawmaking, but does history work in that fashion? Consider Walter Benjamin's "angel of history," his winged figure caught in the maelstrom of events. It gazes at the wreckage of the past left in its wake as it is swept backward into the future by the winds of time. Central to the conception is amazement over past events.[7]

Law thinks through codes and the case-by-case method to cage the chaotic present and to shape the past to reason. It relies on pattern to minimize historical discrepancy, and the lawyers who study those patterns see continuation and precedent as mechanisms of control. Inasmuch as Madison's imperative in *Federalist No. 37* asks for novelty in meaning to be liquidated and ascertained by particular adjudications, law puts its own historical stamp on previously uncertain events.

These controls in legal determination are as they should be, but they seldom reach for a deeper understanding of events. Even legal history rarely reaches history as those in the second discipline understand it. The first modern historian, Giambattista Vico, saw the legal sphere as a powerful but incomplete means of understanding, and he pinned its limitations on its focus on internal rules.[8]

The critic Kenneth Burke, echoing Vico, explains that "legality, in all its forms, makes for the 'efficiency' of rational isolation," while protecting itself institutionally through larger frames of reference. We can see this in the way "*individual* judges are felt to act in their *corporate* identity alone."[9] The two-step—the individual articulation of legal thought up against its corporate mantle of authority—easily turns into holistic social explanation. A particular legal decision comes to stand for the past, for the present, and, until challenged, for all future concerns. The largest problem in *Noriega* is of this nature.

The historical theorist Fernand Braudel makes two crucial observations that apply to this expansive control over thought and events. "It often happens, he writes first, "[that] a whole generation, influenced by strong and rich traditions, can traverse the fertile period of an intellectual revolution without ever being affected by it."[10] American legal thought has been susceptible in this way. It can be centrally engaged and still not see a need for strategic change for what it is.[11]

Braudel's second observation in historical construction ("breaking down time past") concentrates on a different problem of connection, that of *nouvelle sonnante* (a resounding current event or matter of the moment) with *longue durée* (extended movement or understanding across time).[12] Legal investigation is peculiarly vulnerable to simplification in its treatment of this temporal dialectic. The temptations are to concentrate on a seminal

case for answers, or on decisions in the moment to prove an overall consequence, or on a string of cases in a claim of development—approaches that
ignore Lewis Namier's idea of the highest skill in historical study. Namier
insists on "an intuitive understanding of how things do *not* happen."[13]

Law answers, without really answering, by imposing itself through the
record that was said and done, and this does indeed shape history. *United
States v. Noriega* lends itself to just such a linguistic approach, but its
importance turns not so much on what was said and done as on what was
left unsaid. Its significance resides in pages not given, and that is cause for
historical inquiry. Buried in the interstices of Manuel Noriega's trial are
conceptions of the United States of America up for grabs.

Designating Noriega a public enemy in the late 1980s could not be done
without some embarrassment. Panama's military strongman had risen to
power as a longtime ally of the United States. Formal charges against his
ruthless elimination of critics, his terror tactics in suppressing domestic
unrest, and his drug smuggling could not be made without revealing his
longtime collusion of the United States, including under-the-table pay-
ments reaching as high as $250,000 a year, enormous sums at the time.
Noriega's brutal methods were his own. His unseemly success came with
American military, political, and financial support.[14]

During the 1960s Noriega had been trained in counterintelligence at
Fort Gulick, the American installation in the Panama Canal Zone, and in
psychological warfare at Fort Bragg in North Carolina. He worked with
the Central Intelligence Agency (CIA) from the 1960s into the 1980s,
providing information on Cuba, exposing drug operations throughout
Latin America, aiding American-backed guerillas in El Salvador and Nicaragua, and permitting American installations in Panama that violated
treaty obligations.

The State Department's sardonic nickname for Noriega during these
years was "Rent-a-Colonel," but those who used the phrase forgot that to
rent is not to own.[15] Long after he became a known double agent, State and
Defense Department officials protected Noriega from serious inquiry. As
late as the summer of 1985, a year after Noriega had openly falsified election
results in Panama and allegedly arranged for the kidnapping, torture, and
death of his major political foe (Hugo Spadafora), cabinet members in the
federal government ignored direct warnings from the highest-placed diplo-
mats in Panama.[16]

Two decades too late in 2007, the ambassador to Panama during Noriega's rise, Everett Ellis Briggs, revealed the lesson that was never learned. "Mr. Noriega's rise and fall is instructive only insofar as it tells us how the United States should not conduct itself when faced with a thuggish foreign dictator who happens also to have been a longtime intelligence 'asset.' "[17] Noriega still retained official U.S. support in late 1987. However, a sealed federal indictment against him (with the object of seizing him unawares during one of his regular trips to Florida or Las Vegas) backfired when it became public in February 1988. Clumsy efforts in the same month to bribe Noriega into accepting exile also failed.

Noriega responded with a tightened reign of terror against political attempts to replace him. On May 10, 1989, he went so far as to nullify the presidential election of May 7 when it went against his figurehead candidate, and two days later he had paramilitary thugs physically beat winning opposition leaders in the midst of their victory parade. Video images of this assault were broadcast widely in the spring of 1989, forcing the United States to respond to world opinion as well as Noriega.[18]

American pressure began with trade sanctions against a country totally dependent on American commerce, but an induced collapse of the Panamanian economy failed to accomplish its goal. More failures in foreign policy followed. A military coup openly backed and botched by the United States on October 3, 1989, ended miserably when Noriega outmaneuvered the junior officers at the center of the conspiracy and had seventy of them summarily executed. The leader of the coup, Major Moises Giroldi, was tortured at length in Noriega's presence before being finally dispatched.[19]

Two incidents in mid-December 1989 gave the final impetus to invasion. On the December 15, amidst U.S. military maneuvers in the region and growing economic chaos in Panama, the increasingly desperate Noriega announced "a state of war" existed between the United States and his country. The next day, December 16, episodic harassment of American military personnel in Panama led to the kind of tragic incident that turns into a public relations bonanza for controlling opinion. One U.S. marine was shot to death and another was wounded by Noriega's soldiers when a group of marines fled from an aggressive street checkpoint.

Four days later, starting at 12:45 A.M. on December 20, twenty-four thousand American troops invaded Panama, bringing enormous firepower to bear and conquering the country in a matter of hours. Even so, the surprise attack met stiffer resistance than anticipated from Noriega's "Dignity Battalions," and casualties were higher than expected. Twenty-three American troops died, along with three civilians, but the exactitude in these tragedies paled next to uncertainties on the other side. In the wildly contradictory figures released, somewhere between three hundred and four thousand Panamanians also died.

The huge discrepancy in reports of the Panamanian war dead depended on who supplied the body counts, the United States or less official aid sources in Panama. While related figures were also in dispute, the size of them suggests more catastrophe than the United States was officially willing to admit. Some eighteen thousand civilian homes were destroyed, and as many as fifty thousand Panamanians were left homeless in the wreckage of well over $1 billion in property damages.[20]

The overwhelming use of force and quick military victory did not, however, yield the desired result. Noriega, the *raison d'être* for the entire invasion, managed to avoid capture for two weeks even after the United States, searching diligently with an added $1 million bounty on his head, took over his nation. The leader turned fugitive eluded everyone within a tiny sector of the conquered country, and it implied continuing support for Noriega among at least part of the Panamanian population. Why would no one give him up?

Taking stock on the run, Noriega could not have liked the options before him. He faced capture on humiliating terms, elimination by enemy fire, or death at the hands of a mob, but the man that everyone was looking for escaped them all. Armed with an Uzi submachine gun and a hand grenade, on December 24 he managed to slip inside the Apostolic Nunciature, the Roman Catholic Church's embassy in Panama requesting asylum. On Christmas Eve, the Holy See was not in a position to deny him room in the inn.

Noriega was now everyone's problem. He had refused exile and death, the honorable alternatives, and frustration showed in those who had been stymied in the massive manhunt to get him. Military imposition is always cultural imposition, but it took a weird turn in the week that ensued. U.S. troops surrounding the Vatican's embassy played deafening rock-and-roll music for three straight days and nights in a bravado attempt to flush their prey out of his sanctuary; a favorite tune, presumably for its power to taunt, was "Nowhere to Run" by Martha and the Vandellas.[21]

American military prowess had descended into farce. The intrusive music stopped only when the president of the United States, after personal pleas from the Vatican itself, ordered it stopped. Finally, on January 3, after ten days of negotiations involving the Vatican, Nicaragua, the Soviet Union, a quickly installed new government in Panama, and the United States, Noriega agreed to turn himself over to American forces, but only under specific terms and conditions very much in his favor.

Noriega would appear only in the appropriate military uniform that showed his full rank and that implicitly recognized his right to rule over Panama. He could not be put to death, and he was to be treated with all due respect while engaging in a voluntary surrender. Finally, his official captor had to be General Maxwell Thurman, chief of the United States Army's Southern Command. He gave himself up as an honorably overmatched prisoner of war. Faced with one embarrassment after another, increasing ridicule, and needing things to end for both military and financial reasons, the United States agreed to his conditions, and every agreement had legal consequences.

The invasion officially came to an end on the same day with Noriega finally in custody. He was quickly flown by military transport to Florida, where he was arraigned on January 4 on charges of drug trafficking, a sharp reduction in dramatic and political scope. President Bush celebrated the captive's presence on American soil as "a clear signal" in the war on drugs, but the truest afterthought, one that would soon become the main story, took place on February 8, 1990. On that day the United States District Court for the Southern District of Florida renewed its claim of jurisdiction over Noriega on criminal charges.[22]

The official justifications given by President George H. W. Bush for the invasion had the ring of political necessity but a much shakier foundation in law. The United States was safeguarding the lives of its citizens in Panama after that country's declaration of war. It was saving democracy for the people of Panama by putting the presumed winner of the aborted presidential election of May 7, Guillermo Endara, in office. It was meeting a threat to national security by protecting the Panama Canal, and it was seizing Noriega to face criminal indictments for drug-related offenses.

None of these political concerns legally authorized the extremity of unilateral invasion of one country by another. Established international law ran absolutely against the invasion, and related claims by President Bush that the United States had acted in self-defense rang hollow. The disparities were simply too great. An invading Goliath had traveled far beyond its own borders, trampling thousands of innocent people in its path and destroying the infrastructure of an entire country to grab Panama's fugitive version of David—a version with no theological but plenty of political status.

The leading American scholar in international law at the time, Louis Henkin, said as much. The invasion had been "a gross violation" of international law, a conclusion already reached by the United Nations and the Organization of American States (OAS).[23] Nine days into "Operation Just Cause" the UN General Assembly condemned the invasion as a violation of Article 2(4) of the United Nations Charter, which categorically prohibits "the threat or use of force against the territorial integrity or political independence of any state or in any other manner inconsistent with the Purposes of the United Nations." Condemnation came with a hefty majority on December 29, 75 to 20 with 40 abstentions.[24]

Comparable OAS repudiation carried with stronger numbers. The vote in that organization was 20 to 1 with just 6 abstentions—the one negative vote coming logically enough from the United States and the abstentions from weaker states heavily dependent on American support.[25] The OAS charter explains the intensity of this reaction. Article 17 of the charter states that "the territory of a State is inviolable; it may not be the object, even temporarily, of military occupation or of other measures of force taken by another State, directly or indirectly, on any grounds whatsoever. No territorial assertions or special advantages obtained either by force or by other means of coercion shall be recognized."[26]

While those elsewhere thought in terms of law as a control on military power, most Americans accepted the political exigencies as their president decided to articulate them. But what about the bases of those exigencies? Taken one at a time, and beyond the crisis mentality that made them plausible, none of them hold up well to even casual examination.

The threats to Americans in Panama were episodic in nature rather than an aspect of Panamanian policy, and they warranted diplomatic address and international pressure before military action. Panama had *not* declared war on the United as President Bush claimed it had in a press conference on December 21, 1989. Noriega *assumed*, correctly as it turned out, that the United States was about to wage war on Panama, and he made the mistake of acknowledging the assumption as fact. He said a state of war *existed* between the United States and Panama and instructed his legislators to agree with that finding.[27]

Nor had the Noriega regime threatened normal use of the Panama Canal. Although it played well in the United States, "saving Panama" for democracy had even less to do with realities on the ground. The new government in Panama would be a democracy only on paper, just as it had been before. Nine months into it, Guillermo "Billy" Ford, the newly installed vice president, had to admit, "Democracy is only a baby. It hasn't even learned to crawl." More objective observers thought the baby stillborn.[28]

A figurehead after the invasion with very low approval ratings, President Endara owed his place to foreign military imposition and his authority to the same domestic militia that ruled under Noriega. The Panamanian military remained the strongest institution in the country. More than 900 of the previous 1,069 ruling officers were kept in place through a mere exchange of ID cards. The same patterns of corruption continued in daily operations, and despite much talk about success in "the war on drugs," the removal of Noriega had no effect on drug trafficking. Crime actually rose when prisons were opened, with "robbers in post-invasion Panama . . . having a field day."[29]

Against these facts, the United States had one truly credible rationale on which everything hung. Manuel Noriega was someone who deserved to be brought to justice on many counts, but where? By whom? The sleight of hand required to answer these questions depended on reversals of law and politics, on the one hand, and rearrangement of domestic and international orientations, on the other.

Here is how that worked. When captured, the outsized international public enemy and tyrant of Panama shriveled into a common criminal; he was just "another crooked cop" facing legal charges in a federal courtroom.[30] The goal at this level was to normalize treatment of Noriega while minimizing the focus on international complications. Success in that courtroom, the government's conviction of Noriega, then allowed a return to panoramic scale; it put the stamp of approval on the earlier invasion through the closure of legal event. In the words of President Bush, carefully timed for Noriega's conviction on April 9, 1992, "[the invasion] enabled justice to be served."[31]

The reasons *not* given for invading Panama help to explain why the sleight of hand to legalize "Operation Just Cause" was so essential. Bush, as president, could declare "justice to be served" as often as he wanted, but neither his well-timed comment in 1992 nor his original justifications for the invasion in 1989 rose to the level of legal verification. The gap between politics and law over the invasion needed to be answered, and the whole force of modern international law stood in the way.

There was another dimension to the president's needs. In closing the gap between law and politics, it was important that the invasion be *depersonalized* and, again, law was the problem and the solution. Since the beginning of the Cold War, military action in another country has been initiated by a president of the United States with some form of acquiescence from Congress. The formal legality required for warfare—a congressional declaration specified under Article 1, Section 8 of the Constitution of the United States—has not been used since World War II. For more than half a century and counting, the wars of the United States all have been presidential wars.

George H. W. Bush relied on this pattern of executive prerogative for the invasion of Panama. Without seeking prior congressional authorization— he wrote only *after* the invasion had taken place—the president sent a letter to leaders in Congress *notifying* them by way of "report on the deployment of U.S. Armed Forces in Panama" to overthrow the Noriega regime. The degree of prerogative assumed in *reporting* becomes clear in a more casual reference. President Bush tells Congress that he has written "in accordance with my desire that Congress be fully informed on this matter."[32]

Legislative acquiescence followed the usual modern form: a grumbling "yes" with no one in Congress raising a level of objection that seriously questioned the president's actions.[33] Compliance when the executive branch defines an international crisis involving troop deployment has become a *de facto* test of a politician's patriotic integrity. Yes, approval has its limits. The political safety valve for any legislator who disagrees later has been to label questionable engagement "the President's war," a self-serving formulation that should trouble even the users of it.

This personalization of American warfare has not been without insidious aspects. The technology of modern warfare gives the capacity to send large numbers of American troops anywhere in the world almost immediately, and the means often creates the necessity. The related need for perpetual readiness in this standing army magnifies the role of commander in chief within the many duties of the presidential office. This places the effective decision for war in an office that was not expected to hold it to the extent that now applies.

Congress faces military resources and capacities too enormous and widespread to be effectively monitored. Its ability to resist military action is symbolic rather than practical in significance. Congress does retain influence in the self-interested minutia of contracts, which are arranged for politicians with committee clout, but these intimate relations only give the military complex more license. Corruption is everywhere in defense budgets.

Presidents now decide not just how but when and where to engage in modern warfare with predictable results. The pressure to invade Panama was not on the collective federal government anywhere near as much as it was very personally on the president of the United States, and George H. W. Bush was not helped by circumstances beyond his control. A new president in 1989, he was assumed to be a weaker, more suspect figure than his magnetic predecessor and former chief, Ronald Reagan.

Bush, a far more sophisticated thinker in international affairs and a seasoned diplomat before becoming the forty-first president, had that assertive example before him without any of the personal leverage. Worse still, as vice president under Reagan, he was tied to every mistake made in previous dealings with Noriega.

Experience and sophistication in this situation had ironic liabilities. Bush, when he served as U.S. ambassador to the United Nations in the early 1970s and as director of the Central Intelligence Agency in 1976, had direct connections to the policies that advanced Noriega. He had conducted personal interviews with Noriega as CIA director and as vice president, and he had authorized some of the strongman's sordid retainers for hundreds of thousands of dollars. Foreign policy was supposed to be the new president's strength. When economic reprisals and the coup against Noriega failed miserably, both on Bush's watch, they led to speculation about his competence as president.

Throughout 1988 and 1989, media coverage of the dissolving Panamanian situation became very personal, even crude in tone. Panama was everyone's problem but Bush's embarrassment, and it brought mocking attention to "poor George Bush" in the election campaign of 1988 against Michael Dukakis. "Of all the Men of Principle, Bush is the last one who should be up on his high horse right now," wrote the *New Republic* on

June 13, 1988. "He, after all, was part of the administration that knowingly tolerated Noriega's drug trafficking for years."[34]

Many of these jibes questioned whether Bush was "someone capable of leadership."[35] A month before the election, he was "Incurious George," evading the Panama question at every turn. When cornered by reporters into saying anything at all, he was accused of lying about "subterranean dealings with unsavory characters." There were "questions of judgment, competence, and simple honesty," and they raised growing worries about "the nation's future under a Bush administration."[36]

The same articles and many others like them demanded action against Noriega and found Bush wanting, first as a candidate and then as president. Headlines ran "Can We Get It Right This Time?," "Shoot or Get Off the Pot," "Surrender, Manny," and "Get It Over With."[37] On October 30, 1989, after the failed coup attempt, the *New Republic* sneered, "Bush has made ample use of his Presidency as a pulpit, but much of what emanates from it is more bull than bully," and, "As befits a Texan who's really from Kennebunkport, he's all hat and no cattle."[38]

Critics discovered a congenital fecklessness in their temporizing president. His identity was said to welcome "the widespread joke, 'George Bush reminds every woman of her first husband.'" In a contest to explain the best interpretation of the joke, he became "the husband who never recovered from the shock of finding wifey isn't mommie."[39] Bush showed his own awareness by trying to joke about it. "Let the others have the charisma. I've got the class," he remarked in one aside. "What's wrong with being a boring kind of guy?" he wondered against media derision about "a wimp factor."[40]

The invasion of Panama changed all of that in an instant. Connecting the search for reputation to a hidden rationale for the attack, Arthur Schlesinger Jr. made it as blunt as possible: "the message intended to be conveyed by Bush's invasion of Panama is 'I'm not a wimp.'"[41] A later biographer confirms the jibe and the assumption behind it. Bush appears there as "stung" by "'wimp' criticism" and tries to rectify it in Panama. The point in this account of the life is that Bush succeeds in the attempt.[42]

This kind of success and the motivations behind it are things to worry about. The extraordinary military capabilities of American armed forces today encourage presidential options in executive management of itself. The press granted President Bush a new identity and gave it a lot of spin from the invasion. *Newsweek* discovered strength under fire. Its lead photograph of the invasion placed its millions of readers looking up at a formidable "commander in chief." Pictorially, Bush stands firmly above with stern face and arms folded. He also responds forcefully: "Yes," he says, "it has been worth it."[43]

Worth it for whom? If the previous reputation of presidential vacillation slipped into the past with the invasion, it was not exactly forgotten. *Newsweek* held onto a whiff of implication. Any further dithering would have meant "a tacit confession of impotence," and the magazine coupled this qualification to a far more troubling one. Deep within its accounts, *Newsweek* quietly observed that justifications for the invasion had little credence; "the incidents cited were mostly pretext."[44]

Despite what would seem to be a serious charge, *Newsweek* nonetheless extolled Bush. He had shown "tight control," great expertise as commander in chief, proper planning ("the President probed and prodded, demanding more and more information"), and the ability to act "without hesitation" in a crisis. "Bush's invasion," as it was headlined everywhere, had somehow made a difference in *the person*. No longer "dogged by the suspicion that he was a little too pliant and passive, not quite his own man . . . not a real leader," the forty-first president had undergone an "apparent transformation from meekness to macho." "Suddenly Bush seems bold and decisive," the magazine applauded, before adding a final accolade, "George Bush has shown that he is in charge."[45]

These views and many others like them in the popular press present a puzzle. How could an invasion costing so much in international prestige and bringing such devastation to so many create a better identity for a president accused of acting mostly on pretext? The issues behind this question open in several directions.

They surface first in the legal forum, where the trial of Noriega could ease questions about the successful invasion only if it, too, proved to be successful. The alternative of losing in court had unthinkable consequences. Failure to convict Noriega would open a Pandora's box of renewed ridicule, and the invasion would devolve into something worse than meaningless. This fear of a "not guilty" verdict was heavy enough to influence the government's behavior in court. The cost of losing was so high, so unacceptable, that federal prosecutors adopted extreme measures and a level of overkill that became problems in themselves.

The same puzzle—praise for the military action against accusations of insufficient reasons for conducting it—had long-lasting implications, and as such, the invasion of Panama reaches beyond any meaning that the trial of Manuel Noriega can provide. What was really at work here? The law in this situation seemed reduced: more symptom than solution, a palliative rather than an answer even as it provided the claim of an answer. The historical problem of method re-enters at this level. How does Braudel's *nouvelle sonnante*, the resounding or special matter of the moment (in this case, the trial of Noriega), inform *longue durée*, or longevity (in this case, an evolving conception of the United States of America)?[46]

No one denied that a trial of Manuel Noriega on criminal charges in an American courtroom involved new legal issues, and skirmishing over the legitimacy of the attempt began long before Noriega's actual capture. As early as the original indictment of February 4, 1988, the United States District Court for the Southern District of Florida, with District Judge William Hoeveler presiding, tried to forestall difficulties with an artful evasion: "Manuel Antonio Noriega was and is a high ranking officer in the military forces of the Republic of Panama."[47]

Noriega, actually *ruling* Panama at the time, countered through counsel on April 28, 1988. He claimed that he could not be prosecuted because of his "unique status as the *de facto* head of a foreign government" and because he was charged with illegal activities taking place *outside* of the territorial bounds of the United States. He could not, therefore, be sought as an "'ordinary' fugitive fleeing United States justice."[48]

Judge Hoeveler in his response agreed and disagreed. His court "and several other District Courts" recognized Arturo Delvalle (the Panamanian president at the time) "as the legitimate head of the Panamanian government," but "despite this official recognition," he agreed that General Noriega had to be treated as "the *de facto* head of the Panamanian government." This confirmed status meant, against government objections, that the judge would exercise his own discretion "in allowing Noriega to present arguments attacking the validity of this indictment and challenging the jurisdiction of the court."[49]

Brought to Miami and formally charged in the first week of January 1990, Noriega immediately seized the opportunity offered him. He challenged the indictment and the jurisdiction of the court on a number of grounds. Taking his time, Hoeveler answered five months later on June 8 with the most important decisions in a trial that would not be resolved for two more years of legal wrangling. Again, as presiding judge, he gave even as he took away.[50]

Noriega argued most cogently that he came to the United States as a captured prisoner of war and was thus not subject to civil jurisdiction or conventional penal conditions. Judge Hoeveler accepted the part of the argument that supplied material benefits but not the part that conferred legal remedies. Noriega *was* a P.O.W. entitled to internment conditions of military decorum, which under the Geneva Convention included inspection by the International Red Cross, separation from prisoners of other countries, exemption from conventional penal discipline or settings, treatment with every dignity of status in place, and the right to appear in uniform. The agreed-upon status did *not* exempt Noriega from charges for illegal conduct that had nothing to do with his military obligations—in this case, drug trafficking.

Safer on American soil than in Panama, the captured Noriega received and reveled in his privileged surroundings. He had a suite with full amenities (including color television), unusual levels of privacy, his own telephone, regular visits from international organizations, the right to appear in court in full uniform, and expansive exercise opportunities. He even joked about these benefits: "Tennis at 11:00. Tea at 3:00."[51]

Although other challenges by Noriega had intricate permutations, they can be summarized quickly. The accused deserved diplomatic immunity as a foreign dignitary. He could not be tried for alleged offenses committed outside of the United States. He could not lawfully face charges based on an invasion that was unlawful under international law. Since both his arrest and the means of taking him had been illegal, no court could claim clean hands in proceedings against him. To conduct a trial under these circumstances would demean the integrity of the American rule of law.

Judge Hoeveler handled each of these claims adroitly, and an initial assertion gave his responses permanent influence. He declared at the outset that the court faced "several issues of first impression"; among them were "the first time that a leader or de facto leader of a sovereign nation has been forcibly brought to the United States to face criminal charges." The trial presented "a drama of international proportions" and a defendant under "difficult circumstances."[52]

A revealing addendum followed, and it qualified the important phrase "forcibly brought to the United States." Hoeveler granted that "the motives behind the military action are open to speculation," adding that "the Government's asserted rationales for the invasion are not beyond challenge and need not be blindly accepted by this Court," but he also refused to offer his own conjectures on the subject. "There are other forums," ran his evasion, "in which complaints about our Government's political activities can be made."[53] Not for the last time, an inextricable connection between law and politics was severed in an arrangement that helped politics more than it helped law.

Some of Noriega's challenges were easier to handle than others. The defendant's criminal activities did have an impact on the United States, and so he was subject to indictment in the United States for them. A request for diplomatic immunity of a high official in a foreign country had to come from that diplomat's head of state. Noriega had never been the official head of state and such a request had not come from the current head of state, President Endara. In any event, Noriega had drug connections in the United States, and could be considered a coconspirator. Even the alleged illegality of Noriega's original arrest presented minor problems. It was "well settled that the manner by which a defendant is brought before the court normally does not affect the ability of the government to try him."[54]

It was the illegality of the invasion under international law that continued to give trouble. Judge Hoeveler handled this ticklish problem by indicating that Noriega, an individual rather than a state entity, lacked standing to raise the objection. He conceded that dodging substance made him uncomfortable. "It can perhaps be argued that reliance on the above body of law [Noriega's lack of standing to object], under the unusual circumstances of this case, is a form of legal bootstrapping."[55]

The circumstances *were* unusual, and it *could* be argued that Hoeveler should recognize not just the form but the substance of legal bootstrapping. What if those "unusual circumstances" included direct governmental illegality on the part of the United States? What control could there be upon such behavior? Who could decide? How clean were the hands of a court that did not decide? The court had no substantive answers to these questions, and Hoeveler's integrity in allowing a glimpse of them forced him toward a larger abdication. The court tried to clean its hands by ducking them in a convenient doctrinal finger bowl.

Noriega argued that "the supervisory power doctrine" should keep a court from dealing with a case that made it an accomplice to governmental misconduct. Forced into this judicial corner, Hoeveler conceded that the doctrine applied to conduct that a court "finds repugnant to fairness and justice and is loath to tolerate." Why, then, did it not apply here? Hoeveler's answer stunned in its scope. "Because the President ordered Noriega arrested 'in the course of carrying out the military operations in Panama,'" Hoeveler writes, "the capture of Noriega was incident to the broader conduct of foreign policy." Foreign policy—the illegal invasion of Panama—trumped legal investigation and hence any real prospect of legal determination! [56]

The powers thus given to the President of the United States were more than sweeping; they were unreachable. "In this case," the court explained, quoting *Marbury v. Madison*, "the decision to send troops into Panama was made by the President in his capacity as Commander in chief, and he is on this matter 'accountable only to his country in his political character, and his own conscience.' "[57]

No matter that illegality might actually be present; it need not be contemplated much less judged. "The Court," Hoeveler concludes, "therefore does not face the task of resolving the exact motives behind the invasion, a question which may well be beyond its expertise and resources." The hedge in this declarative sentence—"may well be beyond its expertise"—lends itself to the referent, "a question." Just how far beyond the court's expertise and resources was American behavior during the invasion?[58]

Hoeveler gives no answer to a question he refuses to ask directly. Instead, he leaves *the idea* of a question hanging by describing a "military war in which innocent lives were unfortunately lost"—a war instigated by the United States. The judge saw no need for an answer. Doctrine can be used to avoid as well as clarify, and here the doctrine of separation of powers gave a prudent exit. "That foreign policy objectives rather than just law enforcement goals are implicated," Hoeveler reasons, "radically changes the Court's consideration of the government conduct complained of."[59]

Looked at closely, the "change" alluded to had more than one "radical" meaning. If a president of the United States is accountable only in his political character and to his own conscience when engaged in questionable foreign policy initiatives, where, if at all, does the subject of law enter when law enforcement goals *are* implicated? Where, if at all, do foreign policy objectives give way to law in a globally impinging world? Judge Hoeveler continued to exclude these questions from the ongoing trial. The conviction of Manuel Noriega would function instead as the last chapter in an American success story.

But success came with a price. With all military and political issues removed by preliminary decisions from the bench, interest in the finding of guilt eclipsed serious concerns over the nature of war powers and unilateral executive action. Internal scandal, elements of farce, and an unforeseen contingency would dominate superficial coverage of the Noriega trial— when it was covered at all in the American press—in the two years that resolution would take.

Delay after tedious delay led most observers to lose interest in everything but the official result. Against the legal complexities, courtroom antics filled the newspapers. In 1990, the government inexcusably risked the challenge of a mistrial when it eavesdropped on telephone conversations between Noriega and his counsel. Prolonged treatment of related issues would reach all of the way to the Supreme Court. In 1991, the screams of Noriega's high-priced but unpaid lawyers dominated press coverage; defense counsel threatened to resign when the general's twenty-million-dollar treasure chest in ill-gotten assets remained frozen in foreign banks. Then, at the end of 1991, Judge Hoeveler required emergency open-heart surgery, forcing yet another postponement for months on end.[60]

Still, the trial remained the available stage for interpreting the Panamanian event even as it was only partially understood. Taking no chances on conviction, the prosecution, with administrative connivance, issued a rash of pardons to coconspirators in exchange for often questionable testimony against Noriega. Many of those rewarded were out-and-out thugs in drug trafficking, men who were demonstrably as bad as the defendant and sometimes worse considering the charges debated before the court.

Major criminals facing life in prison without parole were released after short sentences, granted immunity on murder charges, obtained frozen pension funds, allowed to keep property obtained by drug dealing, enjoyed witness protection plans with their families, and received unspecified means of government support. Each of these testifiers had credibility problems. Only one (who would be impugned) could claim to witness a direct act by Noriega.[61]

A narrower and more politically mundane focus in media coverage could exist because earlier events had been taken off the table. The invasion was never mentioned at trial; the only references to it were implied during jury selection. A preliminary question that Hoeveler asked of every juror was indicative: "I suppose the question that I want to ask you—and I'm having a little difficulty getting to it—is this: is there anyone among you who would let the question of how he [Noriega] was brought here affect you in any way in arriving at your verdict in this case?"

Doubters over such circumlocutions received further assurance from the judge: "There will be nothing, as far as I'm concerned, about this case that has anything to do with politics." Nothing? Not anything? It took a prospective and soon rejected juror to cut to the chase: "We sent our military over there to get this man. I have a hard time. You just don't send our United States army to go pick somebody up."[62] That got to the root of the matter in a way that neither the government nor the court wanted to hear.

Enforced courtroom silence over the invasion allowed the government to have its cake and eat it too. Noriega appeared at trial in the uniform that reminded everyone of the military action required to get him while prosecutors cut him down to size as an ordinary drug offender. As the government explained in opening statements, Noriega was "just another crooked cop," "a small man in his general's uniform."[63] Greater epithets, like "international outlaw" under the Reagan administration, dropped into the eliminated past.[64]

The questions about what had been done in Panama correspondingly shrank with the man diminished in court. On April 9, 1992, Manuel Noriega received a guilty verdict on eight of ten counts with the prospect of 120 years in prison. Prosecutors boasted of "a slam dunk" with the claim "it was all worth it." The attorney general of the United States echoed the president's boast of "victory against drug lords," and the New York Times announced closure for all by headlining " 'Appalling Chapter' Ends for Panama."[65]

It was left to Noriega's chief defense counsel to raise the issues prohibited in court. On the courthouse steps, Frank A. Rubino railed against "the restrictions placed upon us." Finally unleashed from a court gag rule by the verdict, he condemned the invasion as "a modern day version of the Crusades" and warned that "the United States will now trample across the entire world, imposing its will upon the so-called independent, sovereign nations."[66] This prediction, an embittered exaggeration born of defeat, would have future applications. Panama was a glimpse of what would become "the Cheney doctrine of preventive war."[67]

Identifying blame is not the point here. Manuel Noriega was an obvious villain brought to justice, and telling the story of his unprecedented conviction in the United States should not be about finding more villains. The American participants in these events played as their interests dictated from the invasion, to capture, to court trial. People play by the rules of the institutions that they inhabit. The more important story is about communal perceptions—about how a nation has come to think about itself and its obligations.

Something within the *longue durée* of American acceptance of law has changed when it comes to military action. The elements that dictate the way reasoned thought becomes a reasonable conclusion and then legitimate action have shifted. The "ability to trust and to cooperate with other people" under a rule of law remains in place, but it has taken on what pragmatists call a "bad coherence," a complacency in thought that resists existing or preexisting ideals that should apply when questions of legality are in play.[68]

What happened confirmed new directions for those making decisions, greater largesse for military action, new political benchmarks for the public, and legal precedents for how the nation would continue to conduct its affairs.[69] The power of circumstance seemed to control this change in communal thinking as much as individual volition or capacity, the kind of distinction that historians rather than legal theorists want to discuss.

Four factors, each with a deeper background, turned circumstance into need and, all too quickly, into uniform consent: first, the president of the United States felt compelled to act in a unilateral military fashion out of political necessity; second, the president, in acting, received an expected but still extraordinary rise in political and personal capital from the power elite around him, including all leading media sources; third, the American people accepted the invasion with reactions ranging from complacency to enthusiasm; and fourth, the rule of law deferred absolutely to behavior that was highly questionable on legal grounds.

The impact of the *longue durée* might be framed in the following way: Why did such a one-sided military display by the world's greatest superpower count for so much on so many levels when inflicted on an opponent of such weakness and total vulnerability? Military success was a foregone conclusion. Why did a cheap but actually sloppy victory in a questionable context garner so much support in political, military, popular, and legal terms?

The answers to these questions can begin with the way contemporary Americans regard the use of military power within ideological and technological shifts of historic proportions. Since the Civil War, and partially in response to its colossal bloodletting, the United States has moved from a federated republic defined by a right of revolution (curbed only by concepts of justice and the force of law) into a modern nation-state where the test of membership has become one of loyalty.[70]

By extension, victories in war and armed readiness have carried the idea of loyalty toward close identification with military might. There are few Americans today who are not at least subliminally proud of U.S. military power as one core of national identity and, with it, a concomitant right to act positively in the world. The invasion of Panama fed primal urges. In writing about it at the time, a syndicated columnist for the *New York Daily News* summarized the mentality and the problems it presents: "America's message to the world is that we are strong, we are good, we are moral and we will do whatever we think is right. Most Americans will probably agree with this. Just don't be surprised if nobody else does."[71]

The 1980s represent a watershed moment in such thinking. The victorious Reagan presidential campaign in 1980, with its "politics of defense" against the incumbent Jimmy Carter, manipulated the popularity bestowed on American armed forces by emphasizing against the facts that the Carter Administration had neglected America's defense posture.[72] During the same time period, Americans would express greater confidence in their military than in their government or even in organized religion, and this confidence has come to rest in a professional soldiery rather than what had once been a citizen army.

Calls for "victory" and accusations of "defeatism" are now staples in political commentary over military action abroad. "Global America" may be an oxymoron, but it bespeaks powerful sentiments in the body politic and similarly powerful reactions from abroad. Indeed, "global economic and informational systems have not noticeably weakened deeply emotional *nationalisms*—least of all that of the United States." One upshot has been "an upsurge of triumphalism that seemed to display to the rest of the world the most feared features of modern American nationalism: its universalism and its militarism."[73]

Such military chauvinism in international affairs may have been predetermined, the byproduct of victories abroad and the claim of superpower status at home. Be that as it may, the size, readiness, and flexibility of a professional standing army with extraordinary weaponry and stupendous instruments of surveillance have created a new situation entrusted almost solely to executive control to the president of the United States as commander in chief.[74]

The past has not dealt kindly for long with regimes in this situation. History has a way of striking back against military triumphalism. Earlier republicans in the act of ratifying the U.S. Constitution agreed that "the veteran legions of Rome . . . rendered her the mistress of the world." But Madison added a prescient warning: "Not the less true is it, that the liberties of Rome proved the final victim to her military triumphs."[75]

These words are not without some resonance in American history.[76] They should be understood in light of a second warning to those enthralled with military might, power, and weaponry. In still the most comprehensive articulation of American political philosophy, John Jay in *Federalist No. 4* deplores the frequent tendencies of a ruler "to engage in wars not sanctified by justice or the voice and interests of his people."[77] Nor, in a third warning within current mentalities, need such a ruler be guilty of any other vice than too much faith in military might when there is such an enormous capacity within reach.

The necessary requirement of a broad global perspective in leadership easily misreads a world of complexity with multiple needs. Military action has the flavor, if not always the reality, of a clear-cut response and, as the proverbial expression goes, "when your tool is a hammer, everything looks like a nail."[78] The checks and balances on these issues and the mentality behind them are not what they once were.

How will American courts deal with a constitutional imbalance for which there is no end in sight? That is a question to watch after *United States of America v. Manuel Antonio Noriega, et al.* Although Judge Hoeveler in acceding to the invasion of Panama provided no guidelines, he did include some lines from Justice Louis Brandeis's "eloquent dissent" in *Olmstead v. United States*. The words quoted by him from 1928 did not apply to the situation in 1990 so much as they gazed into the future: "In a government of laws, existence of the government will be imperiled if it fails to observe the law scrupulously" and "against that pernicious doctrine [of the end justifying the means] this court should resolutely set its face."[79]

When might that happen? Judge Hoeveler said that a court "may someday have occasion to apply Justice Brandeis' wise words, but this is not that day."[80] *United States v. Noriega* moved away from such a confrontation between law and politics in 1990, and its levels of deference to executive authority made the issue less judiciable on future occasions. By the same token, the growth of military identifications in American culture, the magnified presidential role of commander in chief, and the power of circumstance in the twenty-first century all suggest that the day will come.

Coda

MOST CITIZENS LEARN ABOUT LAW through media sources, cinema, and fiction, and the most intricate and detailed of these recognitions comes through fiction. The great popularity of the courtroom novel today—its regular best-seller status—is one of the features in modern attitudes toward law. Many Americans have come to doubt the fairness of law, and the regularity with which novels project legal corruption in a plot helps to explain contemporary fascination with a genre that used to attract a more select readership.

How that corruption is rendered thus becomes important beyond itself. How realistic are contemporary fictional portrayals of the legal process? The answer is not very realistic, even as the props to make law seem real are very much so. Law and fiction about law both rely on the visual aspects in courtrooms to convey a search for justice. By reducing visual courtroom performance to the simplifying page, the courtroom novel distorts these iconographic aspects for its own purposes, usually ones of protest. The reader interested in law should know how these manipulations actually work.

Meanwhile debate between legal and literary scholars compounds the already vexed relationship between fact and fiction. The professional claim that "there are better places to learn about law than novels" was and remains undeniable if one wishes to learn about "the enforcement of a contract that contains a penalty clause" or any other specific legal application. But what if one is looking beyond that level of particulars? The debate has been fierce at times, so fierce that established figures in law have been called "uninvited guests" when debate on the relevance of courtroom fiction comes up.[1]

These internecine quarrels do have some common ground. Everyone realizes that fictional representations of the legal process have influence on public opinion. Most people do not enter a courtroom, but they do read about them in this way. So the real question changes. "How fairly do novelists' render law?" becomes "How should a reader gauge fairness in those renderings?" The second question is more interesting because of the double bind that it presents. A novelist's first interest centers necessarily on providing entertainment, and this requirement leads in two directions applicable to the question of fairness.

For if courtroom novels raise a problem in legal action by definition, they invariably add a problem in the law itself to generate more concern. Fairly or unfairly? That is the question. A problem created in law had better be realistic enough to hold a reader, and it holds that reader best if the novelist touches a raw legal nerve. The ideal way to do this is to articulate a problem in legal authority that law would just as soon leave unanswered. Moreover, the easiest and often the most subtle device turns on the manipulation of spatial metaphors that expose what remains silent in a courtroom.[2]

These metaphors, "thick descriptions" of scenes in a courtroom, are quickly absorbed, but just as easily overlooked for their actual impact. They shape a reader's perspective on legal behavior and themes in covert ways. They also reach beyond the fiction to question current grounding of law in the world at large.[3] No courtroom novel is without these manipulations, and readers are better served—and perhaps even more knowing citizens— if they know how these devices dictate their surface awareness and inclinations across plot development.

We must first recognize how completely law is dominated by visual and therefore spatial metaphors. Combatants in a courtroom have "standing"; they are seen. The law is "a seamless web." Evidence, a word derived from *evidēns* (that which is apparent), is "presented." Higher courts "review" lower courts. Titles are "searched." Lawyers draw "bright-line distinctions." Constitutional protections emerge from the shadowy realm of "penumbras." A property claim has "color of title," and on and on.[4]

Sight is the most immediately instructive organ of the five senses, and the dependence of law on it, though often overlooked, should surprise no one. Time and again legal authority emphasizes the connection. Why else would judicial decision making insist so compulsively on precision in language through the concept of clarity?[5]

There is more. The reliance of law on the power of the visual only begins in the specificity of descriptive metaphors. The legal process relies on the classification and resolution of conflict within a method that is at once visually frozen and just as visually mobile. It is frozen in that all present must see and accept the forum chosen as the legitimate location for conflict to be resolved. It moves in that a resolution through ceremony must resolve the conflict that identified parties before higher authority have been unable to handle themselves.[6]

In order to convey the legitimacy of these elements in action, law must *show* itself at work in both a fixed and a mobile manner, and its favorite metaphors of spatial representation for doing so are familiar ones. We speak of the "drama" (a cast of settled characters on stage but also an unfolding dénouement) in a courtroom. We hear of the "geometry" (design through structure and principle but toward an ongoing proof) in law. We cannot avoid casting law as a structure (order and ceremony in the unfolding of procedural integrities).[7]

Above all, we are asked to think of "the balance in justice," a metaphor that neatly combines the values of stasis (the scale in equipoise), conflict (the opposing elements that allow the balance), expertise (the skill in achieving it and maintaining it), and human control (the implied figure or hand holding the scale).[8] All of these metaphors are especially useful in relation to each other. They share a reinforcing basis in formation and legitimation, which is to say that they come together on the physical level of display, the psychological level of discourse, and the legal level of unavoidable need.

In physical terms, "the geometry of a courtroom" is all about the balances in play. A judge presides on high and at an equal distance from prosecutorial and defense counsel ranged on either side below. Figuratively, a fair trial can be seen as a vertical equilateral triangle. The exactitude of space between the most active officials suggests the evenhandedness of proceedings taking place there.

The raised platform of the presiding judge reaches down in a series of levels, from the bench to the slightly raised jury box and the counsel tables in "the well" of a courtroom to the rows of lower-placed arranged public benches, sometimes banked, beyond the court railing. Everything about this grid or structure enables spectatorial recognition. The artifacts of note—flags, portraits, tables, even doorways and architectural ornaments—are set to convey balance in justice through their placement.

Psychologically, the same spatial metaphors—drama, geometry, grid, and balance—cohere to suggest the certainty that the law requires of itself in the decisions it makes. No decision can appear to be arbitrary. Legal solutions are tonally about a rhetoric of certainty in the name of clarity no matter how close the previous conflict has been. Consciously or unconsciously, judicial language unifies the metaphors in adversarial debate to secure itself from doubt. Drama, in the oral delivery of a judicial opinion, yields to the satisfaction of a final curtain ringing down on an unhappy event now resolved.

In the language of law, *geometry* lives in the proof offered: *quod erat demonstrandum*. The *grid* finds its place in the generic structure of the judicial opinion as the observable integrity of legal discourse. The *balanced scale* appears everywhere in the act of deliberation as pros and cons are weighed and parsed in a sequential order that leads to the unavoidable decision. Nothing, it must be said, is wrong with these propensities. The law must do what it can to legitimize the answers it supplies against the entanglements that come before it, but these propensities can be misleading when it comes to the mechanics in actual practice.

The spatial metaphors embedded in courtroom ceremony and expository prose conceal a deeper reality that imaginative literature finds and the law tries to hide. The hard fact of adversarial conflict is that it is never pleasant, often ugly, and frequently acrimonious. No one leaves a courtroom enthralled by the ways of law. Asked to comment on "the one thing Americans still don't know about the law," Dahlia Lithwick, reporter on the Supreme Court for *Slate*, answers, "The legal system might be the single worst place to seek 'closure,' whatever closure is. Nobody is ever happy after a trip to court."[9]

A moment's reflection will verify the truth of this statement. Why do disputants in law rarely emerge from the courtroom with the sense of settled resolution that the law proclaims? Consider the situation for what it is. If you have won your case, usually after considerable delay and much expense, you question why it was necessary to go through the process to begin with. Was it not obvious from the start that you should have won, and did you really need a lawyer to get justice? From the other side, defeat is never welcome, and it is twice as expensive, terrible for one's reputation, and sometimes precarious for one's freedom. Most losers in court assume that the law failed to get them the justice they deserved.

Law makes its decisions through prescribed procedural arrangements for both winners and losers, a state of affairs that underscores the frustration often felt on both sides. Faced with everything translated into legal discourse, many disputants have not been able to tell the story the way they experienced it or the way they would like to have told it themselves. The assumed clarity of the judicial decision glosses over these difficulties as the final word that all must accept. Formal record of a trial ends with this final word from the bench both at trial and on appeal.

A courtroom novel seizes on these elements of unhappiness. It has the license, not available in a courtroom, to delve into the underbelly of feelings in conflict against the objectifying rules of procedure, and while law is not always the villain in these fictional renderings, it is rarely the full answer given in court either. The novelist's psychological perspective gives a reader knowledge beyond what a court of law can entertain or ascertain. Most stories of this kind have extralegal solutions or solutions that break legal rules, and they cause the law to look superficial when it is not actually wrong.

The emotional vortices in fiction allow a novelist to find a different answer to the one offered in court or, alternatively, to give the court's decision in a different light. Imaginative interpretation thrives on these tensions. Questioning the limits and rigidities in legal decision making and the partial justice they mete out, the novelist finds flexibility in remedies that might bring a better result.

At work is an aesthetic of contrasts that nonetheless depends on coordination. Samuel Taylor Coleridge in his critical observations liked to distinguish between straight lines and curves when thinking about mechanical and organic forms in nature, art, and thought. Straight lines bespeak reason, order, and rigidity; curves signify motion, energy, and creativity. The straight line represents "confining form"; the curve adds "free life." Together they can form a "perfect reconciliation" in nature and encourage the deepest insight in thought. Proper intellectual use of both promotes "sportive wildness."[10] Think of courtroom fiction as playing with the arrangements in law in a similar fashion.

A novel by C. P. Snow explains how this works, and it is especially useful in its challenge to the constitutive metaphor of balance that so dominates legal thought. *The Affair* (1960) is the last of a series of academic novels set in a mythical Cambridge college named Oxbridge. The narrator, as in the previous stories, is Lewis Eliot, a barrister who moves back and forth between "the corridors of power" of government in Whitehall and the petty but fascinating politics of Oxbridge College.[11]

Eliot has been called in to help solve a case of scientific fraud that threatens to bring scandal to the college and to the British scientific establishment in general—not least because the fraud has been exposed by a team of American scientists. Much of the novel need not concern us. The plot turns on a junior research fellow named Donald Howard, who has been dismissed for submitting a thesis of fraudulent work that does not hold up to proof and examination. Now, at the last minute and for the first time, Howard seeks a second hearing protesting his innocence and placing blame on his former mentor, a beloved figure in the college. Eliot has been retained without fee to be Howard's legal counsel.

The first hearing against the accused, conducted by the tenured faculty serving as "a Court of Seniors," delivered a quick summary judgment condemning Howard before Eliot appears on the scene. Their dispatch sought to keep the scandal within the college while protecting the stellar reputation of Howard's mentor, an eminent and wealthy but now deceased scientist named C. J. B. Palairet. A world authority on his subject, Palairet also left his entire fortune to the college, an act of such generosity that the senior fellows have thought of having a new building named after him at Oxbridge (27–31).

Fraud there has been, but different possibilities can explain it. Either Howard falsified an experiment and presented it as truth or he has taken work from the official notebooks of his supervisor Palairet, with or without Palairet's permission, and published the material. If the latter case and with permission, the false experiments are actually Palairet's. Howard is still at fault for publishing the work as his own and without adequate attribution or confirmation of the findings with his own experiments, but if that is all, the Court of Seniors has come to an unfair conclusion in punishment on insufficient evidence.

To further complicate the picture, the accused in *The Affair* has no redeeming virtues. Donald Howard is a disagreeable lout as well as a narrow careerist who lacks any intellectual sparkle or even serious curiosity about his field. Like many another unpopular defendant, he is unattractive, and it is significant that he remains partially at fault no matter what the verdict. Even his tepid supporters admit that Howard's work "wasn't even second-rate, it was tenth-rate" (343). Snow uses these faults cleverly; they hinder the senior fellows from entertaining any leniency toward one whom they consider a total inferior.

Snow has created a story in which every character in the novel appears unlikable and partial in some way, and this unpleasantness is reified in a final decision. In the end, the Court of Seniors acts mostly to protect itself. It reverses its previous dismissal but does not restore the time lost on Howard's fellowship between the two court hearings. The accused's reinstatement coincides with the end of his fellowship, which the college has no intention of renewing. The court hopes Howard will go away with "half a loaf," and he does (334, 347). It is, however, a hollow victory. Lost in the senior fellows' decision is a favorite maxim of the law: "Do justice and not by halves."[12]

The Affair wants to convey every facet of what Snow calls "the sarcasms of justice," and his titular parallel to the famous Dreyfus Affair is deliberate (339, 152). The last section of the novel, named "The Curves of Justice," comes to a head in the following words: "One started trying to get a wrong righted; one started, granted the human limits, with clean hands and good will; and one finished with the finite chance of having done a wrong to someone else" (339). This predicament lives everywhere in law. What Snow does, possibly unfairly in his search for "inner consistencies" against real uncertainties, is to bring out the worst in everyone engaged in the process (303–14).

No one is spared. Even the narrating protagonist becomes less appealing as the crisis develops. Barrister Eliot believes "no body of men I knew of would have been more punctilious and fair," but he soon realizes that prejudice, politics, previous investments, and fluctuations in "the stock exchange of college reputations" really control what happens (31, 168). He grudgingly acknowledges that his colleagues will accept "a certain amount of individual injustice" in the name of their own comforts and in their fear of "a much larger amount of damage to us all" (133). How accurate is this point in real life? It certainly applies to many punishment regimes that law manages today.

Snow rubs it in. Eliot in action uses his knowledge of moral corruption in the college to influence the comfort level of the senior fellows. In a campaign of insinuation and innuendo, he forces their hand. Judgment, when it comes, has intrinsic problems on all sides. Snow means for us to see that even "upright men" are not at their best in wielding judgment, particularly when governed by feelings of superiority:

> One was grateful for their passion to be just, but its warmth was all inside themselves. They were not feeling as equals: it was *de haut en bas* [from top to bottom]: and, not only towards those who had perpetrated the injustice, but also, and often more coldly, towards the victim, there was directed this component of contempt.
>
> (70)

The Affair has been worth contemplating at some length because it exhibits "the curves of justice" for what they are. Litigants can end in any one of a number of places on a curve of mere reckoning rather than on a precisely calibrated scale of justice. Legal decisions often shade the difference between a bad and a worse result. True enough, but with a catch. The seaminess of Snow's depiction does not question the validity of law, although casual readers might draw that conclusion, so much as it rejects complacency in legal outcomes. All of this unpleasantness also adds a cautionary note that applies everywhere in all legal endeavor. An unattractive or a lower-class individual is at a disadvantage and had best beware of extraneous perceptions when caught in the web of law.

By opening the registers of judgment, the courtroom novel exposes what an actual court manages to hide. Most imaginative depictions of a trial encourage some form of protest over what is done to the accused. Punishment is either too heavy or too light, or wrongly applied or mistakenly withheld altogether.

Excessive punishment is the prevalent but not the only recourse in imagined courtrooms. Shylock in Shakespeare's *The Merchant of Venice* must be disciplined for planning to kill his commercial enemy, the merchant Antonio, but can it be just on any scale to force him to lose his Jewish identity through enforced conversion to Christianity? From the other side of the question, a murderer goes free in Robert Traver's *Anatomy of a Murderer* (1958), and again no one is punished for an even more obvious murder in Scott Turow's novel *Presumed Innocent* (1987). Of greater concern, an entirely innocent man is convicted and killed in Harper Lee's *To Kill a Mockingbird* (1960).

In each case, the distortion in punishment is the reader's key to interpretation, but the important point, for present purposes, is more subtle: in every instance the outcome of the case is already predetermined by the author's knowing manipulation of the geometry of the courtroom. An imbalance in spatial form (or an exaggerated balance in form) tells us what will happen if not exactly how it will happen.

We know, for example, that Shylock will lose in *The Merchant of Venice* well before Portia appears in disguise as a lawyer to challenge him. Clever Portia is the means but not the source of final judgment in the trial scene of act 4, scene 1. The duke, the symbol of absolute authority in Venice, distorts the equilateral triangle of justice from the outset by pulling it upward. He condemns Shylock as "an inhuman wretch, uncapable of pity, void and empty from any dram of mercy," and threatens him directly with a warning that is also a sneer: "We all expect a gentle answer, Jew."[13] Established power will not allow this pariah to kill his social better, no matter what the law says. Shylock's real mistake? He thinks law will protect him from disapproving authority.

The so-called balances are overly convenient in *Anatomy of a Murder*. The moment the amiable and evenly matched attorneys agree that the judge is a "nice old guy" and "a real lawyer," one who will "give both sides a fair shake," we know that things are working far more routinely than a courtroom novel can tolerate. Judge Harlan Weaver does indeed appear to be a likable judge. He regards the world "thoughtfully with his calm blue eyes," and it is telling that he is the one who identifies the hidden imbalance in his courtroom, not the lawyers.[14] He quietly congratulates defense counsel, a previous district attorney, for getting his client off by turning prosecutor in a "blame the victim" strategy: "You're just an old unreconstructed D. A. at heart."[15]

Just as wise judges see the imbalances, so unwise judges are part of them. In Scott Turow's *Presumed Innocent* the equilateral courtroom triangle is flattened by a corrupt judge who throws the case against the defendant out when threatened with exposure by defense counsel. Turow's novel has imbalances running wild. Rusty Sabich, the defendant, is also an assistant district attorney, so he sees all sides of the case and gives the theme when he says, "I have the feeling things were bent well out of shape." The actual murderer, Barbara Sabich, is the defendant's jealous wife; she gets off scot-free despite her husband's knowledge of her crime. A clever reader can figure

out the mystery early on by solving a misogynistic puzzle. Just listen pho-
netically to the name of the true murderer: "Barbara's a bitch."[16]

Good judges make better courtroom novels because a corrupt judge is
the cheap way to go after the imbalances in justice. *To Kill a Mockingbird*
is such a classic because we do have a good judge on the bench, though
not everyone realizes it. Judge Taylor "looks like a sleepy old shark," but he
is deceptively vigilant on the bench. "The impression of dozing" gets "dis-
pelled forever when a lawyer once deliberately pushed a pile of books to the
floor in a desperate effort to wake him up" and is instantly threatened with
contempt of court. Yet justice *does* sleep in this courtroom, and the imbalance at issue can be seen from the moment the courtroom is described by
author Harper Lee.[17]

Everyone remembers the name of the defense counsel who fails to get a
racist jury to find the black defendant Tom Robinson not guilty of raping
the white girl Mayella Ewell even though all of the facts point to Robinson's
innocence. Atticus Finch serves as an exemplum far beyond law and literature. Everyone in law knows the name. Oddly though, very few can come
up with the name of the prosecutor in *To Kill a Mockingbird* or anything
else about him. Is it just because the man is so nondescript? Mr. Gilmer
appears as "a balding, smooth-faced man" with "a slight cast in one of his
eyes" that makes him seem "to be looking at a person when actually he was
actually doing nothing of the kind."[18]

No one remembers Gilmer because we don't need that part of the official triangle except for the distortion it supplies. The whole town pros-
ecutes Tom Robinson. Gilmer's "cast eye" sees in another direction from
legal inquiry because it is the racist gaze that the town and the law at large
brings to the trial. We don't receive Gilmer's extended statements. All we
require is his racist cross-examination of the defendant, which bothers no
one except a small child too young to have caught the town's "usual disease."
Another imbalance in the same opening moment in court tells us that the
defense has no real case in this courtroom. The prosecutor's table is filled
with books and papers; "Atticus's was bare."[19]

For good and bad reasons, the geometry of this courtroom is askew,
and Harper Lee gives us both dimensions. Atticus Finch overwhelms the
rest of officialdom as the town's intellectual leader, but he is rhetorically
magnified as the tragic loser of a case that should have been won. A never
fully developed character, Judge Taylor overrules Gilmer when he can

and helps Finch when he can in a losing cause that everyone, including the judge but excluding the children (who bring a more literal sense of fairness into the courtroom), knows is lost. Defense counsel is the only angle in the triangle of this process that we really see. As town leader, Finch represents "the handful of people in this town who say that fair play is not marked." It is as the losing lawyer that he is important: "He's the only man in these parts who can keep a jury out for so long in a case like that."[20]

Against the expectation of symmetry, most novelists rely on a slow build-up to an appearance in court and turn that moment into a primal scene. Conventional legal imagery is readily available for these purposes.[21] Novelists, but not necessarily readers, know that even a minimal distortion in familiar balances will establish narrative momentum in the story being told at the expense of an independent understanding.

Take Bernard Schlink's novel *The Reader*, an allegory about the second generation in postwar Germany dealing with knowledge of the Holocaust. Through deadpan narrative, Schlink's youthful protagonist, a law student, describes the opening scene of defendants accused of helping to exterminate Jews in Nazi Germany and discovers that one of them is his former female lover, a much older woman with whom he had a clandestine affair in his teens. Schlink tells us that "the prosecutors sat in front of the windows, and against the bright spring and summer daylight they were no more than black silhouettes." Across the room sit "so many" defendants, they stretch "into the middle of the room in front of the public seats."[22] The prosecutors are just silhouettes because the whole world is prosecuting. The defendants stretch well into the public seats to indicate the complicity of the German people.

Schlink wields imbalance in the usual fashion, but the greatest American courtroom novel—even critics of law and literature call it "a minor classic"— eschews the device while holding onto the metaphor.[23] James Gould Cozzens writes *The Just and the Unjust* (1942) as the Bildüngsroman of a young lawyer who loses his big case as a prosecutor. Cozzens wants no part of conventional plot development, a story that celebrates defense counsel winning against impossible odds with an eloquent closing statement.[24]

Cozzens writes as a confirmed realist, and he is trying to get it right instead of festooning the law in melodrama. The story opens in court with dry docket entries and an opening statement too mundane to be recorded. *The Just and the Unjust* follows assistant district attorney Abner Coates in a small New England town from 10:40 A.M. on a Tuesday morning (the opening statement) to just after midnight on Friday night. During that time Coates, the son and grandson of judges, makes some mistakes, handles a host of smaller problems, decides to run for district attorney, and asks his girlfriend to marry him.

The Just and the Unjust is a classic because, in the words of one of its earliest and most distinguished reviewers, Harvard Law professor Zechariah Chafee Jr., it is "one of the best accounts I know of the daily life of ordinary lawyers."[25] Cozzens works with the balances that make the law what it is instead of against them. He gives us the most sophisticated grasp we are likely to receive in fiction on how the balances in law do indeed reflect "the curves in justice" rather than a mythical balance.

The judges in the novel are invariably decent, usually wise, full of integrity, but troubled by minor human flaws (illness, a temper, nameless anxiety). Abner Coates and his opposite number, defense counsel Harry Wurts, are carefully matched when practicing before these judges. They are the same age at thirty-one, from the same town, with the same schooling all of the way through law school. They are made to differ only in how law defines their assigned roles as defense counsel and prosecutor. Wurts is mercurial, funny, pugnacious, litigious, verbose, and devious. Coates is earnest, direct, sincere, and stolid. They symbolize the adage from antiquity of the philosopher Archílochus: the fox knows many tricks, the hedgehog one—a good one.[26] Coates must tell one very believable story well to convict. Wurts tells many stories; he uses as many tricks and alternatives as he can to create a reasonable doubt in the story the prosecution presents.

This is exactly what happens in *The Just and the Unjust*. Defense counsel convinces a runaway jury to disobey the law by appealing to their resentment of authority. Still, the balances in the courtroom remain in place. The twelve jurors quite logically decide not to send two gangsters to the electric chair on a felony murder charge where neither of them wanted to kill or actually pulled the trigger. They accept that second-degree murder—twenty years in prison!—will suffice in this case, a decision that bothers few readers. As one of the judges opines, "Justice is an inexact science."[27]

Embedded within these procedural balances are two philosophical ones that explain the ultimate but very different triumph of balance in legal thought. Yes, justice takes place on a curve instead of a balance. The defendants in this case could just as easily have been sentenced to death, but through good luck they find themselves elsewhere on the curve with prison time—justifiably, given the balances, a lot of prison time.

On a dialectical level, Cozzens's sense of the balance comes through his title, *The Just and the Unjust* based on a line from the Sermon on the Mount: "[God] maketh his sun to rise on the evil and on the good and sendeth rain on the just and on the unjust."[28] Even so, that is not where he leaves it. Cozzens has his flamboyant defense counsel argue with other court personnel after the decision. Harry Wurts wants everyone to accept how he overstepped in his summary to the jury. The unjust, it turns out, have "a great hankering for the approval of the just."[29] A balance exists against misconduct. There are rules. Those who bend them seek the approval of those who abide by them.

On a more internal level, Coates has changed across the pages of *The Just and the Unjust*, through his growth in professionalism. Early on he agonizes over what others think about him and makes awkward mistakes. Later he realizes he can trust to the compass that professionalism has given him. He has learned it is enough when he knows he has acted ethically. Instead of worrying about what others think, he rests in the expertise that those who question him do not have.

Cozzens puts this proof of growth through the internal thought processes that every good lawyer must have. "It was not possible to be above the reasonable calumny of a suspicious man's suspicions," Coates thinks. Although he squirms inwardly when pushed aggressively by a local newspaperman, he quickly settles these qualms. The retained wisdom gained from his elders, the judges in the novel, saves him from embarrassment. They have said to him, "You know whether it's a bargain or not. You know what you take and what you give." Their words guard him against a show of anger or any need for a defensive response.[30]

Against the more pernicious aspects of the curve in justice, the standard of what one will do must come from within as well as without. This double perspective, within and without, is what every lawyer needs to have in order to see all sides of a dilemma and to find where integrity lies in the incessant conflicts of legal engagement. Cozzens's protagonist trusts the courage of his own convictions through the experience and knowledge that law requires but also instills in him. Here, if anywhere, the balance meets the curve in justice.

What obligation do novelists have to convey such a nuanced level of reality? Obviously none if their only goal is to entertain and garner a readership. On the other hand, the courtroom novel is a novel of manners in Lionel Trilling's strict understanding of that form. It is about how people behave in a moral sense—what we can translate into a normative legal sense—and Trilling assigns responsibilities or obligations to it. By manners, he means "a culture's hum and buzz of implication," with the insight that "our attitude toward manners is the expression of a particular conception of reality."[31]

The courtroom novel should do more than entertain in this light. Trilling argues that "to scale the moral and aesthetic heights in the novel one had to use the ladder of social observation" in order to "report the social fact with the kind of accuracy it needs."[32] Why is accurate reportage on social fact so hard to achieve? In the courtroom novel, the compounding element is justice, whether searched for, enacted, or lost. However cynical the novelist, there is always a sense of justice present to be realized or tampered with.

Trilling senses as much when he describes the novel as "a perpetual quest for reality"; there is a moral dimension in that quest, and he raises the issue of "social justice" as one of its central moral concerns. What he sees, and what many courtroom novelists shy away from, is that social justice "does not settle all moral problems, but on the contrary generates new ones of an especially difficult sort."[33] Here is the true mission of the courtroom novel. The difficulties in law is where interest should lie in fiction, and that should be the standard for any novelist who hopes to join the best that has been said or thought.

INTRODUCTION: THE LETTERS IN LAW

1   See, for example, Shoshana Felman, *The Juridical Unconscious: Trials and Traumas in the Twentieth Century* (Cambridge, Mass.: Harvard University Press, 2002), 95–96. On "insularity" and "alterity" in law, literature, and philosophy, see Robert Cover, "The Supreme Court, 1982 Term—Foreword: *Nomos* and Narrative," *Harvard Law Review* 97 (1983): 4–68.

2   Herman Melville, *Billy Budd, Sailor (An Inside Narrative)*, eds. Harrison Hayford and Merton M. Sealts Jr. (Chicago: University of Chicago Press, 1962), 43, 123–24, and Robert A. Ferguson, *Inferno: An Anatomy of American Punishment* (Cambridge, Mass.: Harvard University Press, 2014), 199–208.

3   E. M. Forster, *Aspects of the Novel* (New York: Harcourt, 1927), 23.

4   The quoted phrases are from James Wood, *How Fiction Works* (New York: Farrar, Straus and Giroux, 2008), 67, and Wolfgang Iser, *The Implied Reader: Patterns of Communication in Prose Fiction from Bunyan to Beckett* (Baltimore: Johns Hopkins University Press, 1974), 290.

5   John Dewey, "The Historical Background of Corporate Personality," *Yale Law Journal* 35 (1925–26): 655.

6   Robert Scholes, *The Crafty Reader* (New Haven: Yale University Press, 2001), 242.

7   Kenji Yoshino, *A Thousand Times More Fair: What Shakespeare's Plays Teach Us about Justice* (New York: HarperCollins, 2011), ix–xi. Forster says we can only know a character perfectly in fiction. *Aspects of the Novel*, 55, 63.

8   Frank Kermode, *The Sense of an Ending: Studies in the Theory of Fiction* (New York: Oxford University Press, 1967).

9   Austin Sarat, Matthew Anderson, and Cathrine O. Frank, eds., "Introduction: On the Origins and Prospects of the Humanistic Study of Law," in *Law and the Humanities: An Introduction* (Cambridge: Cambridge University Press, 2010), 11–19.

10 I distinguish between "law and literature" as a field of inquiry and "law &
    literature" as a movement within the field.

11 For an excellent explanation of how law works by reducing analogies in human
    experience to its own case terms in the name of legal reason, see Lloyd L. Wein-
    reb, "Analogy and Inductive and Deductive Reasoning," in *Legal Reason: The
    Use of Analogy in Legal Argument* (New York: Cambridge University Press,
    2005), 19–39.

12 Richard A. Posner, "The Decline of Law as an Autonomous Discipline:
    1962–1987," *Harvard Law Review* 100 (1987): 761–80.

13 Clifford Geertz, "Thick Description: Toward an Interpretive Theory of
    Culture," in *The Interpretation of Cultures* (New York: Basic Books, 1973),
    3–4.

14 Christopher D. Stone, "From a Language Perspective," *Yale Law Journal* 90
    (1981): 1154.

15 Wood, *How Fiction Works*, 236.

16 Ibid., 106.

17 Lenora Ledwon, ed., preface to *Law and Literature: Text and Theory* (New
    York: Garland Publishing, 1996), ix–x.

18 James Boyd White, "Law as Language: Reading Law and Reading Literature,"
    Texas Law Review 60 (1982): 429–30, 444–45.

19 Kieran Dolin, introduction to *A Critical Introduction to Law and Literature*
    (Cambridge: Cambridge University Press, 2007), 10.

20 Anthony Julius, introduction to *Law and Literature: Current Legal Issues*, eds.
    Michael Freeman and Andrew Lewis (Oxford: Oxford University Press, 1999),
    2:xiv–xv.

21 Robert A. Ferguson, *Law and Letters in American Culture* (Cambridge, Mass.:
    Harvard University Press, 1984).

22 Robert A. Ferguson, *The American Enlightenment, 1750–1820* (Cambridge,
    Mass.: Harvard University Press, 1997).

23 Robert A. Ferguson, *The Trial in American Life* (Chicago: University of
    Chicago Press, 2007).

24 Robert A. Ferguson, *Inferno: An Anatomy of American Punishment* (Cambridge.
    Mass.: Harvard University Press, 2014).

25 Oliver Wendell Holmes Jr., *The Common Law* (Boston: Little, Brown, 1881).

26 See Thomas L. Haskell, ed., *The Authority of Experts: Studies in History and
    Theory* (Bloomington: Indiana University Press, 1984).

27 Ronald Dworkin, *Law's Empire* (Cambridge, Mass.: Harvard University Press, 1986), 380.

28 The Latin reads *juris praecepta sunt: honeste vivere, alterum non laedere, suum cuique tribuere.* Paul Krueger, ed., *Justinian's Institutes* (Ithaca: Cornell University Press, 1987), 1. The *Institutes* were first published in 533 C.E.

29 Paul Kahn, *The Cultural Study of Law: Reconstructing Legal Scholarship* (Chicago: University of Chicago Press, 2000), 31–33, 71–83.

PART I. LITERARY COMPONENTS IN THE LEGAL IMAGINATION

1 Stephen Crane, "An Eloquence of Grief," in *The Complete Short Stories and Sketches of Stephen Crane*, ed. Thomas A. Gullason (Garden City, NY: Doubleday, 1963), 321–22, and *The Works of Stephen Crane*, ed. Fredson Bowers, vol. 8, *Tales, Sketches, and Reports* (Charlottesville: University Press of Virginia, 1969–75), 382–84.

2 Hans Kelsen, *Introduction to the Problems of Legal Theory* (Oxford: Clarendon Press, 1992), xix, 87.

3 These quotations reflect an ongoing controversy between pragmatic and philosophical interpretations. See Richard A. Posner, *How Judges Think* (Cambridge, Mass.: Harvard University Press, 2008), 252, and Ronald Dworkin, *Taking Rights Seriously* (Cambridge, Mass.: Harvard University Press, 1977), 106.

4 Robert A. Dahl, *How Democratic is the American Constitution?* (New Haven: Yale University Press, 2001), 7, 141–57.

5 Garrett Epps, *American Epic: Reading the U.S. Constitution* (New York: Oxford University Press, 2013), and John E. Finn, *Peopling the Constitution* (Lawrence: University Press of Kansas, 2014).

6 Linda Ross Meyer, *The Justice of Mercy* (Ann Arbor: University of Michigan Press, 2010), and Bryan Stevenson, *Just Mercy: A Story of Justice and Redemption* (New York: Spiegal & Grau, 2014).

1. THE U.S. CONSTITUTION AS LITERATURE

1 *The Works of Benjamin Franklin*, ed. Jared Sparks (Boston: Hilliard, Gray, 1840), 1:408.

2 The Declaration of Independence, in *The Documentary History of the Ratification of the Constitution*, ed. Merrill Jensen, vol. 1, *Constitutional Documents and*

Records, 1776–1787 (Madison: State Historical Society of Wisconsin), 1976), 73–75.

3 Max Farrand, ed., *The Records of the Federal Convention of 1787* (New Haven: Yale University Press, 1966), 2:648. All further references to this work will be through parenthetical reference in the text.

4 James Madison, *Federalist No. 10* and *Federalist No. 37*, in *The Federalist Papers*, ed. Roy P. Fairfield, 2nd ed. (Baltimore: Johns Hopkins Press, 1981), 23, 101. All further references to *The Federalist Papers* will be to this edition by editor, paper number, and page number.

5 Fairfield, ed., *Federalist No. 37*, 102–3.

6 Ibid., 103.

7 *The Works of John Adams*, ed. Charles Francis Adams (Boston: Little, Brown, 1851), 4:283–85, 292–94.

8 There are "seven seals" in biblical lore, seven days in the week, seven deadly sins, and seven wonders of the ancient world. Seven is the most frequent number to appear in two six-sided dice games, and it is the lowest natural number that cannot be represented as the sum of the squares of three integers.

9 Articles of Confederation and Perpetual Union, article XIII, in Jensen, ed., *Documentary History*, 1:93.

10 See Clinton Rossiter, *1787: The Grand Convention* (New York: Macmillan, 1966), 274–98.

11 Articles of Confederation, in Jensen, ed., *Documentary History*, 1: 86.

12 Fairfield, ed., *Federalist No. 51*, 160.

13 Samuel Johnson, *A Dictionary of the English Language*, 1st ed. (London: W. Strahan, 1755).

14 *The Papers of James Madison*, eds. Robert A. Rutland, Charles F. Hobson, William M. E. Rachal, and Frederika J. Teute, vol. 10, *27 May 1787–3 March 1788* (Chicago: University of Chicago Press, 1977), 355.

15 *The Works of John Adams*, ed. Charles Francis Adams (Boston: Little, Brown, 1856), 6:220

16 *The Papers of James Madison*, 10:208

17 *The Writings of Benjamin Franklin*, ed. Albert Henry Smyth, vol. 9, *1783–1788* (New York: Macmillan, 1907), 658–59.

18 *The Works of John Adams*, ed. Charles Francis Adams (Boston: Little, Brown, 1856), 10:283.

19 *The Papers of Thomas Jefferson*, ed. Julian P. Boyd, vol. 11, *1 January–6 August 1787* (Princeton: Princeton University Press, 1955), 251.

20 *The Works of John Adams*, 10:397–98.

21 Francis Newton Thorpe, ed., *The Federal and State Constitutions, Colonial Charters, and Other Organic Laws of the States, Territories, and Colonies Now or Heretofore Forming the United States of America*, vol. 3, *Kentucky–Massachusetts* (Washington, D.C.: Government Printing Office, 1909), 1841, and Earl Gregg Swem, ed., *Jamestown 350th Anniversary Historical Booklets* (Williamsburg, Va.: Garrett & Massie, 1957), 4:126–28.

22 Jensen, ed., *Documentary History*, 1:306.

23 Francis Newton Thorpe, ed., *The Federal and State Constitutions, Colonial Charters, and Other Organic Laws of the States, Territories, and Colonies Now or Heretofore Forming the United States of America*, vol. 7, *Virginia–Wyoming* (Washington, D.C.: Government Printing Office, 1909), 3815.

24 Rossiter, *1787*, 145–46.

25 *The Works of John Adams*, 10:149.

26 Benjamin Franklin, *Information to Those Who Would Remove to America*, in *The Writings of Benjamin Franklin*, ed. Albert Henry Smyth, vol. 8, *1780–1782* (New York: Macmillan), 603.

27 George Washington, *Circular to the States*, in *The Writings of George Washington*, ed. John C. Fitzpatrick, vol. 26, *January 1, 1783–June 10, 1783* (Washington, D.C.: Government Printing Office, 1938), 483–86.

28 John Adams, *Defense of the Constitutions of Government of the United States of America*, in *The Works of John Adams*, 6:219–20.

29 Forrest McDonald, *Novus Ordo Seclorum: The Intellectual Origins of the Constitution* (Lawrence: University Press of Kansas, 1985), 211, and Gary Wills, *Explaining America: "The Federalist"* (Garden City, N.Y.: Doubleday, 1981).

30 Robert N. Bellah, *Beyond Belief: Essays on Religion in a Post-Traditional World* (Berkeley: University of California Press, 1970), 175.

31 Stephen Botein, "Religious Dimensions of the Early American State," in *Beyond Confederation: Origins of the Constitution and American National Identity*, eds. Richard Beeman, Stephen Botein, and Edward C. Carter II (Chapel Hill: University of North Carolina Press, 1987), 315–30.

32 *The Papers of James Madison*, 10:208.

33 *The Papers of James Madison*, eds. Robert A. Rutland and Thomas A. Mason, vol. 14, *6 April 1791–16 March 1793* (Charlottesville: University Press of Virginia, 1983), 191–92.

34 Ibid., 191–92.

35 *The Works of John Adams*, 4:219–20.

2. THE PLACE OF MERCY IN LEGAL DISCOURSE

1   Norman Mailer, *The Executioner's Song* (Boston: Little, Brown, 1979), 91. See also Elaine Scarry, *The Body in Pain: The Making and Unmaking of the World* (New York: Oxford University Press, 1985), 5–16, 53–60.

2   Melissa Barden Dowling, *Clemency and Cruelty in the Roman World* (Ann Arbor: University of Michigan Press, 2006).

3   Suetonius, "Nero," in *The Twelve Caesars*, trans. Robert Graves (London: Penguin Classics, 1957), 209–41.

4   Seneca, *De Clementia*, trans. and ed. Susanna Braund (New York: Oxford University Press, 2009), 103 [1.5.3]. Standard scholarly recognition of paragraph and section indications in further references to this text is provided in brackets.

5   James Morwood, ed., *The Pocket Oxford Latin Dictionary* (New York: Oxford University Press, 1994), 26, 85.

6   Seneca, *De Clementia*, 145, 115, 103 [2.5.1; 1.11.2; 1.5.3].

7   Ibid., 145, 143 [2.5.1; 2.3.2].

8   Ibid., 105, 145 [1.6.2; 2.4.1].

9   Ibid., 149 [2.6.3].

10 Ibid., 105 [1.6.1].

11 Ibid., 107, 105, 115 [1.7.2–3; 1.6.1; 1.11.4].

12 Ibid., 151 [2.7.3–5].

13 See the account in Tacitus, *The Annals of Imperial Rome*, trans. Michael Grant (New York: Penguin Books, 1972), 376 [15.62].

14 Marcus Aurelius, *Meditations*, trans. Maxwell Staniforth (New York: Penguin Books, 1964), 122, 69, 114 [8.5; 4.25; 7.54]. Standard scholarly recognition of paragraph and section indications in further references to this text is provided in brackets.

15 Ibid., 38, 116, 156 [1.11, 7.65, 10.12].

16 Ibid., 114, 172–73, 130, 169, 148–49 [7.55; 11.19; 8.43; 11.9; 9.42].

17 Ibid., 152, 57, 110 [10.6; 3.5; 7.29].

18 Ibid., 182–83 [12.16].

19 Martha Nussbaum, "Equity and Mercy," *Philosophy and Public Affairs* 22, no. 2 (1993): 85–88, 91–92, 96.

20 Consider, among many other examples, Matthew 7:1–2 and Matthew 25:34–46.

21 For philosophical debate over the double meaning of dignity, see Oscar Schachter, "Human Dignity as a Normative Concept," *American Journal of Sociology* 77, no. 4 (1983): 848–54; Aurel Kolnai, "Dignity," *Philosophy* 51, no. 197 (1976): 251–71; and Jeremy Waldron, "Dignity and Rank," *European Journal of Sociology* 48, no. 2 (2007): 201–37. See also Steven Pinker, "The Stupidity of Dignity," *New Republic*, May 28, 2008, 28–31.

22 See Jeffrie G. Murphy and Jean Hampton, *Forgiveness and Mercy* (Cambridge: Cambridge University Press, 1988), 168–69, 180–81; Carol S. Steiker, "Tempering or Tampering? Mercy and the Administration of Criminal Justice," in *Forgiveness, Mercy, and Clemency*, eds. Austin Sarat and Nasser Hussain (Stanford: Stanford University Press, 2007), 20–21, 28; Dan Markel, "Against Mercy," *Minnesota Law Review* 88 (2004): 1441; Robert L. Misner, "A Strategy for Mercy," *William & Mary Law Review* 41, no. 4 (2000): 1309–21, and Linda Ross Meyer, *The Justice of Mercy* (Ann Arbor: University of Michigan Press, 2010), 1, 48, 95. The quotation in the text is from Steiker, "Tempering or Tampering?," 21.

23 St. Anselm, *Proslogium; Monologium: An Appendix in Behalf of the Fool by Gaunilon; and Cur Deus Homo*, trans. Sidney Norton Deane (Chicago: Open Court, 1903), 14, 17, 18, 19 [chap. 9; chap. 10; chap. 11]. Standard scholarly recognition of chapters in further references to this text is provided in brackets.

24 Oliver O'Donovan, *Common Objects of Love: Moral Reflection and the Shaping of Community* (Grand Rapids, Mi.: William B. Eerdmans, 2002), 2–3.

25 Anselm, *Proslogium*, 17 [chap. 10].

26 Ibid., 17, 14–15 [chap. 10; chap. 9].

27 Ibid., 19 [chap. 11].

28 John Stuart Mill, "Of the Liberty of Thought and Discussion," in *On Liberty* (Boston: Ticknor and Fields, 1863), 95–97.

29 J. L. Austin, *How To Do Things with Words*, eds. Marina Sbisà and J. O. Urmson (1962; repr., Cambridge, Mass.: Harvard University Press, 1975), 4–7, 99–109.

30 I paraphrase from the Model Penal Code § 305.10.

31 Joan Petersilia, "Parole and Prisoner Reentry in the United States," *Crime and Justice* 26 (1990): 479–529 at 487ff.

32 Escoe v. Zerbst, 295 U.S. 490 (1935) at 492, and Biddle v. Pervovich, 274 U.S. 480 (1927) at 486.

33 Katherine Skolnick, ed., "Parole," in *A Jailhouse Lawyer's Manual*, 8th ed. (New York: Columbia Human Rights Law Review, 2009), 972–97.

34 A. Keith Bottomley, "Parole in Transition: A Comparative Study of Origins, Developments, and Prospects for the 1990s," *Crime and Justice* 12 (1990): 319–74.

35 Kathleen Dean Moore, "How to Distinguish Forgiveness, Mercy, and Pardon," in *Pardons: Justice, Mercy, and the Public Interest* (New York: Oxford University Press, 1989), 181–96.

36 Austin, *How To Do Things with Words*, 14–15, 84.

37 Quotations to Shakespeare's plays are by act, scene, and line and from the following editions: *The Merchant of Venice*, ed. David Bevington (New York: Bantam Books, 1980); *Measure for Measure*, ed. J. W. Lever (London: Methuen, 1965); and *The Tempest*, eds. Peter Hulme and William H. Sherman (New York: Norton, 2004).

38 Kenji Yoshino, "The Lawyer of Belmont," *Yale Journal of Law & the Humanities* 9, no. 1 (1997): 183–216, and Yoshino, *A Thousand Times More Fair: What Shakespeare's Plays Teach Us About Justice* (New York: Harper Collins, 2011).

39 Henry Campbell Black, *Black's Law Dictionary*, 6th ed. (St. Paul, Minn.: West Publishing, 1990), 1029.

40 Daniel J. Kornstein, "Fie Upon Your Law!" *Cardozo Studies in Law & Literature* 5 (1993): 35–46, particularly 45.

41 Yoshino, "The Lawyer of Belmont," 207.

42 Matthew 2:1–12.

43 See William Blackstone, *Commentaries on the Laws of England*, book 4, *Of Public Wrongs* (Oxford: Clarendon Press: 1769), 92, 370, 374, 380–81.

44 Alywnne Smart, "Mercy," *Philosophy* 43 (1968): 345.

45 Ibid., 351–52, 356–59.

46 See P. Twembley, "Mercy and Forgiveness," *Analysis* 36 (1976): 87.

47 See Claudia Card, "On Mercy," *Philosophical Review* 81, no. 2 (1972): 183–84, 194–96, 205–7. See, as well, Heidi M. Hurd, "The Morality of Mercy," *Ohio State Journal of Criminal Law* 4 (2007): 405–7, and Moore, "How to Distinguish Forgiveness, Mercy, and Pardon," 181–96. For privileging retribution over utilitarianism on the subject of mercy in Shakespeare, see, Stephen P. Garvey, "'As the Gentle Rain from Heaven': Mercy in Capital Sentencing," *Cornell Law Review* 81, no. 5 (1996): 1013ff.

48 Murphy and Hampton, *Forgiveness and Mercy*, 164–66.

49 Ibid., 65, 119, 129.

50 Markel, "Against Mercy," 1464; Robert F. Schopp, *Justification Defenses and Just Convictions* (Cambridge: Cambridge University Press, 2008), 182; and Twembley, "Mercy and Forgiveness," 85.

51 James Q. Whitman, *Harsh Justice: Criminal Punishment and the Widening Divide Between America and Europe* (Oxford: Oxford University Press, 2003), 201, 13.

52 H. Scott Hestevold, "Justice to Mercy," *Philosophy and Phenomenological Research* 46, no. 2 (1985): 281, and Hestevold, "On the Moral Status of Punishment," *Law and Philosophy* 6, no. 2 (1987): 251.

53 George W. Rainbolt, "Mercy: An Independent, Imperfect Virtue," *American Philosophical Quarterly* 27 (1990): 169–73, and Card, "On Mercy," 188.

54 Hurd, "The Morality of Mercy," 395.

55 Markel, "Against Mercy," 1442, 1429, 1453.

56 Misner, "A Strategy for Mercy," 1303–1400, particularly 1303–4, 1400.

57 Ibid., 1318, 1325.

58 Markel, "Against Mercy," 1440–41, esp. n. 64.

59 Melissa Beach, " 'When Mercy Seasons Justice,' " *St. John's Journal of Legal Commentary* 23, no. 3 (2008): 918.

60 Hurd, "The Morality of Mercy," 413.

61 Card, "On Mercy," 195–97, 202.

62 Robert Weisberg, "Apology, Legislation, and Mercy," *North Carolina Law Review* 82, no. 4 (2004): 1415–40, particularly 1420–21.

63 Garvey, " 'As the Gentle Rain from Heaven,' " 990–92, and Weisberg, "Apology, Legislation, and Mercy," 1429–30.

64 Gregg v. Georgia, 428 U.S. 153 (1976).

65 See Justice Sandra Day O'Connor's majority opinion in Penry v. Lynaugh, 492 U.S. 302 (1989) at 326–27.

66 Nussbaum, "Equity and Mercy," 115–18. Nussbaum bases her analysis on close readings of two Supreme Court cases, Walton v. Arizona, 110 S. Ct. 3047 (1990) and California v. Brown, 479 U.S. 538 (1987).

67 Walton v. Arizona, 497 U.D. 639 (1990) at 641–42, 718.

68 Franklin v. Lynaugh, 487 U.S. 164 (1998) at 190.

69 Wilson v. Kemp, 777 F.2d 621 (11th Cir. 1985), 621, 624.

70 *Brown*, 479 U.S. 538 at 837, 849–50.

71 Ibid., at 850.

72 Bertolotti v. Dugger, 883 F.2d 1503 (11th Cir. 1989) at 1526.

73 Lusk v. Singletary, 965 F.2d 946 (11th Cir. 1992) at 950–51.

74 Johnson v. Texas, 509 U.S. 350 (1993) at 371–72.

75 Ibid.

76 Kansas v. Marsh, 548 U.S. 163 (2006) at 165–66, 176.

77 Graham v. Florida, 560 U.S. _ (2010).

78 Ibid., 8–11, 14–16, 19–23, 26–29, 31.

79 See United States v. Smith, 359 F. Supp.2d 771 (E.D. Wis. 2005); Kimbrough
    v. United States, 552 U.S. 85 (2007); Spears v. United States, 129 S. Ct. 840
    (2009).

80 *Brown*, 479 U.S. 538, at 850.

81 I quote and paraphrase in this paragraph from Seneca, *De Clementia*, 151, 133
    [2.7.3; 1.22.2–4].

82 Whitman, *Harsh Justice*; Michael Tonry and David P. Farrington, "Punishment
    and Crime Across Space and Time," *Crime and Justice* 33 (2005): 1–39; Marie
    Gottschalk, "The Long Reach of the Carceral State: The Politics of Crime,
    Mass Imprisonment, and Penal Reform in the United States and Abroad,"
    Social Inquiry 34, no. 2 (2009): 439–72; and David Nelken, "Patterns of Puni-
    tiveness," *Modern Law Review* 69, no. 2 (2006): 262–77.

3. IMMIGRATION LAW: AN ANSWER TO INTRACTABILITY

1   Louis Buller Gohmert Jr., U.S. representative from Texas, made this charge on
    the floor of Congress on June 24, 2010, and repeated it on *Anderson Cooper
    360°*, a television news show, on August 12, 2010. See Elise Hu, "TX Rep. Louie
    Gohmert Warns of Terrorist Babies," *Texas Tribune*, June 28, 2010, and Hu,
    "Gohmert Debates 'Terror Babies' on CNN," *Texas Tribune*, August 13, 2010.

2   These quotations, said by several state representatives, are taken from Charles
    M. Blow, "Silliness and Sleight of Hand," *New York Times*, April 29, 2011,
    A21.

3   Kenneth Burke, *Permanence and Change: An Anatomy of Purpose* (1935; repr.,
    Berkeley: University of California Press, 1984), 49.

4   Oscar Handlin, *Statue of Liberty* (New York: Newsweek Book Division, 1971),
    61–65.

5   On the innate human need for a feeling of superiority, see the following works
    by Friedrich Nietzsche: *Thus Spoke Zarathustra*, trans. Thomas Common (New
    York: Modern Library, 1917), 62–63, 202–20; and *Beyond Good and Evil*, trans.
    Marianne Cowen (Chicago: Henry Regnery, 1955), 56–57, 69–72, 104, 132–37,
    200–201, 214–15, 231–32. See also Jonathan Glover, "Nietzsche's Challenge," in
    Humanity: A Moral History of the Twentieth Century (New Haven: Yale Uni-
    versity Press, 1999), 11–17.

6   The most accurate figures on immigration come from the Pew Hispanic Center
    of the Pew Research Center. Senior Demographer Jeffrey S. Passel and Senior

Writer D'Vera Cohn, both at Pew, put the figure at 11.9 million in 2008. Passel and Cohn, *A Portrait of Unauthorized Immigrants in the United States*, April 14, 2009, 1–2, http://www.pewhispanic.org/files/reports/107.pdf.

7   Daniel Aaron, *The Unwritten War: American Writers in the Civil War* (New York: Alfred A. Knopf, 1973), 333.

8   Lewis P. Simpson, "The Civil War and the Failure of Literary Mind in America," in *The Brazen Face of History* (Athens: University of Georgia Press, 1997), 109–10.

9   Derrick A. Bell Jr., "The Racial Imperative in American Law," in *The Age of Segregation: Race Relations in the South, 1890–1945*, ed. Robert Haws (Jackson: University Press of Mississippi, 1978), 3–28.

10 Herbert Blumer, "Race Prejudice As a Sense of Group Position," *Pacific Sociological Review* 1, no. 1 (1958): 3–7, and Ryan D. King and Darren Wheelock, "Group Threat and Social Control: Race, Perceptions of Minorities, and the Desire to Punish," *Social Forces* 85, no. 3 (2007): 1255–79.

11 The quotations are from Hubert M. Blalock Jr., "Theoretical Propositions," in *Toward a Theory of Minority-Group Relations* (New York: John Wiley, 1967), 204.

12 Ian Hacking, "Why Race Still Matters," *Daedalus* 134, no. 1 (2005): 114.

13 Ibid., 102, 114; Cornel West, "A Genealogy of Modern Racism," in *Prophesy Deliverance! An Afro-American Revolutionary Christianity* (Philadelphia: Westminster Press, 1982), 47–65; and Lawrence Hirschfeld, *Race in the Making: Cognition, Culture, and the Child's Conception of Human Kinds* (Cambridge: Mass.: MIT Press, 1996).

14 Mae M. Ngai, *Impossible Subjects: Illegal Aliens and the Making of Modern America* (Princeton: Princeton University Press, 2004), xx.

15 Roger Daniels, *Guarding the Golden Door: American Immigration Policy and Immigrants Since 1882* (New York: Hill and Wang, 2004), 261, 263–64.

16 Mae M. Ngai, "Notes on Language and Terminology," in *Impossible Subjects*, xix. Emphasis added.

17 See Daniel J. Boorstin, "From Ideal to Image: The Search for Self-Fulfilling Prophecies," in *The Image: A Guide to Pseudo-Events in America* (New York: Athenaeum, 1978), 181–238.

18 For popular movies within the *Alien* series that connect with the equally negative idea of "Predator," another form of alien, see *Alien* (1979), *Aliens* (1986), *Alien 3* (1993), *Alien Resurrection* (1997), as well as *Predator* (1987), *Predator 2* (1990), *Alien vs. Predator* (2004), *Aliens vs. Predator: Requiem* (2007), and

Predators (2010). These movies spawn ever multiplying books, video games, spin-offs, and toys—all tied to the pejorative meaning of "alien."

19 Mae M. Ngai, "The Johnson-Reed Act of 1924 and the Reconstruction of Race in Immigration Law," in *Impossible Subjects*, 21–55, and Ngai, "The Architecture of Race in American Immigration Law: A Reexamination of the Immigration Act of 1924," *Journal of American History* 86 (1999): 67–91.

20 For an examination of the veiled racist appeals in anti-immigration organizations, see Jason De Parle, "Anti-Immigration Crusader," *New York Times*, April 17, 2011, A1.

21 Ross Douthat and Jenny Woodson, "The Border," *Atlantic Monthly*, January/February 2006, 54–55.

22 John B. Judis, "Phantom Menace," *New Republic*, February 13, 2008, 21–23, and De Parle, "Anti-Immigration Crusader," A1.

23 A. G. Sulzberger, "Growing Anti-Immigrant Sentiments in an Unlikely State," *New York Times*, October 3, 2010, 16.

24 Julia Preston, "Political Battle on Immigration Shifts to States," *New York Times*, January 1, 2011, A1, A11.

25 Judis, "Phantom Menace," 21–23.

26 Gail Collins, "The Great Undebate," *New York Times*, September 4, 2010, A19.

27 Peter Skerry and Devin Fernandes, "Citizen Pain," *New Republic*, May 8, 2006, 14.

28 For the problems in defining *illegal alien*, see Gerald L. Neuman, "Aliens as Outlaws: Government Services, Proposition 187, and the Structure of Equal Protection Doctrine," *UCLA Law Review* 42 (1995): 1440–45. See also Immigration and Nationality Act [hereafter referred to as "I.N.A."] at 8 U.S.C. [United States Code] § 1101 and 8 U.S.C. § 1365(b)d, and 29 C.F.R. [Code of Federal Regulations] § 500.20(n).

29 The plenary power doctrine is first articulated in the Chinese Exclusion Case, or Chae Chan Ping v. United States, 130 U.S. 581 (1889). See, as well, Hiroshi Motomura, "Immigration Law after a Century of Plenary Power: Phantom Constitutional Norms and Statutory Interpretation," *Yale Law Journal* 100 (1990): 546–613; and Gabriel J. Chin, "Is There a Plenary Power Doctrine? A Tentative Apology and Prediction for Our Strange But Unexceptional Constitutional Immigration Law," *Georgetown Immigration Law Journal* 14, no. 2 (2000): 257–87.

30 See the editorial "Borderline Ridiculous," *New York Times*, September 17, 2011, A20.

31 See I. N. A., § 318 Prerequisite to Naturalization; Burden of Proof [8 U.S.C.A. (United States Code Annotated) § 1430]. See also I.N.A. § 237 Deportable Aliens [8 U.S.C.A. § 1227].

32 Preston, "Political Battle on Immigration Shifts to States," A1, A11; and Marc Lacey, "On Immigration, Birthright Fight in U.S. is Looming," *New York Times*, January 5, 2011, A1, A15.

33 For "self-deportation," see Neuman, "Aliens as Outlaws," 1445. See also Kim Severson, "Southern Lawmakers Focus on Illegal Immigrants," *New York Times*, March 20, 2011, A13, and Cristina M. Rodriguez, "The Significance of the Local in Immigration Regulation," *Michigan Law Review* 106 (2008): 567–642.

34 Campbell Robertson, "Alabama Wins in Ruling on Its Immigration Law: State's Statute Is Now the Nation's Strictest," *New York Times*, September 29, 2011, A16; Campbell Robertson, "After Ruling, Hispanics Flee an Alabama Town," *New York Times*, October 4, 2011, A1, A16; "Alabama's Shame: A Harsh Immigration Law Spreads Fear and Punishes the Vulnerable," *New York Times*, October 4, 2011, A26.

35 Campbell Robertson, "In Alabama, Calls for Revamping Immigration Law," *New York Times*, November 17, 2011, A15; "Alabama's Second Thoughts," *New York Times* December 18, 2011, SR18.

36 Luis V. Gutierrez, U.S. representative from Illinois, quoted by Julia Preston, "House Backs Legal Status for Many Young Immigrants," *New York Times*, December 9, 2010, A38.

37 Daniels, *Guarding the Golden Door*, 226–27; Ngai, *Impossible Subjects*, 265–66.

38 Julia Preston, "Immigration Vote Leaves Obama's Policy in Disarray," *New York Times*, December 18, 2010, A1.

39 Kirk Semple, "In a Study, Judges Express a Bleak View of Lawyers Representing Immigrants," *New York Times*, December 11, 2011, A24; "For Want of a Good Lawyer: Deportation Without Representation," *New York Times*, December 25, 2011, SR14.

40 Julia Preston and Robert Gebeloff, "Some Unlicensed Drivers Risk More Than a Fine," *New York Times*, December 9, 2010.

41 Michael de Certeau, *The Practice of Everyday Life*, trans. Steven F. Rendall (Berkeley: University of California Press, 1984).

42 Julia Preston, "Deportation Halted for Some Students as Lawmakers Seek New Policy," *New York Times*, April 27, 2011, A20.

43 "Development, Relief, and Education for Alien Minors Acts of 2010" at 156 Cong. Rec. H8221–H8243 (daily ed., December 8, 2010); and "Dream Act," at 156 Cong. Rec. S8548–S8550 (daily ed. December 6, 2010), 156 Cong. Rec. S8660–S8661 (daily ed. December 9, 2010), and S10498–S104504 (daily ed. December 17, 2010).

44 People often advocate for the death penalty but refuse to support it if asked to do so in a particular case. See John Futty, "Death Penalty Cases in Franklin County Becoming Rarer," *Columbus Dispatch*, November 3, 2008; Gary Goodpaster, "The Trial for Life: Effective Assistance of Counsel in Death Penalty Cases," *New York University Law Review* 58 (1983): 299–362; Michelle E. Barnett, Stanley L. Brodsky, and Cali Manning Davis, "When Mitigation Evidence Makes A Difference: Effects of Psychological Mitigating Evidence on Sentencing Decisions in Capital Trials," *Behavioral Sciences and the Law* 22, no. 6 (2004): 751–70; and Carol S. Steiker, "The Marshall Hypothesis Revisited," *Howard Law Journal* 52 (2009), 525–55.

45 Michael Winerip, "Dream Act Advocate Turns Failure into Hope," *New York Times*, February 20, 2011.

46 Julia Preston, "After a False Dawn, Anxiety for Illegal Immigrant Students," *New York Times*, February 8, 2011, A15.

47 Preston, "After a False Dawn," A15.

48 Harriet Beecher Stowe, "In Which It Appears That a Senator Is but a Man," in *Uncle Tom's Cabin, or Life Among the Lowly* (New York: Penguin Classics, 1986), 9, 141–61.

49 Ibid., 155–56.

50 *The Oxford Pocket Latin Dictionary*, ed. James Morwood (New York: Oxford University Press, 1994), 139.

51 *Black's Law Dictionary*, 6th ed. (St. Paul, Minn.: West, 1990), s.vv. "ripeness doctrine," "standing to sue doctrine." See, as well, Steven L. Winter, "The Metaphor of Standing and the Problem of Self-Governance," *Stanford Law Review* 40 (July 1988): 1417–57.

52 James Boyd White, introduction to *Justice as Translation: An Essay in Cultural and Legal Criticism* (Chicago: University of Chicago Press, 1990), xiii.

53 Soshana Felman and Dori Laub, foreword to *Testimony: Crises of Witnessing in Literature, Psychoanalysis and History* (New York: Routledge, 1992), xviii.

54 Martha C. Nussbaum, "The Literary Imagination," in *Poetic Justice: The Literary Imagination and Public Life* (Boston: Beacon Press, 1995), 8–10.

55 Richard A. Posner, "Conclusion," in *Law and Literature: A Misunderstood Relation* (Cambridge, Mass.: Harvard University Press, 1988), 354.

56 Brook Thomas, "An Opening Statement," in *Cross-Examinations of Law and Literature: Cooper, Hawthorne, Stowe, and Melville* (Cambridge: Cambridge University Press, 1987), 13–16.

57 Walter Benjamin, "The Storyteller: Reflections on the Works of Nikolai Leskov," in *Illuminations: Essays and Reflections*, ed. Hannah Arendt, trans. Harry Zohn (New York: Schocken Books, 1969), 86–90.

58 Colin McGinn, *Ethics, Evil, and Fiction* (Oxford: Clarendon Press, 1997), 3.

59 Robert Penn Warren, "Why Do We Read Fiction?," in *New and Selected Essays* (New York: Random House, 1989), 55–56.

60 E. L. Doctorow, "False Documents," in *E. L. Doctorow: Essays and Conversations*, ed. Richard Trenner (Princeton, N.J.: Ontario Review Press, 1983), 16

61 See Ann Hagedorn, *The Untold Story of the Heroes of the Underground Railroad* (New York: Simon & Schuster, 2002), 135–39.

62 Cindy Weinstein, introduction to *The Cambridge Companion to Harriet Beecher Stowe*, ed. Cindy Weinstein (New York: Cambridge University Press, 2004), 1.

63 David S. Reynolds, introduction to *Mightier than the Sword: "Uncle Tom's Cabin" and the Battle for America* (New York: Norton, 2011), xi.

64 Leslie Fiedler, "The Many Myths of Henry Roth," in *New Essays on Call It Sleep*, ed. Hana Wirth-Nesher (New York: Cambridge University Press, 1996), 28.

65 Fredric Jameson, *Postmodernism, or, The Cultural Logic of Late Capitalism* (Durham: Duke University Press, 1991), 67, 88–89.

66 Wolfgang Iser, *The Implied Reader: Patterns of Communication in Prose Fiction from Bunyan to Beckett* (Baltimore: Johns Hopkins Press, 1974), 57–59, 81, xiii, 290.

67 *A Dictionary of Literary Terms*, ed. J. A. Cuddon (Garden City, N.Y.: Doubleday, 1977), s.v. "modernism."

68 Ezra Pound, "Hugh Selwyn Mauberly," in *The Norton Anthology of Modern Poetry*, eds. Richard Ellmann and Robert O'Clair (New York: Norton, 1973), 346, lines 91, 84–85.

69 Michael H. Levenson, *A Genealogy of Modernism: A Study of English Literary Doctrine, 1908–1922* (New York: Cambridge University Press, 1984), 201–6, and Ruth Wisse, "The Classic of Disinheritance," in *New Essays on "Call It*

Sleep," ed. Hana Wirth-Nesher (New York: Cambridge University Press, 1996), 61–62.

70 Henry Roth, *Call It Sleep*, 1st Picador Ed. (New York: Farrar, Straus, and Giroux, 2005), 27, 401–2. All further references to the novel are to this edition by page number in parentheses in the text.

71 For more about protests against the Fugitive Slave Law when it reached a legal forum, see Gordon S. Barker, *Imperfect Revolution: Anthony Burns and the Landscape of Race in Antebellum America* (Kent, Ohio: Kent State University Press, 2010), and Don E. Fehrenbacher, *The Slaveholding Republic: An Account of the United States Government's Relations to Slavery* (New York: Oxford University Press, 2001), 231–51. For evidence of extended public discussions over severe new state restrictions on undocumented immigrants, see Robertson, "In Alabama, Calls for Revamping Immigration Law," A15.

72 See Robertson, "Alabama Wins in Ruling on Its Immigration Law," A16; "Alabama: Judge Blocks Part of Immigration Law," *New York Times*, December 13, 2011, A22; Robbie Brown, "Parts of Immigration Law Blocked in South Carolina," *New York Times*, December 23, 2011, A18.

73 John C. Calhoun, "On the Reception of Abolition Petitions," in *The Works of John C. Calhoun*, ed. Richard K. Crallé, vol. 2., *Speeches of John C. Calhoun Delivered in the House of Representatives and the Senate of the United States* (New York: D. Appleton, 1854–1856), 629–30. This speech was made before the U.S. Senate on February 6, 1847.

74 Calhoun, *A Disquisition on Government*, in *The Works of John C. Calhoun*, ed. Richard K. Crallé, vol. 1., *A Disquisition on Government and a Discourse on the Constitution and Government of the United States* (New York: D. Appleton, 1854–1856), 52–54.

75 Robert Cover, "Nomos and Narrative," *Harvard Law Review* 97 (1983): 102–3.

76 Graham v. Richardson, 403 U.S. 365–383 (1971), and Mathews v. Diaz, 426 U.S. 67–87 (1976). References to quotations in these decisions in the next two paragraphs will be by page number in parentheses in the text.

77 The 1860 United States Census finds a total population of 31,443,321. The best informed estimate for the slave population in 1860 is 3,953,760. See Donald B. Dodd, ed., *Historical Statistics of the State of the United States: Two Centuries of the Census, 1790–1990* (Westport, Conn.: Greenwood Press, 1993), 103, and John Cummings and James A. Hill, ed., *Negro Population, 1790–1915* (Washington, D.C.: Government Printing Office, 1918), 53. Current U.S. Census figures place the nation's total population at 311,090,451.

PART II. THE NATURE OF JUDGMENT

1 Paul O. Carrese, *The Cloaking of Power: Montesquieu, Blackstone, and the Rise of Judicial Activism* (Chicago: University of Chicago, 2003), 1–4; Ronald Dworkin, *Law's Empire* (Cambridge, Mass.: Harvard University Press, 1986), 407, 401–10.

2 Dworkin, *Law's Empire*, 11.

3 Richard A. Posner, *How Judges Think* (Cambridge, Mass.: Harvard University Press, 2008), 1–2, 19–55.

4 Nastasya Tay, "Thokozile Masipa: The World Awaits Her Verdict on Oscar Pistorius, *Observer*, August 9, 2014, http://www.theguardian.com/theobserver /2014/aug/10/thokozile-masipa-world-awaits-her-verdict.

5 "Oscar Pistorius Trial," YouTube video, 27:18–30:38, posted by SABC News on April 11, 2014, http://www.youtube.com/watch?v=eBvvA4cL5Zc. These insights about the trial of Pistorius in this paragraph and the next were formed and refined with two of my students, Alison Gordon and David Adam Moss, in conversation and writing during the fall semester of 2014.

6 *In the Matter Between the State and Oscar Leonard Carl Pistorius*, No. CC113– 2013 (September 11–12, 2014) at 3280–81, 3326–27.

7 Ian McEwan, *The Children Act* (New York: Doubleday, 2014). All references in the text to the novel are from this edition.

8 *The Journals and Miscellaneous Notebooks of Ralph Waldo Emerson*, ed. Merton M. Sealts Jr., vol. 10, *1847–1848* (Cambridge, Mass.: Belknap Press of Harvard University Press, 1973), 343.

4. HOLMES AND THE JUDICIAL FIGURE

1 Quoted in Michael Herz, "'Do Justice': Variations on a Thrice-Told Tale," *Virginia Law Review* 82 (1996): 111. See, as well, Lester E. Denonn, ed., *The Wit and Wisdom of Oliver Wendell Holmes, Father and Son* (Boston: Beacon Press, 1953), 46, 58.

2 Every commentator notes Holmes's "felicitous way with words" and "dazzling skills" somewhere. This is the judge who "made the dullest case a literary adventure." See David P. Currie, "The Constitution in the Supreme Court: 1910–1921," *Duke Law Journal* 34, no. 6 (1985): 1111, 1161; David P. Currie, "The Constitution in the Supreme Court: Full Faith and the Bill of Rights, 1889– 1910," *University of Chicago Law Review* 52 (1985): 867, 899–900.

3 For Holmes's management of his career, see Felix Frankfurter, *Of Law and Men: Papers and Addresses, 1939–1956* (New York: Harcourt, Brace, 1956), 162. "It would be difficult," observes Frankfurter, "to conceive a life more self-conscious of its directions."

4 Judges represent "the counter-majoritarian difficulty." See Alexander Bickel, *The Least Dangerous Branch: The Supreme Court at the Bar of Politics* (Indianapolis: Bobbs-Merrill, 1962), 16–28.

5 Frankfurter, *Of Law and Men*, 39, 200.

6 Ibid., 182, 177.

7 Jerome Frank, *Courts on Trial* (Princeton: Princeton University Press, 1949), 62–79.

8 For some judicial testimonials, see *The Miscellaneous Writings of Joseph Story*, ed. William W. Story (Boston: Little, Brown, 1852), 781–828; Oliver Wendell Holmes Jr., "John Marshall: From the Bench, February 4, 1901," in *Collected Legal Papers* (New York: Harcourt, Brace, 1920), 266–71; Felix Frankfurter, "Mr. Justice Holmes," *Harvard Law Review* 44, no. 5 (1931); Learned Hand, *The Spirit of Liberty: Papers and Addresses*, 3rd ed. (New York: Alfred A. Knopf, 1960), 24–29, 57–65, 129–33, 166–79, 201–24, 263–73; Henry J. Friendly, *Benchmarks* (Chicago: University of Chicago Press, 1967), 196–234, 285–324.

9 Hand, *The Spirit of Liberty*, 130.

10 Quoted from Henry J. Abraham, *The Judicial Process: An Introductory Analysis of the Courts of the United States, England, and France*, 5th ed. (New York: Oxford University Press, 1986), 55.

11 Frankfurter, "Mr. Justice Holmes," 54, 118, 85; Frankfurter, *Of Law and Men*, 159–60; Hand, *The Spirit of Liberty*, 29, 25; Jerome Frank, *Law and the Modern Mind* (New Brunswick, N.J.: Transactions Publishers, 1970), 253–26.

12 Harold J. Laski, introduction to *Representative Opinions of Mr. Justice Holmes*, ed. Alfred Lief (New York: Vanguard Press, 1931), ix, xviii; Max Lerner, ed., *The Mind and Faith of Justice Holmes* (Boston: Little, Brown, 1943), vii; Dean Acheson, *Morning and Noon* (Boston: Houghton Mifflin, 1965), 62; Frankfurter, *Of Law and Men*, 201, 278; Benjamin N. Cardozo, "Mr. Justice Holmes," *Harvard Law Review* 44, no. 5 (1931), 682, 691, 684, 682.

13 Frankfurter, *Of Law and Men*, 183.

14 Oliver Wendell Holmes Jr., *The Common Law* (Boston: Little, Brown, 1881), 1. For Holmes's life, see Mark DeWolfe Howe, *Justice Oliver Wendell Holmes*, vol. 1, *The Shaping Years, 1841–1870* (Cambridge, Mass.: Harvard University

Press, 1957), and *Justice Oliver Wendell Holmes*, vol. 2. *The Proving Years, 1870–1882* (Cambridge, Mass.: Harvard University Press, 1963).

15 See David H. Burton, ed., *Oliver Wendell Holmes, Jr.: What Manner of Liberal?* (Huntington, N.Y.: R. E. Krieger, 1979), particularly Harold R. McKinnon, "The Secret of Mr. Justice Holmes," 91–105, and Daniel J. Boorstin, "The Elusiveness of Mr. Justice Holmes," 129–34.

16 Lerner, ed., *The Mind and Faith of Justice Holmes*, 367.

17 Robert W. Gordon, "Holmes' *Common Law* as Legal and Social Science," *Hofstra Law Review* 10, no. 3 (1982): 719–721, 742, 746.

18 G. Edward White, "The Rise and Fall of Justice Holmes," *University of Chicago Law Review* 39 (1971): 51, 54. See also Currie, "The Constitution in the Supreme Court, 1910–1921," *Duke Law Journal* (1985): 1161, and Currie, "The Constitution in the Supreme Court," *University of Chicago Law Review* (1985): 900. For the question about apotheosis, see Yosal Rogat, "The Judge as Spectator," *University of Chicago Law Review* 31 (1964): 213, 256.

19 Frank, *Law and the Modern Mind*, 253; Lerner, ed., *The Mind and Faith of Justice Holmes*, vii; Cardozo, "Mr. Justice Holmes," 682; Frankfurter, *Of Law and Men*, 165.

20 Holmes's entry in the *Album of the Harvard College Class of 1861* is reprinted in Lerner, ed., *The Mind and Faith of Justice Holmes*, 6–8.

21 Quoted in David H. Burton, introduction to Burton, ed., *Oliver Wendell Holmes, Jr.: What Manner of Liberal?*, 1.

22 Mark DeWolfe Howe, ed., *Holmes–Pollock Letters: The Correspondence of Justice Holmes and Sir Frederick Pollock, 1874–1932*, 2 vols. (Cambridge, Mass.: Harvard University Press, 1951), 1:106; 2:173.

23 Quoted in Lerner, *The Mind and Faith of Justice Holmes*, 399–400. For Emerson's influence on Holmes, see Howe, *Justice Oliver Wendell Holmes*, 1: 44, 54, 59, 203. For the last quotation in this paragraph, see Oliver Wendell Holmes Jr., "Ideals and Doubts, 1915" in *Collected Legal Papers*, 306.

24 Quoted in Frankfurter, *Of Law and Men*, 177–78, and Howe, ed., *Holmes–Pollock Letters*, 1:106.

25 Southern Pacific Co. v. Jensen, 244 U.S. 205, 222 (1917). (Holmes dissenting).

26 Felix Frankfurter, "The Supreme Court in the Mirror of Justices," *University of Pennsylvania Law Review* 105, no. 6 (1957): 781, 784.

27 See Holmes's Civil War writings in Mark DeWolfe Howe, ed., *Touched with Fire: Civil War Letters and Diary of Oliver Wendell Holmes, Jr., 1861–1864* (New York: Da Capo Press, 1969), 27–28, 54, 60, 64, 71, 142–43, 149.

28 Mark DeWolfe Howe, ed., *The Occasional Speeches of Justice Oliver Wendell Holmes* (Cambridge, Mass.: Harvard University Press, 1962), 75; Edmund Wilson, *Patriotic Gore: Studies in the Literature of the American Civil War* (New York: Oxford University, Press, 1962), 743–96; George M. Fredrickson, *The Inner Civil War: Northern Intellectuals and the Crisis in Union* (New York: Harper & Row, 1965), 168–71, 218–22.

29 Oliver Wendell Holmes Jr., "The Class of 1861: A Poem," in Lerner, ed., *The Mind and Faith of Justice Holmes*, 8. Holmes said the Civil War made him and his comrades "citizens of the world and not of a little town." Oliver Wendell Holmes Jr., "The Fraternity of Arms," in Howe, ed., *The Occasional Speeches*, 100–101.

30 The quotations are from Saul Touster, "In Search of Holmes from Within," *Vanderbilt Law Review* 18 (1965): 437, 464, 470, 459. For Holmes's descriptions of his experiences at the Battle of Fredericksburg (December 11–15, 1862), ones that show how "the rhetoric of later years is moulded," see Howe, ed., *Touched with Fire*, 76–77, and Howe, ed., *The Occasional Speeches*, 11–12.

31 Charles E. Wyzanski Jr., "The Democracy of Justice Oliver Wendell Holmes," *Vanderbilt Law Review* 7 (1954): 311, 322; Howe, *Justice Oliver Wendell Holmes*, 2: 4, 253–56.

32 Howe, ed., *The Occasional Speeches*, 168.

33 Howe, ed., *Touched with Fire*, 79–80. The son's reproof of the father is a recurring pattern. See also 67, 86, 91, 123, 148.

34 Quoted in Howe, *Justice Oliver Wendell Holmes*, 1:19.

35 For Oliver Wendell Holmes Sr.'s literary career, see Martin Green, *The Problem of Boston: Some Readings in Cultural History* (New York: Norton, 1966), 74–75, 115, 169–70, 186–87.

36 Howe, ed., *Touched with Fire*, 90–91, and quoted in Howe, *Justice Oliver Wendell Holmes*, 1:19.

37 Quoted in Howe, *Justice Oliver Wendell Holmes*, 2:25.

38 Oliver Wendell Holmes Jr., "The Path of the Law," in *Collected Legal Papers*, 202

39 John Gross, *The Rise and Fall of the Man of Letters: A Study of the Idiosyncratic and the Humane in Modern Literature* (New York: Macmillan, 1969), 62–97, and John Tomsich, *A Genteel Endeavor: American Culture and Politics in the Gilded Age* (Stanford: Stanford University Press, 1971).

40 Thomas Carlyle, *On Heroes, Hero-Worship, and the Heroic in History* (New York: D. Appleton, 1841), 249, 316, 328, 266, 274.

41 Holmes, "The Path of the Law," 167–68.

42 Ibid., 167–68, 173.

43 Ibid., 169, 186, 170–71, 201.

44 Ibid., 276–77.

45 Archibald Cox, *The Court and the Constitution* (Boston: Houghton Mifflin, 1987), 134, and G. Edward White, *The American Judicial Tradition: Priorities of Leading American Judges* (New York: Oxford University Press, 1988), 178–229.

46 Oliver Wendell Holmes Jr., "Law and the Court," in *Collected Legal Papers*, 291–97. The quotations appear on 292, 296.

47 Ibid., 296–97.

48 William K. Wimsatt Jr. and Cleanth Brooks, *Literary Criticism: A Short History* (New York: Alfred A. Knopf, 1957), 74.

49 See Howe, ed., *The Occasional Speeches*, 9, 41, 151, 161.

50 Howe, ed., *Holmes–Pollock Letters*, 2:253, 268, and Mark DeWolfe Howe, ed. *Holmes–Laski Letters: The Correspondence of Mr. Justice Holmes and Harold J. Laski*, vol. 2., *1926–1935* (Cambridge, Mass.: Harvard University Press, 1952), 1188, 1183.

51 Quoted in Catherine Drinker Bowen, *Yankee From Olympus: Justice Holmes and His Family* (Boston: Little, Brown, 1944), 408.

52 Holmes, "John Marshall: From the Bench, February 4, 1901," 270, 267–68, 271.

53 Ibid.

54 Howe, ed., *Holmes-Pollock Letters*, 2:36. See also Ex Parte Indiana Transportation Co., 244 U.S. 456, 457 (1917).

55 Oliver Wendell Holmes Jr., in "Address at Northwestern University Law School, 1902," in *Collected Legal Papers*, 274. See, as well, "The Path of the Law," 169–70; "Law in Science and Science in Law," 225–26; and "Speech at Bar Association, 1900," 248, all in *Collected Legal Papers*.

56 Harry C. Shriver, *What Gusto: Stories and Anecdotes About Justice Oliver Wendell Holmes* (Potomac, Md.: Fox Hills Press, 1970), 23, 29, and Shriver, ed., *Justice Oliver Wendell Holmes: His Book Notices and Uncollected Letters and Papers* (New York: Central Book, 1936), 200.

57 See J .G. A. Pocock, *Politics, Language and Time: Essays on Political Thought and History* (London: Methuen, 1972), 202–72, particularly 230–31 and 240–41.

58 See Andrew Oliver, *The Portraits of John Marshall* (Charlottesville: University Press of Virginia, 1977), 75.

59 Howe, ed., *Holmes–Pollock Letters*, 2:11, and Acheson, *Morning and Noon*, 62.

60 David H. Burton, *Oliver Wendell Holmes, Jr.* (Boston: Twayne, 1980), 143–45, 105–7. Majority opinions and concurrences outnumber dissents more than eight to one, a record that lends some support to Holmes's courtroom contention: "I think it useless and undesirable, as a rule, to express dissent." Northern Securities Co. v. United States, 193 U.S. 197, at 400 (1904).

61 Richard A. Posner, *Law & Literature: A Misunderstood Relation* (Cambridge, Mass.: Harvard University Press, 1988), 281, 285.

62 Lochner v. New York, 198 U.S. 45, 74–75 (1904) (Holmes dissenting). The quotations in this paragraph and the next three are from 74–76.

63 Holmes, "The Path of the Law," 187.

64 For the ironies in this accusation, see Cass R. Sunstein, "Lochner's Legacy," *Columbia Law Review* 87, no. 5 (1987): 879–80.

65 For the quotations in this paragraph and the next three, see Frank v. Mangum, 237 U.S. 304, 345–49 (1915).

66 Arthur Garfield Hays, *Trial by Prejudice* (New York: Covici, Friede, 1933), 296–315, and John J. O'Connor, "Murder of Mary Phagan on NBC," *New York Times*, January 22, 1988, 20.

67 Walter Benjamin, *Illuminations: Essays and Reflections*, ed. Hannah Arendt, trans. Harry Zohn (New York: Schocken Books, 1969), 90, 108–9.

68 *Frank*, 237 U.S. 304, at 349.

69 For the complete account of Holmes's dissent in *Abrams*, see Thomas Healy, *The Great Dissent: How Oliver Wendell Holmes Changes His Mind—and Changed the History of Free Speech in America* (New York: Henry Holt, 2013).

70 Wyzanski, "The Democracy of Justice Oliver Wendell Holmes," 318–19.

71 Abrams v. United States, 250 U.S. 616, 630 (1919) (Holmes dissenting).

72 See Samuel J. Konefsky, *The Legacy of Holmes and Brandeis; A Study in the Influence of Ideas* (New York: Macmillan, 1956), 202–10.

73 *Abrams*, 250 U.S. at 616–24.

74 Schenck v. United States, 249 U.S. 47, 52 (1919).

75 For the quotations from Holmes's dissent in *Abrams* in the rest of this paragraph and the next two, see, in order, *Abrams*, 250 U.S. at 626, 628, 629, 629, 630, 631.

76 Towne v. Eisner, 245 U.S. 418, 425 (1918).

77 Howe, *Justice Oliver Wendell Holmes*, 2:282.

78 Holmes to John Wu, May 14, 1923, quoted in Lerner, ed., *The Mind and Faith of Justice Holmes*, 421.

79 Holmes, "Law in Science and Science in Law," 455.

80 Ibid.

5. THE OPINION AS LITERARY GENRE

1 See Alastair Fowler, *Kinds of Literature: An Introduction to the Theory of Genres and Modes* (Cambridge, Mass.: Harvard University Press, 1982), and Adena Rosmarin, *The Power of Genre* (Minneapolis: University of Minnesota Press, 1985).

2 Minersville School District v. Gobitis, 310 U.S. 586 (1940), and West Virginia State Board of Education v. Barnette, 319 U.S. 624 (1943).

3 Linda Greenhouse, "Patriotism and the Pledge," *New York Times*, August 27, 1988, 4; Jon C. Blue, "One Nation, Divisible, With Liberty for None," *New York Times*, September 2, 1988, 27; "Quayle Embraces Patriotic Themes and Attacks Dukakis on Pledge," *New York Times*, September 6, 1988; "Dukakis Likens G.O.P. Attacks to McCarthy's," *New York Times*, September 10, 1988; and "The Presidential Debate: Transcript of the First TV Debate Between Bush and Dukakis," *New York Times*, September 26, 1988, 17.

4 Archibald Cox, *The Court and the Constitution* (Boston: Houghton Mifflin, 1987), 192–98, and Edward F. Waite, "The Debt of Constitutional Law to Jehovah's Witnesses," *Minnesota Law Review* 28 (1944): 209–46.

5 See William Raymond Smith, *The Rhetoric of American Politics: A Study of Documents* (Westport: Conn.: Greenwood, 1969), 407–17; and Benjamin N. Cardozo, "Law and Literature," in *Selected Writings of Benjamin Nathan Cardozo*, ed. Margaret E. Hall (New York: Fallon, 1947), 339–56.

6 Fowler, *Kinds of Literature*, 37–39, 256–76.

7 Mikhail. M. Bakhtin, *The Dialogic Imagination: Four Essays,* ed. Michael Holquist, trans. Caryl Emerson and Michael Holquist (Austin: University of Texas Press, 1981), 349–50.

8 Richard A. Posner, *The Federal Courts: Crisis and Reform* (Cambridge, Mass.: Harvard University Press, 1985), 119–27.

9 Bakhtin, *The Dialogic Imagination*, 294, 264–71, 342–44.

10 *Gobitis*, 310 U.S. 586 at 591.

11 Rosmarin, *The Power of Genre*, 46–47, and more generally, Robert Langbaum, *The Poetry of Experience: The Dramatic Monologue in Modern Literary Theory* (New York: Norton, 1957).

12 *Barnette*, 319 U.S. 624 at 646–47, and *Gobitis*, 310 U.S. at 596.

13 *Barnette*, 319 U.S. 624 at 636.

14 Ibid., 645.

15 Stephen J. Greenblatt, *Renaissance Self-Fashioning: From More to Shakespeare* (Chicago: University of Chicago Press, 1980), and James Clifford, *The Predicament of Culture: Twentieth-Century Ethnography* (Cambridge, Mass.: Harvard University Press, 1988), 92–113.

16 Walter Benjamin, *Illuminations: Essays and Reflections*, ed. Hannah Arendt, trans. Harry Zohn (New York: Schocken Books, 1969), 93, 106–9.

17 *Gobitis*, 310 U.S. 586 at 596, and *Barnette*, 319 U.S. 624 at 647.

18 John Hart Ely, *Democracy and Distrust: A Theory of Judicial Review* (Cambridge, Mass.: Harvard University Press, 1980), 5.

19 See Owen Fiss, "Objectivity and Interpretation," *Stanford Law Review* 34, no. 4 (1982): 739, 744–45.

20 *A Handlist of Rhetorical Terms*, ed. Richard A. Lanham, 2nd ed. (Berkeley: University of California Press, 1991), s.v. "hypophora."

21 See William Chambliss's paraphrases of Francis Bacon in *The Politics of Law: A Progressive Critique*, ed. David Kairys (New York: Pantheon Books, 1982), 230. See, as well, *The Philosophical Works of Francis Bacon*, ed. John M. Robertson (London: Routledge, 1905), 271.

22 Elias Canetti, *Crowds and Power*, trans. Carol Stewart (New York: Farrar, Straus & Giroux, 1984), 284–89.

23 I rely in part on Richard Danzig, "How Questions Begot Answers in Felix Frankfurter's First Flag Salute Opinion," *Supreme Court Review* (1977): 257–74.

24 *Gobitis*, 310 U.S. 586 at 592–93.

25 Ibid., 593.

26 Ibid., 595, 597.

27 Cardozo," Law and Literature," 346.

28 Bakhtin, *The Dialogic Imagination*, 280.

29 *Barnette*, 319 U.S. 624 at 635–36. Emphasis in the text.

30 See ibid., 659–61.

31 Ibid., 639–40.

32 See Bakhtin, *The Dialogic Imagination*, 253.

33 Clifford Geertz, *Local Knowledge: Further Essays in Interpretive Anthropology* (New York: Basic Books, 1983), 48.

34 *Gobitis*, 310 U.S. 586 at 597, emphasis added. See also Danzig, "How Questions Begot Answers," 261–64.

35 By June 1940, when the *Gobitis* decision was announced, Germany had swallowed up Austria, Czechoslovakia, Poland, Denmark, Luxembourg, the Netherlands, and Belgium and had successfully invaded France. The Allied

forces were evacuating from Dunkirk and the Soviet-German nonaggression pact of August 1939 was still in force. In England and the United States, these were the darkest moments of World War II.

36 *Gobitis*, 310 U.S. 586 at 591, 595, 598, 600.

37 *Barnette*, 319 U.S. 624 at 641.

38 Ibid., 642.

39 See Cox, *The Court and the Constitution*, 194–95, and Blue, "One Nation, Divisible, With Liberty for None," 27.

40 *Barnette*, 319 U.S. 624 at 643.

41 For recognition of the term used originally in this essay, see Richard A. Posner, *Cardozo: A Study in Reputation* (Chicago: University of Chicago Press, 1990), 45 and 45n.

42 Kenneth Burke, *A Grammar of Motives* (1945; repr., Berkeley: University of California Press, 1969), 258–59, 379–80.

43 Leo Tolstoy, *War and Peace*, trans. Rosemary Edmonds, 2 vols. (Baltimore: Penguin Books, 1961), 2:1433–34, 1438–39.

44 See J. G. A. Pocock, "Burke and the Ancient Constitution: A Problem in the History of Ideas," in *Politics, Language, and Time: Essays in Political Thought and History* (New York: Atheneum, 1973), 202–32.

45 Alexander M. Bickel, *The Morality of Consent* (New Haven: Yale University Press, 1975), 24, and generally, 11–25.

46 Michel Foucault, *Discipline & Punish: The Birth of the Prison*, trans. Alan Sheridan (New York: Random House, 1979), 20–21.

47 *Gobitis*, 310 U.S. 586 at 593, 594, 598.

48 Ibid., 601, 604.

49 *Barnette*, 319 U.S. 624 at 637, 640.

50 Ibid., 664, 660–61.

51 See *Gobitis*, 310 U.S. 586 at 596, 594n3, 589, 604–5, and *Barnette*, 319 U.S. 624 at 653, 667, 649–50, 636, 639–40, 646.

52 *Barnette*, 319 U.S. 624 at 666.

53 *Gobitis*, 310 U.S. 586 at 596

54 *Barnette*, 319 U.S. 624 at 655, and *Gobitis*, 310 U.S. 586 at 596.

55 Burke, *A Grammar of Motives*, 441–42.

56 Bruce Ackerman, "Foreword: Law in an Activist State," *Yale Law Journal* 92, no. 7 (1983): 1083–85, 1098–99.

57 Henry David Thoreau, *Walden*, ed. J. Lyndon Shanley (Princeton: Princeton University Press, 1971), 101.

6. ULYSSES IN GOVERNMENT HANDS

1   United States v. One Book Called "Ulysses," 5 F. Supp.182–185 (S.D.N.Y. 1933).

2   See Marisa Anne Pagnattaro, "Carving a Literary Exception: The Obscenity
    Standard and *Ulysses*," *Twentieth-Century Literature* 47, no. 2 (2001): 223–25.
    Well before the actual trial, involved lawyers began to use the phrase "law and
    literature" as a central concept. Alexander Lindey, memo to Morris Ernst,
    August 6, 1931, in *The United States of America vs. One Book Entitled "Ulysses"
    by James Joyce: Documents and Commentary—A 50-Year Retrospective*, eds.
    Michael Moscato and Leslie LeBlanc (Frederick, Md.: University Publications
    of America, 1984), 77.

3   The defects in a decision filled with "well-intentioned lies" are first noted in
    Leslie Fiedler, "To Whom Does Joyce Belong? *Ulysses* as Parody, Pop, and
    Porn," in *Light Rays: James Joyce and Modernism*, ed. Heyward Ehrlich (New
    York: New Horizon Press, 1984), 29; and later by Paul Vanderham, "The Well-
    intentioned Lies of the Woolsey Decision," in *James Joyce and Censorship: The
    Trials of Ulysses* (New York; New York University Press, 1998), 115–31; Stephen
    Gillers, "A Tendency to Deprave and Corrupt: The Transformation of American
    Obscenity Law from *Hicklin* to *Ulysses II*," *Washington University Law Review*
    85, no. 2 (2007): 284.

4   United States v. One Book, Entitled Ulysses by James Joyce, 72 F. 2d 705 (2nd
    Cir. 1934).

5   Benjamin Cardozo, *Law and Literature and Other Essays and Addresses*
    (New York: Harcourt, Brace, 1931), 7.

6   Cardozo, a Democrat, was nominated by President Herbert Hoover, a Repub-
    lican, and confirmed unanimously by the Senate in 1932.

7   For how an accomplished opinion might not be "scrupulous in its treatment . . .
    of precedent" and employ "inaccuracy" in "statement of facts" while "gliding
    too quickly" over legal analysis" in analyses that discuss Cardozo's opinion in
    Palsgraf v. Long Island R. Co., 248 N.Y. 339, 162 N.E. 99 (1928), see Richard A.
    Posner, "Law and Literature: A Relation Reargued," *Virginia Law Review* 72,
    no. 8 (1986): 1380–83, and Richard A. Posner, *Cardozo: A Study in Reputation*
    (Chicago: University of Chicago Press, 1990), 33–57.

8   Aristotle, *On Rhetoric: A Theory of Civic Discourse*, trans. George A Kennedy,
    2nd ed., (New York: Oxford University Press, 2007), 33 [1.1.1355a].

9   Cicero, *Brutus, Orator*, trans. G. L. Hendrickson and H. M. Hubbell, Loeb
    Classical Library ed. (Cambridge, Mass.: Harvard University Press, 1939),

356–57 [xx.68–xxi.71], and Kenneth Burke, *A Rhetoric of Motives* (Berkeley: University of California Press, 1969), 71–73.

10   Aristotle, *On Rhetoric*, 121 [2.3.1380a]. "Let calmness [*praünsis*] be [defined as] a settling down and quieting of anger."

11   Cardozo, *Law and Literature*, 8.

12   See chapter 5 for treatment of this subject.

13   John A Jenkins, "A Candid Talk with Justice Blackmun," *New York Times*, February 20, 1983, 20.

14   Timothy Wu of the Columbia Law School quoted in Peter Lattman, "A Paean to the Opinions of the Prolific Judge Posner," *Law Blog: On Cases, Trends, and Personalities in Business* (blog), *Wall Street Journal*, October 10, 2006, http://blogs.wsj.com/law/2006/10/10/a-paean-to-the-opinions-of-the -prolific-judge-posner/.

15   Richard A. Posner, *How Judges Think* (Cambridge, Mass.: Harvard University Press, 2008), 230–31, 176, 203.

16   Stephen E. Toulmin, *The Uses of Argument* (Cambridge: Cambridge University Press, 2003), 33–36. See also Dennis Patterson, *Law & Truth* (New York: Oxford University Press, 1996), 150.

17   Toulmin, *The Uses of Argument*, 31.

18   David Weissman, *Truth's Debt to Value* (New Haven: Yale University Press, 1993), 148, 329ff.

19   Bernard Williams, *Truth and Truthfulness: An Essay in Genealogy* (Princeton: Princeton University Press, 2002), 11. Williams names accuracy and sincerity as "the two basic virtues of truth."

20   Ibid., 10–11.

21   19 U.S.C.A. § 1305(a). The provision states "all persons are prohibited from importing in the United States from any foreign country . . . any obscene book, pamphlet, paper, writing, advertisement, circular, print, picture, drawing, or other representation, figure, or image on or of paper or other material, or any cast, instrument or other article which is obscene or immoral." Section 1305(b) then follows: "Upon the adjudication that such book or matter thus seized is of the character of the entry of which is by this section prohibited, it shall be ordered destroyed and shall be destroyed."

22   Regina v. Hicklin, 3 Q.B. 360, 371 (1868).

23   *Hicklin*, 3 Q.B. 360, 371 (1868). See, as well, Cara L. Newman, "Eyes Wide Open, Minds Wide Shut: Art, Obscenity, and the First Amendment in Contemporary America," *DePaul Law Review* 53, no. 1 (2003): 134.

24 Michael Moscato and Leslie LeBlanc, eds., *The United States of America vs. One Book Entitled "Ulysses" by James Joyce: Documents and Commentary*, 284, and *"Ulysses* Case Reaches Court After 10 Years," *New York Herald-Tribune*, November 26, 1933. For facts on Woolsey's life, see Paul Vanderham, *James Joyce and Censorship: The Trials of Ulysses* (New York; New York University Press, 1998), 110.

25 Vanderham, *James Joyce and Censorship*, 109.

26 Clifford Geertz, *Local Knowledge: Further Essays in Interpretive Anthropology* (New York: Basic Books, 1983), and Louis Joughin and Edmund M. Morgan, *The Legacy of Sacco and Vanzetti* (1948; repr., Princeton: Princeton University Press, 1978), 196.

27 "The confiscated copy of *Ulysses* reveals that the US Attorney's Office deemed a total of 260 passages over 198 pages, roughly 25 percent of the pages, to be obscene by the standards of 1932–33." Vanderham, *James Joyce and Censorship*, 108–9.

28 The Tariff Act of 1930 reaches beyond books to also include as obscene "any paper, writing, advertisement, circular, print, picture, drawing, or other representation, figure, or image on or of paper or other material."

29 *One Book Called "Ulysses"* dominates Woolsey's later reputation despite other very significant cases he weighed on. For how single high-profile trials shape legal careers, see Robert A. Ferguson, "Where Courtrooms and Communities Meet," in *The Trial in American Life* (Chicago: University of Chicago Press, 2007), 5–28.

30 Some writers celebrate the lack of a meaningful standard in obscenity law. See Stephen Gillers, "A Tendency to Deprave and Corrupt," 295–96.

31 United States v. One Obscene Book, Entitled "Married Love," 48 F.2d 821 (S.D.N.Y. 1931), and United States v. One Book, Entitled "Contraception," 51 F.2d 525 (S.D.N.Y. 1931).

32 Richard A. Posner, *How Judges Think* (Cambridge, Mass.: Harvard University Press, 2008), 65–67.

33 United States v. One Book Called "Ulysses," 5 F. Supp. 182 (S.D.N.Y. 1933) at 182. All further quotations from the opinion will be from this source and given parenthetically by page number in the text.

34 Reviews of the book were pasted into the copy of *Ulysses* that Judge Woolsey used by the defense. Also, against Woolsey's order, the defense supplied relevant essays and books of criticism. See Vanderham, *James Joyce and Censorship*, 88–93.

35 Vanderham, *James Joyce and Censorship*, 126, 117–20.

36 Fiedler, "To Whom Does Joyce Belong?" 30–33. He describes Joyce in this way: "a coprophile [gaining sexual pleasure from playing with feces] and a voyeur— a sniffer of bicycle seats, a fingerer of the miniature drawers he liked to carry about in his pocket[,] . . . the peddler of his own most shameful erotic fantasies, a writer of dirty letters to the world, in short, once more a pornographer."

37 James Joyce, *Ulysses*, corrected unabridged ed. (New York: Random House, 1946), 357–61, 723–68.

38 Ibid., 360.

39 *One Book, Entitled Ulysses by James Joyce*, 72 F. 2d 705 at 706–7.

40 Ibid.

41 Oliver Wendell Holmes Jr., "The Path of the Law," *Harvard Law Review* 10 (1897): 459.

42 *A Handlist of Rhetorical Terms*, ed. Richard A. Lanham, 2nd ed. (Berkeley: University of California Press, 1991), s.v. "ethos."

43 Henry James, preface to *The Portrait of a Lady, Volume I*, The Novels and Tales of Henry James, 26 vols. (New York: Charles Scribner's, 1908), 3:xi. See also Percy Lubbock, *The Craft of Fiction* (New York: Charles Scribner', 1955).

44 J. M. Lotman, "Point of View in a Text," *New Literary History* 6 (1975): 339–52.

45 See Vanderham, *James Joyce and Censorship*, 124, 228. Vanderham notes that the term *l'homme moyen sensuel* is a term of ridicule for a man of crude sensibilities and that Woolsey gives the term "a remarkable transformation" to suit his own rhetorical needs.

46 *One Book, Entitled Ulysses by James Joyce*, 72 F. 2d 705 at 708.

47 See, for example, Michael Meyer, "The Nature of Rhetoric," in *Rhetoric, Language, and Reason* (University Park: Pennsylvania State University Press, 1994), 155–56.

48 Eugene Garver, *For the Sake of Argument: Practical Reasoning, Character, and the Ethics of Belief* (Chicago: University of Chicago Press, 2004), 135.

49 Edwin Black, "Secrecy and Disclosure as Rhetorical Forms," in *Rhetorical Questions: Studies of Public Discourse* (Chicago: University of Chicago Press, 1992), 51–78.

50 Charles Sanders Peirce, "How to Make Our Ideas Clear," in *The Nature of Truth: Classic and Contemporary Perspectives*, ed. Michael P. Lynch (Cambridge, Mass.: MIT Press, 2001), 193, 208–9. The essay first appeared in *Popular Science Monthly* 12 (January 1878): 286–302.

51 Williams, *Truth and Truthfulness*, 11, 75, 126–127.

52 Harry G. Frankfurt, *On Truth* (Princeton: Princeton University Press, 2006), 7–8.

53 Bertrand Russell, "Truth and Falsehood," in *The Problems of Philosophy* (1912; repr., Oxford: Oxford University Press, 1974), 121.

54 William James, "Pragmatism's Conception of Truth," in *Essays in Pragmatism*, ed. Alburey Castell (1907; repr., New York: Hafner, 1948), 159–60. "Pragmatism's Conception of Truth" first appeared in William James, *Pragmatism: A New Name for Some Old Ways of Thinking* (New York: Longmans, 1907), 197–236.

55 Charles Taylor, *The Ethics of Authenticity* (Cambridge, Mass.: Harvard University Press, 1991), 33, 51–53, 45.

56 Henry David Thoreau, "Wednesday," in *A Week on the Concord and Merrimack Rivers*, eds. Carl F. Hovde, William L. Howarth, and Elizabeth Hall Witherell (1849; repr., Princeton, N.J.: Princeton University Press, 1980), 267.

57 Taylor, *The Ethics of Authenticity*, 81–84.

58 Weissman, *Truth's Debt to Value*, 128.

59 Garver, *For the Sake of Argument*, 131.

60 Williams, *Truth and Truthfulness*, 219–34.

61 Raymond Geuss, *The Ideal of a Critical Theory* (Cambridge: Cambridge University Press, 1981), 65ff.

62 Taylor, *The Ethics of Authenticity*, 34, and Charles Taylor, *Sources of the Self: The Making of the Modern Identity* (Cambridge, Mass.: Harvard University Press, 1989), 72.

63 For a discussion about the engaged over the passive citizen, see Michael J. Sandel, "Justice and the Common Good," in *Justice: What's The Right Thing to Do?* (New York: Farrar, Straus and Giroux, 2009), 244–69.

64 Kent Greenawalt, *Law and Objectivity* (New York: Oxford University Press, 1992), 46.

65 James, preface to *The Portrait of a Lady*, xi.

PART III. THE PUBLIC USES OF LEGAL ELOQUENCE

1 Shakespeare's abiding interest in legal discourse and problems has long been noted. See in general but also specifically, Kenji Yoshino, *A Thousand Times More Fair: What Shakespeare's Plays Teach Us about Justice* (New York: HarperCollins, 2011), 59–88, and Quentin Skinner, *Forensic Shakespeare* (Oxford: Oxford University Press, 2014), 89–97, 129–35.

2   Harold Bloom, "Measure for Measure," in *Shakespeare: The Invention of the Human* (New York: Penguin, 1998), 358–66."

3   Samuel Taylor Coleridge, *Lectures and Notes on Shakespeare and Other English Poets*, ed. T. Ashe (London: George Bell, 1902), 299. Coleridge first published these lectures in 1819.

4   William Shakespeare, *Measure for Measure*, ed. J. W. Lever, Arden Shakespeare, 2nd series (London: Thomson Learning, 2000), 1.3.26–31, 2.1.1–4. All references to the play are to this edition and identified, as here, by act, scene, and line in the text.

5   See Edward W. Tayler, "Measure for Measure: Its Glassy Essence," *Cithara* 37, no. 1 (1997): 3–21.

7. LAWYER LINCOLN: THE MAKING OF ELOQUENCE

1   Ronald C. White Jr., *The Eloquent President: A Portrait of Lincoln through Words* (New York: Random House, 2005), xix. See also James Wood, "A Critic's Notebook: Verbage," *New Yorker*, October 13, 2008, 74–75.

2   "Second Inaugural Address, March 4, 1865," in *The Collected Works of Abraham Lincoln*, ed. Roy P. Basler, 8 vols. (New Brunswick, N. J.: Rutgers University Press, 1953), 8:333. All further references to Lincoln's words, unless otherwise indicated, will be to this edition and indicated by volume and page number in the text.

3   See Gabor S. Boritt, ed., *The Lincoln Enigma: The Changing Faces of an American Icon* (New York: Oxford University Press, 2001). Lincoln was proud of the independency of mind that came from self-education. "He studied with nobody," he announced in a short autobiography. Basler, ed., *Collected Works of Abraham Lincoln*, 4:65.

4   Joshua Wolf Shenk, *Lincoln's Melancholy: How Depression Challenged a President and Fueled His Greatness* (Boston: Houghton Mifflin, 2005), and earlier, George B. Forgie, *Patricide in the House Divided: A Psychological Interpretation of Lincoln and His Age* (New York: Norton, 1979). But see also Doris Kearns Goodwin, *Team of Rivals: The Political Genius of Abraham Lincoln* (New York: Simon & Schuster, 2005).

5   Quoted in Benjamin P. Thomas, *Abraham Lincoln: A Biography* (New York: Alfred A. Knopf, 1960), 498. For the facts in Lincoln's life, I rely on this biography and David Herbert Donald, *Lincoln* (New York: Simon & Schuster,

1995). I also rely on Lincoln's "Autobiography Written for John L. Scripps," in Basler, ed., *Collected Works of Abraham Lincoln*, 4:60–67.

6   See Robert A. Ferguson, *Law and Letters in American Culture* (Cambridge, Mass.: Harvard University Press, 1984).

7   "When I read aloud my two senses catch the idea—1st I see what I am reading and 2dly I hear it read; and I can thus remember what I read the better." Quoted in Donald, *Lincoln*, 145. See, as well, William H. Herndon to Jesse W. Weik, February 18, 1887, in Herndon-Weik Collection, Library of Congress.

8   Don Edward Fehrenbacher, "The Words of Lincoln," in *Lincoln in Text and Context* (Stanford: Stanford University Press, 1987), 285. For Lincoln's emendations, see Douglas L. Wilson, *Lincoln's Sword: The Presidency and the Power of Words* (New York: Vintage, 2007), 59–69.

9   Daniel Boorstin, preface to the Beacon Press Edition of *The Mysterious Science of the Law: An Essay on Blackstone's Commentaries Showing How Blackstone Made of the Law at Once a Conservative and a Mysterious Science* (Boston: Beacon Press, 1958); William Blackstone, "Of the Nature of Laws in General," in *Commentaries on the Laws of England*, 4 vols. (1765–1769; repr., Chicago: University of Chicago Press, 1979), 1:4, 35, 41. See, as well, Ferguson, *Law and Letters in American Culture*, 11, 14–15, 30–33, 212, 290.

10 In "Autobiography Written for John L. Scripps," Lincoln wrote that "all his schooling did not amount to one year," and that "he regrets his want of education, and does what he can to supply the want." Basler, ed., *Collected Works of Abraham Lincoln*, 4:62.

11 See Mark E. Steiner, *An Honest Calling: The Law Practice of Abraham Lincoln* (DeKalb: Northern Illinois University Press, 2006), 33. See also Thomas, *Abraham Lincoln*, 66–67.

12 Donald, *Lincoln*, 149.

13 For these quotations and a general discussion of Lincoln's simple but effective manner and his willingness to concede on peripheral points, see Allen D. Spiegel, *A. Lincoln, Esquire: A Shrewd, Sophisticated Lawyer in His Time* (Macon, Ga.: Mercer University Press, 2002), 45–46, and Steiner, *An Honest Calling*, 8–10.

14 For the negative press reaction, see Herbert Mitgang, ed., *Abraham Lincoln, A Press Portrait* (Chicago: Quadrangle Books, 1971), 92–96.

15 For Lincoln's difficulties, see Paul M. Angle, introduction to *Created Equal? The Complete Lincoln–Douglas Debates of 1858* (Chicago: University of Chicago Press, 1958), x–xxx, 18, 106–13.

16 See also Basler, ed., *Collected Works of Abraham Lincoln*, 3:311–18.

17 James Oakes, "They Soared Above the Din," review of *Lincoln and Douglas: The Debates That Defined America*, by Allen C. Guelzo, and of *The Lincoln–Douglas Debates*, edited by Rodney O. Davis and Douglas L. Wilson, *New York Review of Books* 55 (October 23, 2008): 37–40.

18 Quoted in Angle, introduction to *Created Equal?*, xxx. Lincoln worked hard to get the debates published. Basler, ed., *Collected Works of Abraham Lincoln*, 3:339, 345, 349, 372–74, 516.

19 See David Herbert Donald, "A. Lincoln, Politician," in *Lincoln Reconsidered: Essays on the Civil War Era* (New York: Random House, 1956), 71–81; Donald, *Lincoln*, 398–405; and Goodwin, *Team of Rivals*.

20 Quoted in White, *The Eloquent President*, 139, and 139–52 generally.

21 Donald, *Lincoln*, 369, and Mitgang, *Abraham Lincoln, A Press Portrait*, 300–302.

22 See, most obviously, "First Inaugural Address, March 4, 1861," in Basler, ed., *Collected Works of Abraham Lincoln*, 4:261.

23 For the dialectic of law and religion, see Robert A. Ferguson, "The Dialectic of Liberty," in *Reading the Early Republic* (Cambridge, Mass.: Harvard University Press, 2004), 51–83.

24 For Lincoln's adeptness and imagination before juries, see Brian Dirck, *Lincoln the Lawyer* (Urbana: University of Illinois Press, 2007), 99–105.

25 These statistics come from Frank J. Williams, "Abraham Lincoln: Commander in Chief or 'Attorney in Chief'?" in *Judging Lincoln* (Carbondale: Southern Illinois University Press, 2002), 39.

26 Horace Greeley, *New York Tribune*, March 6, 1861, quoted in full in Mitgang, *Abraham Lincoln, A Press Portrait*, 238–39.

27 Lincoln asked all of his cabinet members to sign a sealed letter on August 23, 1864, in which he bound them to continue working "to save the Union" if he failed to be reelected in November. Basler, ed., *Collected Works of Abraham Lincoln*, 7:514, and Kearns, *Team of Rivals*, 648–49.

28 See Garry Wills, *Lincoln at Gettysburg: The Words That Remade America* (New York: Simon & Schuster, 1992), and Ronald C. White Jr., *Lincoln's Greatest Speech: The Second Inaugural* (New York: Simon & Schuster, 2002).

29 For Lincoln's "dispassionate" professional nature, his "high degree of emotional distance," and his desire "not to be led from the region of reason into that of hot blood," see Dirck, *Lincoln the Lawyer*, 161–70. Riding the legal circuit, Judge David Davis wrote that "Mr. Lincoln was not a sociable man by

any means," and also that Lincoln had "no strong emotional feelings for any person—mankind or thing." Donald, *Lincoln*, 146, 153.

30 I give what is known as the "Bliss Copy," the final public version that Lincoln wrote out in March 1864.

31 For more on how Lincoln "built the Gettysburg Address upon a structure of past, present, and future time," see White, *The Eloquent President*, 243.

32 Edwin Black, "The Ultimate Voice of Lincoln," *Rhetoric & Public Affairs* 3 (Spring 2000): 49ff. "The 'single most important instance of rhetorical leadership by Lincoln during his presidency' was his disappearance . . . in the place of his vanished ego, he proposed a set of principles of which he became the personification."

33 See Basler, ed. *Collected Works of Abraham Lincoln*, 2:81. See, as well, Dirck, *Lincoln the Lawyer*, 67, 158, 160–61.

34 See Wills, *Lincoln at Gettysburg*, 148–75, and Michael Leff and Jean Goodwin, "Dialogic Figures and Dialectical Argument in Lincoln's Rhetoric," *Rhetoric & Public Affairs* 3 (Spring 2000): 59–69. See also "Rhetorick" and "Style" in Samuel Kirkham, *English Grammar in Familiar Lectures* (Rochester, N.Y.: Marshall & Dean, 1832), 219–20ff, a work Lincoln studied with great care.

35 Michael Billig, "Imagining 'Us' as the National Community," in *Banal Nationalism* (London: Sage, 1995), 70–73.

36 Wills, Lincoln at Gettysburg, 100–101, 146–47.

37 Lincoln knew aspects of Samuel Kirkham's *English Grammar* (1832) and William Scott's *Lessons in Elocution* (1806) by heart. See White, *The Eloquent President*, 103–4; Donald, *Abraham Lincoln*, 48–49; and Wills, *Lincoln at Gettysburg*, 160–67. "Lincoln may have known [Hugh] Blair directly; he certainly new his principles from derivative sources (Wills, *Lincoln at Gettysburg*, 160). The six parts that were said to compose "a regular formal oration" that Lincoln employs are found in Hugh Blair, "Lecture 31," in *Lectures on Rhetoric and Belles Lettres* (1783; repr., Brooklyn: Thomas Kirk, 1807), 2:86–87. For Blair's profound impact on nineteenth-century American oratory, see William Norwood Brigance, ed., *A History and Criticism of American Public Address* (New York: McGraw-Hill, 1943), 1:21, 202–4, 330, 333, 485.

38 The *Springfield Republican* observed, "Turn back and read it over, it will repay study as a model speech." Quoted in Earl Wellington Wiley, *Abraham Lincoln: Portrait of a Speaker* (New York: Vantage Press, 1979), 538–39.

39 Lincoln's bold reworking of the date of national formation did not go unchallenged. The *Illinois State Register*, in quoting the first sentence of the address,

announced: "Lincoln began his dedicatory address by the enumeration of the following political falsehood." See Wiley, *Abraham Lincoln*, 537.

40   Look to the "necessary and proper" clause of the U.S. Constitution [article 1, section 8, number 18]. In this case, and again in the "Second Inaugural Address," Lincoln uses the device to show what cannot be done.

41   Lincoln was proud of having "studied and nearly mastered the Six-books of Euclid." He used the term "proposition" in its technical meaning, as something to be proved. See Basler, ed., *Collected Works of Abraham Lincoln*, 4:62.

42   See Tzvetan Todorov, *The Poetics of Prose*, trans. Richard Howard (Ithaca, N.Y.: Cornell University Press, 1977), 111. Narrative moves from equilibrium, to disequilibrium, and then to a higher form of equilibrium.

43   Frederick Douglass, *Autobiographies* (1893; repr., New York: Library of America, 1994), 802.

44   White, *Lincoln's Greatest Speech*, 101, 114. John Quincy Adams quotes from Psalm 127:1: "Except the Lord keep the city, the watchman waketh but in vain."

45   George Washington's "Second Inaugural" was only 135 words long. He spoke only of taking the oath. Jared Sparks, ed., *The Writings of George Washington*, vol. 10, *1782–1785* (Boston: Little, Brown, 1858), 321–23.

46   Exodus 21:24.

47   Spiegel, *A. Lincoln, Esquire*, 45.

48   Donald, "A Pumpkin in Each End of My Bag," "With Charity For All," "I Will Take Care of Myself," in *Lincoln*, 377–406, 558–64, 589–92.

49   Jeremy Waldron, "Kant's Legal Positivism," *Harvard Law Review* 109, no. 7 (1996): 1566.

50   *Hamlet, Prince of Denmark*, 3.3.36–71 (reference to act, scene, and line). Lincoln memorized the soliloquies of *Hamlet* in William Scott's *Lessons on Elocution*, and claimed Claudius's speech to be a personal favorite. See William Scott, *Lessons on Elocution; Or, A Selection of Pieces in Prose and Verse for the Improvement of Youth in Reading and Speaking* (Wilmington: Peter Brynberg, 1797), 343–44, and Donald, *Lincoln*, 15, 31, 337, 569.

51   *A Handlist of Rhetorical Terms*, ed. Richard A. Lanham, 2nd ed. (Berkeley: University of California Press, 1991), s.v. "hypophora."

52   Gideon Welles, *Diary of Gideon Welles, Secretary of the Navy Under Lincoln and Johnson*, vol. 2, *April 1, 1864–December 31, 1866* (Boston: Houghton Mifflin, 1911), 190.

53   Steiner, *An Honest Calling*, 3.

54 John Rawls, "The Idea of Public Reason Revisited," *University of Chicago Law Review* 64 (Summer 1997), 777–78.

55 David Zarefsky, "Lincoln's 1862 Annual Message: A Paradigm of Rhetorical Leadership," *Rhetoric & Public Affairs 3* (Spring 2000): 5–14.

56 The quotation is from *New York Times*, November 7, 1862.

57 Ecclesiastes 1:4 (AV): "One generation passeth away and another generation cometh, but the earth abideth forever." The passage appears in Lincoln's message. See Basler, ed., *Collected Works of Abraham Lincoln*, 5:527.

58 The formal definitions of "enthrall" and "disenthrall" appear in both *Webster's Third Unabridged New International Dictionary of the English Language Unabridged* (Springfield, Mass.: Merriam-Webster, 1993), 757, 648, and *The Compact Edition of the Oxford English Dictionary* (New York: Oxford University Press, 1971), 1:749, 876. Lincoln's lifelong interest in etymology came from his study of Samuel Kirkham, "Etymology," in *English Grammar in Familiar Lectures*, 26ff.

8. MEMORIALIZATION AND THE SPIRIT OF LAW

1 Jean-Paul Sartre, *No Exit*, in *No Exit and Three Other Plays* (New York: Random House, 1976), 45.

2 The familiar trope, "the spirit of the laws," comes from the title of Montesquieu's *De l'esprit des loix* (1748).

3 See Jonathan Glover, *Humanity: A Moral History of the Twentieth Century* (New Haven: Yale University Press, 2000), and Derrick A. Bell Jr., "The Racial Imperative in American Law," in *The Age of Segregation: Race Relations in the South, 1890–1945*, ed. Robert Haws (Jackson: University Press of Mississippi, 1978), 3–28.

4 The mural was painted in 1962 by J. William Myers.

5 Information about the two paintings in the Metropolitan Museum of Art can be found at www.metmuseum.org.

6 For the legal importance of John Brown, see Robert A. Ferguson, "John Brown: Defendant on the Loose," in *The Trial in American Life* (Chicago: University of Chicago Press, 2007), 117–52.

7 For legal complicity in the Holocaust, see Richard Weisberg, "Lawtalk in France: The Challenge to Democracy," in *Poethics and Other Strategies of Law and Literature* (New York: Columbia University Press, 1992), 127–87.

8   Hannah Arendt, *Eichmann in Jerusalem: A Report on the Banality of Evil*, revised and enlarged edition (1963; repr., New York: Penguin Books, 1965), 12.

9   Arendt, *Eichmann in Jerusalem*, and Haim Gouri, *Facing the Glass Booth: The Jerusalem Trial of Adolf Eichmann*, trans. Michael Swirsky (Detroit: Wayne State Press, 2004).

10 Arendt, *Eichmann in Jerusalem*, 1–150.

11 John Rawls, *A Theory of Justice* (Cambridge, Mass.: Harvard University Press, 1971), 12, 19, 136–42, and John Rawls, *Justice as Fairness, A Restatement* (Cambridge, Mass.: Harvard University Press, 2001), 3, 15, 18.

12 James Baldwin, *No Name in the Street* (New York: Dial Press, 1972), 63, 149. See, as well, James Baldwin, *The Fire Next Time* (New York: Dial Press, 1963), 102.

13 Aristotle, *Nichomachean Ethics*, trans. Martin Ostwald (New York: Bobbs-Merrill, 1962), 111–30 [5.1–6].

9. PRECISION IN PERSUASION

1   Peter M. Tiersma, *Legal Language* (Chicago: University of Chicago Press, 1999), 115–17, 243.

2   For disciplinary approaches to evidence, see James Chandler, Arnold I. Davidson, and Harry Harootunian, "Editors' Introduction: Questions of Evidence," *Critical Inquiry* 17, no. 4 (Summer 1991): 738–867, and *Critical Inquiry* 18 (Autumn 1991): 76–153.

3   Pierre N. Leval, "Judicial Opinions as Literature," in *Law's Stories: Narrative and Rhetoric in the Law*, eds. Peter Brooks and Paul Gewirtz (New Haven: Yale University Press, 1996), 207.

4   Bryan A. Garner, *The Elements of Legal Style*, 2nd ed. (Oxford: Oxford University Press, 2002), 53–58.

5   T. S. Eliot, "The Love Song of J. Alfred Prufrock," in *Collected Poems, 1909–1962* (New York: Harcourt, Brace, 1975), 4.

6   Alex Ayres, ed., *The Wit and Wisdom of Mark Twain* (New York: Harper & Row, 1987), and George Bainton, ed., *The Art of Authorship* (New York: D. Appleton, 1891), 87–88.

7   T. S. Eliot, "The Four Quartets," in *Collected Poems, 1909–1962* (New York: Harcourt, Brace, 1975), 188–89.

8   Paul Kahn, *The Cultural Study of Law: Reconstructing Legal Scholarship* (Chicago: University of Chicago Press, 1999), 7–8, 22–27.

9   Michael Oakeshott, "The Rule of Law," in *On History and Other Essays* (Indianapolis: Liberty Fund, 1999), 129–31, 174–78.

10 See Joseph Raz, "The Rule of Law and its Virtues," in *The Authority of Law: Essays in Law and Morality* (Oxford: Oxford University Press, 1979), 214, and Lon Fuller, *The Morality of Law* (New Haven: Yale University Press, 1964), 33–94.

11 Meir Dan-Cohen, "Decision Rules and Conduct Rules: On Acoustic Separation in Criminal Law," *Harvard Law Review* 97 (1984): 625–26.

12 This approval rating comes from Gallup poll figures conducted from June 5–8, 2014, reported in Charles M. Blow, "The Frustration Doctrine," *New York Times*, June 23, 2014, A21.

13 Leval, "Judicial Opinions as Literature," 207, 209.

14 Walter Probert, "Law and Persuasion: The Language-Behavior of Lawyers," *University of Pennsylvania Law Review* 35, no. 1 (1959): 58. Probert paraphrases Cohen from Felix S. Cohen, *Ethical Systems and Legal Ideals: An Essay on the Foundation of Legal Criticism* (Westport, Conn: Greenwood Press, 1933), 21–28. See also Felix S. Cohen, "Modern Ethics and the Law," *Brooklyn Law Review* 4, no. 1 (1934): 33.

15 Felix S. Cohen, "Field Theory and Judicial Logics," *Yale Law Journal* 59 (1950): 238.

16 Leval, "Judicial Opinions as Literature," 207. 239

17 Tiersma, *Legal Language*, 51.

18 George C. Christie, "Vagueness and Legal Language," *Minnesota Law Review* 48 (1964): 885–911, at 887.

19 "The misuse of legal language is both rampant and problematic." Bradley Scott Shannon, "Action Is an Action Is an Action Is an Action," *Washington Law Review* 77 (2002): 65–167, at 65–67.

20 Tiersma, *Legal Language*, 107.

21 Reddy v. Community Health Foundation of Man, 171 W. Va. 368 (1982) at 372.

22 John V. Orth, "Requiem for the Rule in Shelley's Case," *North Carolina Law Review* 67 (1989): 681–93.

23 Mitu Gulati and Robert E. Scott, *The Three and a Half Minute Transaction* (Chicago: University of Chicago Press, 2013). Gulati and Scott give a book-length analysis of this problem of lost meaning over the *pari passu* clause in contract law.

24 See Mahoney v. Grainger, 283 Mass. 189 (1933) at 191–92.

25 Palsgraf v. Long Island Railroad Co., 248 N.Y. 339 (1928). Judge William Andrews, the dissenter in this case, writes: "These two words [proximate cause] have never been given an inclusive definition."

26 Sandra F. Sperino, "Statutory Proximate Cause," *Notre Dame Law Review* 88, no. 3 (2013): 1199, 1200, 1202.

27 Campbell v. Acuff-Rose Music, Inc., 510 U.S. 569 (1994) at 580–581, 581n. See also Suntrust Bank v. Houghton Mifflin Co., 268 F.3d. 1257 (11th Cir. 2001) at 1269n23.

28 Simon Dentith, *Parody (The New Critical Idiom)* (London: Routledge, 2000), 6, 189.

29 *Campbell*, 510 U.S. 569 (1994) at 580, and Mikhail Bakhtin, "From the Prehistory of Novelistic Discourse," in *Theory of the Novel*, ed. Michael McKeon (Baltimore: Johns Hopkins University Press, 2000), 338. See, as well, *A Dictionary of Literary Terms*, ed. J. A. Cuddon (Garden City, N.Y.: Doubleday, 1977), s.v.v. "parody," "satire."

30 Brenda Danet, "Language in the Legal Process," *Law & Society Review* 14, no. 3 (1980): 545.

31 Peter M. Tiersma, "The Judge as Linguist," *Loyola of Los Angeles Law Review* 27 (1993): 283, and Jill C. Anderson, "Misreading like a Lawyer: Cognitive Bias in Statutory Interpretation," *Harvard Law Review* 127, no. 6 (2014): 1522–91.

32 Anil Gupta, "Remarks on Definitions and the Concept of Truth," *Proceedings of the Aristotelian Society*, New Series 89 (1988–1989): 240.

33 Fred R. Shapiro, "The Most-Cited Legal Scholars," *Journal of Legal Studies* 29 (2000): 409–26.

34 Joel Cohen, "An Interview with Judge Richard A. Posner," *ABA Journal*, July 2014, 53–60.

35 United States v. Delaney, No. 12–2849 (7th Cir. 2013) at 1–14. All further reference to this case will be by page number in the text.

36 Richard A. Posner, *Law & Literature: A Misunderstood Relation* (Cambridge, Mass.: Harvard University Press, 1988), 268, 272, 274, 286, 290, 303. Emphasis in the original.

37 Mark Twain, "Swimming in Glory: Pudd'nhead Wilson's Calendar," in *Pudd'nhead Wilson and Those Extraordinary Twins*, ed. Sidney E. Berger (1894; repr., New York: Norton Critical Edition, 1980), 27.

38 Matthew Arnold, preface to *Culture & Anarchy*, ed. J. Dover Wilson (Cambridge: Cambridge University Press, 1971), 6.

39 Samuel Johnson, "Abraham Cowley," in *Dr. Johnson: Prose and Poetry*, ed. Mona Wilson (Cambridge, Mass.: Harvard University Press, 1967), 818–19, 809, 814.

40 Ezra Pound, *How to Read* (London: D. Harmsworth, 1931), 21; Ezra Pound, *The ABC of Reading* (New Haven: Yale University Press, 1934), 15.

PART IV. WHEN THE LAW FAILS

1   Arthur Schopenhauer, "Human Nature," in *The Complete Essays of Schopenhauer*, trans. T. Bailey Saunders (New York: Willey, 1942), 14–15.

2   I borrow terminology here from Naomi Mezey, "Approaches to the Cultural Study of Law: Law as Culture," *Yale Journal of Law & the Humanities* 13, no. 1 (2001): 35–38.

3   Also, "he who serves a revolution ploughs the sea" ("The Final Cry of Despair," in *The Liberator, Simón Bolívar: Man and Image*, ed. David Bushnell [New York: Alfred A. Knopf, 1970], 86). See also Octavio Paz Lozano, *The Labyrinth of Solitude* (1950); Jorge Luis Borges, *A Universal History of Infamy* (1954); and Mario Vargas Llosa, *The Feast of the Goat* (2001).

4   Gabriel García Márquez, *Chronicle of a Death Foretold*, trans. Gregory Rabassa (New York: Vintage Books, 1982). All quotations given parenthetically in the text are to this edition.

5   See Maria Aristodemou, *Law and Literature: Journeys from Her to Eternity* (Oxford: Oxford University Press, 2000), 178–203, and Rosanna Cavallaro, "Solution to Dissolution: Detective Fiction from Wilkie Collins to Gabriel García Márquez," *Texas Journal of Women and the Law* 15, no. 1 (Fall 2005): 25–41.

6   For a treatment of the many clues pointing to Angela's abuse, see Pablo Sánchez Iglesias, "*Chronicle of a Death Foretold*: Collective Guilt Disguised as Fatality," *ISLL (Italian Society of Law and Literature) Papers* 6 (2013), http://www.lawandliterature.org/area/documenti/Iglesias%202013.pdf.

7   Randolph Bourne, "Politics, State, and Society," in *The Radical Will: Selected Writings, 1911–1918* (New York: Urizen, 1977), 354.

8   See Senate Select Committee on Intelligence Committee Study of the Central Intelligence Agency's Detention and Interrogation Program, S. Rpt. 113-288 (2014), http://www.intelligence.senate.gov/study2014.html.

10. THE SOMERS MUTINY AND THE AMERICAN SHIP OF STATE

1   See Philip McFarland, *Sea Dangers: The Affair of the Somers* (New York: Schocken Books, 1985), and Buckner F. Melton Jr., *A Hanging Offense: The Strange Affair of the Warship "Somers"* (New York: Free Press, 2003). For articles and chapters on the subject, see William R. Wendt, "The *Somers* Affair," *Marine Corps Gazette* 39, no. 5 (May 1955): 46–51; Frederic F. Van de Water, "Panic Rides The High Seas," *American Heritage* 12, no. 4 (1961): 1–15; Samuel Eliot Morison, "The *Somers* Mutiny, 1842–1843," in *Sailor Historian: The Best of Samuel Eliot Morison*, ed. Emily Morison Beck (Boston: Houghton Mifflin, 1977), 181–202; Hugh Egan, "The Mackenzie Court-Martial Trial: Cooper's Secret Correspondence with William H. Norris," *Studies in the American Renaissance* (1990): 149–58; and Leonard F. Guttridge, "Seven: The *Somers*," in *Mutiny: A History of Naval Insurrection* (Annapolis, Md.: Naval Institute Press, 1992), 87–97.

2   See Newton Arvin, "A Note on the Background of *Billy Budd*," *American Literature* 20 (1948): 51–55. First Lieutenant Guert Gansevoort was the first cousin who was second-in-command.

3   Herman Melville, *Billy Budd, Sailor (An Inside Narrative)*, ed. Harrison Hayford and Merton M. Sealts Jr. (Chicago: University of Chicago Press, 1962), 113–14.

4   Ibid., 110.

5   Ibid., 43, 76.

6   Robert A. Ferguson, *The Trial in American Life* (Chicago: University of Chicago Press, 2007), 2–3.

7   I take these uncontested facts from the two modern accounts of the *Somers* affair, McFarland, *Sea Dangers*, 48–49, and Melton, *A Hanging Affair*, 82, 88–89, 103–10.

8   *Proceedings of the Naval Court Martial of Alexander Slidell Mackenzie, A Commander in the Navy of the United States, &c., Including the Charges and Specifications of Charges Preferred Against Him by the Secretary of the Navy* (New York: Henry G. Langley, 1844), 194–97 (hereafter *Proceedings*), and Harrison Hayford, ed., *The Somers Mutiny Affair: A Book of Primary Sources* (Englewood Cliffs, N.J.: Prentice-Hall, 1959). All further references to *Proceedings* will be through parenthetical expression by page number in the text or cited in the notes when many pages are cited.

9   For the *Somers* affair and its role in the establishment of the United States
    Naval Academy, see Melton, *A Hanging Offense*, 255–56.

10 Gail Hamilton, "The Murder of Philip Spencer," *Cosmopolitan* (June, July,
    August, 1889), 133–40, 248–55, 345–54.

11 See Joseph F. Kett, *Rites of Passage: Adolescence in America, 1790 to the Present*
    (New York: Basic Books, 1977).

12 See Karen Sanchez-Eppler, *Dependent States: The Child's Part in Nineteenth-*
    Century America (Chicago: University of Chicago, Press, 2005); Laurence
    Lerner, *Angels and Absences: Child Deaths in the Nineteenth Century* (Nash-
    ville: Vanderbilt University Press, 1997); and Robert A. Ferguson, "Louisa
    May Alcott Meets Mark Twain Over the Young Face of Change," in *Alone*
    in America: The Stories That Matter (Cambridge, Mass.: Harvard University
    Press, 2013), 61–89.

13 Theodore Sedgwick to Charles Sumner, July 6, 1843, quoted in McFarland,
    Sea Dangers, 181, 281.

14 See "An Act for the Government of the Navy of the United States," 5th Cong.
    (March 2, 1799), sess. 3, ch. 24, Stat. 1, 24 at 709, 711. "Any officer, seaman,
    mariner, or other person who shall disobey the order of his superior, or begin,
    excite, cause or join in any mutiny or sedition in the ship to which he belongs,
    or in any other ship or vessel in the service of the United States, on any pre-
    tence whatsoever, shall suffer death, or such other punishment *as a court mar-*
    tial shall direct; and further, any person in any ship or vessel belonging to the
    service aforesaid, who shall utter any words of sedition and mutiny, or endeav-
    our to make any mutinous assembly on any pretence whatsoever, shall suffer
    such punishment *as a court martial shall inflict*." Emphasis added.

    See also "An Act for the Better Government of the Navy of the United
    States," 6th Cong. (April 23, 1800), sess. 1, ch. 33, article 13, at 47. "If any person
    in the navy shall make or attempt to make any mutinous assembly, he shall *on*
    conviction thereof by a court martial, suffer death; and if any person as aforesaid
    shall utter any seditious or mutinous words, or shall conceal or connive at any
    mutinous or seditious practices, or shall treat with contempt his superior, being
    in the execution of his office, or being witness to any mutiny or sedition, shall
    not do his utmost to suppress it, he shall be punished *at the discretion of a court*
    martial." Emphasis added.

15 *Proceedings*, 16, 35, 41, 51, 54, 58, 61, 62, 66, 76, 78, 131, 158.

16 *Proceedings*, 20, 39, 40, 72, 158, 211, 240.

17 Even the judge advocate prosecuting the case praised Mackenzie (*Proceedings*,
    258).

18 See "Power Is a Tool," *New York Times Magazine*, March 16, 2014, 12; Robin Toner, "Trust in the Military Heightens Among Baby Boomers' Children," *New York Times*, May 27, 2003, A1; and Charles M. Blow, "The Frustration Doctrine," *New York Times*, June 23, 2014, A21. See also Edwin A. Miles, "The Whig Party and the Menace of Caesar," *Tennessee Historical Quarterly* 27, no. 4 (Winter 1968): 361–79.

19 Melton, *A Hanging Offense*, 212–17.

20 "Collateral Attack on Courts-Martial in the Federal Courts," *Yale Law Journal* 57, no. 3 (1948): 483–89, Richard A. Oppel Jr., "Army General Reaches Deal on Sex Counts," *New York Times*, March 17, 2014, A1, A15; and "A Broken Military Justice System," *New York Times*, March 18, 2014, A22. For Supreme Court cases upholding the immunity from civil prosecution of military officers, see Feres v. United States, 340 U.S. 135 (1950); Chappell et al. v. Wallace et al., 462 U.S. 296 (1983); United States et al. v. Stanley 483 U.S. 669 (1987); and Edward F. Sherman, "The Civilianization of Military Law," *Maine Law Review* 22 (1970): 3–103.

21 Charles Sumner to Lt. Charles H. Davis, January 3, 1843, in *Memoir and Letters of Charles Sumner*, ed. Edward L. Pierce (London: Low, Marston, Searle, and Rivington, 1878), 2:225.

22 Jeremiah Hughes, ed., *Niles National Register*, vol. 64, *March 1843 to September 1843* (Baltimore, n.d.), 32 (March 11, 1843). See, as well, Melton, *A Hanging Offense*, 216.

23 Edward P. Crapol, *John Tyler, the Accidental President* (Chapel Hill: University of North Carolina Press, 2006), 2, 26, 27, 36–37, 56.

24 Horace Bushnell., "Views of Christian Virtue," in *The American Intellectual Tradition*, eds. David A. Hollinger and Charles Capper, vol. 1, *1630–1865*, 3rd ed (New York: Oxford University Press, 1997), 363, 365–66, 368, and generally 363–73; and Gillian Brown, *Domestic Individualism: Imagining Self in Nineteenth-Century America* (Berkeley: University of California Press, 1990)

25 Bushnell, "Views of Christian Virtue," 304–5, 372.

26 For a similar familial leave-taking offered Cromwell, see *Proceedings*, 56.

27 Bushnell, "Views of Christian Virtue," 369.

28 "December 29, 1842," in *The Diary of Philip Hone, 1828–1851*, ed. Allan Nevins (New York: Dodd, Mead, 1927), 2:642.

29 The ardent support of Dana, Sumner, and the Sedgwicks is documented in Hayford, ed., *The Somers Mutiny Affair*, 75–76, 83, 87–89, 102–6, 117, 129, 163–64. Dana's January 11 letter to Catharine Sedgwick in support of Mackenzie, first published in the *New York Evening Post* on January 13, 1843, was widely

reprinted. See also Charles Sumner, "The Mutiny of the *Somers*," *North American Review* 57 (July 1843): 195–241.

30 Richard Henry Dana Jr. to A. S. Mackenzie, April 16, 1843, in Hayford, *The Somers Mutiny Affair*, 159.

31 *Proceedings*, 26, 80, 90, 91, 112, 113, 152, 153.

32 See Don E. Fehrenbacher, *The Slaveholding Republic: An Account of the United States Government's Relations to Slavery* (Oxford: Oxford University Press, 2002); Albert J. von Frank, *The Trials of Anthony Burns: Freedom and Slavery in Emerson's Boston* (Cambridge, Mass.: Harvard University Press, 1998); and Robert A. Ferguson, "John Brown: Defendant on the Loose," in *The Trial in American Life* (Chicago: University of Chicago Press, 2007), 117–52.

33 These arguments would prevail only through Abraham Lincoln in 1865 with the narrow passage of the Thirteenth Amendment abolishing slavery.

34 Richard H. Dana Jr., to Catharine M. Sedgwick, January 11, 1843, in *Richard Henry Dana: A Biography*, ed. Charles Francis Adams (Boston: Houghton Mifflin, 1890), 1:52.

35 Ibid., 55–57.

36 Sumner, "The Mutiny of the *Somers*," 236–37.

37 Ibid.

38 Ibid., 236–37, 238–39.

39 Ibid., 239.

40 Richard Henry Dana Jr. to Catharine M. Sedgwick, 1:56.

41 Stephen E. Toulmin, *The Uses of Argument*, updated ed. (Cambridge: Cambridge University Press, 2003), 15, 33–36, 154.

42 Roger Fisher and William Ury, "Focus on Interests, Not Positions," in *Getting to Yes: Negotiating Agreement Without Giving In*, 2nd ed. (New York Penguin Books, 1991), 40–55; and Richard Shell, "A World of Different Cultures," in *Bargaining for Advantage: Negotiation Strategies for Reasonable People* (New York: Penguin Books, 2006), 18–20.

11. INVADING PANAMA: CIRCUMSTANCE AND THE RULE OF LAW

1 Arthur Schlesinger Jr., *Journals: 1952–2000*, eds. Andrew Schlesinger and Stephen Schlesinger (New York: Penguin Press, 2007), 684.

2 For Dick Cheney's central role in the 1989 invasion of Panama, see "Fighting in Panama: The Pentagon; Excerpts from Briefings on U.S. Military Action in Panama," *New York Times*, December 21, 1989, A20.

3   For the official version of the five justifications listed below, see George
     H. W. Bush to Thomas S. Foley (Speaker of the House of Representatives),
     December 21, 1989, H.R. Doc. No. 127, 101st Cong., 2d Sess. (1990). For exten-
     sive documentation and analyses of the justifications given by the George H.
     W. Bush Administration, see Louis Henkin, "The Invasion of Panama Under
     International Law: A Gross Violation," *Columbia Journal of Transnational Law*
     29 (1991): 293ff, and Frances Y. F. Ma, "Noriega's Abduction from Panama:
     Is Military Invasion an Appropriate Substitute for International Extradition?,"
     Loyola of Los Angeles International and Comparative Law Journal 13 (June 1991):
     935ff. For President George W. Bush's parallel but far more perfunctory claims
     for invading Iraq in 2003, see "Presidential Letter to the Speaker of the House of
     Representatives and the President Pro Tempore of the Senate," March 18, 2003,
     at http://www.whitehouse.gov/news/releases/2003/03/20030319-1.html.

4   At a hastily arranged White House briefing at 9:40 P.M. on January 3, 1990,
     the day Noriega was captured, President Bush reinforced these objectives
     with slight variations after some criticism of them. He would also claim that
     they all had been met. "On December 20, I ordered U.S. troops to Panama
     with four objectives: to safeguard the lives of American citizens, to help restore
     democracy, to protect the integrity of the Panama Canal treaty, and to bring
     General Manuel Noriega to justice. All of these objectives have now been
     achieved." "Noriega's Surrender: The President; Text of Bush Announcement
     on the General's Surrender," *New York Times*, January 4, 1990, http://www.
     nytimes.com/1990/01/04/world/noriega-s-surrender-president-text-bush
     -announcement-general-s-surrender.html.

5   *Newsweek* poll conducted by the Gallup Organization on December 23, 1989,
     and published in *Newsweek*, January 1, 1990, 22.

6   James Madison, "The Federalist No. 37," in *The Federalist: A Commentary
     on the Constitution of the United States*, ed. Edward Mead Earle (New York:
     Random House, 1937), 229.

7   Walter Benjamin, "Thesis on the Philosophy of History: IX," in *Illuminations:
     Essays and Reflections*, trans. Harry Zohn (New York: Schocken Books, 1969),
     257–58.

8   See Leon Pompa, "Vico: The Ideal Eternal History," in *Human Nature and
     Historical Knowledge: Hume, Hegel, and Vico* (Cambridge: Cambridge Univer-
     sity Press, 1990), 139–40.

9   For Burke's understanding of "legality," see Kenneth Burke, *Attitudes Toward
     History* (Los Altos, Ca.: Hermes Publications, 1959), 291–92.

10 Fernand Braudel, *On History*, trans. Sarah Matthews (Chicago: University of Chicago, 1980), 18.

11 See Morton J. Horwitz. *The Transformation of American Law, 1780–1860* (Cambridge, Mass.: Harvard University Press, 1977), and Morton J. Horwitz, *The Transformation of American Law, 1870–1960: The Crisis of Legal Orthodoxy* (Oxford: Oxford University Press, 1992).

12 Braudel, *On History*, 27–34.

13 Quoted in Fritz Stern, "The Goldhagen Controversy: One Nation, One People, One Theory," *Foreign Affairs*, November/December 1996, 128–29, and Richard Gid Powers, review of *Wild Man: The Life and Times of Daniel Ellsberg*, by Tom Wells, *Journal of American History* 89, no. 2 (September 2002): 726–27.

14 Rae Corelli, "Lifestyle of a Dictator," *Maclean's*, January 1, 1990, 55; Tina Rosenberg, "The Panama Perplex," *New Republic*, January 25, 1988, 17–23; G. Pope Atkins, "Panama Situation and Conflict," in *Encyclopedia of the Inter-American System* (Westport, Conn.: Greenwood Press, 1997), 404–7; Frederick Kempe, "Ties That Blind: U.S. Taught Noriega to Spy, But the Pupil Had His Own Agenda," *Wall Street Journal*, October 18, 1989, 1, 20; and *Infoplease.com*, s.v. "Manuel Antonio Noriega," http://www.infoplease.com/ce6/people/A0835878.html.

15 Reported by Kempe, "Ties That Blind," 20.

16 Guillermo Sanchez Borbón, "Hugo Spadafora's Last Day," *Harper's Magazine*, June 1988, 56–62.

17 Everett Ellis Briggs, "Op-Ed: Our Man in Panama," *New York Times*, September 9, 2007, W15.

18 *Time* put an image of the beating on the cover of its May 22, 1989, issue, with the headline "Politics, Panama-Style."

19 Kempe, "Ties That Blind," 1, 20.

20 Ma, "Noriega's Abduction from Panama," 939–40; Periscope, "How Many Civilians Died?" *Newsweek*, January 15, 1990, 8; and Independent Commission of Inquiry on the U.S. Invasion of Panama, *The U.S. Invasion of Panama: The Trial behind Operation "Just Cause"* (Boston: South End Press, 1991), 40ff.

21 George J. Church, "Panama: No Place to Run," *Time*, January 8, 1990, 38.

22 "Noriega's Surrender: The President; Text of Bush Announcement on the General's Surrender."

23 Henkin, "The Invasion of Panama Under International Law," 293–317; Ma, "Noriega's Abduction from Panama," 925–53. See also Daniel Patrick

Moynihan, *On the Law of Nations* (Cambridge, Mass.: Harvard University Press, 1990), 169–77.

24 The UN General Assembly "strongly deplores" the invasion of Panama as a "flagrant violation of international law." UN General Assembly, Resolution 240, "Effects of the military intervention by the United States of America in Panama on the situation in Central America," 44, and UN General Assembly Supp. at 52, U.N. Doc. a/44/L/63, and Add.1 (1989).

25 "OAS Voices 'Regret' on Panama Invasion," *Los Angeles Times*, December 22, 1989, 2, and Atkins, "Panama Situation and Conflict," 406.

26 Organization of American States Permanent Council, Resolution 534 (800/89), "Serious Events in the Republic of Panama," December 22, 1989; Henkin, "The Invasion of Panama Under International Law," 312n76; and "OAS Voices 'Regret' on Panama Invasion," 2.

27 Theodore H. Draper, "Did Noriega Declare War?" *New York Review of Books*, March 29, 1990, 13.

28 David Johnston, "No Victory for Panama," *New York Times*, April 11, 1992, 1, 12. For discussions on the lack of democracy in Panama, see: Andres Oppenheimer, "Day of the Gringo," *New Republic*, February 28, 1990, 14–15; Amy Wilentz, "Slippery Blades," *New Republic*, November 1, 1993, 10–11, and "Learning to Crawl," *Economist*, September 22, 1990, 49–52.

29 Carla Anne Robbins, "What Kind of a Country Kept Noriega in Power," *New Republic*, May 28, 1990, 28–36; Oppenheimer, "Day of the Gringo," 14–15; Ross Laver, Joseph Gannon, and William Lowther, "The Last Stand," *Maclean's* (January 8, 1990), 16; Jill Smolowe, "Panama's Would-Be President," *Time*, January 1, 1990, 30–31; and "Learning to Crawl," 49–52.

30 "Opening Statement by Prosecution," *Transcript of Trial Proceedings: United States of America vs. Manuel Antonio Noriega, et al.* (September 16, 1991), vol. 7: 1397.

31 Johnston, "No Victory for Panama," 1.

32 See Bush to Foley, and Henkin, "The Invasion of Panama Under International Law," 293nn1–2.

33 Moynihan, *On the Law of Nations*, 171.

34 "Get It Over With," *New Republic*, June 13, 1988, 7–9.

35 Ibid.

36 "Incurious George," *New Republic*, October 17, 1988, 7–8.

37 Tina Rosenberg, "Can We Get It Right This Time?," *New Republic*, January 25, 1988, 17; Morton M. Kondracke, "Shoot or Get Off The Pot," May 2, 1988, 12; "Surrender, Manny," June 5, 1989, 9; "Get It Over With," 7.

38 "Fiasco in Panama," *New Republic*, October 30, 1989, 5–6.

39 "The Editors," "A Mystery Solved," *New Republic*, October 17, 1988, 9.

40 Quoted in Terry Coleman, "A Touch of Yankee Class," *Guardian*, December 3, 1988, and in *Daily Telegraph*, April 28, 1988. See also Steve A. Yetiv, "The Agent-Structure Question in Theory: President Bush's Role during the Persian Gulf Crisis," and Douglas G. Brinkley, "The Bush Administration and Panama," in *From Cold War to New World Order: The Foreign Policy of George H. W. Bush*, eds. Meena Bose and Rosanna Perotti (Westport, Conn.: Greenwood Press, 2002), 138, 182.

41 Schlesinger, *Journals: 1952–2000*, 684.

42 Timothy Naftali, *George H. W. Bush* (New York: Henry Holt, 2007), 88.

43 "Invasion," *Newsweek*, January 1, 1990, 12–15; George J. Church, "Showing Muscle," *Time*, January 1, 1990, 20–23; "Bush Bags Noriega," *Human Events*, January 13, 1990, 3–4.

44 Nathan Alter, "For Bush, the Best of a Bad Bargain," *Newsweek*, January 1, 1990, 23.

45 Thomas M. DeFrank and Ann McDaniel, "Bush: The Secret Presidency," *Newsweek*, January 1, 1990, 26–27.

46 Braudel, *On History*, 27–34.

47 United States of America v. Manuel Antonio Noriega, et al., Defendants, No. 88-0079-CR, OR-HOEVELER (February 4, 1988), 1988 WL 168666 (S.D. Fla.).

48 United States of America v. Manuel Antonio Noriega, et al., Defendants, No. 88-0079-CR (April 28, 1988), 683 F. Supp.1373.

49 Ibid.

50 Unless otherwise indicated, all of Judge Hoeveler's comments in this paragraph and the paragraphs to follow are from United States v. Noriega (hereafter referred to as *Noriega*), 746 F. Supp. 1506–1541 (June 8, 1990). For the convenience of readers, I give pagination at the end of each paragraph.

51 Noriega was quoted in "Private Phone That Wasn't Private," *Economist*, November 17, 1990, 30.

52 *Noriega*, 746 F. Supp., 1510–11.

53 Ibid., 1537, 1539.

54 Ibid., 1529.

55 Ibid., 1534.

56 Ibid., 1535, 1537.

57 Ibid., 1539.

58 Ibid., 1537n40.

59 Ibid., 1537, 1538.

60 David Johnston, "A Year Old, the Noriega Case Is Far From Closed," *New York Times*, December 14, 1990, B8, and "5 Years from Accusation to Conviction," *New York Times*, April 10, 1992, A24.

61 The revelations of overly generous plea deals for major drug dealers and other serious criminals came out during cross-examination by defense counsel. See *Transcript of Trial Proceedings: United States of America vs. Manuel Antonio Noriega, et al.*, vol. 7:1502–vol. 8:1739; vol. 8:1740–vol. 12:2300; vol. 12:2301–vol. 15:2956; vol. 12:2961; vol. 18:3508. See also Cathy Booth, "Canned Pineapple: Noriega on Trial," *New Republic*, March 30, 1992, 13–14.

62 *Transcript of Trial Proceedings*, vol. 1:103–4, vol. 2:275.

63 "Opening Statement of Prosecution," *Transcript of Trial Proceedings*, vol. 7: 1397, 1367.

64 For the Reagan administration's use of this label, see Larry Rohter, "U.S. Jury Convicts Noriega of Drug-Trafficking Role as the Leader of Panama," *New York Times*, April 10, 1992, 1.

65 Rohter, "U.S. Jury Convicts Noriega," 1, 24; Larry Rohter, "Victory in Noriega Case Stunned Even Prosecutors," *New York Times*, April 17, 1992, B16.

66 Rohter, "U.S. Jury Convicts Noriega," 24, and Shirley Christian, " 'Appalling Chapter' Ends for Panama," in *New York Times*, April 10, 1992, A24.

67 For a full account of the doctrine of preventive war, see David Bromwich, "The Co-President at Work," *New York Review of Books*, November 20, 2008, 29–33.

68 Richard Rorty, preface and "The Banality of Pragmatism and the Poetry of Justice," in *Philosophy and Social Hope* (New York: Penguin Books, 1999), xiii, 99, 100, and Margaret Radin, "The Pragmatist and the Feminist," *Southern California Law Review* 63 (1990): 1710.

69 For how *Noriega* "set a powerful precedent, rejecting traditional immunity and jurisdiction defenses," see Adam Isaac Hasson, "Extraterritorial Jurisdiction and Sovereign Immunity on Trial: Noriega, Pinochet, and Milosevic—Trends in Political Accountability and Transnational Criminal Law," *Boston College International & Comparative Law Review* 25 (2002): 125–58.

70 For George H. W. Bush's own insistence on absolute loyalty over facts, see, "Road to the White House," *Newsweek*, August 15, 1988, 15.

71 Lars-Erik Nelson, " 'Rules' of International Law Depend on Who's Winning the Game," *New York Daily News*, December 29, 1989, 17.

72 Larry M. Bartels, "Constituency Opinion and Congressional Policy Making: The Reagan Defense Build Up," *American Political Science Review* 85, no. 2 (1991), 457–74, at 459.

73 D. W. Meinig, *The Shaping of America: A Geographical Perspective on 500 Years of History*, vol. 4, *Global America, 1915–2000* (New Haven: Yale University Press, 2004), 394–96.

74 Moynihan, *On the Law of Nations*, 177.

75 James Madison, "The Federalist No. 41," in Earle, ed., *The Federalist*, 262.

76 Thus, in the Cuban Missile Crisis, scholarship suggests that the Russians agreed to remove their nuclear missiles from Cuba only when President John F. Kennedy warned that he was losing control of his own military machine if there was not an accommodation very soon. See Richard Holbrooke, "Real W.M.D.'s," *New York Times Book Review*, June 22, 2008, 1, 8–9, and Michael Dobbs, *One Minute to Midnight: Kennedy, Khrushchev, and Castro on the Brink of Nuclear War* (New York: Alfred A. Knopf, 2008).

77 John Jay, "The Federalist No. 4," in Earle, ed., *The Federalist*, 18.

78 Traced to Abraham H. Maslow, *The Psychology of Science: A Reconnaissance* (New York; Harper & Row, 1966), 15.

79 *Noriega*, 746 F. Supp. 1506 (June 8, 1990) at 1537. See also Olmstead v. United States, 277 U.S. 438 (1928), 485; 48 S.Ct. 564 (1928), 575.

80 *Noriega*, 746 F. Supp. 1506 (June 8, 1990) at 1537. Judge Hoeveler's warning has judicial authority behind it. See Atlee v. Laird, 347 F. Supp. 689 (E.D.Pa. 1972) at 702; Crockett v. Reagan, 558 F. Supp. 893 (D.D.C.1982) at 898; and Ma, "Noriega's Abduction from Panama," 925, 950n185.

CODA: HOW TO READ A COURTROOM NOVEL

1 Richard A. Posner, "Law and Literature: A Relation Reargued," *Virginia Law Review* 72 (1986): 1356–57, and Richard A. Posner, *Law and Literature: A Misunderstood Relation* (Cambridge, Mass.: Harvard University Press, 1988), 15, 353, 355. See David Ray Papke, "Problems with an Uninvited Guest: Richard A. Posner and the Law and Literature Movement," review of *Law and Literature: A Misunderstood Relation*, by Richard A. Posner, *Boston University Law Review* 69 (1989): 1067–88.

2 Aristotle, *Aristotle's Poetics: A Translation and Commentary for Students of Literature*, trans. Leon Golden (Englewood Cliffs, N.J.: Prentice-Hall, 1968), 37 [21.1457b], and Alexander Preminger, ed., *Princeton Encyclopedia of*

Poetry and Poetics, enlarged ed. (Princeton: Princeton University Press, 1974), 490–95.

3 Clifford Geertz, "Thick Description: Toward an Interpretive Theory of Culture," in *The Interpretation of Cultures* (New York: Basic Books, 1973), 4–30.

4 Bernard J. Hibbitts, "Making Sense of Metaphors: Visuality, Aurality, and the Reconfiguration of American Legal Discourse," *Cardozo Law Review* 16 (1994): 230–31.

5 Pierre N. Leval, "Judicial Opinions as Literature," in *Law's Stories: Narrative and Rhetoric in the Law*, eds. Peter Brooks and Paul Gewirtz (New Haven: Yale University Press, 1996), 206–10. Leval is a leading federal judge on the United States Court of Appeals for the Second Circuit.

6 As early as Achilles's shield in book 18 of *The Iliad*, legal decisions are made within a distinct "sacred circle." *The Iliad of Homer*, trans. Richmond Lattimore (Chicago: University of Chicago Press, 1961), 388.

7 Milner S. Ball, "The Play's the Thing: An Unscientific Reflection on Courts Under the Rubric of Theater," *Stanford Law Review* 28 (1975): 81ff; Boris Kozolchyk, "On the State of Commercial Law at the End of the 20th Century," *Arizona Journal of International and Comparative Law* 8, no. 1 (1991): 4–5; and Pierre Schlag, "The Aesthetics of American Law," *Harvard Law Review* 115 (2001): 1955–1066.

8 Dennis E. Curtis and Judith Resnik, "Images of Justice," *Yale Law Journal* 96 (1987): 1727–72.

9 Dahlia Lithwick, "Up Front," *New York Times Book Review*, February 14, 2010, 4.

10 "Anima Poetae [December 16, 1804]," in *Anima Poetae: From the Unpublished Note-Books of Samuel Taylor Coleridge*, ed. Ernest Hartley Coleridge (Boston: Houghton Mifflin, 1895), 83, and Samuel Taylor Coleridge, *Miscellanies, Aesthetic and Literary to Which Is Added the Theory of Life* (London: G. Bell, 1911), 22–23.

11 C. P. Snow, *The Affair* (1960; repr., Kelly Bray, UK: Stratus Books, 2000), 102. Further references to the novel are given parenthetically in the text.

12 William Mack and Howard Pervear Nash, eds., *Cyclopedia of Law and Procedure* (New York: America Law Book, 1905), 16:134.

13 William Shakespeare, *The Merchant of Venice* (New York: Penguin Books, 1970), 93–94 [4.1.3–34].

14 Robert Traver, *Anatomy of a Murder* (New York: St. Martin's Press, 1958), 193–94, 195–199, 88, 239, 218. "Robert Traver" is the pen name of Judge John D. Voelker of the Michigan Supreme Court.

15 Ibid., 431.

16 Scott Turow, *Presumed Innocent* (New York: Farrar, Straus and Giroux, 1987), 374–75, 384–89, 410–11.

17 Harper Lee, *To Kill A Mockingbird* (1960; repr., New York: Warner Books, 1982), 167.

18 Ibid., 167–69.

19 Ibid., 195–99, 88.

20 Ibid., 239, 218.

21 Costas Douzinas and Lynda Nead, eds., *Law and the Image* (Chicago: University of Chicago Press, 1999).

22 Bernhard Schlink, *The Reader*, trans. Carol Brown Janeway (New York: Pantheon Books, 1997), 95.

23 Posner, *Law and Literature*, 79.

24 Mark Twain, *Pudd'nhead Wilson and Those Extraordinary Twins*, ed. Sidney E. Berger (1894; repr., New York: Norton, 1980); John Grisham, *A Time to Kill* (New York: Dell, 1989); and the movie *The Verdict* (1982), directed by Sidney Lumet and starring Paul Newman, Charlotte Rampling, Jack Warden, and James Mason.

25 Lynne Wilson, "Book Review," review of *Zechariah Chafee Jr.: Defender of Liberty and Law*, by Donald L. Smith, *Harvard Law Review* 56 (1943): 833.

26 Richmond Lattimore, ed., *Greek Lyrics*, 2nd ed. (Chicago: University of Chicago Press, 1960), 4.

27 James Gould Cozzens, *The Just and the Unjust* (New York: Harcourt, Brace, 1942), 109, 262, 341–46, 411, 427.

28 Matthew 5:45.

29 Cozzens, *The Just and the Unjust*, 420.

30 Ibid., 396.

31 Trilling, "Manners, Morals, and the Novel," in *The Liberal Imagination: Essays on Literature and Society* (1950; repr., Garden City, N.Y.: Doubleday, 1953), 200–201.

32 Ibid., 206–7.

33 Ibid., 205, 213.

Abrams v. United States, 250 U.S. 616, 630 (1919)

Bertolotti v. Dugger, 883 F.2d 1503 (11th Cir. 1989)

California v. Brown, 479 U.S. 538 (1987)

Dred Scott v. Sandford, 60 U.S. 393 (1857)

Frank v. Mangum, 237 U.S. 304, 345–49 (1915)

Franklin v. Lynaugh, 487 U.S. 164 (1998)

Graham v. Florida, 560 U.S. ___ (2010)

Graham v. Richardson, 403 U.S. 365–383 (1971)

Gregg v. Georgia, 428 U.S. 153 (1976)

Johnson v. Texas, 509 U.S. 350 (1993)

Kansas v. Marsh, 548 U.S. 163 (2006)

Lochner v. New York, 198 U.S. 45 (1905)

Lusk v. Singletary, 965 F.2d. 946 (11th Cir. 1992)

Marbury v. Madison, 5 U.S. 37 (1803)

Mathews v. Diaz, 426 U.S. 67–87 (1976)

Minersville School District v. Gobitis, 310 U.S. 586 (1940)

Olmstead v. United States, 277 U.S. 438 (1928), 485; 48 S. Ct. 564 (1928)

Palsgraf v. Long Island Railroad Co., 248 N.Y. 339 (1928)

Regina v. Hicklin, 3 Q.B. 360, 371 (1868)

Schenck v. United States, 249 U.S. 47, 52 (1919)

Southern Pacific Co. v. Jensen, 244 U.S. 205 (1917)

State of Tennessee v. John Thomas Scopes (1925)

United States of America v. Manuel Antonio Noriega, et al., Defendants, No. 88–0079-CR, OR-HOEVELER (February 4, 1988), 1988 WL 168666, (S.D. Fla.)

United States v. Delaney (2013)

United States v. Noriega, 746 F. Supp. 1506–1541 (June 8, 1990)

United States v. One Book Called "Ulysses," 5 F. Supp.182–185 (S.D.N.Y., 1933)

United States v. One Book, Entitled Ulysses by James Joyce, 72 F. 2d 705 (2nd Cir. 1934)

Walton v. Arizona, 497 U.D. 639 (1990)

West Virginia State Board of Education v. Barnette, 319 U.S. 624 (1943)

Wilson v. Kemp, 777 F.2d 621 (11th Cir. 1985)

Abrams v. United States, 109, 111–12

Achilles's shield, as sacred circle for legal decisions, 329n6

Affair, The (Snow), 269–72

alien, terminology in immigration, 67–70

Alien (film series), 289n18

Anatomy of a Murderer (Traver), 272–73

"angel of history," 243–44

anthropology: explaining the scene of conflict, 123; in idea formation, 4; as a relevant discipline, 1, 8, 198; use of thick description in, 266

Aristotle, 132, 134, 195

Austin, J. L., 44, 46–47, 62

Bacon, Francis, 120

Bakhtin, Mikhail, 122

Baldwin, James, 193–94

Beach, Melissa, 56

Benjamin, Walter. See "angel of history"

Bertolotti v. Dugger, 59

Bible, 33, 74, 101, 135; Lincoln's use of, 162–67, 176–80, 206

Billy Budd, Sailor (Melville), 1, 7, 217–19

Black, Hugo, 116, 125, 133

Blackmun, Harry, 59, 82, 133

Bolívar, Simón, 212

Braudel, Fernand, 244–45

Burke, Edmund, 126

Burke, Kenneth, 66, 126, 244

Bush, George H. W., 343–54

Bush, George W., 242, 323n3, 323n4

Bushnell, Horace, 233–35

California v. Brown, 58, 62

Call It Sleep (Roth), 77–81

Canetti, Elias, 120

Cardozo, Benjamin, 94; discussion of opinion in *Palsgraf,* 304n7; on Holmes, 96–97, 122, 131–33, 193; on proximate cause, 202;

Carlyle, Thomas, 102

Cheney, Dick, 241–42, 261, 322n2

Children Act, The (McEwan), 88–90

Chronicle of a Death Foretold (Márquez), 212–15

Cicero, 132

Cohen, Felix, 200

Coleridge, Samuel Taylor, 152; and straight lines vs. curves in thought, 269

communal pressures on law, 2–8, 8–9, 188, 215; in *Barnette,* 124; and challenges to authority, 152; and competing stories, 262; and immigration, 65–67, 72, 82; and judicial rhetoric, 132, 136; translation into legal terms, 12–13, 62–63

Constitution of the United States, 15, 17–34; craft of, 21–24; Lincoln and, 165–66, 169, 173–74, 192, 251, 263; and state constitutions, 26, 29, 112–13, 124, 129

court martial: conflicts over, 321n20, statute, 320n14. See also *Somers* mutiny

courtroom novel: *The Just and the Unjust* as greatest American example of, 275; as novel of manners, 278

Cozzens, James Gould, 89, 275
Crane, Stephen, 12–14
Crowds and Power (Canetti), 120
Cuban Missile Crisis, U.S. military out of control during, 328n76
Cultural Study of Law, The (Kahn), 198

De Clementia (Seneca), 37–39
death penalty, inconsistency of advocacy, 292n44
Declaration of Independence, of the United States, 18–19; Lincoln's use of, 164, 173–74
Douglas, Stephen A., 164–65
Douglas, William, 116, 125
Dred Scott v. Sandford, 164–65
Dworkin, Ronald, 9, 281n5

Eliot, T. S., 198, 203
"Eloquence of Grief, An" (Crane), 12–14
Emerson, Ralph Waldo, 90, 98
evidence, disciplinary approaches to, 315n2
experts, authority of, 9

failure: of audience to see judge's way, 98; in *Chronicle of a Death Foretold*, 213–15; and Holocaust, 190, 195; of language, 21, 44, 113; of law, 65–66, 70; in *Measure for Measure*, 153–55; of mercy, 55; in *Scopes* trial, 189; to see injustice, 75
Federalist, The: No. 4, 263; *No. 10*, 20; *No. 37*, 20–21, 243–44; *No. 51*, 24
Felman, Shoshana, 279n1
fiction, 1–2, 6–7, 14; apprehending society through, 265; courtroom novel as sportive wildness in law, 269, 276; and literary criticism, 6, 90; power of, 75–76; rendering of injustice in, 2; utility of in Constitutional thinking, 20, 29
Fiedler, Leslie, 77; on defects of *Ulysses* decision, 304n3; on Joyce as pornographer, 307n36
field invariant, vs. field-dependent, in rhetoric, 134
Frank, Jerome, 95
Frank v. Mangum, 109–111

Frankfurter, Felix, 94–95, 99, 116, 126–28
Franklin, Benjamin, 19–20, 26, 29–30, 127
Franklin v. Lynaugh, 58

Geertz, Clifford, 4
Graham v. Florida, 60–61
Graham v. Richardson, 82
Gregg v. Georgia, 57
Grisham, John, 7

Hampton, Jean, 54–55
Hand, Augustus, 141, 145–46
Hand, Learned, 95, 130, 141
Henkin, Louis, 323n11
history: blended with fiction, 70; in explanation of legal controversy, 82; on ideas, 120; and inevitability, 128, 243; in judging, 94, 118, 126–28; knowledge of, 33–34; legal misunderstanding of, 243–45, 255, 261; literary implications of, 8; looking beyond, 61; as relevant discipline, 1, 3, 17–18; and understanding of time, 244–45
Holmes, Oliver Wendell, Jr., 9, 93–114; Cardozo on, 96; comparison to John Marshall, 95, 106, 108; portrait of, 104–9; 126, 132–33, 141; and U.S. Civil War, 298n29; as writer, 93, 98–99, 113–14
Holmes, Oliver Wendell, Sr., 100–101
Hone, Philip, 235
Hopkinson, Charles, 104–9
Hurd, Heidi, 56

imagery of law: in eloquence, 268; in fiction, 75; geometric design in opinion writing, 138; geometry of courtrooms, 267, 273–74; and iconicity, 24; iconography in law, 104; image culture and law, 34, 69; as legal framing, 24; in legal writing, 109, 118, 143; in memorialization of a legal event, 104; in reputation of Holmes, 93, 98, 106–9; video influence of, 246; and visual studies, as relevant discipline, 1, 198
immigrants, terms for, 67–69, 70

immigration: congressional debates over, 73; politics and, 65, 68, 70–71
interdisciplinarity, as a tool, 1–10, 15, 93, 156, 243; in the study of mercy, 15, 35–36; in understanding judging, 94, 208
Interpretation of Cultures, The (Geertz), 4

Jackson, Robert, 116, 127–28
James, Henry, 142, 149
James, William, 147
Jay, John, 64
Jefferson, Thomas, 26, 104, 127; Lincoln on, 173
Johnson v. Texas, 59
Joyce, James, 140, 142–44; Fiedler's description of, 307n36
judges: ambivalence toward, 86; in courtroom novel, 273; criticisms of, 87; Felix Frankfurter on, 94; Learned Hand on, 95; writing of, 93, 113;
judicial rhetoric, controlling elements of, 132–33
Just and the Unjust, The (Cozzens), 89, 275–77

Kahn, Paul, 198
Kansas v. Marsh, 60
Kennedy, Anthony, 59–61
Kill a Mockingbird, To (Lee), 7, 272–75

l'homme moyen sensuel (the average feeling man), as term of ridicule, 307n45
Laski, Harold, 95
law & literature (movement), 3–4, 7–8, 280n10; early use of concept of, 130, 304n2
law and literature: claims for, 9, 75; as field of inquiry, 280n10
law review writing, 5–6, 56
Lazarus, Emma, 66–67
Lee, Harper, 7, 272–74
legal eloquence, 152–57, 196–210; of Constitution, 34; definition of, 159–60, 184; Gettysburg Address and Second Inaugural as models of, 170–83; and Holocaust memorials, 192–95;

importance of hearing in Lincoln's, 161; in *Measure for Measure*, 153–55; and Oliver Wendell Holmes Jr., 113; of Richard Posner, 207–8
legal language: and literary criticism, 196–97; Mark Twain on, 197–98; misuse of, 316n19; Supreme Court's trust in, 202
legal positivism, 1; Kant's notion of, 181
legal realism, 100, 137
Lincoln, Abraham, 27, 77, 104, 127, 156; criticisms of, 312n39; Gettysburg Address, 112, 170–76, 184; and *Hamlet* soliloquies, 313n50; importance of reading aloud for, 310n7; lament on his lack of education, 310n10; as lawyer, 159–87, 311n29; and life-long interest in etymology, 314n58; pledge from cabinet members to save the union, 311n27; pride in knowledge of Euclid, 313n41; pride in self-education, 309n3; professional distance as lawyer, 311n29; Second Annual Message to Congress, 184–87; Second Inaugural Speech, 159–60, 176–83; training in elocution, 312n37
Lithwick, Dahlia, 268
Lochner v. New York, 109
Lusk v. Singletary, 59

Madison, James, 19–33, 127; and *Federalist No. 37*, 243, 245, 263
Marbury v. Madison, 258
Marcus Aurelius, 39–40, 63
Markel, Dan, 55–56
Márquez, Gabriel García, 212–15
Masipa, Thokozile, 87–88
Mathews v. Diaz, 82
McEwan, Ian, 88–90
Measure for Measure (Shakespeare), 36, 47, 50, 152–56
media influences: on abolition, 166; on coverage of trials, 7, 8, 145; on immigration controversies, 74; on military misbehavior, 227, 231; on the Panamanian crisis, 252–55, 259, 261

Meditations (Marcus Aurelius), 39–40

Melville, Herman, 1, 217–19

Merchant of Venice, The (Shakespeare), 15,
    36; Portia's speech, 46–50; Shylock's
    punishment, 272–73

mercy: Christian, 40–42, 47, 56;
    definitions of, 34–36, 44, 63; in law
    as fulfilled speech act, 44; for Marcus
    Aurelius, 40; nexus law and mercy in
    Shakespeare, 47

militarism, and law: Holmes on, 96, 100;
    on immigration issues, 70; and invasion
    of Panama, 241–42; and national
    security, 215–16; in *Somers* case, 220,
    228, 231

Minersville School District v. Gobitis,
    115–28; and World War II, 302n35

Misner, Robert, 55–56

Morris, Gouverneur, 20, 30–31

Murphy, Jeffrie, 54–55

Namier, Lewis, 245

national security, and law, 124, 215–18,
    238–40, 248

Noriega, Manuel Antonio, contested legal
    status of, 256–57

Nussbaum, Martha, 57

obscenity law, 132–35, 141, 146

obscenity statute, 305n21

Olmstead v. United States, 264

Palsgraf v. Long Island Railroad Co., 131;
    discussion of opinion, 304n7

Panama, invasion of: court on, 258; loyalty
    over facts, 327n70; President Bush on,
    323n4; rationale for, 242, 246, 261

Peirce, Charles Sanders, 147

philosophy: influence on judging, 94;
    influence on social distinctions and
    justice, 193; lawyers as, 9; as relevant
    discipline, 1, 198

Pistorius, Oscar, trial of, 87–88

plea deals, generosity of, 327n61

plenary power doctrine, 290n29

point of view, 9, 12, 76, 78, 99, 137, 142–44,
    198, 238

Posner, Richard A., 87, 133–34, 157; on
    Palsgraf, 304n7; on *United States v.
    Delaney*, 204–9; works by, 203

Pound, Ezra, 78

pragmatic, vs. philosophical interpretations
    of the law, 281n3

Presumed Innocent (Turow), 272–74

Proslogium (St. Anselm), 42–43

psychology: in death penalty views,
    292n44; in fiction about law, 269; in
    the immigrant's plight, 60; in legal
    framing, 27; as relevant discipline, 1,
    198

Randolph, Edmund, 20, 22, 26, 28, 30

Rawls, John, 184, 193

Reader, The (Schlink), 7, 275

Regina v. Hicklin, 135–37, 141, 148

religion: civil, 32; in conflict with law, 189;
    in the cult of domesticity, 233–34; as
    influence on Lincoln, 166–67; legal
    misunderstanding of, 41–43; as source
    of freedom, 118; theology as relevant
    discipline, 1, 198

retributive theory: debates over, 54–56,
    286n47; and mercy, 54

Roman law, principles of, 9

Roth, Henry, 77

Russell, Bertrand, 147

Saint Anselm, 42–43

Scalia, Antonin, 58

Schenck v. United States, 112

Schlesinger, Arthur, Jr., 241

Schlink, Bernard, 7, 275

Schopenhauer, Arthur, 212

Seneca, 37–39

seven, as symbolic number, 282n8

Shakespeare, William, 15, 35, 36, 46–49,
    50–53, 61, 155, 162; abiding interest in
    legal discourse, 308n1

slave population, 294n77

Smart, Alwynne, 54

Snow, C. P., 269

sociology: on discriminatory practices,
    67–68; as a relevant discipline, 1, 8,
    198

Somers mutiny case, 215, 216–39; and anti-slavery discourse, 235–39; Captain Mackenzie's defense in, 226–28, 230, 235; Charles Sumner and Richard Henry Dana Jr. on, 236, 238–39; code of honor invoked, 220, 228, 231; court martial statute, 320n14; familial narrative in, 219, 226–27, 232–35; Joseph Story on, 231; mothers in, 219, 233–34; Philip Hone on, 235; women in, 229, 234

Southern Pacific Co. v. Jensen, 99

speech act theory, 44, 46–47, 156

State of Tennessee v. John Thomas Scopes, 189

Stevens, John Paul, 58

Stone, Harlan, 116, 127–28

Stowe, Harriet Beecher, 74–77

superiority, human need for, 288n5

superiority complex, 193

Supreme Court, 71; confused approach to mercy, 57–60; crucial wording of opening question in cases before, 120; decisions of, 82–83, 115–16, 124, 164, 199; Holmes's dissents in cases, 109–110; necessary qualities in decisions of, 125; on parody, 202

Taylor, Charles, 147–48

Tempest, The (Shakespeare), 36, 47, 50–53

Thoreau, Henry David, 90, 129, 145, 149

Time to Kill, A (Grisham), 7

Tolstoy, Leo, 126

Traver, Robert, 272

trial: and competing stories, 327; and entertainment, 13; high-profile, 7; and ideological conflict, 8, 145; as measure of communal thought, 240; mutually exclusive discursive space in, 227; of Oscar Pistorius, 87; *Somers* Mutiny, 217, 219; *Ulysses*, 136; unanswered questions in, 218

Trilling, Lionel, 278

Turow, Scott, 272

Twain, Mark, on language, 197–98, 203, 209

Ulysses (Joyce), 130–49

Uncle Tom's Cabin (Stowe), 74–77

United States of America v. Manuel Antonio Noriega, et al., 243, 245; conceptions of America revealed in, 245, 261–63; credibility of witnesses, 259–60

United States v. Delaney, 204–9

United States v. One Book called "Ulysses": defects in decision, 304n3; obscenity statute in, 305n21

U.S. Constitution. *See* Constitution of the United States

U.S. Declaration of Independence. *See* Declaration of Independence

U.S. Supreme Court. *See* Supreme Court

utilitarian theory, 54–55, 286n47

Vico, Giambattista, 244

Walton v. Arizona, 58

Warren, Robert Penn, 76, 90, 93

Washington, George, 30–32

Weinreb, Lloyd, 280n11

Weisberg, Richard, on legal complexity in Holocaust, 314n7

Weisberg, Robert, 56–57

West Virginia State Board of Education v. Barnette, 115–28

Whitman, James Q., 55

Wilson, James, 22, 30

Wilson v. Kemp, 58

Woolsey, John, 130–49

Wyzanski, Charles, 111